SECRET WAR

By the same author

Spy! (with Richard Deacon)
MI5: British Security Service Operations 1909–45
MI6: British Secret Intelligence Service Operations 1909–45
A Matter of Trust: MI5 1945–72
Unreliable Witness: Espionage Myths of the Second World War
The Branch: A History of the Metropolitan Police Special Branch
GARBO (with Juan Pujol)
GCHQ: The Secret Wireless War 1900–86
Molehunt
The Friends: Britain's Post-war Secret Intelligence Operations
Games of Intelligence
Seven Spies Who Changed the World

FICTION
The Blue List
Cuban Bluff

SECRET WAR

The Story of SOE,
Britain's Wartime Sabotage Organisation

Nigel West

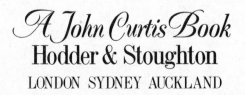
A John Curtis Book
Hodder & Stoughton
LONDON SYDNEY AUCKLAND

British Library Cataloguing in Publication Data

West, Nigel
  Secret war: The story of SOE, Britain's wartime
  sabotage organisation.
  I. Title
  940.54

  ISBN 0-340-51870-7

Published by Hodder and Stoughton,
a division of Hodder and Stoughton Ltd,
Mill Road, Dunton Green, Sevenoaks, Kent TN13 2YA.
Editorial Office: 47 Bedford Square, London WC1B 3DP.

Designed by Tim Higgins
Photoset in Linotron Ehrhardt by Rowland Phototypesetting Ltd,
Bury St Edmunds, Suffolk
Printed in Great Britain by
St Edmundsbury Press Ltd, Bury St Edmunds, Suffolk

Dedication

I first came into indirect contact with Special Operations Executive (SOE) through the late Ronald Seth, to whose memory this book is dedicated. He was an extraordinarily gifted individual, who, like so many of his wartime colleagues, underwent appalling privations to pursue the mission with which he had been entrusted.

In retrospect almost everything about his mission was sheer folly. He had no reception committee to arrange a safe landing, and his experience of parachuting and wireless was minimal. He never knew the real names of the SOE staff officers who planned his lonely mission, but he was sure that none of them had even the slightest knowledge of the mines in Silesia he was despatched to sabotage on 24 October 1942.

Seth's unique adventures, recounted in his classic *A Spy Has No Friends*, were bizarre even by the remarkable standards set by so many others who operated in enemy-occupied territory and suffered betrayal and torture. Nevertheless, he received no thanks whatever when, after four years of German captivity, he eventually made his way back to England.

Seth was found in Paris, wearing the uniform of a *Luftwaffe* officer, which took some explaining, as did the complaint of a British prisoner of war in his camp who claimed that he was a German stool-pigeon. But, as ever, Seth answered every charge with characteristic good humour. He then had to take his fight for back-pay to the Commons before the War Office reluctantly conceded his entitlement. Although his health had been broken, Seth's spirit and tenacity survived unscathed, apparently unaffected by either the Gestapo or the Whitehall bureaucrats.

He was a warm, colourful personality, who also happened to be a writer of great wit and talent, and is sadly missed by those privileged to have known him.

Nigel West

The warfare between SOE and SIS . . . is a lamentable but perhaps inevitable feature of our affairs.

Winston Churchill to General Ismay, 10 February 1944

Though SOE and SIS were nominally on the same side in the war, they were generally speaking more abhorrent to one another than the *Abwehr* was to either of them.

Malcolm Muggeridge, *The Infernal Grove*

All available experience shows that the only real pleasure to be got from war is to quarrel with your own side.

Basil Davidson, *Special Operations Europe*

Contents

Maps and Tables   VIII

Abbreviations   IX

Introduction   1

1 The First Two Years   7

2 A Branch of the Secret Service? SOE in
   the Middle East   49

3 Suspicion and Misgiving: Scandinavian Operations   73

4 'Der Englandspiel': SOE in Holland, Belgium
   and Czechoslovakia   88

5 A Deep and Abiding Jealousy: French Operations   105

6 A Hot Humid Summer: SOE in North Africa and
   the Balkans   131

7 Pass Down the Blame: SOE in Greece   157

8 Exorbitant Cost: The Oriental Mission   173

9 Too Many Plans: The India Mission   184

10 Bitter and Unfruitful Arguments: SOE in
   South-East Asia   195

11 Clandestine Bodies: SOE in 1944   218

Conclusion   246

Appendices
   1 SOE's Organisation, Structure and Personnel   255
   2 SOE's Special Training Schools   267
   3 JEDBURGHS   270

Source Notes   274

Index   285

Maps and Tables

Section D   10

MI(R)   15

SOE's Charter   20

SOE HQ Organisation   23

SIS/SOE Country Sections   26

French Operations   31

SOE Cairo   54

Yugoslav Country Section, Cairo   61

Czech Operations 1941–2   91

Map from *They Fought Alone*   117

SOE-trained Agents Arrested in France   126

Yugoslav Operations   149

Force 136 (Meerut and Kandy)   197

SOE's Circuits Active on D-Day   224

Abbreviations

AFO	Anti-Fascist Organisation
AK	*Armia Krajowa* (Polish Home Army)
BCRA	*Bureau Central de Renseignements et d'Action*
BNA	Burmese National Army
BSC	British Security Co-ordination
CD	Head of SOE
CNR	*Conseil National de la Résistance*
CPGB	Communist Party of Great Britain
EAM	Greek national resistance front
EDES	Greek anti-monarchist resistance movement
ELAS	Guerrilla wing of the Greek national resistance front
FANY	First Aid Nursing Yeomanry
FSM	Free Siamese Movement
GCHQ	Government Communications Headquarters
ISLD	Inter-Services Liaison Department
MCP	Malayan Communist Party
MI(R)	Military Intelligence (Research)
MI5	British Security Service
MI6	British Secret Intelligence Service
MI9	Escape and Evasion Service
OSS	Office of Strategic Services
PCO	Passport Control Office
PWE	Political Warfare Executive
SA	*Service Action* (French intelligence service)
SAS	Special Air Service
SD	*Sicherheitsdienst* (Nazi security service)
SI	Secret Intelligence
SIS	Secret Intelligence Service (MI6)
SO	Special Operations
SOE	Special Operations Executive
STS	Special Training School
SFHQ	Special Forces Headquarters

Heads of SOE

Sir Frank Nelson	July 1940–May 1942
Sir Charles Hambro	May 1942–September 1943
Major-General Colin Gubbins	September 1943–June 1946

Introduction

Of all Britain's secret services, the one created by the War Cabinet on 22 July 1940 was, and remains to this day, the most controversial. Special Operations Executive began its short life in an air of mystery, headed by Sir Frank Nelson, a Secret Intelligence Service (SIS) officer and the former Conservative MP for Stroud. In the seventy-one months of its existence, until it was officially disbanded on 30 June 1946, it trained and equipped more than nine thousand agents, and inserted them into enemy-occupied territory with varying degrees of success. It operated on a global basis, running missions in China, Malaya, Africa, South America and the Middle East as well as in nineteen European countries.

Initially SOE was an amalgam of two existing clandestine units: the black propaganda staff known as Electra House, which was headed by Sir Campbell Stuart; and SIS's sabotage branch, Section D, which consisted of 140 hastily recruited intelligence officers. Together they formed the foundation of SOE, an ad hoc organisation created to foment subversion across the world and, in Churchill's famous phrase, 'set Europe ablaze'. It was also to precipitate an enduring wrangle over what exactly happened during its short existence. All three of its executive directors, who adopted the letters 'CD' to conceal their identities, went to their graves without having written anything substantial about their wartime work. Nelson retired to his country home near Kidlington, Oxfordshire, his role entirely unknown outside Whitehall's secret corridors: his entry in *Kelly's Handbook* noted only that he had served in the Royal Air Force Volunteer Reserve during the war, joining with the rank of pilot officer in 1940 and being promoted to squadron leader the following year. His successor, Sir Charles Hambro, of the merchant banking family, who had started SOE's Scandinavian country sections, died on 28 August 1963 with his daughter at his bedside stoking a small bonfire of his secret papers which he had demanded should be burned.[1] Sir Colin Gubbins, a regular army officer with unconventional ideas about guerrilla warfare, alone mentioned SOE in a short lecture to the Royal United Services Institute in January 1948,[2] and authorised his

Norwegian wife to publish his biography after his death on 11 February 1976. As yet, her task has not been completed.[3]

Unlike Britain's other secret services, MI5 and SIS, SOE did not shun publicity at the end of the war and even co-operated with the Ministry of Information on a full-length film entitled *Now It Can Be Told*, featuring authentic SOE personnel.[4] Nor did the Foreign Office raise any objection when several of SOE's former agents published their recollections, even though the majority of those released were far from accurate. Among the first into print was Maurice Buckmaster, who had headed F Section, the French country section, between September 1941 and June 1945. His first book, *Specially Employed*, was published in 1952 and gave a glowing account of what he purported to be his Section's successes, while admitting in the foreword that it was not completely factually accurate.[5] There were others who wrote in a similar vein, but it was not until Jean Overton Fuller wrote *Double Webs* in 1958 that serious questions were raised about F Section's integrity.[6] Having been the executor of the will left by her friend Noor Inayat Khan (*Madeleine*), she had researched Khan's biography.[7] Her investigations took her to Germany, where she met many of SOE's wartime adversaries and unearthed the appalling truth that F Section's Air Movements Officer, Henri Dericourt, had worked as a double agent for the *Sicherheitsdienst* (SD), the Nazi Party's security service. Because he was still alive and had been convicted of no serious crime, Miss Fuller could only refer to him by his SOE nom de guerre, *Gilbert*. Her discovery, combined with the severe criticisms of the way F Section had recruited and run seven women agents who had been betrayed to the Nazis, made by Elizabeth Nicholas in *Death Be Not Proud*,[8] caused questions to be tabled in the Commons.

Suddenly SOE was not the glorious story of the triumph of British improvisation over the unscrupulous Nazis. It had been transformed into a tale of unprecedented treachery, betrayal and criminal incompetence, exploited by a resourceful enemy, which, the evidence suggested, rarely had to resort to physical torture. Indeed, as Miss Fuller revealed, captured SOE agents were greeted at the SD's notorious Paris headquarters in the Avenue Foch by a genial British officer, Captain John Starr, an SOE turncoat who had given the Germans his parole in 1943 following his second ill-fated mission to France. Once welcomed by a colleague who knew their real names, other F Section agents abandoned their cover identities, exasperated by the obvious depth of the enemy's knowledge of SOE. A few who survived promised to kill Starr, but after the war he narrowly escaped prosecution for treason and went to live in Paris. His case received absolutely no publicity and set the tone for the bizarre, sometimes labyrinthine, intrigue which was to mark the way SOE was to be treated in the future.

During the immediate post-war years successive British governments maintained a discreet silence on the issue of classified wartime operations, having been advised to do so by their secret civil servants, who were no doubt very sensitive to the possible consequences of disclosure and debate on matters that, by convention, were kept out of the public arena. On 15 December 1958 John Profumo MP, then a junior minister in the Foreign Office, acknowledged the growing criticism of SOE and announced his intention, following pressure from the redoubtable Dame Irene Ward MP, to appoint 'a former officer with wartime experience of the Executive to advise and assist inquirers and in general to deal with questions regarding the release of information on the Special Operations Executive'. While Dame Irene was delighted by the Foreign Office's apparent co-operation, Profumo's reply engendered nothing but hostility from Colonel John Cordeaux, the Conservative MP for Nottingham Central, who denounced the Minister's decision as 'beyond a joke' and cited 'the harm done by these amateur spies cashing in on their war experiences by turning amateur authors': 'Will he ensure that what has not yet been disclosed of Services technique and practice remains secret from now on? Will he deny access to these files to all historians, professional or amateur, or other unauthorised persons?'[9]

Those in the Strangers' Gallery of the House of Commons listening to these exchanges might have been forgiven for wondering why Cordeaux felt so passionately about this issue. Although *Who's Who* listed only his 'attachment to the Foreign Office 1942–6', Cordeaux was in fact a senior SIS officer and the author of a secret report into one of the most serious of SOE's wartime catastrophes, the double-agent 'game' perpetrated by the Germans in Holland, which led to the deaths of over forty agents.

Following more lobbying from Dame Irene, the Prime Minister, Harold Macmillan, authorised research to determine whether an official account of SOE's activities in France could be published. In the autumn of 1960 Professor M. R. D. Foot embarked upon two years of work, which resulted in a parliamentary reply on 13 April 1964 announcing that his history, *SOE in France*, was to be released in April 1966. However, when the first draft was circulated to various interested parties, it provoked a furious response. References to Odette Sansom were changed in the second edition at the request of her lawyers, and both Nicholas Bodington, F Section's long-serving deputy head, and Peter Churchill brought actions for defamation against the Crown and the author.[10] Churchill had his claim settled out of court, but Bodington died before the matter could come before a jury.

Foot's book remains the standard work of reference on SOE although the text inevitably contains some errors. Brian Stonehouse, a radio operator who parachuted into France in July 1942, is but one survivor with strong views who complained that virtually all the references to him were incorrect.[11] Although Foot had been granted full access to what remained of SOE's records, his research was done under the ever vigilant supervision of Colonel Edward Boxshall, a veteran SIS officer, whose pre-war experience in Bucharest had, according to intelligence folklore, made him indispensable to SIS and an obvious candidate to be the Foreign Office's first SOE Adviser.[12] However, as Foot himself admitted, his account was bound to be incomplete because of the lack of certain key files, including SOE's entire financial records and the North African archives. Some had been 'weeded' out, many had been destroyed deliberately, and others had perished in the mysterious fire which had engulfed SOE's Baker Street headquarters in January 1946. In addition, security considerations had prevented him from studying papers relating to some of the more contentious episodes in SOE's history, such as the bitter dispute perpetuated by SIS's Frank Slocum, who had denied SOE facilities to get its agents across the Channel by boat. SIS had played a crucial, but largely unknown, role in SOE's development and, since that arcane body had become the custodian of SOE's archives, it is hardly surprising that it exercised complete control over certain names and particular events. Nevertheless, despite the need for caution in this delicate area, SIS evidently had no qualms about other secret departments. Tony Brooks, for example, who had moved from SOE to SIS after the war, and later joined MI5, was still working for the counter-espionage branch of the Security Service when *SOE in France* was published and his exploits divulged.[13]

The fact that a proportion of SOE's records had gone missing was first made known in October 1949, when a Dutch parliamentary commission arrived in London to launch an investigation into the disastrous performance of N Section, the Netherlands country section, which had previously been the subject of John Cordeaux's secret enquiry. SIS had had to admit that 'the bulk' of the relevant archive had been destroyed, leaving the commission to cross-examine six senior SOE officers and three of their SIS counterparts. The commission concluded that there was not 'the slightest grounds for believing that there was treachery on either the British or the Netherlands side'. However, the fact that the visiting parliamentarians were never informed of the existence of the Cordeaux report makes one wonder how valid their conclusions were. It also leaves room for speculation about

Cordeaux's motive for opposing the release of material from SOE's vaults.

It is Foot's belief that, while he was still preparing his final version of *SOE in France*, a copy was made available to Edward Spiro, a journalist of Austrian origin, who, in parallel, had been researching *Inside SOE* under the pen-name of E. H. Cookridge.[14] A year earlier Spiro had published *They Came from the Sky*, the stories of three F Section agents, with a foreword by Buckmaster, but *Inside SOE* was to be a much more comprehensive history, containing a short statement from Buckmaster attacking the criticisms levelled by Jean Overton Fuller and Elizabeth Nicholas.[15]

What is truly astonishing about the frequently bitter machinations that went on behind the scenes to protect reputations and enhance previously established fiction was that SIS itself possessed two documents which, if released, could have set the record straight once and for all. Colonel R. A. Bourne-Paterson, F Section's Planning Officer (and later Buckmaster's deputy), wrote a secret 136-page history of F Section's operations entitled *The 'British' Circuits in France*, which remains classified to this day and was evidently one of Professor Foot's principal sources.[16] It is dated 30 June 1946, the very day that SOE was wound up, which suggests that it has stayed in SIS's hands ever since. Its contents can be judged by the author's opening remarks: 'I would urge that this work be treated as confidential and be given a strictly limited circulation. Complete frankness has been observed in its composition in order that, in the right hands, its utility may be as great as possible.'

Cookridge had no knowledge of Bourne-Paterson's work. Nor did he know that a distinguished Scottish academic, Professor William Mackenzie, had spent three years writing a detailed, warts-and-all account of SOE for SIS. Now eighty-one years old, Mackenzie says that he 'was reasonably paid for the job, and . . . the typescript belongs to some branch or other of Her Majesty's Government'.[17] According to the current Secretary of the Cabinet, Sir Robin Butler, 'there are at present no plans to declassify and release it'.[18]

Sir Robin's predecessor in the Cabinet Office, Lord Armstrong, commissioned another academic, the late Charles Cruickshank, to write *SOE in Scandinavia* and *SOE in the Far East*,[19] both of which were submitted for editorial attention by the Government before publication. In addition, three further officially sanctioned studies, on SOE operations in Italy, Yugoslavia and the Low Countries, are now under way. What makes these projects so unsatisfactory is that they have been sponsored by the Cabinet Office, and it is widely believed that when the present Lord Armstrong was Cabinet Secretary he acted to ensure that they contained only a part of SOE's story. This, of course, was the more creditable aspect of the organisation's performance, with only minimal references to SIS, which had waged an undeclared war with SOE from the moment of the latter's inception. What follows is in part the remarkable story of that conflict and the extraordinary heroism of the men and women recruited into what was known to the *cognoscenti* as 'the racket'.

At the conclusion of the Cold War it is sometimes hard for those in the West to recall the full horror of the totalitarian regimes that have dominated Eastern Europe during the past forty-five years. It is harder still for a younger generation to imagine the sacrifices made by SOE's personnel who undertook clandestine missions into enemy-occupied countries. Nor were the harrowing ordeals limited to the agents in the field, for the headquarters staff invariably shouldered a heavy burden of responsibility for their welfare, frequently having to weigh up the conflicting evidence and decide whether a particular wireless link had fallen under enemy control. Nor were these crucial assessments made in ideal conditions by ruthlessly pragmatic staff with no operational experience despite the bitter protests of individual agents who have written of being abandoned in hostile territory, ignored by their country section desk officers. Briefing and planning officers have complained equally of slap-dash security and reckless behaviour in the field. This account is intended to strike a balance between the two apparently incompatible extremes and explain how a small covert sabotage service, financed from the British Government's secret vote and a mining magnate's private fortune, was transformed into a global organisation that actively assisted despotic tyrannies to seize power in so much of Eastern Europe.

I · The First Two Years

The whole concept of secret warfare, embracing espionage, counter-espionage, guerrilla warfare, secret para-military and para-naval operations, was an anathema to some. Such secret activities involved varying degrees of illegal or unethical methods which would violate normal peacetime morality and would not only be improper but often criminal; untruths, deceptions, bribery, forgeries of passports, permits or currencies, acts of violence, mayhem and murder.

Jack Beevor, Assistant to CD, Sir Charles Hambro, June 1941–July 1943[1]

Given Britain's multiplicity of secret services in 1940, why was yet another branch needed? Why had SIS, the clandestine organisation which had been responsible for the country's covert intelligence activities since 1909, not responded to the Nazi challenge? Certainly SIS's hierarchy would have preferred this alternative, but political, as well as operational, considerations were taken into account when the decision was made to create SOE.

The politics involved were complicated. The Labour Party had long been suspicious of MI5's and SIS's professionals, a distrust which dated back to the Zinoviev Letter affair in 1924 and domestic surveillance of trade union members suspected of being disloyal. Both organisations had, to a greater or lesser extent, failed to remain aloof from politics. The long-serving Director-General of the Security Service, Sir Vernon Kell, had once threatened to burn every file in MI5's extensive registry rather than let the contents fall into the hands of a left-wing government; and before the war the Chief of SIS, Admiral Sir Hugh Sinclair, had once forced Stanley Baldwin back to the Commons to retract a misleading statement he had made on German air strength. Moreover, the only significant pre-war espionage cases, those of Percy Glading and Wilfred Macartney, had both involved political activists of the Left.

Both MI5 and SIS were in the hands of Conservative ministers. MI5 answered to the Home Secretary, Sir John Anderson, through the mechanism of the newly created Home Defence (Security) Executive, headed by another Tory politician, Lord Swinton. The Security Executive had been set up on the Prime Minister's instructions to supervise MI5's anti-Fifth Column activities, but Swinton had swiftly taken control of the entire organisation, which was then in a state of chaotic expansion. SIS, on the other hand, was the responsibility of the Foreign Secretary, Lord Halifax. The Labour Party was not well-inclined to the burgeoning ranks of solicitors and City businessmen all headed for safe desk jobs in intelligence. It also believed itself to be better placed to liaise with foreign resistance groups, especially those that were predominantly Socialist, and those with which the Labour Party already enjoyed fraternal links.

There were also strong operational reasons for separating the functions of 'secret intelligence' from 'special operations'. SIS had previously undertaken both roles, but with only limited success, for a catastrophe early in the war had virtually neutralised SIS's European infrastructure. SIS's acquisition of intelligence relied upon two principal sources: the regular SIS officers posted abroad under Passport Control cover to liaise with their respective host countries, and the Z organisation, a clandestine network which operated in parallel with, but remotely from, the local Passport Control Office (PCO). At the outbreak of hostilities in September 1939, individual Z representatives had been instructed to disclose their existence to their counterparts at the local PCO. This directive had been intended to allow them to run in tandem, but the reality was a loss of their in-built compartmented security, combined with rivalry, jealousy and recriminations that followed the Venlo fiasco: the kidnapping of a senior Z officer and his PCO counterpart by the *Sicherheitsdienst* at Venlo on the Dutch–German frontier in November 1939. Captain Sigismund Best and Major Richard Stevens were enticed to the frontier with the promise of meeting a senior anti-Nazi *Luftwaffe* officer, but the whole operation turned out to be an elaborate trap: they were both abducted and endured lengthy interrogation.[2] In consequence, SIS's management had good reason to fear that its dependence upon the chain of European British PCOs had been compromised, and that Z's undercover assets, such as they were, had become vulnerable liabilities.

These fears were to be compounded by the swiftness with which the *Wehrmacht* had overrun France and the Low Countries, leaving SIS devoid of bases from which to direct operations. It had almost no connections with the anti-Nazi movements on the Continent, nor had it established any stay-behind networks. The few abortive sabotage missions that were launched in an effort to deny certain strategic commodities to the advancing enemy were mounted by a strange, semi-autonomous group known as Section D, which worked under SIS's auspices and was led by a charismatic army officer, Major Laurence Grand of the Royal Engineers, who was rarely seen without a perfectly furled umbrella and a red carnation. Although Section D was a relatively new branch, having been founded in March 1938, it was to absorb what remained of the Z network after the Venlo incident and to acquire, for the first time, sufficient staff to undertake its mission. Significantly, many of the Z personnel were retained to run D's outposts, and even the old Z numbers, which had been allocated for identification purposes in ciphered telegrams, remained the same. According to a minute dated 5 June 1939, Grand's 'D for Destruction' unit had been instructed to 'investigate every possibility of attacking potential enemies by means other than the operations of military forces', but Grand had no staff apart from Monty Chidson, an experienced SIS officer who had until the previous year been the Passport Control Officer in The Hague. It had been his successor, Richard Stevens, who had been abducted.

Grand's brief would not have developed beyond the academic if it had not been for his friendship with the American-born tycoon (Sir) Chester Beatty, who, upon being told that the Treasury was restricting SIS's preparations for war, had agreed to finance what was referred to as the 'Sabotage Service'. Beatty produced a large cheque and promised to introduce some reliable men with a knowledge of the Balkans, Section D's target area. Among them was George Taylor, a ruthless Australian businessman, who had supervised the establishment of Section D's principal office at 2 Caxton Street, conveniently close to SIS's headquarters in nearby Broadway, and a Victorian mansion called The Frythe near Hatfield in Hertfordshire. When Chidson and Taylor began their recruitment for Section D, their cover was the War Office's non-existent 'Statistical Research Department'.

Although officially a sub-division of SIS, Section D's remit was sabotage, and its personnel were distributed across Europe to make preparations intended to impede any German advance into the Balkans. Unlike the remainder of its parent organisation, D's task did not concern intelligence-gathering and it operated entirely separately from the compromised SIS stations, whose covers as British PCOs had been blown so comprehensively. D's key figure in the Balkans was Julius Hanau, a South African businessman, who was the Vickers representative in Belgrade and who had close connections with Beatty. Beatty's company, the Selection Trust Group, owned huge holdings in South-East Europe, including the Trepca Mine in Serbia, one of

Section D

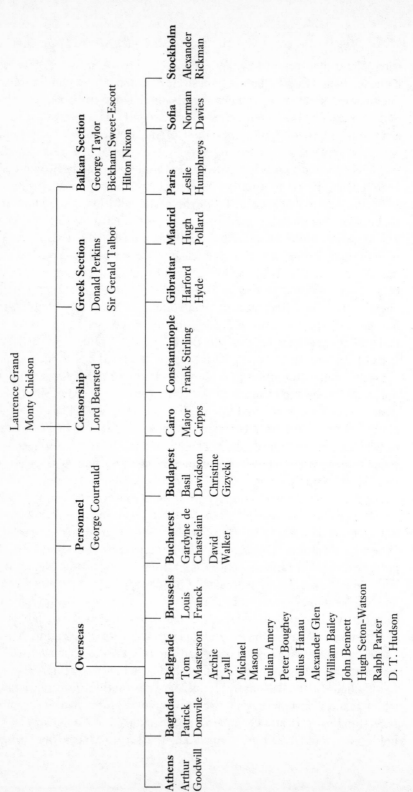

Laurence Grand
Monty Chidson

Overseas

Personnel	**Censorship**	**Greek Section**	**Balkan Section**
George Courtauld	Lord Bearsted	Donald Perkins	George Taylor
		Sir Gerald Talbot	Bickham Sweet-Escott
			Hilton Nixon

Athens	**Baghdad**	**Belgrade**	**Brussels**	**Bucharest**	**Budapest**	**Cairo**	**Constantinople**	**Gibraltar**	**Madrid**	**Paris**	**Sofia**	**Stockholm**
Arthur Goodwill	Patrick Domvile	Tom Masterson	Louis Franck	Gardyne de Chastelain	Basil Davidson	Major Cripps	Frank Stirling	Harford Hyde	Hugh Pollard	Leslie Humphreys	Norman Davies	Alexander Rickman
		Archie Lyall		David Walker	Christine Gizycki							
		Michael Mason										
		Julian Amery										
		Peter Boughey										
		Julius Hanau										
		Alexander Glen										
		William Bailey										
		John Bennett										
		Hugh Seton-Watson										
		Ralph Parker										
		D. T. Hudson										

the richest mineral deposits in Europe, which at that time employed some three thousand miners and is still in production fifty years later.[3]

That Beatty wished to protect his investment is hardly surprising. The entire enterprise was an enormous undertaking and was international in its nature. The ore was moved from the main site, a mountain at Stan Trg, to a flotation plant at Zvecan. There it was loaded on to railway wagons and transported to the Greek port of Thessaloniki for shipment to the Antwerp market and to Europe's refineries for smelting. However, there was an additional reason for Beatty's involvement: the Trepca Mine was effectively supporting the German war effort.

This extraordinary situation arose because of a decision by the Yugoslav Government to appropriate seventy per cent of the mine's production and to barter some of its strategic minerals, like zinc and lead, with Germany in return for armaments. Selection Trust had little option but to accept this arrangement, for to have opposed it would have risked a complete take-over by the state. However, it did leave Beatty's all-British management in the embarrassing position of supplying the enemy with vital minerals. Equally unpalatable was the destination for the remainder of the production, the Soviet Union. Once the Mediterranean had been closed to commercial traffic, the mine had been obliged to sell to the Russians, who then shipped the ore in barges down the Danube to the Black Sea.

SIS, and in particular Section D, was fully aware of this situation, and a plan to improve it was hatched by Hanau, in conjunction with two of Beatty's senior staff, who had been recommended to Grand and who were to play important roles in Section D and then SOE: a metallurgist, S. W. (Bill) Bailey, and a South African mining engineer, D. T. (Bill) Hudson. Hanau's scheme was to sabotage the flow of Romanian oil from Giurgiu to Regensburg in Germany by blowing up the Danube gorge known as the Iron Gates. The Trepca Mine had plenty of gelignite, Bailey had the necessary expertise, and the British Legation could give a measure of diplomatic protection to some of the saboteurs, or so the theory went.

In practice the operation turned out to be rather more complicated, but in March 1940 a very determined effort was made to cut off the oil. The first step was the creation of the Goeland Shipping Company, run by William Harris-Burland, which began to buy up or charter the Danube's barges so as to deny them to the Germans. These were then manned by Australian and British naval volunteers and moved to Sulina, at the river's mouth, to rendezvous with the SS *Ardinian*, which was carrying a cargo of weapons, explosives and more naval ratings led by an eccentric British naval intelligence officer, Merlin Minshall. The intention, according to David

Walker, who was a roving Section D agent working under *Daily Mirror* cover, was to transfer the illicit cargo, documented as oil equipment, on to lighters and then to take them up river towards Budapest in ninety-four barges towed by five tugs. However, one shipment, on the *Tormonde*, was discovered by the Romanians to consist of several three-pounder guns, six tons of gelignite and a quantity of grenades. Twelve naval ratings were detained and then deported, having been escorted on to a British tanker bound for Istanbul. The remainder of the team were subsequently rounded up and allowed to leave Romania without charge. Section D bowed to the outrage expressed by the Foreign Office and abandoned the entire operation. Minshall, who had conducted a clandestine survey of the Iron Gates from his yacht before the war, succeeded in extricating himself from the Romanian security police, largely due to his status as a British vice-consul, and made a swift exit into the Black Sea aboard a fast launch, after having abandoned his own explosives-packed ship, the *Oxford*.[4] Harris-Burland was also evacuated to Istanbul, albeit under less dramatic circumstances, where he was later to succeed Gardyne de Chastelain as head of SOE's local Romanian sub-section.

Section D's performance elsewhere was equally unimpressive. On 29 May it launched a mission in an eleven-ton Norwegian fishing boat, the *Lady*, which sailed from Lerwick in Scotland with Simon Field as first mate, intending to wreak havoc around the Hardanger Fjord. A hydroelectric plant at Ålvik was badly damaged, and the crew of the *Lady* returned safely. A second attempt, to establish a wireless set in Norway, ended with the arrest of Konrad Lindberg and Frithof Pedersen. Both men were executed the following year, on 11 August 1941. As Frank Nelson minuted, 'In Norway we have at the moment literally no one in the field at all.'[5]

Another mission, this time to Sweden, also ended in disaster. Alexander Rickman, of Section D's Scandinavian Section, had been sent to Stockholm under journalistic cover early in 1938. In August 1939 Faber & Faber had published his book, *Swedish Iron Ore*, which had enhanced his local standing, and he had started recruiting a network based on two members of the expatriate business community, Ernest Biggs, a one-legged tea importer, and Harry Gill, British Petroleum's representative.

Rickman's objective had been to plant explosives in the iron-ore port of Oxelösund in anticipation of a German invasion, and Gerald Holdsworth had flown to Stockholm to assist, when, on 9 April, the *Wehrmacht* entered Denmark and Norway. However, while Rickman was still in the preparatory stages of moving his sabotage material to his target, he was arrested by the Swedish police. Convicted of attempted sabotage, he was sentenced to eight years' hard labour; Biggs, who was caught carrying two suitcases packed with dynamite, received five years.[6] Two other fellow-conspirators, Elsa Johansson and Arno Behrisch, got three and a half years.

This disaster might not have been so bad if the Passport Control Officer, John Martin, had not been aware that Biggs had been under constant Swedish surveillance. Martin had been tipped off by a sympathetic police-man that Biggs had been compromised by an informant and was likely to be arrested. However, the SIS officer had failed to alert Rickman in time because he had been anxious not to lose a valued source. Instead, Rickman's group was rounded up and imprisoned. Harry Gill resisted interrogation and managed to escape with a fine, and Holdsworth sought temporary sanctuary in the British Legation before fleeing to Finland for repatriation to England.

Despite these disheartening setbacks, Section D persevered by deploying its personnel further afield. In Rome the SIS Head of Station, Humphrey Plowden, and the local Z representative, Graham Maingot, combined forces to recruit an anti-Fascist stay-behind network, but their efforts were to come to nought. Section D also made contact with Moshe Sharett of the Jewish Agency, and sent another young recruit from the Z network, John Codrington, to establish an office in Paris,[7] while Arthur Goodwill took up residence in the British Legation in Athens. The sudden Nazi attack in May 1940 gave the Section, which had by now reached a strength of 140 members, an opportunity to demonstrate its ability to conduct clandestine operations. In two particularly successful undertakings, Monty Chidson returned to Holland to recover Amsterdam's reserves of industrial dia-monds,[8] and Louis Franck, a Belgian-born banker, removed a quantity of gold from Brussels just as the enemy entered the city.

At the end of May 1940 George Taylor opened a branch in Cairo, leaving the London end in the hands of Bickham Sweet-Escott and an Australian, Hilton Nixon. To accommodate the additional staff, Section D expanded into the fourth floor of the St Ermin's Hotel. Meanwhile, the military setbacks on the Continent forced D into a series of rearguard actions: the rescue of Madame de Gaulle from France by Norman Hope, and Peter Wilkinson's mission to Biscarosse Plage, south of Bordeaux, to exfiltrate General Sikorski and what remained of the Polish General Staff after the French collapse. Thereafter, D's role became entirely defensive, preparing for a Nazi invasion and creating an embryonic resistance network across Britain. In addition to The Frythe, a further country estate, Coleshill House, near Faringdon on the Wiltshire–Berkshire border, was acquired for the training of saboteurs. There the Auxiliary Units were organised into individual patrols and, after intensive instruction in the art of silent killing, subversion and other arcane skills, posted to areas likely to fall under enemy occupation after a successful German landing.[9]

The 'invasion summer' of 1940 saw an amalgamation between Section D and another irregular unit known as MI (Research). Headed by a sapper, Colonel John (Joe) Holland, and based at 7 Whitehall Place, conveniently close to its cover address, 'Room 365, The War Office', MI(R) was intended to develop guerrilla warfare techniques and to circulate pamphlets on the subject. Holland's own military experience had been far from ordinary: he had won the DFC as a pilot, had fought with T. E. Lawrence in the Middle East and later had been wounded during the Troubles in Ireland. As MI(R) became operational, advocating the use of the elite, uniformed specialist formations which were eventually to evolve into the commandos, it moved from the realm of the theoretical and despatched military missions to the Continent. Each remained in contact with a headquarters staff in London (see table opposite), and a sub-office headed by Peter Wilkinson was opened at 88 rue de Varennes in Paris. The largest group, under the leadership of a gunner and a contemporary of Holland's at Sandhurst, Colin Gubbins, which was sent to Warsaw in September 1939, only just managed to escape capture and eventually made its way home via Romania and Cairo. There MI(R) operated a local branch under the leadership of Colonel Adrian Simpson, an old Russian hand who had been deputy managing director of Marconi.

MI(R) boasted its own research centre, known as Station XII, at Aston House, near Knebworth in Hertfordshire. This highly secret establishment was run by a colourful teacher, Commander Arthur Langley RN, a scholar from Downing College, Cambridge, who had been appointed the senior science master at King Edward's School, Birmingham, after having headed the Royal Navy Experimental Station at Stratford during the First World War. He was later to be succeeded by another munitions expert, Colonel (Sir) Ernest Wood, who specialised in the development of anti-tank weapons such as the 'sticky bomb', which could be used by relatively unskilled partisans.

Such interest was generated by the work done by Holland's boffins that a sub-branch, MI(R)(c), was formed under Stuart Macrae, who opened a workshop in the International Broadcasting Company's studios at 35 Portland Place and in a small warehouse in Hendon.[10] It seems that Macrae and Quintin Hogg, another MI(R) luminary, had simultaneously heard that, as the IBC's two stations, Radio Normandie and Radio Fécamp, were going off the air for the duration, their premises would be available for

MI(R)

Head	John Holland

London

Western Europe	Tommy Davies	Central Europe	Douglas Dodds-Parker
Scandinavia	Peter Fleming	Supply	Ralph Gregg
South Russia	Douglas Roberts	Personnel	John Kennedy

Missions

Gibraltar	Peter Kemp	Poland	Colin Gubbins
Greece	Ian Pirie	Palestine	Arthur Lawrence
France	Peter Wilkinson	Romania	Geoffrey Household
Crete	John Pendlebury	Egypt	Adrian Simpson
Norway	J. Watt Torrance		Oliver Baldwin
	Anthony Palmer		Terence Airey
	Andrew Croft		Charles Richardson
	Malcolm Munthe	Finland	E. R. W. Whittington-Moe
			J. C. Scott-Harston

requisitioning. Both successfully manipulated the War Office bureaucracy and acquired a suite of offices above the IBC's well-equipped workshops.

By an administrative oversight, not uncommon in those chaotic days, many of the IBC staff were absorbed into MI(R)(c), which resulted in entertainers and broadcasting technicians being involved in the construction of ingenious, if unorthodox, instruments of sabotage. Indeed, the arrangement worked so well that the IBC's Chief Engineer, Norman Angier, built a revolutionary 20mm spigot mortar known as the Blacker Bombard after its MI(R) inventor, Colonel Stewart Blacker. This eccentric Irishman had a truly remarkable history. He was a pioneer of wireless telegraphy, having raised and commanded the 1st Divisional Signals in 1910, and thereafter had learned to fly, joining the Royal Flying Corps. Severely wounded in 1916, he transferred to Turkestan, where he joined a detachment of Indian guides. In later life, as an explorer, he climbed Mount Everest twice and walked across most of Russia and Central Asia. His one frustration, solved by the creation of MI(R)(c), was the inability of the top hierarchy to adopt his novel ideas. His proposal in 1922 to equip infantry with parachutes was a little ahead of its time, but some of his other brainchildren, such as the

Hedgehog anti-submarine mortar and the PIAT anti-tank weapon, were eventually put into production.

Moral, political and financial support for MI(R)(c)'s unconventional research came from an unusual source: Winston Churchill, the new Prime Minister, and his scientific adviser, Professor Frederick Lindemann. Ever since his experiences in the Boer War, Churchill had been interested in guerrilla tactics and he retained a fascination for novelties, especially of the exploding variety. It was not unusual for (Sir) Millis Jefferis, another of MI(R)(c)'s boffins seconded from the Royal Engineers, to be summoned to Chequers to give a fireworks' display on Sunday afternoons. On one memorable occasion, on 18 August 1940, the Blacker Bombard was demonstrated in the garden at Chequers by Ralph Farrant. It misfired and sent the twenty-three-pound projectile perilously close to the group of VIPs gathered around the Prime Minister. Having narrowly missed General Smuts, it exploded close to General de Gaulle, leading Churchill to promptly authorise expenditure of a further £5,000 for perfecting the device. The episode did no harm to the careers of those involved, as both Farrant and Jefferis were later promoted to the rank of major-general. In another similar incident King Haakon was chased across the golf links at Roehampton by a prototype, remote-controlled contraption, known as the Mobile Mine, which ran out of control. The Norwegian monarch fled to the first green and was only saved when the wheels of the infernal invention sank into the sand of a strategically sited bunker.

Incendiaries from German air raids eventually destroyed MI(R)(c)'s stores at Hendon and put the Portland Place offices out of action, so new accommodation was found in the country, in a secluded house called The Firs, at Whitchurch, just north of Aylesbury in Buckinghamshire. Owned by a wealthy stockbroker, (Sir) Arthur Abrahams, The Firs became a production centre for numerous imaginative aids to unconventional warfare, such as magnetic limpet mines and pencil fuses.

MI(R) began life as a one-man undertaking, with Joe Holland fighting the military intelligence establishment and the Ministry of Supply for recognition. Gradually, as the Norwegian campaign faltered, and the principles of *Blitzkrieg* were understood, his ideas gained acceptance. Some of his early subordinates, like Norman Crockatt and Clayton Hutton,[11] accepted Holland's doctrines and moved sideways to set up other new organisations, in their case an escape and evasion service designated MI9. Following the cancellation of Operation KNIFE, an MI(R) sabotage mission to the Sogne Fjord, two of its members, Brian Mayfield and Bill Stirling, obtained permission to open a training facility at Inverailort House, twenty-five miles west of Fort William in Inverness-shire. This modest establishment was to become the first of dozens of SOE's Special Training Schools (STSs).

Thus, by the beginning of May 1940, there was no shortage of enthusiastic volunteers willing to indulge in unconventional warfare. However, it soon became clear that these buccaneers needed supervision, and this became manifest during the last desperate days of the month when both MI(R) and Section D were operational in France. Leslie Humphreys, the head of D's French Section, was active in northern France, concealing ten dumps of arms and ammunition, each guarded by two local recruits, in a somewhat optimistic attempt to build a stay-behind network, while MI(R) landed a party of four near Etaples on a raid which Churchill described in his memoirs as a 'pinprick' and a 'silly fiasco'.[12] Led by Alan Warren of the Royal Marines, it consisted of three French-speaking officer cadets from Woolwich and was intended to make contact and organise the remnants of the British Expeditionary Force, who were believed to be wandering aimlessly in the French hinterland.

MI(R)'s plan did not go entirely as expected. Warren and his team spent three weeks in enemy-occupied territory, but failed to find a single straggler. Their main preoccupation was avoiding the many German patrols and, after the failure of their wireless, trying to find a way back across the Channel. Eventually they commandeered a rowing boat and set off towards England. They were finally rescued, exhausted and demoralised, by the Dungeness Lightship. This humiliating episode was a matter of acute embarrassment to MI(R), and virtually no records of the débâcle exist, apart from Warren's own candid account of it.[13] He was subsequently transferred to the Auxiliary Units and, thereafter, to SOE's headquarters in Singapore.

The crucial date in SOE's genesis is 13 June 1940, when Lord Hankey called in Holland and Grand 'to discuss certain questions arising out of a possible collapse of France'. Hankey, a Cabinet member by virtue of his position as Chancellor of the Duchy of Lancaster, fulfilled the function of Churchill's co-ordinator of intelligence. Seeing the potential for muddle and wasteful duplication with MI(R) and Section D, he recommended that a Directorate of Combined Operations be created. This was a new proposal, based on an MI(R) paper outlining solutions to the obvious need to integrate the covert warfare specialists. The new Director of Military Intelligence, Paddy Beaumont-Nesbitt, endorsed the document calling for a new War Office directorate of 'irregular activities', as did his Minister, Anthony Eden. Two days after Hankey's consultation, General Sir Alan Bourne RM was appointed to the new post of Director of Combined Operations, but he too echoed demands for a separate body to liaise between SIS, Electra House, the Admiralty, the Foreign Office and the Air Ministry.

Quite how much Section D or MI(R) actually achieved during the first six months of the war is difficult to assess. According to Bickham Sweet-Escott:

> our record of positive achievement was unimpressive. There were a few successful operations to our credit, but certainly not many; and we had something which could be called an organisation on the ground in the Balkans. But even there we had failed to do anything spectacular. The oil of Romania continued to arrive in Germany punctually and without much in the way of let or hindrance, and our essays in Balkan subversion had succeeded only in making the Foreign Office jumpy. As for Western Europe, though there was much to excuse it, the record was lamentable for we did not possess one single agent between the Balkans and the English Channel.[14]

Gubbins has also confirmed that 'in 1940, when British forces were evacuated from Western Europe, there was not a single contact of any kind with occupied Western Europe until somebody was dropped back there'.[15]

In short, SIS was at a disadvantage when attempting to justify its own intelligence-gathering performance. The Venlo disaster had jeopardised the PCO system, and the Z network, which had only produced reports of the most dubious variety, had been dismantled hastily. No provision had been made to leave agents in place, ready to be activated after the *Wehrmacht* had 'rolled over', and no contact had been established with the few remaining opposition cells in Germany. SIS's paucity of worthwhile assets obliged it to concentrate on building a relationship with the various governments-in-exile transplanted to London. This was to pay dividends in the future, with SIS exercising control over their intelligence operations and total mastery of their communications. The trump card SIS retained, and continued to exploit for the remainder of the war, was the signals analysis work carried out at its 'war station' at Bletchley Park.

It was in this climate of failure that the Foreign Secretary, Lord Halifax, called a meeting in his room on Monday, 1 July 1940, just as the news came through that the *Wehrmacht* had occupied the Channel Islands. Sir Alexander Cadogan, the Permanent Under-Secretary at the Foreign Office, was there, as was his private secretary, Gladwyn Jebb. So too was Hugh Dalton, Minister of Economic Warfare, Hankey, the Colonial Secretary Lord Lloyd, the Director of Military Intelligence and (Sir) Desmond Morton, who represented the Industrial Intelligence Centre and Number Ten. The discussion focused on the overlapping responsibilities of the numerous separate units all with interests in subversion, and highlighted once again the need for centralised departmental control. The debate led Dalton to write to Halifax the next day:

What is needed is a new organisation to co-ordinate, inspire, control and assist the nationals of the oppressed countries who must themselves be the direct participants. We need absolute secrecy, a certain fanatical enthusiasm, willingness to work with people of different nationalities, complete political reliability. Some of these quali- ties are certainly to be found in some military officers and, if such men are available, they should undoubtedly be used. But the organisation should, in my view, be entirely independent of the War Office machine.[16]

Halifax conferred with Churchill on 11 July, in a meeting attended by Cadogan; the Lord President, Neville Chamberlain; and the Leader of the Labour Party, Clement Attlee. According to Cadogan's diaries:

The Prime Minister (put up to it by Morton) is against Dalton taking over and wants to lump the whole thing under Swinton. This is sloppy: we want to get someone to get a grip on sabotage, etcetera, and pull it into shape. I think Dalton the best man. And the meeting agreed to recommend this.[17]

This elevated group also proposed Sir Robert Vansittart as Dalton's Chief of Staff, and suggested the recently replaced Ambassador in Madrid, Sir Maurice Peterson, as a possible alternative. There was a brief pause for thought, and possibly some political interference by Brendan Bracken (or so Dalton suspected), before Churchill asked Chamberlain to prepare a formal plan, which has subsequently become SOE's founding charter.[18] It 'envisaged an organisation to co-ordinate all action by way of subversion and sabotage, against the enemy overseas'. The document was circulated briefly in Whitehall, and then the Prime Minister sent a copy to Dalton on 16 July, inviting him to take charge of it, with Vansittart as Chief of Staff, and the Lord President acting as an arbitrator in any difficulties arising from other government departments.[19]

This historic document, which has never previously been published, sug- gests that SOE would take on a co-ordinating role, following the example of the Security Executive. Thus, with Dalton's appointment, Churchill had neatly fulfilled an operational need and been politically expedient. This combination, achieved with Chamberlain's help, must have seemed irre- sistible at the time and was formally approved by the War Cabinet on 22 July, complete with the rider that 'it would be very undesirable' for any parliamentary questions to be tabled on the issue.

What makes this decision so odd is the apparent lack of any consultation with those supposedly already in this field. SIS regarded itself as enjoying direct responsibility for the kind of activities envisaged for SOE; it might

SOE's Charter

The original Cabinet memorandum, drafted by Neville Chamberlain in July 1940, which created SOE. Never previously published, it was misplaced in SOE's files and has recently come to light in another secret archive.

MOST SECRET.   C O P Y.   11·3·   2·>|7

W.P. (40) 271.   ———
                                                        71c
19th JULY 1940.   W A R   C A B I N E T.

HOME DEFENCE (SECURITY) EXECUTIVE.

SPECIAL OPERATIONS EXECUTIVE.

Memorandum by the Lord President of the Council.

1.   The memorandum which I circulated to the Cabinet on 27th May (W.P. (40) 172) gave particulars of the organisation of the Home Defence (Security) Executive, which was set up under the chairmanship of Lord Swinton to co-ordinate action against the Fifth Column.

2.   In addition to presiding over the Home Defence (Security) Executive, Lord Swinton has been entrusted with executive control of M.I.5 and is thus responsible for counter espionage activities in Great Britain.

3.   The Prime Minister has now decided that Lord Swinton shall also exercise operational control over the work of M.I.6 in respect of all the activities of M.I.6 in Great Britain and in Eire. M.I.6 will also continue to place at the disposal of Lord Swinton all information in their possession which may have a bearing on Fifth Column activities in Great Britain or Eire.

4.   The Prime Minister has further decided, after consultation with the Ministers concerned, that a new organisation shall be established forthwith to co-ordinate all action, by way of subversion and sabotage, against the enemy overseas. The Prime Minister requested me to set on foot this new organisation in consultation with those concerned. Action is accordingly being taken as follows: -

(a) An organisation is being established to co-ordinate all action, by way of subversion and sabotage, against the enemy overseas. This organisation will be known as the Special Operations Executive.

(b) The Special Operations Executive will be under the chairmanship of Mr. Dalton, the Minister for Economic Warfare.

(c) Mr. Dalton will have the assistance of Sir Robert Vansittart.

(d) The Special Operations Executive will be provided with such additional staff as the Chairman and Sir Robert Vansittart may find necessary.

(e) The various departments and bodies taking part in underground activities will, for the time being, continue to be administered by the Ministers at present responsible for them.

(f) The departments and bodies affected which will now be coordinated by Mr. Dalton are:

Title	Alternative title	Administrative Authority.
Sabotage Service.	"D"	F.O.
M.I.R.	–	W.O.
* Department Electra House.	Sir Campbell Stuart's Organisation.	Joint F.O. and Minister of Information.

-2-

Mr. Dalton will also have the cooperation of the Directors of Intelligence of the three Service Departments and of the Secret Intelligence Service (M.I.6) for the purpose of the work entrusted to him. Mr. Dalton will also keep in touch with Lord Hankey.

(g) The planning and direction of raids by formed bodies of British or Allied ships, troops or aircraft will remain the function of the Military authorities, but Mr. Dalton will maintain touch with Departments planning such raids in order to afford any possible assistance through the channels he coordinates.

(h) Any Department obtaining information likely to be of value to Mr. Dalton will place their information at his disposal.

(i) All operations of sabotage, secret subversive propaganda, the encouragement of civil resistance in occupied areas, the stirring up of insurrection, strikes, etc., in Germany or areas occupied by her will be submitted before being undertaken by any Department, to Mr. Dalton for his approval.

(j) Mr. Dalton will co-ordinate the planning operations of underground warfare and will direct which organisation is to carry them out. He will be responsible for obtaining th agreement of the Secretary of State for Foreign Affairs or other Minister interested to any operation which is likely to affect their interests.

(k) It will be important that the general plan for irregular offensive operations should be in step with the general strategical conduct of the war. With this end in view, Mr. Dalton will consult the Chiefs of Staff as necessary, keeping them informed in general terms of his plans, and, in turn, receiving from them the broad strategic picture.

5.   Lord Swinton and Mr. Dalton will arrange for any consultation that may be mutually helpful or may be necessary to prevent overlapping between the Home Defence (Security) Executive and the Special Operations Executive. Normally, no doubt, consultation between their respective staffs will suffice for this purpose.

6.   The Prime Minister has requested that Lord Swinton and Mr. Dalton should regard me as the member of the War Cabinet who they should consult and to whom any inter-Departmental difficult_es, should they arise, would be referred.

(Int'd) N.C.

Privy Council Office, S.W.1.

19th July, 1940.

* Note: The organisation of this Department is being reviewed.

also fairly be said that, even if Section D had not pulled off any major coups recently, it did at least represent a structure that already had some experience of clandestine operations or, in the words of the official historian, Professor Sir Harry Hinsley, was 'not unlike itself in mode and sphere of activity'.[20] Certainly Stewart Menzies, who had only been installed as Chief of SIS for a matter of months, had played no part in SOE's creation. Indeed, he had been excluded from the deliberations, which may account for MI6's subsequent hostility. To what extent this is a reflection of Menzies's personal position, or the one adopted by his loyal subordinates, is still a matter of controversy. After all, the majority of SOE's personnel who had had overseas service were in Section D, a branch of MI6 which presumably owed its departmental allegiance to Menzies. Those in D who had been involved in the old Z network had all been recruited by Claude Dansey or his deputy, Kenneth Cohen. Both men were to acquire formid-able reputations within the Allied intelligence community as skilful but manipulative operators. Dansey, always a controversial figure because of his legendary ruthlessness, was to become Menzies's deputy. Frank Nelson, of course, the first man to be designated CD as head of SOE, was himself a former SIS hand from Basle, where he had worked for Dansey. According to Sweet-Escott, the key to SOE's future problems was SIS's retention, at this crucial moment, of the new organisation's communications. The politicians had invented a new body to act as an umbrella for a sabotage and subversion service, but had not provided it with the facilities needed to execute its brief. 'A fundamental conflict thus arose at the start,' said Sweet-Escott, who pointed out that SIS's and SOE's roles were so different that they were bound to cause conflict:

The man who is interested in obtaining intelligence must have peace and quiet, and the agents he employs must never, if possible, be found out. But the man who has to carry out operations will produce loud noises if he is successful, and it is only too likely that some of the men he uses will not escape.[21]

•   •   •   •   •   •

Despite the separation of interests between SIS and SOE, the new organis-ation set about developing a structure which almost exactly paralleled SIS. The most striking example is in the case of the French Section, which was started by Section D's representative in Paris, Leslie Humphreys, upon his evacuation to London in June 1940. He had been quite unsuccessful in one of his principal tasks, namely the development of a stay-behind network in France. All his attempts had been deliberately frustrated by Colonels

SOE HQ Organisation

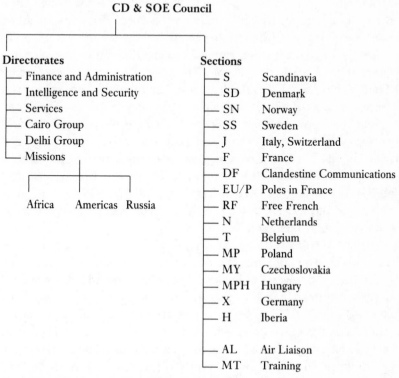

CD & SOE Council

Directorates
— Finance and Administration
— Intelligence and Security
— Services
— Cairo Group
— Delhi Group
— Missions

Africa   Americas Russia

Sections
— S   Scandinavia
— SD   Denmark
— SN   Norway
— SS   Sweden
— J   Italy, Switzerland
— F   France
— DF   Clandestine Communications
— EU/P   Poles in France
— RF   Free French
— N   Netherlands
— T   Belgium
— MP   Poland
— MY   Czechoslovakia
— MPH   Hungary
— X   Germany
— H   Iberia

— AL   Air Liaison
— MT   Training

For details of personnel, refer to Appendix I.

Louis Rivet and de Villeneuve of the *Service de Renseignements*, who had their own reasons for discouraging Peter Wilkinson's contacts with the Poles in France. Accordingly, the official liaison between the Free French in London was channelled through Dansey and Cohen. When Humphreys's SIS counterpart in Paris, Wilfred Dunderdale, returned to London, he concentrated not so much on the French but on the Poles left in France, of whom there were a very large number, including some well-disciplined groups with military backgrounds. Dunderdale cultivated these, via his SIS section designated P5,[22] while in December 1940 SOE started a parallel section, known as EU/P. Typically, Polish political intrigues prevented EU/P from making any progress until July 1941, when it was taken over by Ronald Hazell, a former Baltic shipbroker, who spoke perfect Polish and

German but absolutely no French. This combination proved ideal, and Hazell remained in his post until September 1944. Thus, during the first critical months of the secret war, while the *Wehrmacht* established itself across Western Europe, SIS had three compartmented groups operating into occupied France: Dansey and Cohen picking up the pieces of Z; Major Keyser's French Section running a regular liaison unit, designated P1b; and a Free French sub-section, P1c under Lieutenant-Commander J. E. Gentry. On the SOE side there was Humphreys's F Section, with a sub-section designated DF to run escape lines from the Continent. Supervising both was MO, an operations section under Richard (Dick) Barry, a regular soldier who had just graduated from staff college and who was later to become Chief of Staff to Colin Gubbins. In addition to the above, the Belgian (T) Section and Dutch (N) Section also had an interest in the region. Accordingly, in November 1941 a regional controller was introduced into the chain of command to supervise all the country section operations.

By the time SOE moved from St Ermin's Hotel into its headquarters at 64 Baker Street, a building recently vacated by HM Prison Commissioners, on 31 October 1940, several additional sections had been added to what had originally been termed 'SO 2' to distinguish it from 'SO 1', the propaganda branch. This caused SOE to seek accommodation in several neighbouring office blocks in the same street – Norgeby House at number 83, and St Michael's House at number 82 – and to occupy a proportion of the flats in nearby Montagu Mansions and Berkeley Court. Cover was maintained by the adoption of the name 'Inter-Services Research Bureau', a suitably anonymous title fixed on a plaque outside 64 Baker Street. However, the entrance used most was a small back doorway at the rear, which led on to Kendrick Place.

Among the Sections were MO, under Barry, and F, which was initially under Humphreys, who moved to DF in December 1940 and was replaced by Tommy Davies and Henry Marriott, formerly the Courtauld's representative in Paris, who had been recommended by George Courtauld. The latter had been the personnel officer in the old Section D, and Davies had been a MI(R) veteran and a Courtauld's employee, who had stripped the Courtauld factory in Calais of its valuable stock of platinum to prevent it from falling into German hands in May 1940.

However, the most active part of SOE was its Scandinavian Section, with Charles Hambro, Nelson's deputy and a distinguished banker, as regional controller. The Scandinavian Section had grown out of James Chaworth-Musters's activities when he had been at the British Consulate in Bergen during the German invasion in April 1940. He had linked up with an ill-fated MI(R) mission led by Andrew Croft, but little had been accomplished before they had made their escape. Malcolm Munthe had been captured, but eventually managed to reach Stockholm and the SIS Head of Station at the British Legation, John Martin. Anthony Palmer was arrested by the Germans in Trondheim, and Captain Torrance retreated from Narvik and was evacuated with the rest of the unsuccessful Allied force. In November 1940 Chaworth-Musters's embryonic section was expanded into a regional organisation, headed by a City solicitor, Harry Sporborg, with Frank Stagg as his assistant.

Although the Scandinavian Section existed on paper, it had very little to show for its efforts in terms of manpower. While SOE did have half-a-dozen Norwegians undergoing training at Brickendonbury Hall, two others had been excluded for 'insubordination'[23] and had been handed over to MI5's tender mercies for internment. They had learned too much about Britain's newest, secret organisation, and SOE had not yet acquired suitable accommodation for difficult customers. Such a facility was later obtained, a remote country house at Inverlair. The Scandinavian Section's principal asset during this period was a steady flow of volunteers who landed on the Shetland Islands, the nearest British territory to Norway. SIS had already decided to mobilise these Norwegians and had created a secret base, headed by Leslie Mitchell of SIS's P13 Section, at a secluded but dilapidated farm property called Flemington. Early in 1941 Mitchell was joined by David Howarth of SOE, and the legendary 'Shetland Bus' began operations from Cat Firth, a sheltered anchorage fifteen miles north of the nearest town, Lerwick. In the years that followed, Flemington was to be one of the few successful examples of SIS/SOE co-operation. (For an illustration of the inevitable duplication between their respective country sections, see below.)

That the Scandinavian Section should have established itself so quickly is partly a reflection of the dedication and connections of the SOE personalities involved, and a tacit acknowledgment by SIS that the region, in strategic terms, was a relative backwater.

The Rickman débâcle had left SOE severely disadvantaged in the Baltic and, therefore, in October 1940 Hambro paid a flying visit to the region. He appointed (Sir) Peter Tennent, the Press Attaché, as SOE's representative for Sweden, Denmark and Germany, with Malcolm Munthe liaising with the Norwegians under assistant military attaché cover. This arrangement was to continue until March 1941, when Ronald Turnbull finally reached Stockholm to take command. The full details of the Rickman episode were only disclosed to a handful of people in London, and there

SIS/SOE Country Sections

The responsibilities and jurisdiction of SOE and SIS country sections overlapped, which inevitably led to unnecessary confusion and rivalry in the field and much friction in London. This chart identifies the key headquarters personnel of each organisation together with their assigned territories.

Territory	SIS Section	SIS Personnel	SOE Section	SOE Personnel
France	P1		F/ADM	Major I. J. Mackenzie
North Africa	P1a		AMX	Major E. H. Sherren
Non-Free French	P1b	Lt Dekkers Lt Butler ('Buckley')	F	Col M. Buckmaster Major N. Bodington
Free French	P1c	Lt-Cmdr J. E. Gentry F/O Luce	RF	Col J. R. Hutchison Col L. H. Dismore Fl/Lt F. Yeo-Thomas
Training		Major Bertram		
Iberia	P2	Basil Fenwick	H	R. G. Head
Italy	P4	Major E. J. Robertson	J	Col C. L. Roseberry
Poland and French Lines	P5	Wilfred Dunderdale Fl/Lt Philipson ('Schneidau')	MP EU/P	Col H. P. Perkins Major C. B. Ince
Germany and Czech Liaison	P6	Simon Gallienne Major Day Fl/Lt White	X MY	Major R. H. Thornley F. E. Keary
Belgium	P7	Captain Slater Captain Conway Captain Manning ('Martin')	T	Major C. T. Knight
Holland	P8	Euen Rabagliati Charles Seymour Douglas Child Kenneth Dulling Lt G. A. J. Druce Lt Dixon	N	Major S. Bingham
Norway, Faroes and Iceland	P9	Eric Welsh Captain Turner Captain Cope	SN	Sir George Pollock Captain A. Brogger Captain J. M. Carr
Baltic	P13	Leslie Mitchell	S	G. O. Wiskeman
PoW/MI9	P15	James Langley Airey Neave Ian Garrow Captain Windham-Wright	DF	L. A. L. Humphreys Fl/Lt R. M. Archibald Lt F. Pickering Captain U. Walmsley
Photographic Unit	P19	Professor Henry Briscoe	DSR	Professor Newitt
Yugoslavia	Y/S	John Ennals	D/H	Major E. C. Last

was no mention of the affair in the newspapers, despite quite comprehensive coverage in the Swedish media of the prosecution's case. Naturally, SIS was anxious to conceal the role of its Head of Station, John Martin, and in particular the fact that he had known that Rickman's star agent had come under hostile surveillance a full eighteen months before the Swedish police eventually closed in. It was, undoubtedly, an early manifestation of the dilemma which would overshadow SOE's relations with SIS. This was not the 'confusion and friction' that Sweet-Escott talks of, but a deliberate decision, taken by a professional intelligence officer, to sacrifice an amateur operation to protect a long-term source. It highlights the conflict of interest inherent in clandestine operations, which was to characterise the lack of affinity between the two covert organisations.

As well as finding politics complicated, SOE's staff demonstrated some naïveté in believing that, in the face of a common enemy, local differences of opinion and strategy would be overcome or at least overlooked. Certainly this was not the experience of Sweet-Escott, the first head of SOE's Polish Section, under the overall regional control of Peter Wilkinson. In fact, P Section was little more than a liaison office for maintaining contact with, and providing facilities for, the Fifth Bureau of the Polish General Staff. Relocated in the Rubens Hotel in Victoria in July 1940, it retained control over the *Armia Krajowa* (AK) or Home Army, the principal underground movement in occupied Poland. From SOE's standpoint, the Fifth Bureau represented a ready-made organisation led by Colonel Jozef Smolenski, which enjoyed a wireless link, supervised by SIS, with Poland via Bucharest and Budapest. The London headquarters consisted of a technical branch, under Captain Jan Jazwinski, and an operations branch, under Lieutenant Zygmunt Oranowski; it was later to expand considerably.

The overlap of interests and responsibility between SOE and SIS, and the Polish networks spread across Europe, is highlighted by the first official operations conducted by the two British rivals. For example, the first airborne mission into occupied France took place on the night of 9/10 October 1940, when a Whitley from 419 Flight at Stradishall dropped Phillip Schneidau near Montigny le Roi in France. He was picked up ten days later by a Lysander, flown by Flight Lieutenant Wally Farley from Tangmere. A bullet through the compass on take-off prevented Farley from navigating, and they eventually crash-landed at Oban, on the west coast of Scotland. Schneidau, an international hockey player with dual British–French nationality, who subsequently adopted the nom de guerre of Philipson, was given an RAF commission and went to work in Dunderdale's P5 section as a conducting officer, escorting SIS agents around the country.

Due mainly to inclement weather, and a shortage of suitable aircraft, the first SOE flight to Poland was not to take place until 15/16 February 1941, when three Polish agents – Flight Lieutenant Stanislaw Krzymowski, Lieutenant Jozef Zabielski and a courier, Czeslaw Raczkowski – were dropped by a specially modified Whitley near Bielsko. Zabielski made a bad landing and injured his legs, and all their equipment was lost. Worse still, the group discovered that it had been dropped more than sixty miles from its intended target, but it did eventually find its AK reception committee, and the mission was judged a success by the Polish government-in-exile, as well as SOE. However, the Air Ministry was less impressed, and very few operations were conducted thereafter during 1941. It was not until July 1942 that three Halifax aircraft were allocated to the Poles of 138 Squadron at Tempsford, but under RAF control.

SOE's early efforts to run agents into France met with similar, limited success, and were dogged by poor relations with SIS. F Section in particular was handicapped by three difficulties: it was a secret organisation and, therefore, had no contact with the Free French, which made recruitment difficult; it had no direct access to aircraft; and it depended upon a 'private navy' run under the auspices of the Naval Intelligence Division for clandestine transport across the Channel.

Section D had never had its own naval unit, and on the one occasion it had mounted a seaborne operation, in the Baltic in 1939, it had used seventeen volunteer yachtsmen, members of the Royal Cruising Club, to sail along the Norwegian and Swedish coastline and to chart the inshore waters. Organised by Lieutenant Frank Carr RN, the results of the survey had been passed to Section D, where they had been collated with data from Gerald Holdsworth's observations of possible amphibious landing sites around Bergen. Since then there had been no requirement for boats, but after the collapse of France the need manifested itself very quickly. The first attempt to infiltrate an agent into enemy-occupied territory was made by the *Service de Renseignements* on 17 July 1940 with a borrowed fast craft, and was completed successfully a few days later using a fishing boat. This at least proved that such undertakings were possible, and subsequently a forty-one-foot seaplane tender was extracted from the RAF and found a berth in the Helford River. Here a senior SIS officer, Commander Frank Slocum RN, started what amounted to a private navy for SIS and SOE.

SOE's local representative was Gerald Holdsworth, who had escaped from Finland after the Rickman fiasco in April and had finally arrived at Barrow-in-Furness in June. Reunited with his wife, another Section D veteran, he had gone straight down to Helford and taken over a house near the river large enough to accommodate boat crews, agents and their conducting officers. Like so many of Section D's original personnel, Holdsworth had already enjoyed an unusual career as a rubber planter in Borneo and as a film producer for Philips of Eindhoven's advertising department. In the latter job he had been approached by Section D to work in Norway under commercial cover, as a herring buyer. Holdsworth's deputy was Francis Brooks Richards, a young naval officer who had transferred to SOE after an explosion on a minesweeper had left him badly injured. They were to be joined by Nigel Warington-Smyth, a well-known, one-legged boat designer and yachtsman, who established himself in a magnificent three-masted schooner, the *Sunbeam*, on the river near Helford village.

Over a very short period a diverse party of enthusiasts, smugglers and fishermen were gathered together, along with a sixty-five-foot Breton tunny-man, the *Mutin*, and a French drifter. These vessels were to comprise the Helford Flotilla, but it was to experience many frustrations before it could be put to good use. The main difficulty was, as M. R. D. Foot describes it, 'jealous rivalry with the intelligence service'.[24] Slocum was 'determined to keep Brittany as quiet as possible'[25] so as to avoid interfering with SIS's agent-running sorties, which also encompassed MI9's activities. The escape and evasion service was later to develop a covert ferry route, codenamed SHELBURNE, from Falmouth to a secluded beach near Plouha in Brittany, and SIS insisted that nothing should occur in this part of the Channel which would attract the lethal German E-boat patrols. Slocum's first responsibility was to his own fleet, a fifty-foot trawler, the *N51*, run by Steven Mackenzie and Daniel Lomenech from an advance base in the Scillies. This was to be SIS's principal line of communication with André Dewavrin, who ran the *Service de Renseignements*, and Cohen's star agent, Gilbert Renault-Roulier, who had begun to build his circuit in France. Any mischief by SOE in Brittany would, SIS considered, be bound to compromise Slocum's work, and in a meeting held in London on 16 December 1940, attended by the Director of Combined Operations, General Sir Alan Bourne, and representatives of SOE and SIS, specifically to plan the future co-ordination of the three organisations, SIS expressed the view that SOE's seaborne activities 'might interfere with their organisation for getting agents into enemy-occupied territory'.[26] Accordingly, SIS 'did their best' to restrict their rival, and Bourne issued a formal ban on SOE operations on the French coastline between the Channel Islands and St Nazaire.

Unlike SIS, which had cultivated a close relationship with the Free French, SOE's F Section operated independently, and a pretence was maintained that the organisation did not actually exist. This fooled the

French for only the shortest time and, following pressure from the Foreign Office, it was suggested that a new sub-section be created to overcome the risks presented by contact with Raymond Lagier's notoriously leaky *Service Action* (SA).* Whether the French agency deserved this reputation is not a matter for debate here, but it was certainly regarded by SOE as being unprofessional. This view was enhanced by an incident on 14 November 1940, when an F Section agent recruited from the SA was flown by a 419 Flight Whitley to Morlaix, in Brittany, but at the last moment refused to jump. He had been promptly returned to whence he had come – General de Gaulle's headquarters at 4 Carlton Gardens. Although the proposal for a Free French sub-section was first made late in 1940, it only came into formal existence in the spring of 1941, with the designation MO/D.

MO/D, which later became RF Section, was formed at the *Ecu de France*, a restaurant in Jermyn Street, where Harry Sporborg, SOE's regional controller for Northern Europe, hosted a lunch for his choice as head of the new section, Eric Piquet-Wicks, and his two Free French counterparts, Dewavrin and Lagier. At the end of lunch Piquet-Wicks was escorted on a tour of Dewavrin's office, at 3 St James's Square, and then took up residence at 1 Dorset Square, an elegant house on the corner of Gloucester Place, recently vacated by Bertram Mills Circus and lent to SOE by Cyril Mills, who had just joined MI5.

Piquet-Wicks was a new recruit into 'the racket', having previously been garrisoned in Belfast with his regiment, the Royal Inniskilling Fusiliers, and had no experience of clandestine work. Nevertheless, he was briefed by Marriott's deputy, Thomas Cadett, and then informed 'quite casually' by Gubbins that he was to 'work directly with the Free French Forces'. Novice though he was, Piquet-Wicks immediately sized up Dewavrin and 'could see that liaison with [him] would have its difficulties'.[27] This was an astute observation, if something of an understatement, for he had not been told of the very close relationship between SIS and the third senior figure in Dewavrin's apparatus, André Manuel, whose main function was to liaise with that organisation. Since the *Service de Renseignements* depended entirely upon Dansey and Cohen for virtually everything, it is hardly surprising that Piquet-Wicks recalled that 'frequently over questions of policy we found ourselves before an impasse from which it was difficult to find a way out'.[28]

* In addition to the *Deuxième Bureau* of the French General Staff, there existed the *Service de Renseignements* to collect secret intelligence and the *Service Action*, which conducted clandestine operations. In January 1942 both branches were integrated into de Gaulle's *Bureau Central de Renseignements et d'Action* (BCRA).

French Operations

Both SOE and SIS were active in Nazi-occupied France, as were the respective Free French and Polish intelligence services. In total SOE deployed four active country sections in France (RF, F, EU/P and DF), while SIS ran three (P1, P1b and P1c) as well as the Polish liaison unit designated P5 and the MI9 escape and evasion service (known within SIS as P15). Predictably this proliferation of secret units, all operating on the same territory, led to duplication, muddle and some dangerous rivalry.

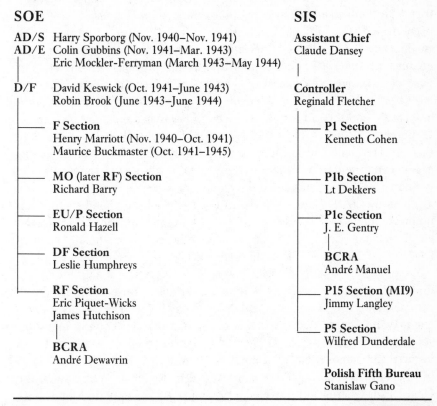

SOE		SIS	
AD/S	Harry Sporborg (Nov. 1940–Nov. 1941)	**Assistant Chief**	
AD/E	Colin Gubbins (Nov. 1941–Mar. 1943)	Claude Dansey	
	Eric Mockler-Ferryman (March 1943–May 1944)		
D/F	David Keswick (Oct. 1941–June 1943)	**Controller**	
	Robin Brook (June 1943–June 1944)	Reginald Fletcher	
	F Section	**P1 Section**	
	Henry Marriott (Nov. 1940–Oct. 1941)	Kenneth Cohen	
	Maurice Buckmaster (Oct. 1941–1945)		
	MO (later RF) Section	**P1b Section**	
	Richard Barry	Lt Dekkers	
	EU/P Section	**P1c Section**	
	Ronald Hazell	J. E. Gentry	
	DF Section	**BCRA**	
	Leslie Humphreys	André Manuel	
	RF Section	**P15 Section (MI9)**	
	Eric Piquet-Wicks	Jimmy Langley	
	James Hutchison		
		P5 Section	
	BCRA	Wilfred Dunderdale	
	André Dewavrin		
		Polish Fifth Bureau	
		Stanislaw Gano	

After all, Dewavrin had commented that 'we had practically no means, while the English had everything available'.[29] Thus, as MO/D depended upon Dewavrin's goodwill, and he was entirely dependent on SIS, some blame for Free French obstruction must be taken by Cohen.

That obstruction was taking place was incontrovertible. SOE had initiated its Special Training School programme and, after a late start, twenty agents had graduated from Wanborough Manor, near Guildford in

Surrey, in the spring of 1941. All were bilingual, usually having been brought up in France by English parents. Each had been selected after a series of interviews held by F Section's two recruiting officers, Lewis Gielgud, formerly a senior official with the Red Cross in Geneva, and Selwyn Jepson, the successful thriller writer. While the agent candidates were being put through their paces, accompanied from one training course to another by specially chosen 'conducting officers', there were demands for paramilitary operations that F Section was unable to meet.

One such request came from the Air Ministry, which reported that a particularly effective *Luftwaffe* pathfinder unit, *Kampfgeschwader* 100, had been located at an airfield outside Meucon, near Vannes. According to Air Intelligence, *KG* 100 was a specialist unit which had played a key role in guiding the *Luftwaffe* bombers to Coventry the previous November. The plan, codenamed SAVANNA, was to ambush the German aircrew's bus on a quiet stretch of road near Meucon, to wipe out the highly trained pilots and crews, and then to withdraw. Five of Dewavrin's men, led by Captain G. Berge, were dropped by a Whitley on 15 March, but they soon discovered that the Germans had abandoned their bus route in favour of individual cars to carry them from Vannes to the airfield. Realising that the plan would not now work, Berge dispersed his group and arranged to rendezvous with a submarine, HMS *Tigris*, on 4/5 April at Les Sables d'Olonne. However, on the appointed night only two of the party turned up, and the sea was so rough that Joel Letac had to be left on the beach. He eventually reached England via Spain, in August, having trekked across the Pyrenees.

Despite SOE's lack of participation in SAVANNA, training continued, under the direction of Colonel John S. Wilson, a former deputy police commissioner in Calcutta, and latterly camp chief of the Boy Scouts Association. Wanborough Manor was one of the first of many country mansions acquired for SOE by Colonel D. T. Wallace, an architect, whose activities inspired the rumour that the initials SOE really stood for 'Stately 'Omes of England'. Wanborough was commanded by Roger de Wesselow of the Coldstream Guards and provided a preliminary training period for F Section agents destined to work in occupied France. The main difficulty, however, was getting them to the Continent. The Helford Flotilla was unable to take them, despite promises to the contrary, and the delay cost three of the agents their lives, when, early in May 1941, they were killed in an air raid; two others were injured. When, on the second attempt, an agent was delivered to Brittany by boat on 27 March, he simply disappeared. This reduced the number of available F Section agents to fourteen.

Morale was not improved when JOSEPHINE, a mission to sabotage the

Pessac power station at Mérignac, went badly wrong. The plan called for six agents to be dropped from a specially converted Whitley of 1419 Flight (419 Flight's new designation, the original number having been allocated to a Royal Canadian Air Force bomber squadron). F Section had nobody suitable for the operation, so six Poles were assigned to MO Section for the task. The plane took off from Tangmere, a fighter base near Chichester, but lost two of its special weapons containers over the Loire due to an electrical failure. The pilot turned back, but crashed on landing, killing or injuring all the crew and agents.

The first F Section agent to make a successful parachute drop was Georges Begue, who landed 'blind', with no reception arrangements, in unoccupied France near Châteauroux, on 5/6 May on a mission planned by Thomas Cadett. Begué signalled his safe arrival and was followed on 10/11 May by Pierre de Vomécourt and Roger Cottin, a former representative of a Paris perfume house. Although de Vomécourt and his two brothers, Philippe and Jean, were to become the foundation on which F Section's first circuit, AUTOGIRO, was to be built, the operation was not an outstanding success.[30] Cottin, codenamed *Bernard*, was spotted by villagers as he landed and reported to the police. He was placed under house arrest, but later managed to talk his way out of trouble, eventually ending up as a civil servant in the Vichy administration, but taking no further active part in the resistance.

Following the failure of the first JOSEPHINE flight, the RAF converted another valuable Whitley bomber, and Gubbins gave this second attempt to Piquet-Wicks and his Free French section, now designated RF. Dick Barry and Dewavrin joined Piquet-Wicks to brief the assignment, codenamed JOSEPHINE B, to be made by three volunteers: R. Cabard, Lieutenant Varnier and a survivor of SAVANNA, Captain A. Forman. They were dropped on 11/12 May and, after a series of misadventures, succeeded in planting their explosives and wrecking Pessac's power station. The team also managed to meet up with Joel Letac in Paris and, having completed their mission and missed a pick-up rendezvous with a Lysander aircraft, made their way to Spain and thence to England, presenting RF with a fairly hefty bill for the travel expenses incurred during their three-month odyssey.

By the middle of 1941 SOE's operations in occupied France totalled F Section's fledgling AUTOGIRO circuit (see below), and RF's triumph of JOSEPHINE B. Their victory was all the greater when it was learned that the *Wehrmacht* had court-martialled and executed a dozen of the power station's guards for negligence. DF Section had concentrated on finding a safe land route into France, and Leslie Humphreys visited Lisbon twice over the winter to confer with DF Section's representative in Lisbon, an expatriate businessman named L. H. Mortimore, who had been recruited by SOE's man in the British Embassy, Jack Beevor.[31] DF Section had inserted a couple of agents into France and one, E. V. Rizzo, a Maltese civil engineer who had taught science in Paris before the war, started the TROY circuit in Perpignan, which operated relatively undisturbed until the Liberation. Rizzo had arrived in France by boat on an EU/P Section mission, which brought a Polish travel agent named Bitner to Lille with the intention of recruiting the former Polish Consul-General there into the Polish Fifth Bureau. Bitner succeeded, and the former diplomat proceeded to organise a circuit. Bitner and Rizzo had been landed on 25 April by HMS *Fidelity*, a 2,400-ton armed merchantman, which, until the previous year, had been called *Le Rhin*, working for the French colonial intelligence service. It had been seized by a Gaullist naval officer in Marseilles at the time of the French collapse and had been sailed to England for enrolment in Slocum's private navy. Renamed HMS *Fidelity*, she had been returned to Gibraltar for agent-running operations, but was eventually to be switched to convoy escort duties.[32] This was the *Fidelity*'s first clandestine infiltration, and both Rizzo and Bitner arrived at their respective destinations safely. However, it is a reflection of the paucity of air and sea links available to SOE at this time that EU/P was obliged to deliver an agent in southern France when his mission was in northern France. Although Rizzo did not have far to go, for Perpignan was just along the coast from the *Fidelity*'s landing site, Lille was some two thousand kilometres away and on the other side of the closely guarded demarcation line. Nor was the exercise entirely without cost. The member of *Fidelity*'s crew who had ferried Rizzo and Bitner ashore capsized while making his way back to the ship and was arrested on the beach an hour later. Far from being the Canadian soldier he claimed to be to the Vichy police, he was actually a Belgian doctor, Albert-Marie Guerisse, who was to become a key figure in MI9's escape lines.[33]

In terms of assets on the ground in occupied France, SOE had little to boast of in the summer of 1941. F Section had started AUTOGIRO and the Vomécourt brothers had set up three sub-branches, with Pierre based in Paris, Jean in Pontarlier and Philippe at the family château at Bas Soleil, near Limoges. On 13 June a Whitley dropped, at the fourth attempt, SOE's first delivery of *matériel*. Unfortunately, some of it was useless, particularly the underwater limpet mines, as Limoges is a considerable distance from the nearest port, but the event did prove that Begué's wireless link with London was effective. It also proved that the Vichy police and the German radio monitoring service were vigilant; therefore, to reduce his transmissions Begué devised a system of innocuous messages to be broadcast by the BBC, each with a particular meaning. This method of communicating with resisters was to be adopted generally by SIS and SOE, and proved both efficient and unjammable. Shortly before each news bulletin the BBC broadcast a series of brief 'personal messages', many of which were authentic phrases, arranged before an individual's escape and used to indicate to families in the occupied zone that a person had reached England safely. However, the texts, which usually consisted of a single sentence, could easily be adapted to contain a hidden meaning, and many of the more innocuous messages were really signals to indicate that a particular operation was under way.

Apart from TROY, which was an escape line still in its early stages, DF Section only had a couple of agents in France, and two neutral travellers working as couriers into France from Lisbon and Berne respectively: Daniel Delignant, a French Jew who had permission to travel to his native country from Portugal; and René Bertholet, who occasionally carried messages to Lyons from Switzerland. In addition, Humphreys thought that he had recruited a Norwegian Quaker named Holst, who had a ship-broking business in Marseilles. Apparently, DF Section did not realise that Holst's English wife, Madge, was an SIS agent, running an escape line for Jimmy Langley's P16 section, also designated MI9. Despite this apparent breach of security, with two separate compartmented services overlapping and employing members of the same family, the Holsts were to mastermind one of the most successful escape lines to operate in France. The other SOE section involved with France, EU/P, was still planning a number of ambitious projects with Polish personnel, but none had resulted in circuits being developed. As for RF Section, a further two-man team in the SAVANNA mould, codenamed TORTURE, was dropped on 5 July 1941 to sabotage a German airfield at Carpiquet, near Caen, but the wireless operator, Lieutenant J. Cartigny, was betrayed by a farmer soon after landing. His partner, Henri Labit, abandoned the operation and made his way to Toulouse, where he started a circuit called FABULOUS, based in the university. This, then, was SOE's rather dubious record to date.

In contrast, SIS was running two big networks in France, one centred on a makeshift Polish stay-behind group in Paris, the other a sophisticated resistance movement politically opposed to de Gaulle, which enjoyed many sympathisers within the Vichy regime. As we shall see, both organisations were to be penetrated by the Germans.

The Polish network, known as INTERALLIÉ, boasted several transmitters and a cell structure designed to ensure internal security. Most of its personnel were displaced Poles with military backgrounds, who were well disciplined, knew what to look out for and recognised what they saw. These were no amateurs, unable to distinguish different types of aircraft or tank models; they were trained observers who had a good grasp of the kind of information required by the intelligence analysts in London. Their productivity was first rate and, perhaps most important of all, was insulated from the domestic political intrigues that had handicapped EU/P Section's activities. INTERALLIÉ was so impressive that its organiser, an air-force officer named Roman Garby-Czerniawski, was invited to London to confer with Dunderdale and the Polish Commander-in-Chief, General Sikorski. A rendezvous with a Lysander from Tempsford was arranged and, on 11 October, Garby-Czerniawski was delivered to London in a flawless operation, the first pick-up from German-occupied territory of the war. Garby-Czerniawski then spent nine days at Broadway (the Poles were at the Rubens Hotel), always accompanied by Philip Schneidau as his conducting officer, before receiving an urgent message from France, alerting him to a bitter quarrel between his mistress, a French nurse named Mathilde Carré, and the organisation's chief radio operator, Gane. Cutting short his visit, Garby-Czerniawski parachuted back 'blind' into the Loire valley and, upon his return to Paris, learned that everything was far from well. Before leaving for England he had unwisely entrusted INTERALLIÉ's secrets to Carré and his cipher clerk, and now they had both fallen out. But worse, on 3 November the *Abwehr* in Cherbourg arrested Raoul Kiffer, one of INTERALLIÉ's principal sub-agents. Under duress, the former French air-force NCO implicated one of Garby-Czerniawski's assistants, Bernard Krutki. When both men were left alone in an interrogation room in the *Abwehr*'s headquarters in the Hôtel Edouard VII in the Avenue de l'Opéra, their conversation was recorded and Krutki unwittingly disclosed Garby-Czerniawski's address in St Germain-en-Laye.

Within three days of arresting Garby-Czerniawski, on 17 November 1941, his entire network had been rounded up. Mathilde Carré swiftly transferred her allegiance to the *Abwehr* and became the mistress of Sergeant Hugo Bleicher, one of the *Abwehr*'s most successful and imaginative investigators. Now in the possession of four of INTERALLIÉ's transmitters, it was his idea to resume contact with London to report the arrest of Garby-Czerniawski. Carré intended to take over the network, but none of the Polish wireless operators would collaborate. However, Carré told her captors of a Frenchman, Henri Tabet, who had previously left INTERALLIÉ after a disagreement. Under duress, he agreed to send a signal, carefully enciphered by Carré. The transmission was duly acknowledged and there then followed three months of a sophisticated radio game, which gave the *Abwehr* a unique insight into SIS's activities.[34] Unfortunately, it also led to the elimination of F Section's main circuit, AUTOGIRO.

On 24 October AUTOGIRO had experienced the loss of its wireless operator, Georges Begué, who had been arrested when he called at a compromised address in Marseilles. This left the circuit with only one operator, Georges Bloch, who had been dropped on 6/7 September. He too was arrested by police equipped with direction-finders in Le Mans on about 13 November, which meant that Pierre de Vomécourt was without any means of communicating with London. Undeterred, he searched Paris for another radio and just after Christmas was introduced to Carré, who revealed her link with London and offered to service AUTOGIRO.

From a security standpoint the idea of allowing a penetrated *réseau* (network) to contaminate another is a cardinal error, and the whole principle of compartmentation is to isolate separate operations. Under normal circumstances such a development would have been vetoed, but SIS took the decision to accept AUTOGIRO's messages via INTERALLIÉ and thereby doubled the Germans' knowledge of the resistance structure. If SIS and SOE had maintained different lines of communication, such a step would probably have been rejected, but SIS had only recently fought and won a bitter bureaucratic struggle in London to retain its control over SOE's signals.

SOE was perfectly aware of the pressures imposed on it by SIS, but was powerless to do anything but protest. Apart from the operational restrictions on SOE's access to the Channel, aircraft and the French coastline, there was a continuing problem over communications. All SOE's radio links were relayed through Whaddon, the main SIS reception station. SOE suspected, quite rightly, that all its most sensitive messages were being read and circulated inside Broadway Buildings. In April 1941 this anxiety had been translated into a formal request for an independent cipher system and a separate communications channel. The proposal had been resisted strenuously, and SIS had prevailed with the assertion that 'SOE's methods were insecure'.[35] There followed, in consequence, a débâcle in France.

Before turning to AUTOGIRO's victims, we should pause a moment to consider SIS's acceptance of Mathilde Carré as a conduit for the circuit's messages. Pierre de Vomécourt made the initial approach to her, via her lawyer, who happened to be known to him. Once London's acknowledgment had been received, via the Canadian Legation in Vichy, de Vomécourt was fully satisfied that Carré was trustworthy. Accordingly, he channelled all his communications through her, which meant that her *Abwehr* lover, Hugo Bleicher, was reading every item.

These events were taking place just as F Section was undergoing a traumatic change of leadership in London which had climaxed in November 1941. Henry Marriott had been dismissed by Harry Sporborg after a lengthy row with Robin Brook, who had been appointed regional controller with responsibility for SOE's French, Dutch and Belgian Sections. Marriott's retirement was supposedly on health grounds and he had been replaced by Maurice Buckmaster, who had transferred to SOE in March as F Section's Information Officer and then been made temporary head of the Belgian Section. Thomas Cadett would have been the obvious internal choice as Marriott's successor, or even Leslie Humphreys from DF Section, but instead Nelson promoted Buckmaster, a former executive with the Ford Motor Company in Paris. Buckmaster recalled:

I was at once conscious of the immense amount of work with which I was faced. As yet we had no organisation, few means of having our agents received by friendly patriots or of accepting messages from them once they had landed. France was without means of speaking to us.[36]

His swift promotion was to lead to Cadett's resignation soon afterwards. Thus, just when AUTOGIRO had lost its wireless operator and was in desperate need of help, the headquarters staff in London was in a state of turmoil and, in the absence of any spare operators, F Section's new management had let SIS's INTERALLIÉ handle AUTOGIRO's signals.

After nearly two months of working with Carré, Pierre de Vomécourt eventually realised that all was not well. He had noticed a strange delay in her transmissions and was suspicious about the arrest of a courier. Also, she seemed to be able to obtain German travel stamps for documents without much difficulty. He therefore challenged her with being in contact with the enemy. Upon being confronted Carré admitted her liaison with the *Abwehr*, which placed de Vomécourt in considerable difficulty. He had no other method of warning London that both AUTOGIRO and INTERALLIÉ had been compromised, and he could neither simply disappear nor take any overt steps to warn the rest of his circuit. Indeed, he had just been sent another agent, Jack Fincken, as an assistant. Nor could he explain to London that INTERALLIÉ's link was being used by the *Abwehr* to supply misleading information, including some false intelligence about the German battle-cruisers *Scharnhorst*, *Gneisenau* and the *Prinz Eugen*, which were able to escape from Brest and return up the Channel to Germany unscathed.

Instead, de Vomécourt persuaded Carré to switch sides again and operate as a triple agent.

It was an extraordinary gamble, but it did lead the Germans to endorse a bold plan: de Vomécourt would be allowed to go to London with Carré, where she proposed to work for the *Abwehr*, and he would later return to France with a British general. Thus, on 12/13 February an SIS fast motor gunboat, the *MGB 314*, with Nicholas Bodington aboard, attempted to collect Carré and de Vomécourt from a beach in Brittany. It failed to pick up the two agents, but it did deliver another F Section pair, Claude Redding and his wireless operator, G. W. Abbott. Both were quickly arrested, together with their Royal Navy escort, Sub-Lieutenant Ivan Black. The *MGB 314*'s commander, a peacetime solicitor and yachtsman, Dunstan Curtis, was unaware of the drama taking place on the beach and, bound by a strict timetable, headed for home with his depleted crew as dawn approached.

A more successful pick-up was fixed for 26/27 February. On this occasion de Vomécourt and Carré were taken to Dartmouth, where they were met on the quay by Buckmaster. De Vomécourt promptly revealed Carré's duplicity and the fate of INTERALLIÉ. This must have been devastating news for SIS, especially when P1 realised the extent to which it had been duped. It had relayed bogus information to the Admiralty about the German battle-cruisers at Brest and, according to Philippe de Vomécourt, who was then still in France, SOE had requested intelligence about St Nazaire, the strategically important French port on Normandy's Atlantic coast and now a vital base for the *Kriegsmarine*.

In 1959 Philippe de Vomécourt disclosed that some of the messages handled by Carré, and therefore the *Abwehr*, had referred to St Nazaire, which had been selected as the target for CHARIOT, an ambitious attack against the lock gates of the port's massive dry dock.[37] SOE had played a vital role in preparing the plans for the operation, and many of the participants had been trained at its school at Aston House, near Hertford, known as 'Station 12'. CHARIOT took place on the night of 28/29 March, nearly a month after SIS and SOE had been notified that all INTERALLIÉ's communications had been betrayed to the *Abwehr*. Whether anyone considered calling off the raid because of the possibility that it might have been compromised is unknown.

Pierre de Vomécourt was given a warm welcome in London and was received by the Chief of the Imperial General Staff, General Sir Alan Brooke, Anthony Eden and Lord Selborne, Dalton's successor at the Ministry of Economic Warfare. Carré, however, was not so lucky. She was interrogated by MI5, SIS and SOE before being imprisoned, first at Holloway and then at Aylesbury.

De Vomécourt's intention had been to return to France with Carré. Once his version of events had been confirmed by another member of AUTOGIRO, Ben Cowburn,[38] who had made his own way to England via Madrid after the failure of the first rendezvous the previous month, he was allowed to parachute back alone on 1 April. He landed on his brother's estate near Limoges and proceeded to Paris, where Roger Cottin had been running AUTOGIRO in his absence. In order to buy time from Bleicher, who had been expecting Carré accompanied by a notional British general, the *Abwehr* was told via its INTERALLIÉ wireless that de Vomécourt had been delayed in London but would be back by the next full moon. Isolated from this dangerous radio link, and without a wireless operator, de Vomécourt was obliged to communicate with F Section by courier via Virginia Hall, an American journalist working for the *New York Post*, who ran a safe-house in Lyons. Despite the handicap of having a wooden leg, Virginia Hall was to be a highly successful F Section agent and, later, a senior officer in the CIA's Latin America division.

Authorising Virginia Hall to work with de Vomécourt, who was himself thoroughly compromised and known to the *Abwehr*, seems an extraordinary risk to have taken. Once her courier had been caught, and Bleicher had realised that de Vomécourt had slipped back into France, AUTOGIRO was doomed. Cottin, who had been kept under constant German surveillance, was arrested immediately; soon afterwards Leon Walters, the Belgian in whose flat de Vomécourt was staying, was taken in for questioning. On 25 April Bleicher caught up with de Vomécourt in a café, where he was meeting Jack Fincken; Noel Burdeyron, who had represented AUTOGIRO in Normandy since the previous July, was next; and then the Comte de Puy. Last of all was Christopher Burney, another F Section agent who was dropped near Le Mans on 31 May with instructions to contact AUTOGIRO's man in Caen and then work for Burdeyron.[39] He was eventually arrested on 1 August, by which time Virginia Hall had learned of the round-up and alerted London.

The AUTOGIRO débâcle led to the capture of Abbott, Redding, Black, Cottin, Burdeyron, Walters, Fincken and de Vomécourt. Altogether fifteen members of AUTOGIRO were arrested, as well as de Vomécourt's brothers, Philippe and Jean. Only the latter did not survive the war.

The fact that so many members of a single *réseau* escaped death is quite extraordinary. In fact, the members of AUTOGIRO who were caught by the Germans and lived amount to nearly a quarter of F Section's total number of surviving prisoners throughout the entire war. The unusually high proportion definitely suggests that a deal was made. Philippe de Vomécourt certainly believed that Pierre had 'once again hoodwinked the Germans and succeeded in saving the lives of all fifteen of his comrades', which implies that at least two arrangements were made with the *Abwehr*: one to get to London with Carré, and a second to have those arrested treated as prisoners of war. This was by no means unique, as we shall see. Circuit leaders were occasionally made these attractive offers by the *Abwehr*, which invariably kept its side of the bargain. As far as AUTOGIRO is concerned, seven of its members, including Pierre de Vomécourt, were liberated from Colditz at the end of the war, together with the 'prominente' hostages. Suspicion that there was much more to the AUTOGIRO story was confirmed when Bleicher was interrogated by MI5 after the war and claimed that de Vomécourt had betrayed his entire network in return for favourable treatment.

A very similar situation was to arise with INTERALLIÉ, which, after the AUTOGIRO collapse, was terminated. The Germans broke off contact with London, but that was not to be the end of the saga. In October 1942 Garby-Czerniawski, INTERALLIÉ's Polish leader, appeared at the British Embassy in Madrid and explained to the astonished SIS Head of Station that he had escaped from Fresnes prison and had trekked across the Pyrenees. He was brought to London, where he was interrogated by SIS and MI5. Although he was reluctant to admit it to his Polish colleagues, he too had made a pact with the *Abwehr*. He had offered to travel to England and spy for the Germans in return for a guarantee of good treatment for his brother, who was a prisoner of war, his mother in Poland, and all INTERALLIÉ's members in German custody. MI5 accepted Garby-Czerniawski's version of events and agreed to enrol him as a double agent with the codename *Brutus*.[40] Wireless contact was established with the *Abwehr* in Paris in December and was continued until the end of hostilities.

The INTERALLIÉ and AUTOGIRO disasters meant that by mid-1942 F Section was virtually back to square one, with hardly any assets left in the field. The same nearly happened to SIS with its principal network, the ALLIANCE.[41] This was Kenneth Cohen's organisation in Vichy, led by Georges Loustaunau-Lacau, a professional army officer who had been badly wounded in 1940. He had developed an impressive circuit, well-equipped with SIS radios supplied via Madrid. Loustaunau-Lacau was himself exceptionally well connected in the political world and enjoyed a measure of protection from friends high in the Vichy regime. ALLIANCE seemed destined for great achievements, especially as it had proved itself capable of handling airdrops from England. The problems began when, on 5 August 1941, SIS sent out a new wireless operator named Bradley Davis. Soon after his arrival he developed appendicitis and underwent surgery, but once he had recovered he was sent to Normandy for ALLIANCE.

Exactly what happened next is unknown, but Davis certainly fell into the *Abwehr*'s hands. He also continued transmitting to SIS, ostensibly from Normandy but actually from Paris. Despite his collaboration with the enemy, SIS failed to notice that he had fallen under hostile control, and Cohen in London seemed more concerned about the way his organisation was collapsing than about what Davis was up to. Henri Schaerrer had been arrested on 11 July, some weeks before Davis had arrived in France, but the Germans only realised two months later that he had been an important member of ALLIANCE. He was shot at Fresnes on 13 November. Gabriel Riviere, Jean Boutron, Lucien Vallet, Maurice Coustenoble, Edmond Poulain, Antoine Hugon and Admiral Pierre Barjot, all key members of ALLIANCE, were also scooped up by the Vichy police, together with four of the circuit's six transmitters. Most endured terrible privations at concentration camps in Germany, although a few, like Loustaunau-Lacau, were still alive when Mauthausen was liberated.

Despite Davis's treachery ALLIANCE did survive under the leadership of Loustaunau-Lacau's principal lieutenant, Marie-Madeleine Fourcade, and eventually numbered some three thousand active supporters spread throughout France, reporting every type of intelligence. In the early days this was information concerning the location of the *Luftwaffe*'s decoy airfields and reports from inside the *Kriegsmarine*'s submarine bases, but later it was to include crucial data about German rocketry. Of that total number of ALLIANCE agents, about five hundred were caught and executed by the Nazis. In praising Marie-Madeleine Fourcade after the war, Cohen called the Davis affair 'a blunder' and noted that it 'did not dim her loyalty to the British'. He also suggested that the remarkable record of another SIS wireless operator, Frederick Rodney, had been sufficiently exemplary to compensate for Davis's behaviour. That the Cockney Londoner had been a traitor, directly responsible for the arrest, torture and death of numerous ALLIANCE agents, is indisputable, and Cohen eventually ordered his death. In 1942 a rendezvous with Davis was arranged in Lyons, where what remained of ALLIANCE planned to snatch him and, after interrogation, kill him. Instead, the Gestapo turned up at the agreed meeting place, and ALLIANCE's hit squad was obliged to withdraw. Eventually, Davis was spotted in Marseilles by another SIS agent named Crawley; Davis was kidnapped, questioned and finally poisoned.

The Davis episode has been referred to obliquely by both Cohen and Fourcade, but his true identity has never been disclosed before. It was not until her death in 1989 that friends of Fourcade felt free to reveal Davis's real name. The fact is that Davis should never have been chosen for work in occupied France, but SIS's agent selection system was about as haphazard as SOE's. Indeed, Buckmaster tells the story of an early agent named Nigel Low, who was a gambler and a confidence trickster with a string of criminal convictions. Despite these obvious handicaps, he was despatched to the South of France by F Section in the spring of 1942 with a large sum of cash, but was never seen again. 'He was, as far as we know, never caught and certainly he betrayed no one,' says Buckmaster.[42]

• • • • • •

A common criticism of SOE was its apparent lethargy in developing its operational capacity in Europe. Before turning to its activities in the rest of Europe, it is worth pausing for a moment to understand the extraordinary handicaps which the organisation was obliged to endure. As we have already seen, SOE's communications with its *réseaux* in France were handled by SIS, in spite of the security implications, and the AUTOGIRO disaster was a direct consequence of the lack of separation between F Section's first circuit and SIS's compromised INTERALLIÉ. But apart from the communications difficulties, SOE found itself hamstrung by a lack of transport facilities.

SOE's naval section in the Helford River continued to experience problems with getting agents across the Channel, and HMS *Fidelity* had been sent to Gibraltar to exploit the relatively unguarded South of France, which, until November 1942, was under Vichy control. However, unquestionably the best method of infiltrating agents and servicing networks in occupied territory was by air, and this was where SOE was at a disadvantage. This is highlighted by two significant dates in SOE's development: the first successful parachute mission into France did not take place until May 1941, and SOE's first Lysander pick-up did not happen until September 1941. This contrasts with SIS's removal of Philip Schneidau in October 1940, eleven months earlier.

Clandestine air operations were, by established convention, unpopular with the Air Ministry and the monopoly of SIS. The Chief of the Air Staff, Air Marshal Sir Charles Portal, told Harry Sporborg that his resources were too limited to risk on SOE's adventures: 'Your work is a gamble which may give us a valuable dividend or may produce nothing. It is anybody's guess . . . I cannot divert aircraft from a certainty to a gamble, which may be a goldmine or may be completely worthless.'[43] Nor was the RAF very enthusiastic about SAVANNA, RF Section's plan to ambush the German aircrew on the way to their airfield in Brittany. On that occasion Portal had minuted that 'there is a vast difference, in ethics, between the time-honoured operation of the dropping of a spy from the air and this entirely new scheme for dropping what one can only call assassins.'[44]

Nor was the RAF's initial experience of SOE very encouraging. F Section's very first parachutist was flown to Brittany on 14 November 1940 and, at the last moment, had refused to jump. Then there had been JOSEPHINE, MO Section's sabotage mission, which had resulted in a large number of casualties and the loss of a Whitley when it had crashed on landing, after the operation itself had been abandoned. Even the RAF's first Lysander pick-up, bringing Schneidau out from France in October 1940, had ended in the loss of the plane which had crashed in Scotland. No further air operations took place until 11/12 April 1941, when a Lysander, using the fighter station at Tangmere as a forward base, collected an SIS agent from the Châteauroux area.

Initially the RAF provided a unit, 419 Flight, based at North Weald, Middlesex, consisting of four Lysanders, two of which were operational and the other two held in forward reserve. The aircraft itself was an obsolescent, slow, single-engined spotter plane, but it was to prove ideal for ferrying agents. During the summer of 1940 North Weald attracted a great deal of attention from the *Luftwaffe*, so in September 419 Flight moved a few miles south to a grass airfield at Stapleford Abbots. On 9 October there was another move, to RAF Stradishall in Suffolk, where three Whitley bombers, converted for parachute operations, were added. In February 1941 there was a further move to Newmarket racecourse, known as Rowley Mile, where some Lysanders, still in their target towing livery, were acquired from 3 Group Gunnery Flight. Until suitable accommodation was found in the town, in the form of some racing stables at Sefton Lodge, the aircrew lived in the racecourse grandstand. It was here that 138 (Special Duties) Squadron was joined by the King's Flight, which adopted the designation 161 (Special Duties) Squadron. On 25 August 1941, 1419 Flight became 138 Squadron and divided into two flights, of eight Whitleys (with two in reserve) and two Lysanders.

138 Squadron's first operational sortie (as opposed to its regular training exercises) took place on 29/30 August 1941, when an RF agent named R. Lencement was dropped by a Whitley near Vichy. He had travelled to England on his own via Spain during his annual vacation and was returned before he was missed. Operation TROMBONE was a success in that Lence-

ment, an electrical engineer, managed to organise some of his neighbours into an embryonic network, but he attracted the attention of the police and was arrested before the end of the year.

SOE's first Lysander pick-up was Operation LEVEE, which took place on 4/5 September 1941, when Gerard Morel was delivered to the north-east of Châteauroux. After he had disembarked, Jacques de Guélis replaced him and was flown back to Tangmere. Morel lasted six weeks before he was betrayed, but he later succeeded in escaping from the Germans and was eventually appointed F Section's operations officer. De Guélis had been an advertising agent in peacetime and had been captured while acting as a liaison officer with the British Expeditionary Force in 1940. He had escaped, made his way to England and then been taken on by Sporborg as F Section's briefing officer. He had been dropped on 6 August, together with Georges Turck, once the *Deuxième Bureau*'s liaison officer with Section D. De Guélis completed his mission, which was principally one of reconnaissance, and made his rendezvous with the Lysander a month later. This operation was to be SOE's only Lysander pick-up during the whole of 1941.

Meanwhile, 161 Squadron, which had moved briefly from Newmarket to Graveley, joined 138 Squadron at Tempsford in April 1942. Tempsford was an unusual place to locate a clandestine base. It was a stretch of low-lying marshy land between the main railway line to Edinburgh and the Great North Road, overlooked by anyone travelling north by rail or road. It was to be found close to the village of Everton, Bedfordshire, and the corner assigned to SOE and SIS was distinguished by a solitary dilapidated barn known as Gibraltar Farm. This was where agents waited with their conducting officers while the aircrew prepared their aircraft for take-off. Construction work had begun on the airstrip late in 1940, but it did not become operational until twelve months later. After the arrival of 138 Squadron on 11 March 1942, no less than thirty-eight Lysander sorties were flown before the end of the year, of which only eleven were on behalf of SOE to France, a figure which includes the loss of one plane and two passengers. In addition to Tempsford's total number of flights, there were an unknown number of highly secret missions flown by two Havoc light bombers, which were deployed as mobile radio stations to receive wireless signals from SIS agents in occupied territory. Unfortunately, no records of these operations survive.

Quite apart from having to fight the RAF for access to aircraft, SOE was also locked into a battle with SIS, with whom the Air Ministry seemed to be on far better terms. Perhaps SOE had been mistaken not to have instituted an Air Liaison Section from the outset, instead of opting for an operations unit, MO Section, which had been intended to look after all the operational needs of each of the organisation's country sections. The arrangement changed in mid-1942, when MO developed into AL (Air Liaison), and C. Grierson took over responsibility for dealing with the Air Ministry through AI 2(c), a sub-section of its intelligence branch. Later Squadron Leader Lord Allerton was transferred to AL from the Polish Section, in the hope of increasing AL's influence over the RAF, especially in respect of the provision of long-range aircraft, but it was to no avail. During 1943 the number of Lysander sorties flown to France for SOE nearly quadrupled on the previous year, to thirty-eight, and a further sixteen sorties were flown by Hudsons. In subsequent years the statistics escalated dramatically, but these were early days for SOE.

In contrast, SIS boasted excellent relations with the RAF, and the regional controller for Europe, Reginald Fletcher, enjoyed contacts at the highest level throughout Whitehall and the Air Ministry. Created Baron Winster in 1942, he had served in the Royal Navy during the First World War and thereafter had headed the Near Eastern Section of the Naval Intelligence Division. He had also been a Labour MP briefly and had co-authored *The Air Defences of Britain* just before the war.[45] No doubt SIS was an extremely useful ally for the Air Ministry, both through the work of Squadron Leader John Perkins, who headed SIS's air liaison unit, Section IV, and courtesy of the valuable signals intelligence from Bletchley Park, which was channelled to the RAF via Group Captain F. W. Winterbotham's liaison organisation. In any event, it is easy to see that while the Air Ministry might have regarded SOE as a dangerous nuisance, it relied heavily upon SIS for intelligence of all types.

Since SOE had no hope of exerting this kind of influence over the Air Ministry, which was insistent that it alone would be the final arbiter over which flights were to receive priority, SOE concentrated instead on its sea links to the Continent. Because of continuing obstruction from Slocum's private navy in Falmouth, these facilities were limited to the Mediterranean. SIS's hostility to SOE's naval activities was so intense that, when the two rivals eventually merged in June 1943, Nigel Warington-Smyth observed: 'It came as a source of great surprise to more than one officer (and to some of the more intelligent ratings) to discover that, contrary to what they had been educated to believe, the principal enemy was Hitler and not their opposite number in the sister organisation.'[46] Perhaps reluctantly, SOE came to recognise the limited opportunities for cross-Channel operations and moved further south, where HMS *Fidelity* operated semi-independently from Gibraltar and carried agents for SIS as well as SOE. However, it was EU/P that provided the *feluccas* that served SOE so well.

SOE's *feluccas* were twenty-ton Portuguese sardine boats, the *Seawolf* and the *Sealog*, run by two Polish naval officers, Lieutenants Marian Kadulski and Jan Buchowski, who made regular visits to the Riviera, even though their slow boats took a fortnight to make the round trip from Gibraltar.

Gibraltar had been a vital centre of intelligence from the moment that Sir Samuel Hoare had been appointed Ambassador in Madrid. His own loyalties were not entirely above suspicion, which may have been part of the reason for his appointment, and Sir Alexander Cadogan had confided to his diary that the appeaser was politically unreliable. Whatever Hoare's motive – and, as a former SIS officer who had operated in Russia during the First World War, he may have been entitled to his prejudices – he banned SIS from undertaking any kind of activity in Spain. He also vetoed SOE's use of any Spanish Republicans, from whose ranks there were plenty of volunteers, for fear of upsetting Franco. Accordingly, Gibraltar acquired a special significance, especially when there was a strong possibility that Hitler might invade Spain through France. The British contingency plan, codenamed MAD DOG, was to sabotage all the road and rail links to the east, and a team from H Section, SOE's Spanish branch, was assembled on the Rock on 5 April 1941 for deployment if the worst happened. SOE already had an office in Gibraltar to supervise operations in Iberia and North-West Africa, headed by Peter Quennell and Harry Morris, but a mission codenamed RELATOR, consisting of John Burton, David Muirhead, Adrian Gallegos and Peter Kemp, was organised for operations in Spain.

Until now H Section's existence has remained a secret and the name of its head, Major L. J. W. Richardson, appears in none of the official histories. Nor, for that matter, do the names of his immediate subordinates, Major J. A. S. Hamilton or Captain K. M. D. Mills. When Adrian Gallegos wrote his wartime memoirs, *From Capri to Oblivion*,[47] he diplomatically omitted any reference to his work in Gibraltar. However, Peter Kemp has given accounts of RELATOR in *No Colours or Crest* and *The Thorns of Memory*,[48] although he is too discreet to name other members of the Section. He was sent to Gibraltar on HMS *Fidelity* with the intention of linking up with local anti-Nazi partisans in Estremadura, but 'Hoare categorically refused to allow SOE to take any measures in Spain to prepare for our operations'.[49] Clearly very little research had gone into RELATOR's planning. Kemp had fought in the Spanish Civil War for nearly three years on the Nationalist side, but any anti-Nazis in the area assigned to him and Butler were likely to have been Republicans. Kemp recalls:

It was difficult for us to feel great enthusiasm for such a vague and ill-planned scheme, or to take much interest in its preparation. The method by which it was proposed that we should reach our areas had the one merit of simplicity: as soon as the German invasion began, each party would climb into its lorry – already loaded with arms, explosives and wireless – and drive by the shortest route to its destination; how many of us would get there, or even succeed in crossing the International Zone to La Linea, was anybody's guess.[50]

RELATOR was eventually disbanded in August 1941, following the German invasion of the Soviet Union, when SOE recognised that there was no further need for MAD DOG. However, another group was assembled in time for Operation TORCH, the invasion of North Africa, the following year.

The lack of planning and preparation for MAD DOG was characteristic of SOE's early existence, when groups of what can only be described as colourful adventurers attempted to thwart the Nazi advance in the most amateurish way. Initially, the effort had been unco-ordinated, with Section D and MI(R) operating independently of each other and at odds with SIS's own activities. The amalgamation of Section D and MI(R) gave SOE an enthusiastic pool of talent on which to draw, but opposition to the new-comers from Whitehall's hidebound military establishment and the more experienced old hands at SIS ensured that SOE got off to a slow start. Contact with occupied Poland and France had been unproductive, not least because of SOE's lack of any means of communicating with the Continent. Wireless was SIS's monopoly and the RAF and Royal Navy could not be persuaded to regard Dalton's desperadoes as a priority. That, of course, is not to say that individual officers did not show great initiative and gallantry while attempting to mount SOE's ill-conceived schemes. It is testimony to their powers of endurance, given the paucity of official encouragement and the frustrating lack of suitable equipment, that SOE was to survive and even expand, particularly overseas, where MI(R) and Section D had scarcely time to develop foundations.

2 · A Branch of the Secret Service? SOE in the Middle East

I do not believe that theatre commanders, as they came to be called, or even Resident Ministers, were ever informed officially by the War Cabinet of the creation of SOE in July 1940; and secondly they were not given any inkling of the charter upon which it was founded. From the beginning quite excessive secrecy was enjoined on SOE itself from above, and I can now begin to understand why GHQ Middle East felt that resistance activities in distant countries (not even on their shores), though within their theatre, were not their direct concern. In this connection I cannot at the same time find anybody who was ever informed officially or in writing of what the charter of SOE was. I think that SOE was looked upon as a sort of branch of the secret service, and of course a secret service with no written charter, but SOE had one written down in the Cabinet minutes, though as far as I can make out it never got beyond that.

Major-General Sir Colin Gubbins, July 1973[1]

SOE's earliest days in the Middle East did not inspire confidence in the organisation, even if it was to conduct more operations in this theatre than anywhere else in the world. The first head in Cairo, which naturally became SOE's regional headquarters because of its proximity to the British Army's Headquarters Middle East, was Arthur Goodwill, an eccentric Wykehamist who had been one of Grand's first band of supporters in Section D and was originally supposed to have run the Section's operations in neutral Athens with Ian Pirie from the safety of the British Legation, concentrating specifically on Albania. Like Belgrade, where Julius Hanau had been so active, Athens had been selected as a key neutral capital from which Section D could stir up anti-Nazi feeling in the Balkans employing expatriate businessmen and individual agents working under commercial and diplomatic cover. However, the swiftness of the German advance through South-East Europe, and Italy's designs on Albania, meant that the Greek police had kept Goodwill and his colleagues under surveillance, and he had been able to achieve little before he had hurriedly embarked for Egypt.

Goodwill had concluded that Section D's efforts could not be directed from London as they had been hitherto and, with the consent of the Middle East Intelligence Centre,[2] then headed by Colonel (Sir) Iltyd Clayton, set up a local office in Cairo. In May 1940 George Taylor flew out to start a Balkan section, but within a short time he was back in London as Sir Frank Nelson's Chief of Staff and, effectively, SOE's first director of operations. Goodwill also returned to London to run SOE's Balkan desk. Their replacement was a barrister, (Sir) George Pollock, who had been a sub-editor on the *Daily Chronicle* before being called to the bar in 1928. Thus, by the time the resourceful Pollock arrived in Egypt in September 1940, SOE Cairo had already been through two senior figures. The Balkans was to become a graveyard of reputations within the organisation, which, owing to over-enthusiasm and poor judgment, soon fell foul of both the civil and military authorities. It certainly did not take long for SOE Cairo to antagonise SIS, which had previously enjoyed a monopoly of political intelligence in the region.

It would seem that Pollock was expected to achieve the impossible, with minimal help from GHQ or anyone else. Apart from a garage full of stores in Alexandria and a tiny staff, there was little else to boast of. One important asset in the region was the collaboration of the Jewish Agency, which had been negotiated with Moshe Sharett, the head of the Agency's political office in Cairo, with the intention of linking Section D to Jewish underground networks in the Balkans. This never really materialised, but an archaeologist, Professor Arthur Lawrence, who had the advantage of being T.E.'s younger half-brother, did open an office in Jerusalem to recruit and train Jewish volunteers, most of whom were members of the paramilitary *Haganah* who had decided to throw in their lot with the British for the duration of the war. An arrangement between the two protagonists was negotiated by Reuven Shiloah, who headed the Jewish Agency's intelligence unit, and in consequence a group of Jewish activists was released on 1 February 1941 from Acre prison where they had been serving sentences for offences against the mandate authorities. Among them was the young Moshe Dayan, who participated in a couple of low-scale operations shortly before the Allied invasion of Syria in June 1941 and who, in a border skirmish, was wounded and lost the sight of one eye. Under Shiloah's supervision and in anticipation of a German occupation of the Middle East, SOE established an impressive stay-behind network across Palestine, with each cell linked by wireless. Once the danger had receded, the same personnel were trained for undercover work in Eastern Europe. Altogether a total of twenty-six Jews from Palestine were to be deployed in Italy, Poland and the Balkans.

There was criticism, however, particularly from General Wavell, that not enough was being done in the Balkans, and that Rashid Ali's pro-German coup in neutral Iraq in April 1941 had been allowed to take place without any apparent British interference, despite a substantial SOE presence there, led by an archaeologist and former monk, Adrian Bishop, whose staff included two Section D veterans: the noted Arabist, (Dame) Freya Stark, and an Anglo-Iranian Oil Company executive, Aidan Philip. In reality, SOE was preoccupied, not with the complexities of Iraqi politics, but in 'fierce interdepartmental warfare'.

The SIS Head of Station in Baghdad was Frank Giffey, who had previously served in Tallinn, and his assistant, Nigel Clive, recalls that 'if fifty per cent of the day could be devoted to trying to defeat Hitler, we were doing quite well and might win the war'.[3] Giffey 'had restricted his contacts with the rest of the intelligence community to an irreducible minimum',[4] but nevertheless claimed to have unearthed Rashid Ali's Nazi-backed plot just in time, leaving SOE no credit whatever, although it undoubtedly enjoyed far better local sources of information. Fortunately for all concerned, Rashid Ali's regime lasted no more than a month and the usurper fled to Iran.

There was also some anxiety about Operation YAK, an over-ambitious scheme dreamed up to screen Italian prisoners of war and recruit those anti-Fascists among them into SOE. This project was developed by Peter Fleming, formerly of MI(R), and Colonel Cudbert Thornhill, a veteran intelligence officer who had been Military Attaché in Petrograd during the Russian Revolution. A large number of Jews of Italian origin were recruited in Palestine for the vetting process and a start was made at four Italian prisoner-of-war camps: Mustafa near Alexandria, Helwan, Ganfieh and Ajami. In addition, a newspaper, the *Corriere d'Italia*, was printed locally and circulated in the camps under SOE's sponsorship. Unfortunately for Thornhill and Fleming, whose brother Ian was to invent James Bond, not a single Italian volunteered to join YAK and become a saboteur. Worse still, the SOE officer in charge of the Italian desk in SOE's psychological warfare division, John de Salis, discovered that the paper was carrying articles which, if not actually Communist inspired, could certainly be interpreted to be very anti-British. One offending item, entitled 'Perfidious Albion', had already been rejected by the censor but was published anyway, lending weight to the prevalent view that, in its naïveté, SOE had allowed itself to be hijacked by Socialists who had used its facilities to disseminate Communist propaganda. The row that followed led to the dismissal of the *Corriere*'s editorial board, headed by Professor Umberto Calosso, and the arrest by the Egyptian police of Enzo Sereni, one of the *Corriere*'s editors and a key SOE agent. Following an eleven-day hunger strike and Moshe Sharett's intervention, Sereni was released from gaol and sent on a secret mission to Baghdad.

This was not the only complaint laid against SOE. Unwisely, Thornhill became entangled with a notorious Arab nationalist, Aziz el-Masri, who had been the Egyptian army's Chief of Staff and was wanted for plotting against British rule. When el-Masri was finally taken into custody, he revealed his embarrassing connection with Thornhill, which prevented him from being put on trial. He was interned instead, but Thornhill was compromised further.

This is not to say that SOE in Cairo was entirely devoid of useful assets. In fact, a valuable clandestine link had been established with Athens, which had been occupied by the *Wehrmacht* in April. This was largely thanks to the work done by Section D, which had cultivated some helpful commercial contacts in Greece early in the war. The head of Section D's Greek desk in London was Donald Perkins, who was assisted by Sir Gerald Talbot, a former naval attaché in Athens at the end of the First World War. Both made frequent visits to Greece, where David Pawson was operating under commercial cover. His efforts were reinforced in March 1941 when Nicholas Hammond, an archaeologist and a Classics don at Cambridge, arrived in time to distribute wireless sets to various stay-behind agents, including Colonel Euripedes Bakirdzis, who had won a DSO during the First World War and had been sentenced to death for his involvement in the anti-monarchist coup attempt in 1935. A republican known as 'the Red Colonel', Bakirdzis had been recruited by Pawson and was given the codename *Prometheus*; using the call-sign 333, the Leftist regular officer had maintained contact with SOE from November 1941 until he was extricated and brought to Cairo for consultations in August 1942. SIS had reluctantly donated seven scarce transmitters to SOE for use in the Balkan theatre and, accordingly, *Prometheus* acquired a special status within SOE (in spite of his politics) for his was the only transmitter to be operated during the winter of 1941/2. The remaining six stayed silent after the Axis had completed its occupation of the region.

As we shall see later in Chapter 7, SOE's link to Bakirdzis was to commit the organisation to him and his republican adherents, while SIS plumped for an entirely different set of resistants who had stayed loyal to the King and the Greek government-in-exile after their evacuation from Crete in May 1941. As well as causing confusion among the Greeks, who could not understand how two clandestine organisations could be operating separately in the same territory, the lack of co-ordination was to have far worse consequences.

Apart from its limited activities on the mainland, Section D had also been active in Crete, where Thomas Dunbabin, a Fellow of All Souls, Oxford, who had been assistant director of the British School of Archaeology since 1936, had taken up a consular appointment. He managed to withdraw to Cairo as the Germans mounted their airborne assault on the island, but one of his colleagues, Professor Jack Hamson, was made a prisoner of war. Fortunately for him the Germans never realised his true role, although, even if he had been interrogated, it is difficult to see what Section D operations might have been jeopardised. There were, in short, simply none to be compromised. In fact, Greece had been invaded and occupied without any significant interference from SOE even though its personnel had been in the area for months.

Growing dissatisfaction with SOE's performance and its administration led Sir Frank Nelson to send a new man to Cairo, but his nominee, a regular soldier, was shot down over the Bay of Biscay and captured, destined to spend the remainder of the war in a prisoner-of-war camp. His substitute, a merchant banker, was vetoed by Dalton, so the third candidate, Terence Maxwell, was despatched to Egypt and was accompanied on the journey by Nelson. Like Pollock, whom he was to replace, Maxwell was a barrister and, like so many other recent recruits into SOE, a merchant banker, being managing director of Glyn, Mills & Co. Before the war he had been a reserve officer and he had just been through a Staff College intelligence course at Minley Manor when Nelson selected him for the task of putting SOE's Cairo branch, which operated under the cover designation of MO4, back on its feet. Pollock, meanwhile, was assigned to SOE's Norwegian Section, presumably on the basis that his new area of responsibility was about as unlike the Middle East as was possible to find.

The task for Maxwell was considerable, but he did not arrive in Egypt with much in the way of status. His official rank was that of counsellor and he operated under rather flimsy Ministry of Economic Warfare cover. The fact that a few weeks earlier he had been a captain in a territorial regiment, and had previously served with the Post Office Rifles, was not publicised. Certainly he was walking into the lions' den in terms of British intelligence controversies. As well as SOE, which had established itself a short distance

SOE Cairo

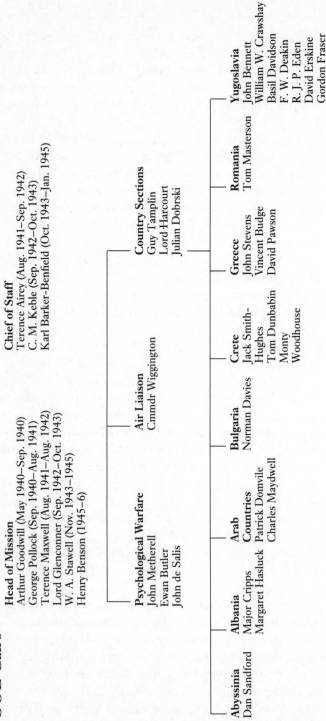

Head of Mission
Arthur Goodwill (May 1940–Sep. 1940)
George Pollock (Sep. 1940–Aug. 1941)
Terence Maxwell (Aug. 1941–Aug. 1942)
Lord Glenconner (Sep. 1942–Oct. 1943)
W. A. Stawell (Nov. 1943–1945)
Henry Benson (1945–6)

Chief of Staff
Terence Airey (Aug. 1941–Sep. 1942)
C. M. Keble (Sep. 1942–Oct. 1943)
Karl Barker-Benfield (Oct. 1943–Jan. 1945)

Psychological Warfare
John Metherell
Ewan Butler
John de Salis

Air Liaison
Cmmdr Wiggington

Country Sections
Guy Tamplin
Lord Harcourt
Julian Dobrski

Abyssinia
Dan Sandford

Albania
Major Cripps
Margaret Hasluck

Arab Countries
Patrick Domvile
Charles Maydwell

Bulgaria
Norman Davies

Crete
Jack Smith-Hughes
Tom Dunbabin
Monty Woodhouse

Greece
John Stevens
Vincent Budge
David Pawson

Romania
Tom Masterson

Yugoslavia
John Bennett
William W. Crawshay
Basil Davidson
F. W. Deakin
R. J. P. Eden
David Erskine
Gordon Fraser
J. W. Hitchen
Roger Inman
Michael Ionides
James Klugmann
R. C. E. Oades
William Wilson

away from GHQ in a large block of flats called Rustum Buildings on the Sharia Kasr-el-Aini, both SIS and MI5 had local organisations and operated from the same modern apartment building in GHQ's compound in Garden City known as 'Grey Pillars'. SIS called itself the Inter-Services Liaison Department (ISLD) and was headed by one of Stewart Menzies's senior aides, Captain Cuthbert Bowlby RN. His Security Service counterpart was Colonel Raymund Maunsell, a younger man but a professional soldier, who had served with the Transjordanian Frontier Force. By mid-1941, when Maxwell appeared on the scene, both Maunsell and Bowlby had developed a wealth of experience in the region, but neither was prepared to share it with the newcomer. Indeed, Maxwell's assistant recalls that 'nobody who did not experience it can possibly imagine the atmosphere of jealousy, suspicion and intrigue which embittered the relations between the various secret and semi-secret departments in Cairo that summer of 1941.'[5] However, tensions eased after Maxwell's arrival, for he promptly sacked the unfortunate Thornhill and a large number of SOE personnel, while John Metherell, a former branch manager of the Bombay Company in Madras, was promoted to Director of Psychological Warfare. (Christopher Sykes, who had been Thornhill's assistant during 1941 before joining Adrian Bishop at SOE's office in Persia, used his own experiences in SOE as background for his first novel, *High Minded Murder*, in which he took the opportunity to portray Metherell, his *bête noire* on SOE's staff, as an easily recognisable loathsome character, named Major Walter Anstey.[6] Astonishingly, the book was published in 1944.)

Maxwell's reorganisation, regarded by its many casualties as a purge, created three separate directorates, of which Metherell's was but one. The second directorate, Political Subversion, was divided into two branches, with Tom Masterson (from Section D in Belgrade) handling Balkan affairs and Patrick Domvile (from Section D in Baghdad) dealing with Arab matters. Previously each individual country in the region had had its own sub-section, which corresponded with a similar desk at Baker Street. However, this arrangement was abolished, only to be reinstated a year later during another purge, which left many believing this annual event had become an institution. The third directorate, Operations, was left to Terence Airey and his team of MI(R) adventurers, who had operated with some success in Ethiopia under their local cover, G(R). As General Wavell remarked at the time, 'SOE think they've taken over GR, and GR think they've taken over SOE, so everybody's happy.'[7] Thus, Cairo revelled in an alphabet soup of secret organisations, each with overlapping responsibilities and minimal co-ordination. Not surprisingly, the inter-agency rivalries were exacerbated, and the resulting bureaucracies were later satirised by Christopher Sykes in *A Song of a Shirt*, published after the war.[8]

Maxwell's empire was not limited to Cairo. SOE ran a substantial branch office in neutral Istanbul, where at least four of the country sections were represented, under the leadership of an oil company executive, Gardyne de Chastelain, who had retreated from Bucharest and retained responsibility for the Romanian Section. Walter (Frank) Stirling, an old Near East hand who had been seconded to the Albanian Government for eight years during the 1920s to train the gendarmerie, and had been appointed the chief censor for Britain's telephone traffic to the Continent in 1939, ran the local Albanian desk, and Tommy Davies of MI(R) dealt with Bulgarian matters. David Pawson, who had been evacuated from Athens, represented the Greek sub-section.

Soon after Maxwell's arrival in Cairo, SOE launched BULLSEYE, a mission to Yugoslavia to establish contact with the only known resistance movement, the Cetniks, led by a regular army officer, Colonel Draza Mihailovic, who was already known to Section D. The operation called for the infiltration of a team of SOE agents and Julian Amery was assigned for the task,[9] on the basis of his experience with Section D in Belgrade. Amery had joined SOE in Cairo following the Italian invasion of Albania and had been appointed deputy head of SOE's Balkan division under Colonel S. William Bailey, formerly one of Chester Beatty's technical men at the Trepca Mine. Amery was supplied with some willing volunteers by Colonel Yovan Jonovic, the exiled Yugoslav Director of Military Intelligence, then resident in Istanbul, but at the last moment the first two agents declined to go through with their mission. Amery therefore turned as a replacement to Bill Hudson, a South African Section D officer who spoke Serbo-Croat and had managed one of Beatty's goldmines in Yugoslavia before the war. Hudson had slipped out of Belgrade, after having organised the sabotage of some German ships with cargoes of manganese ore, and had made his way to Cairo via Istanbul and Cyprus. Amery experienced great difficulty in persuading the Royal Navy to mount a second operation, but eventually the submarine HMS *Triumph* was made available in Malta and Hudson was landed on the Dalmatian coast near Petrovac on 20 September 1941. Soon afterwards he made contact with an unexpected organisation run by Josip Broz, the outlawed Secretary General of the Yugoslav Communist Party, who called himself Tito. Hudson was also accompanied by three Yugoslavs, Majors Zaharije Ostojic and Miro Lalatovic, who had been in Cairo for some months, and an NCO wireless operator, Veljko Dragicevic. They reported on Tito's well-organised group of partisans and received orders to continue their search for Mihailovic, who, coincidentally, had just succeeded in establishing a radio link with Malta, albeit a very insecure one in clear language. Hudson soon found Mihailovic and his Cetniks, and maintained a somewhat erratic radio link with Cairo via Malta until he was extricated in March 1944. He was also to learn of the violent enmity between the two rival groups of guerrillas operating in the mountains.

Although BULLSEYE was officially an SOE mission, Hudson was not aware that his two Serbian companions were under secret orders from SIS. Ostojic had been on the Yugoslav General Staff and his companion, Lalatovic, who had been in the Royal Yugoslav Air Force, had originally intended to return to Yugoslavia alone, under the auspices of SIS, but, with just twelve hours' notice and minimal briefing, Hudson had been assigned the task of going with them. Amery, later to become a Tory MP and Foreign Office minister, had escorted the party all the way to the landing site. According to (Sir) F. W. D. Deakin, who later worked in the Yugoslav country section in Cairo when it was under the command of John Bennett, Hudson's objective had been 'to contact, investigate and report on all groups offering resistance to the enemy, regardless of race, creed or political persuasion'.[10] But the two Serbs 'were pursuing a somewhat different course of action', for they were under secret orders from SIS to deal exclusively with Mihailovic. They 'had secret instructions from their superiors, which were unknown to Hudson', but they attended Hudson's meetings with local Communists and then split up briefly on 9 October, when Hudson had been ordered by Cairo to find Mihailovic. This directive had been sent in response to Mihailovic's own wireless signals. Hudson transmitted another signal on 19 October and then set off with Ostojic to Mihailovic, leaving Lalatovic behind with their remaining Mark III wireless, the batteries of their other set having run out. However, it had already become clear to SOE in Cairo that it was not receiving the full picture. The two Serbs occasionally signalled without Hudson's knowledge, using the single remaining radio, and the messages were, of course, in an SIS cipher which were handled by SIS personnel. Referring to this after the war, General Simovic, who was the head of the first Royal Yugoslav government in London, recalled that SIS 'let it be known that secure communications with Yugoslavia could only be set up if they sent in their people with a W/T set and the necessary ciphers'.[11] In fact, while Hudson headed for west Serbia with Ostojic, Lalatovic 'was clearly bent on establishing channels of communication overland, which would be exclusively nationalist in character'. En route Hudson met Tito and offered to supply him with a radio schedule and a cipher so that he could communicate with SOE in Cairo, using his own Soviet-supplied equipment, but Tito indicated that he was already in touch with Moscow and therefore had no need of SOE. Undeterred, Hudson returned to the Cetniks and established a new wireless link with Malta using the call-sign VILLA RESTA, and it was through this channel that the first airdrop of supplies was organised on 9 November from Luqa in Malta.

This was a considerable milestone in SOE's tangled history. Two Whitley bombers of 138 Squadron had arrived in Malta the previous week from Tempsford, via Portreath, and Pilot Officer Austin, assisted by a Serbian pilot, flew two containers to Hudson's encampment. The operation had been conducted flawlessly, but a second mission, to be led by Ian Mackenzie, was cancelled when his team arrived in Malta by submarine, but without parachutes. As the beleaguered island had none to spare, the mission was postponed and the two Whitleys ordered back to England.

Thus, by the middle of November 1941 SOE had established Hudson with Mihailovic and, in effect, built two wireless links with the Cetniks, one operating to SIS, the other to SOE, but both using the same channel. However, early the following month Hudson suddenly went off the air, leading Cairo to believe that he had fallen victim to a German offensive. Reliable information was so difficult to achieve that SOE decided to send in three missions to report on the situation. HMS *Thorn* carried the first party, codenamed HENNA, which was comprised of two Yugoslavs, Lieutenant Rapotec and Sergeant Stevan Shinko, who left Alexandria on 17 January 1942, destined for the island of Mljet, near Split. The second group, HYDRA, consisting of Major Terence Atherton, Captain Radoje Nedeljkovic of the Royal Yugoslav Air Force, and an Irish wireless operator, Sergeant Patrick O'Donovan, was landed by HMS *Thorn* near Petrovac on 4 February 1942. Nothing was heard of either mission, so a third operation, DISCLAIM, was mounted by air from Malta the following night. Led by Major Kavan Elliott and his operator, Sergeant Robert Chapman, it also included Lieutenant Pavle Crnjanski and Sergeant Miljkovic.

There was no news of the HENNA group for some months, and HYDRA, which was a rare venture, in which SIS had declared its involvement to its rival and had participated in a joint SIS/SOE operation, simply disappeared; DISCLAIM lasted all of three days before its members were surrounded by the pro-Axis Croatian *Ustase* and handed over to the Germans. In fact, Hudson was still in Cetnik hands, but he was held incommunicado for five months because Mihailovic evidently distrusted his contacts with the rival partisans. He was to remain with them until March 1944. Meanwhile, the HYDRA mission had made contact with the partisans, but was unable to use its radio. Atherton, who had previously spent ten years in Belgrade as a journalist before escaping to Cairo, where he had been hired as a war correspondent for the *Daily Mail*, experienced some two months with the partisans and then attempted with O'Donovan to reach Mihailovic. They were not seen alive after 23 April 1942 and the most likely explanation for their disappearance is that they were murdered for the 2,000 gold sovereigns they were carrying. The principal suspect, a Cetnik leader named Spasoje Dakic, was himself killed in action in 1946. The third member of the HYDRA mission, Nedeljkovic, also disappeared, and is believed to have been denounced to the Germans and executed later in Belgrade. The original HENNA mission eventually turned up in Istanbul in July 1942, having failed to reach Hudson. He reported the deaths of Atherton and O'Donovan, and thereafter SOE restricted the amount of currency their agents could carry. The news was received in Cairo just in time for the second major purge which was to shake SOE.

•   •   •   •   •   •

In May 1942, Sir Frank Nelson had left Baker Street, supposedly on the grounds of ill-health, but more likely through sheer exasperation. He had first threatened to resign in November 1941 while fighting off SIS, and had soon been embroiled in three separate controversies: on 19 December Desmond Morton had hinted that Churchill was thinking of letting the recently created Political Warfare Executive, which had already taken over responsibility for propaganda, absorb the rest of SOE, and de Gaulle had demanded that Eden disband SOE's F and RF Sections. Then, in February 1942, Dalton had been replaced by the Third Earl of Selborne at the Ministry of Economic Warfare, and Gladwyn Jebb, who had been the Foreign Office's first nominee to assist Dalton in August 1940, returned to his department. The final imbroglio had been the outcome of a bitter, long-standing dispute with the Belgian intelligence apparatus, which was firmly under SIS's control. The Belgian Prime Minister, H. Pierlot, declined to reach an operating agreement with SOE and terminated their liaison. This, then, was the mantle that Nelson handed to Charles Hambro, together with a knighthood.

The first outward sign of Selborne's new management was the introduction of a special fortnightly meeting with SIS, at which all mutual operational issues could be discussed and resolved. The exact terms of the agreement remain secret, but it can be deduced from other sources that it required Foreign Office approval for all SOE operations in enemy territory, and for the Foreign Office to be informed immediately of any developments of a political nature. There were also changes within SOE's unwieldy structure. Colin Gubbins was named Hambro's deputy with responsibility for overseeing SOE's operations in Western Europe and the Mediterranean, leaving George Taylor to look after Cairo, West Africa and the United States from London. The next step was a further shake-up in Cairo, where Terence Maxwell was replaced by Lord Glenconner, a director of Hambro's Bank.

Glenconner had been working with James Pearson in SOE's Balkans and Middle East Directorate and so knew much of the background to the region. He had also recently spent some months in Istanbul, where he may have gained some knowledge of SOE's difficulties in Greece and Yugoslavia. In any event it was his idea to introduce a Chief of Staff in Cairo, who was to prove a key figure in the drama unfolding in Yugoslavia. Colonel C. M. ('Bolo') Keble had been an intelligence specialist at GHQ and had concentrated on the analysis of that most secret of sources, ULTRA. Astonishingly, no one else in SOE had been cleared for access to this vital signals intelligence, so it gave him an entirely different perspective from which to work. Indeed, having studied SOE's performance in Yugoslavia, Keble assigned two officers from the relevant country section, Bill Deakin and Basil Davidson, to examine the enemy intercepts and develop an order-of-battle for the Balkans. When completed, this clearly demonstrated that there were far more enemy troops tied up in territory controlled by the partisans than in the areas dominated by Mihailovic. This immediately inspired a change in SOE's policy of supporting the Cetniks exclusively, but the decision to do so was to cause unequalled and lasting political controversy.

Before looking at the intelligence available, and the decisions made, we should first turn to the organisational structures of SIS and SOE and take a look at the personalities involved in the decision-making process during this period. As we have seen, from August 1942, SOE in Cairo consisted of a Yugoslav country section in which John Bennett, Basil Davidson and Bill Deakin played important roles. Of the three, Bennett was the senior figure, having been one of Section D's team in Belgrade. Before the war he had stood for Parliament as the Labour Party's candidate against Neville Chamberlain. Davidson was rather more Left-orientated and his background was in journalism, as a writer for the *Economist*, before he was posted to Budapest in January 1940 as Section D's man in Hungary. Deakin's credentials were more academic, having been an Oxford don, and rather better connected: before the war he had helped his friend Winston Churchill research and write his biography of Marlborough.[12]

Yugoslav Country Section, Cairo

Julian Amery	Nov. 1941–July 1942	Dropped into Albania
John Bennett	Feb. 1942–Aug. 1942	
Kenneth Greenlees	Feb. 1942–Oct. 1942	Dropped into Yugoslavia
Basil Davidson	Oct. 1942–July 1943	Dropped into Yugoslavia
David Ionides	Nov. 1942–July 1944	
Hugh Seton-Watson	Nov. 1942–Jan. 1944	
Bill Deakin	Dec. 1942–May 1943	Dropped into Yugoslavia
J. W. Hitchen	Dec. 1942–May 1943	
Roger Inman	April 1943–Jan. 1944	
R. J. P. Eden	May 1943–Sep. 1943	
Gordon Fraser	July 1943–July 1944	
William Wilson	July 1943–Aug. 1944	
R. C. E. Oades	Aug. 1943–Oct. 1943	
William Crawshay	Aug. 1943–Dec. 1943	
Douglas Davidson	Aug. 1943–Dec. 1943	
David Erskine	Sep. 1943–April 1944	
Bill Deakin	Dec. 1943–May 1944	
Peter K. Wright	June 1944–Aug. 1944	

Prior to the 1942 reorganisation SOE had suspended the concept of geographical sub-sections in favour of functional branches, an aberration that only lasted during Maxwell's twelve months at the helm. Of the three main players, only Deakin had served first in London, in the Yugoslav Section, and then in Cairo. He left Baker Street at a crucial moment in October 1942 and did not arrive for two months, when he took over from Davidson in January 1943 before leading TYPICAL, a joint SOE/SIS operation in May 1943 (see page 63). Davidson was to follow him in August, on SAVANNA. Equally influential were Professor Hugh Seton-Watson, an academic of strong Leftist views who had operated for Section D in Belgrade and Bucharest, and James Klugmann, who had joined SOE as a private soldier from the Pioneer Corps. Then there was Bill Bailey, who had fallen victim to the purge of August 1941 and had flown to Canada, at Taylor's behest, to recruit Canadian Croats for participation, principally as interpreters, in the British military missions destined for Yugoslavia.

Seton-Watson, Bennett and Davidson had all been veterans of Section D in the Balkans, and reported to two senior SOE officers in charge of Balkan affairs in London, James Pearson and Edward Boxshall. The latter had previously been associated with SIS in Romania, where, apart from performing as an intelligence officer, he had represented Vickers for the legendary Basil Zaharoff and ICI. He was exceptionally well connected in Bucharest and had married Prince Barbu Stirbey's daughter. His commercial connection with the Vickers Company is not entirely surprising. Allan Monkhouse and five other Vickers employees had been convicted of espionage in the Soviet Union in 1933,[13] and the company had a long-standing relationship with Sir Desmond Morton's Industrial Intelligence Centre. When SOE was wound up after the war, Boxshall returned to SIS to handle Eastern European affairs and to act as guardian of what remained of SOE's records.

At Baker Street Yugoslav country section issues were handled by Bickham Sweet-Escott and Peter Boughey (see table on page 258). For its part, SIS enjoyed a close relationship with the Yugoslav government-in-exile, and the person heading the Yugoslav country section in Broadway, designated Y/S, was John Ennals, a former war correspondent in the Balkans, who, like his brothers David and Martin, was very active in left-wing politics.[14] He was to be succeeded by a Scottish recruit from the Government Communications Headquarters (GCHQ), John Cairncross, who had made a name for himself as an enemy order-of-battle expert specialising in *Wehrmacht* deployments on the eastern front. He also happened to be an NKVD agent, having been recruited by Guy Burgess and Anthony Blunt while still at Cambridge. The Soviets rated his information so highly that they awarded Cairncross the Order of the Red Banner after the Battle of Kursk. SIS's local man in Cairo was James Miller, another left-wing activist who had also been Ennals's contemporary at Cambridge, along with Klugmann and Cairncross. Thus, the weight of intellectual opinion concentrated on the Yugoslav front in both clandestine bodies in London and Cairo, and therefore the principal conduit of advice and information to the political level, was heavily in favour of the Left and Tito's partisans at the expense of Mihailovic's Cetniks.

SIS concentrated its efforts in London, but opened a country section office in Italy run by Aubrey Jones after the Allied invasion. Shortage of aircraft in the region and the loss of Bill Stuart, who was killed with the TYPICAL mission in May 1943, seriously handicapped the organisation.

Stuart had been born in Bosnia of a Scottish father and Hungarian mother, and had worked in Zagreb before the war, having previously been employed in the immigration department of the Canadian Pacific Railway. At the outbreak of war he was in Zagreb, working under British vice-consular cover, and after the Italian invasion he spent six months in internment before being exchanged by the Red Cross as a civilian. He had then been posted to SIS's New York office before returning to participate in TYPICAL. He had been killed in an air raid soon after his arrival, having parachuted into Montenegro while the *Wehrmacht* was launching an offensive against the partisans. His death was one of the few casualties in the war of British SIS personnel.[15]

The issue of SOE's support switching from Mihailovic to Tito was further complicated by the Soviet influence which was exerted directly, through political channels in London, and indirectly by the work of Soviet sympathisers. In brief, Tito was then the Kremlin's man and, having apparently rebuffed the BULLSEYE mission in 1942, or at any rate declined the offer of a communications link with Cairo, accepted the TYPICAL mission in May 1943 and the British Military Mission led by (Sir) Fitzroy Maclean MP, which arrived four months later.

Initially SOE's intention had been to cultivate Mihailovic, but on 7 August 1942 the Cetnik leader had been denounced by the Soviet Ambassador in London, Ivan Maisky, as a Nazi collaborator. Thereafter, SOE's attitude began to undergo a contentious change, but there are two other factors which might account for the conversion. The first is the ULTRA material, which only Keble had access to, and which appeared to shed a new light on the relative strength and value of the partisans and the Cetniks.

However, it is not quite that simple to suggest that, because the boffins at Bletchley Park had managed to solve some of the Enigma cipher machine's many keys, they were able to read all enemy cipher traffic. In reality, the Enigma had numerous variants, which was its intrinsic strength, and different branches of the German forces used their own individual settings. Thus, a breakthrough with one particular category of communications, perhaps the *Sicherheitsdienst*'s messages, would have absolutely no relevance to those from the *Wehrmacht* to the *Luftwaffe*. Nor were all the Enigma keys ever identified, let alone deciphered. Take, for example, the Gestapo's Enigma key, designated TGB at Bletchley, or OYSTER, the U-boat key. Both were monitored throughout the year, but never broken. A huge number were either never linked to a specific service, or were never read. Furthermore, it should be recalled that most of the decrypted data was retrospective in nature and, while being invaluable to the analysts building up a comprehensive picture of the enemy's dispositions, did not necessarily have much impact on the tactical situation in the field at any given moment.

That ULTRA played a part in changing SOE's attitude towards the Cetniks is not disputed, but the fact that this source even existed was not admitted by the British Government until 1974, and those who had been privy to the secret during the war were under an obligation to keep silent about it. Thus, the debate that raged in the post-war era about Mihailovic's treatment at the hands of the Allies could never include some of the most crucial aspects of the argument. However, the full extent of the Allies' knowledge of the enemy's activities, as gleaned from signals intelligence, has now been revealed, and one can survey exactly what was known, and when.

The ULTRA decrypts relevant to the Balkans consist of nine separate sources, all of which were broken at different times, but the dates of the first breaks are important. Each individual source was assigned an unique cryptonym, and the list covers all the fighting services. Thus, the first break was achieved on 20 February 1942, when RAVEN, the main *Wehrmacht* key in the Balkans for the 12th Army, was successfully attacked. GCHQ's cryptanalysts had been concentrating on this cipher since the previous September, when it had first been positively identified, and five months' intense effort was rewarded. Then, on 10 February 1943, MERLIN, the *Wehrmacht*'s Staff key for the Balkans, was read for the first time. Three days later this helped the cryptographers to solve NUTHATCH, the *Wehrmacht*'s channel between Belgrade and Berlin. This was followed in May by BUZZARD, the main *Wehrmacht* key for South-East Europe. On 24 August PEREGRINE gave an insight into the SS *Panzers* stationed in Yugoslavia, as did another similar channel, WRYNECK I, which was broken the next month. In October the *Luftwaffe*'s key for Croatia, YAK, was read, and on 16 November 1943 WOODPECKER surrendered, which was revealed to be another *Wehrmacht* key for South-East Europe. This was followed by LLAMA, the *Luftwaffe*'s key for Albania, in February 1944. Although these highly secret decrypts gave SIS a vein of intelligence of unprecedented quality, it was an opportunity that was not shared by SOE until Keble joined the organisation in August 1942. Up until that point the country section heads had no idea that such a rich source even existed.

Clearly the best breaks into the enemy's signals traffic occurred at a significant juncture for SOE, but before making an assessment of their impact, we should consider briefly the second factor in SOE's change in policy towards Mihailovic, which centres on the motives of some of those directly involved. The issue of undue Soviet influence in support of Tito's partisans has arisen on many occasions. There has also been speculation about the loyalties of certain SOE officers, in particular James Klugmann, who was a lifelong Communist and rose to a high position in the Communist Party of Great Britain (CPGB). As well as serving on the politburo, he also became the Party's official historian.[16] The fact that he was also a Soviet spy has been confirmed by two of his fellow moles, John Cairncross and

Anthony Blunt. Indeed, he never gave up his creed, even when offered a tempting proposition by the Security Service towards the end of his life. Cairncross was persuaded by MI5 to approach Klugmann with an immunity from prosecution in exchange for information, but he had been rejected. Nor was Klugmann the only Soviet agent in SOE's country section in Cairo. According to Professor M. R. D. Foot, John Eyre was also working for the NKVD.[17] Indeed, even Hugh Seton-Watson, who subsequently became a conservative, has described himself in Cairo during this important period as 'a Soviet sympathiser'.[18]

That the Soviets indulged in espionage against SOE at this time is a matter of record. Ormond Uren, who worked for Peter Boughey in the Balkan sub-section dealing with Hungary, was actually convicted of passing secrets to a Soviet contact in October 1943. Uren, who had joined SOE in May 1942, had started supplying Douglas Springhall with information in April 1943. Springhall was a veteran CPGB activist, having been political commissar of the British Battalion of the International Brigade during the Spanish Civil War. He was sentenced to seven years' imprisonment, as was Uren.

Supporters of Mihailovic, who was executed as a Nazi collaborator by the Communist regime after the war, contend that he was the victim of a conspiracy organised by Soviet sympathisers inside SOE to prevent him from receiving the political and logistical aid he deserved and desperately needed. Equally badly treated were the various SOE teams that made contact with the Cetniks and had no knowledge of the political battles raging in Cairo and Whitehall about which side, in what amounted to a civil war, Britain should be backing. They knew that their role was being misrepresented because of the very biased reports being broadcast by the BBC. Most of the original signals received in Cairo have been destroyed, either burnt in July 1942, when there was a real fear that Rommel would reach Cairo, or in 1945, when Henry Benson was closing up SOE for ever, but a few have survived and they make harrowing reading. On 5 October 1943 the NERONIAN mission reported:

On 5 Oct at Jelasnic (?) and Arknjazevac (?) Germans attacked to obtain arms. Killed 14 wounded 20. One wounded was brought back, 40 rifles, 3 MGs one maxim, 2 pistols, one binocs, good supply ammo for weapons captured and equipment from dead. Why no help from Cairo? Three planes as requested be big help. First frost today, no clothing, no money, no food. Help. Help.[19]

The chronic lack of SOE's logistical support for Hudson is highlighted by this pathetic signal, sent on 22 September 1943:

I have been waiting one and a half years for battle dress blouse size 6ft, waiting at least 7 months for boots size 11 and riding breeches size 6ft and large great coat. All repeatedly asked for. It was not funny last year when in lieu of above you sent me my tennis trousers and silk pyjamas, nor this year when you sent your stunted five foot five outfits. In fact ever since you sent me in from Cairo with bum W/T equipment your supply dept has been just plain lousy.[20]

Brigadier Charles Armstrong, who led the British Military Mission to the Cetniks in September 1943, was able to cite specific examples where particular actions had been credited to the wrong side by the BBC, because the fighting had been witnessed by Bill Bailey of SOE. Armstrong sent this message on 16 November:

If you want to get the best out of MIHAILOVIC you must give him fairer press and broadcasts. BAILEY was with MIHAILOVIC forces when took PRIBOJ and PRIJEPOLJE and BERANE. I saw capture VISEGRAD, destruction bridges, and know OSTOJIC took ROGATICA. MIHAILOVIC never credited with any these, although reported to you. On other hand, when PARTISANS drove his forces out, PARTISANS credited on BBC.[21]

Similarly, the ENAMEL mission reported on 30 November 1943:

We are so surrounded by lies and contradictions and so lacking true information that we have lost faith in everything except our ultimate victory, inevitability of which we hammer into SERBS constantly.[22]

On 1 December ALMONER also complained about a distorted news item, broadcast by the BBC, concerning a group of Bulgarian collaborators:

News from London in SERB giving false information. The forty BUGS killed at KALNA were not attacked by PARTISANS but by MIHAILOVIC's forces from SUVA PLANINA. NOVOVOROS is also a MIHAILOVIC affair. Can't you have these points corrected and keep a watching brief over future news in Serb? . . . Why no plane to me here?[23]

Part of the problem may have been the quality of liaison deployed to the two rival forces, for Hudson's BULLSEYE mission had been undermined by the long period that it was off the air, and the fact that the two SIS agents who had gone with him had been sending reports without Hudson's knowledge. Bailey's three-man team had made contact with the Cetniks in December 1942, and Armstrong had arrived to join them in September 1943. A regular soldier who had fought in North Russia and Mesopotamia during the First World War, and had been evacuated from Dunkirk in 1940, Armstrong had been an odd choice to co-ordinate a guerrilla campaign. Certainly neither he nor Bailey was ever given an opportunity to report in person to Cairo. In contrast, the TYPICAL mission, consisting of Deakin and Stuart, went to the partisans in May 1943 and was followed up by Fitzroy Maclean, who had the status of Churchill's personal representative and was accompanied by a comparatively large staff of experienced irregulars, including Gordon Alston, an intelligence officer from the Special Air Service (SAS) who had been on plenty of clandestine missions during the desert war. There can be little doubt which side the politicians had wanted to back and Tito found an eloquent advocate in Maclean, who, despite being the Tory MP for Lancaster, became a warm admirer and friend of the Communist leader.

The question remaining concerns the information the politicians were presented with which made them switch their allegiance from Mihailovic to Tito. One explanation may have been the ULTRA material, which had come on stream during 1942 and had been seen by Keble. SIS went to extraordinary lengths to protect this unique source of intelligence and kept its circulation to a tightly controlled minimum. Even in London, only Hambro and his deputy, Gubbins, were allowed to know of ULTRA's existence, and access was restricted to a single conference, once a week, which directly touched on SOE's operations. It is improbable that either was informed of the full scope of the material. However, before Keble's transfer to SOE, he had been granted access and had been handling this sensitive source on a daily basis. He therefore had a high regard for its value and accuracy, and George Taylor, who visited Cairo on an inspection tour in December 1942, believes that it had been 'pure good fortune' that Keble had 'previously been on the Middle East distribution list for the reception of operational intercepts and that he remained on it after he had left his previous post in intelligence. Nobody took him off, so he continued to get them'.[24] Basil Davidson recalls that

early in January 1943 we began to get intercepts and these arrived on my desk probably at the beginning of January. They were very clearly intercepts of the *Sicherheitsdienst* inside Yugoslavia. i.e. it was extremely valuable information. Unfortunately I cannot specify a date but their arrival was a crucial factor because it marked the beginning of a whole new concept.[25]

Sweet-Escott confirms that SOE 'in Cairo were seeing the intercepts and in London we were not'. [26] Seton-Watson remembers that Keble 'had the right to decide which officers to reveal the information from the intercepts to', but suspects that 'somebody told SIS to release it in Cairo'.[27]

The impact of this vital material on SOE was certainly considerable and prompted Keble to write a long, fifteen-page report dated 30 January 1943 and hand it to Churchill personally, when the Prime Minister passed through Cairo on his way to Adana from North Africa. This single document, whilst omitting any reference to Tito, and denying that Mihailovic had been collaborating with the enemy, effectively altered Britain's policy in Yugoslavia. At any rate, its main recommendation, that British military missions be despatched to both the Cetniks and the partisans, was endorsed by Churchill, the Foreign Office and Lord Selborne. This led to Armstrong being sent to Mihailovic and Deakin to Tito, but during the months that followed the weight of support shifted in both logistical and propaganda terms away from the Cetniks to the partisans. The amount of intrigue then endemic in Cairo is hard to exaggerate. Fitzroy Maclean recalls a visit to Rustum Buildings, where he was left alone in a room to study SOE's Yugoslav files in preparation for a briefing by Seton-Watson. He retrieved one interesting dossier, which

contained a number of signals and memoranda concerning my own appointment. This, I soon found, was full of references to a sinister organisation designated by two letters, let us say PX. From these it appeared that PX was the real enemy and that PX must at all costs be outmanoeuvred and their knavish tricks frustrated. After a bit I came to the conclusion that it must be the Abwehr, or possibly something worse. Then I came on a signal which said that one reason why my appointment could on no account be countenanced was my own connection with PX. That was too much. I pinged my bell and my temporary assistant appeared. 'Tell me,' I said, 'what does PX stand for?' 'Oh, PX,' he said, 'that's the Foreign Office.'[28]

Maclean's mission to the Cetniks was, for him at least, a straightforward affair, or so he thought after receiving his assignment from Churchill at Chequers after an evening of watching cartoons together. His 'task was simply to find out who was killing the most Germans and suggest means by which we could help them kill more. Politics must be a secondary consideration.'[29] He recalls that allegedly very little was known about Tito, and 'no comprehensive report of the situation' had been received from TYPICAL, which, he believed, had been dropped in 'a few weeks before'.[30] This is very odd, considering that Deakin had been at Tito's headquarters since 27 May 1943, nearly four months before Maclean's arrival on 17 September. Equally strange is his recollection that there had been speculation in Cairo about Tito himself:

One school of thought refused to believe he existed at all. The same, they said, stood for *Tajna Teroristicka Organizacija*, or Secret International Terrorist Organisation, and not for any individual leader. Another theory was that it was simply an appointment, and that a new Tito was nominated at frequent intervals. Finally, the more romantically inclined claimed that Tito was not a man, but a young woman of startling beauty and great force of character.[31]

This extraordinary account is contradicted by Deakin, who saw a Mihailovic telegram dated as early as 5 November 1941, which referred to 'the Communist leader in Serbia, under the false name "Tito"',[32] and his own signals to Cairo concerning Tito which commenced soon after arrival and were maintained on a regular schedule. Since Tito and his partisans were clearly known to SOE in Cairo, one wonders why the relevant information was not passed on to Maclean before his arrival. In any event, Maclean's mission ensured that henceforth the partisans would be regarded as Britain's official allies.

The really sinister element in the bizarre conflict conducted in Cairo between SOE and SIS concerns a Foreign Office paper, dated 19 November 1943, which demonstrates that SIS's policy of handling all the communications of the various governments-in-exile had been a wise one. Evidently GCHQ had broken the code used by the Yugoslavs, for the memorandum noted that, earlier the previous month,

MIHAILOVIC has given orders to all CETNIK units to co-operate loyally with the GERMANS. Source comments that this is probably on instructions from the YUGO-SLAV government in exile. This is the more probable, as we know that precisely at the end of October the YUGOSLAV COMMAND in CAIRO sent a message to MIHAILOVIC by its clandestine W/T link in its insecure ciphers.[33]

Needless to say, this was one document that was never passed to SOE, which, at this stage, still had Hudson and Bailey in the field with Mihailovic, together with the hapless Brigadier Armstrong, who supposedly told Keble, just before his departure, that he would not go if his mission was to involve politics!

Perhaps not surprisingly the Yugoslav theatre tended to preoccupy much of SOE, but there were plans afoot to run missions into Albania, Bulgaria, Greece, Romania and Hungary. However, before turning to them, a look should be taken at developments in the rest of the world, including Europe. In closing this chapter, it is worth reviewing the other activities that had taken place during this period in the region.

●　　●　　●　　●　　●　　●

In April 1942 a Special Training School, designated STS 102, was established on the Kibbutz Mishmar Haemek, known as Ranath David, near Haifa, and a neighbouring monastery, atop Mount Carmel, was requisitioned to provide secure accommodation. An old crusader castle at Athlit was converted into a holding camp for undercover agents, and two parachute courses opened for business, one near Nazareth, and the other at Kabrit on the Suez Canal. This support infrastructure was an essential prerequisite for launching missions into enemy-occupied territory, as neither SIS nor SOE had much in the way of assets left in the Balkans. The main exception was in Greece, where Colonel Bakirdzis, codenamed *Prometheus*, had maintained contact by radio and, in November 1941, had passed his wireless to Captain Koutsoyiannopoulos, known as *Prometheus II*. This link, kept open by David Pawson in Istanbul, was to be the foundation of Operation HARLING, a successful sabotage mission to destroy the Gorgopotamos viaduct (see pages 164–5). The Greek country section in Cairo, headed by John Stevens and Vincent Budge, hailed this event as a great achievement, the first of its kind on the mainland of Greece, but there was not to be another until 20 February the following year, when Rufus Sheppard and Nicholas Hammond were dropped into Thessaly.

The other country sections fared less well. The first mission into Romania did not take place until June 1943, when David Russell and Nicolae Turcanu crossed the frontier from Yugoslavia for Operation RANJI and made contact with a Section D agent, Juliu Maniu. Unfortunately, the mission ended in tragedy for, like Terence Atherton, Russell was murdered by a Serb guide for his pouch of gold sovereigns. A second mission, AUTONOMOUS, consisting of Ivor Porter, Charles Maydwell and Silviu Metianu, was delayed, but eventually took off from Tocra, near Benghazi, on 21 December 1943, and will be described on pages 153–4.

The Albanian country section in Cairo was run by Major Cripps and Philip Leake, a former schoolmaster who had run SOE's West African regional office from Lagos. They were later to be joined by Mrs Margaret Hasluck, an anthropologist in her own right and the widow of a distinguished archaeologist, who had lived in Albania, near Elbasan, since 1919. She had been expelled by the Italians for alleged espionage in 1939, a charge of which she was innocent, and had moved first to Athens and then to Istanbul, where she had been recruited to head SOE's local Albanian sub-section. Her knowledge of the country and its leaders was unrivalled, and she briefed the CONSENSUS mission, a four-man team consisting of a regular officer from the Royal Scots Greys, Billy McLean; David Smiley from the commandos; a demolitions expert from the Royal Engineers, Garry Duffy; and a wireless operator, Corporal Williamson. A fifth man, an Albanian named Elmaz, was also supposed to accompany them, but he was detained on security grounds at the last minute. He was interned in the

Sudan for the duration. CONSENSUS took off from Derna by Halifax on 17 April 1943 and was dropped into Greece, where it linked up with another SOE mission, led by Brigadier Myers, before crossing into Albania (see page 140).

The Bulgarian country section, headed by Norman Davies, had got off to an unfortunate start. He had been Section D's man in Sofia, but had been evacuated together with the rest of the British Legation in March 1941. His best contact, Dr Dimitroff, who led the Peasants Party, had been murdered soon after his arrival in Istanbul. Contact was not re-established with Bulgaria until mid-December 1943, when Mostyn Davies returned from SOE New York and parachuted into Yugoslavia with the intention of trekking across the frontier to Bulgaria. Frank Thompson later joined him in Bulgaria, but both men were subsequently captured and shot.

The Hungarian Section, designated MPH, was equally unsuccessful. Undermined by the unmasking of Ormond Uren as a Soviet spy in its midst, it did not achieve a single agent in enemy-occupied territory until Peter Boughey went himself in 1944.

The extent of Soviet influence over SOE's operations in South-East Europe is hard to quantify. There was extreme Soviet sensitivity about British interference in what Stalin regarded as his sphere of influence, and both SOE and the Office of Strategic Services (OSS) (see pages 133–4) were to encounter considerable hostility when attempting to infiltrate teams into Balkan countries later in the war. Yet SOE did have a formal relationship with the NKVD and had exchanged liaison officers. Colonel Ivan Chichaev was the Soviet representative in London, and in 1942 Frank Nelson reciprocated by establishing a Russian Section under Major A. D. Seddon and attaching Robert Guinness and later George Hill to the British Military Mission in Moscow. This may have been an unfortunate choice, for Hill was an old SIS hand who had played a very active role in Russia during the civil war. Worse, his exploits had been widely publicised in his two volumes of memoirs, the first having been published in 1932, entitled *Go Spy the Land: Being the Adventure of IK 8 of the British Secret Service*, and *Dreaded Hour*, released four years later.[34] Both were quite uncompromising about the author's attitude to the Bolshevik regime. Quite what the Soviets made of Hill is hard to tell. However, by coincidence, the initials SOE are, in Russian, an acronym for 'socially dangerous elements'.[35]

The degree of success achieved with the Russian liaison was somewhat limited. Certainly WHISKY, the first airdrop arranged on their behalf, destined for Germany in the autumn of 1941, was a disaster. The heavily laden Whitley crashed on take-off, killing one of the NKVD agents and badly burning the other. Both were German Communists, well equipped with local documentation, which suggested to SOE's own one-man German (X) Section, then headed by an old SIS hand, Major Field-Robinson,[36] an impressive degree of sophistication and experience. A second attempt was made to drop the surviving agent on 20 April 1942, after he had recovered from extensive plastic surgery, but the Halifax, piloted by Wing-Commander Wally Farley, the commanding officer of 138 Squadron, was brought down over Mannheim killing all aboard.

3 · Suspicion and Misgiving: Scandinavian Operations

> We have separate organisations working in absurd wasteful compartments which gives rise to all sorts of suspicion and misgiving – naturally – on both sides. I know it myself from experience abroad. I have a good mind to suggest that we should plainly and straightforwardly put our Heads of Mission in charge of all dirty work and definitely subordinate to them all these people with odd initials and numbers which puzzle me more than the enemy.
>
> Sir Alexander Cadogan, Permanent Under-Secretary at the Foreign Office, 1938–46[1]

The difficulties SOE experienced in France while attempting to establish a credible resistance organisation were to be repeated in Scandinavia. Once again, the main problems were the lack of two vital facilities: radio equipment and boats to transport agents. Both were to be crucial if SOE was to fulfil its charter in a territory that, topographically, was quite unsuited to parachute operations. SOE had good reason to believe that these shortages, which had hampered its development elsewhere, had been exacerbated by an increasingly intransigent SIS. The second issue, that of transport, was not to be overcome until the spring of 1942, when the Dartmouth and Helford Flotillas came under a unified command and the inter-agency rivalry, at least across the Channel, was reduced. The paucity of suitable wireless sets was also eased in 1942, when SOE's Signals Section, under the leadership of Brigadier F. W. Nicholls, started to produce its own lightweight portable version, designed by an ingenious technician, John Brown, from a factory in Stonebridge Park, north London.

One area where SOE had scored highly, and where, perhaps uniquely, SOE and SIS appeared to co-exist, was in Scandinavia. Although as top City businessmen Charles Hambro and Harry Sporborg had quite the best contacts in the region's commercial and banking circles, SOE had started out at a disadvantage. The original Norwegian Section had been headed by James Chaworth-Musters, the owner of a farm in southern Norway who had been attached to the British Consulate in Bergen during the German invasion. Its principal preoccupation, in the absence of any radio equipment, was preparing for Operation CLARIBEL, a somewhat optimistic scheme intended to harass German units while they embarked on barges in anticipation of an invasion of England. Surprisingly, this ambitious contingency plan, which was intended to incorporate similar arrangements in Sweden and Denmark, was not to be shelved until 1942. Chaworth-Musters's Section was expanded in November 1940 to encompass a Scandinavian Section under Sporborg's leadership, with Hambro acting as regional controller.

While Sir Frank Nelson was forced to admit late in 1940 that 'we have at the moment literally no one in the field at all',[2] SIS had already achieved an impressive lead. SIS's Leslie Mitchell, who knew Norway well from before the war, had visited the SIS Head of Station in Oslo, Frank Foley, just prior to the German invasion and had laid the foundations for one of SIS's most successful radio operations. By the end of 1940 he was receiving signals from POLLUX, OLDELL and SKYLARK, the first of nearly a hundred SIS wireless agents, and had set up a base in Shetland to receive Norwegian escapees. He experienced only one mishap. Konrad Lindberg and Frithof Pedersen, who had made their way to Aberdeen in August 1940 and had been sent home with a faulty radio, were arrested soon after their arrival. They were executed by the Germans on 11 August 1941. In contrast, Chaworth-Musters had accomplished just one successful infiltration, that of Odd Starheim, who left England by submarine on 22 December 1940 and by the beginning of the following month had opened a radio link at Agder. There he remained, in the most southern district of Norway, until he returned on a fishing boat five months later.

Despite being handicapped by a lack of facilities, SOE was enthusiastic to begin operations in Scandinavia and seized the opportunity to participate in Operation CLAYMORE, a raid on the Lofoten Islands, even though SOE's senior management was never told the plan's real objective. Located high in the Arctic Circle, the Lofotens appeared to be of no strategic value, but the scheme had been dreamed up by the cryptographers at GCHQ, who were keen to acquire one of the enemy's Enigma cipher machines and, in particular, some of its valuable rotors. GCHQ had calculated that there was a good chance that there were at least three on the remote and barren islands. From analysis of the enemy's radio traffic they established that the *Luftwaffe* operated an airfield there and that the *Wehrmacht* had installed a small garrison. There were also plenty of *Kriegsmarine* signals in the vicinity.

SOE, of course, could not be told the mission's true purpose, and its participation was limited to sixteen SOE personnel led by Martin Linge, a swashbuckling character and former actor, who had created the Norwegian Independent Company No. 1, later to be better known as the Linge Company. He had been Chaworth-Musters's neighbour and had quickly teamed up with SOE when he and his Norwegian compatriots had reached England after the evacuation. Having placed himself and his men at SOE's disposal, he found a kindred spirit in Andrew Croft, formerly MI(R)'s man in Bergen, who, in the winter of 1939/40, had supervised the illicit transfer of military supplies across supposedly neutral Swedish territory to the beleaguered Finns, then fighting the Soviet army.

Linge's forty-eight Norwegian commandos were all graduates of SOE's first sabotage school at Brickendonbury, and he led them ashore on 4 March 1941 accompanied by a large force of commandos. German opposition was quickly quelled and more than two hundred soldiers taken prisoner. Over three hundred of the local population volunteered to return to England, and in propaganda terms at least the mission was judged a success, with eleven German and Norwegian ships sunk in the harbours of Svolvaer and Reine. However, not everyone regarded CLAYMORE as a success. Churchill himself stated that 'the British Empire deserves more than cut-throats', in an apparent reference to SOE's role in the operation, and GCHQ complained that not a single Enigma machine had been retrieved. However, some of the Enigma's rotors and coding documents had been recovered from an armed trawler, the *Krebs*, and these enabled the experts at GCHQ to read some of the *Kriegsmarine*'s signals traffic for the next two months.[3]

SOE's first major involvement in Norwegian territory was also to herald complicated political problems of the kind that it was to experience repeatedly in the future with other foreign governments-in-exile. On 11 December 1940 SOE had prepared a policy document for its campaign in Norway, outlining a programme of sabotage, propaganda and paramilitary raids. The latter had caused some concern among the Norwegians in London, who were anxious about German reprisals. Perhaps in anticipation of émigré opposition, SOE had proceeded with CLAYMORE without any consultation. To add insult to injury, SOE deployed Linge's Norwegian volunteers without even asking the Norwegian authorities in London. Although SOE was to be heavily criticised for this behaviour, neither Hambro nor Sporborg was really to blame because, after all, they had not initiated the plan in the first place. However, the political repercussions must have made some members of SOE wonder about the wisdom of ever having participated in the operation. The Norwegian government-in-exile, which had not been informed of GCHQ's special interest in CLAYMORE, or any other aspect of the plan, was furious about the lack of consultation, and the military resistance movement in Norway, *Milorg*, complained that the provocation had led to the execution of hostages, the destruction of dozens of homes and factories in reprisals, and the transportation of seventy Lofoten Islanders to the notorious Grini concentration camp on the Norwegian mainland. The controversy created immense bad feeling and soon afterwards brought the Linge Company under the control of the Norwegian army. Linge himself was later to be killed during a second raid on the Lofotens, Operation ARCHERY, in December 1941.

By the spring of 1941 Leslie Mitchell had already organised more than a dozen operations and had initiated 'the Shetland bus', a regular route across the inhospitable North Sea between Norway and Cat Firth. Fifteen agents had been landed and eighteen members of the resistance, as well as an additional thirty-nine refugees, had been exfiltrated. Mitchell's exclusively SIS operation had proved so successful that it was decided in London to allow both organisations to collaborate. Thus, the arrival of David Howarth from SOE to act as Mitchell's deputy marked a major turning-point in Scandinavian operations, and a unique landmark in SIS/SOE co-operation.[4] Howarth's appointment coincided with the start of the long summer, with continuous daylight, which made SIS's clandestine missions very vulnerable to enemy air reconnaissance and, therefore, virtually impossible. Instead, they prepared themselves for the new sailing season, working from an isolated farmhouse, Flemington, some miles from Cat Firth, and stored ammunition and explosives in the dungeons of a ruined castle in Scalloway.[5]

To prepare the Norwegian volunteers for their work in occupied territory, they were put through a tough training course over the bleak Highlands, centred on three neighbouring houses near Aviemore, designated STS 26: Glenmore Lodge, Drumintoul Lodge and Forest Lodge, with wireless operators going further south to Fawley Court, Henley (STS 54a). Although these arrangements had been made in conditions of the greatest secrecy, the Germans still managed to penetrate them. Six of the small craft carrying refugees which turned up in Scotland during the summer also concealed *Abwehr* spies. Most were easily identified because the Radio Security Service had broken the *Abwehr*'s hand ciphers and were routinely reading the enemy's intelligence traffic. They therefore knew when to expect an attempt to infiltrate an agent. Three such individuals were arrested on a ship which docked at Lerwick in July 1941, and one was removed from a freighter from Iceland the following month. Unfortunately, three who had arrived on the *Olav* in March 1941 slipped through the net and were recruited by SOE. MI5 only learned of their existence in November and managed to detain them.[6] Their companion, who had been employed ferrying agents back to Norway, had already been arrested by the Germans in Norway in September. However, there was never any further evidence to suggest that he had compromised SOE's activities. It was the first case of German penetration to be investigated by John Senter, a tough Scottish barrister, who had been seconded to Baker Street by MI5 as the organisation's resident Director of Security. It was not to be the last.

With the escalation in activity in Shetland a second safe anchorage was established at Lunna Voe, where about forty Norwegian seamen were supervised by three NCOs, Sergeants Almond, H. W. Olsen and Sherwood, and supported by a small civilian staff. SOE's first operation took place on 30 August 1941, when the *Aksel*, a sixty-five-foot cutter, returned to Bergen to make contact with the local resistance. A single agent named Andorsen was carried on the journey and successfully landed. The plan called for him to be collected a week later, so on 5 September the *Igland* crossed the North Sea and completed the operation. In the following three weeks, no less than eight missions were undertaken without mishap. By the end of the 1941 sailing season forty-three trips had been made, with forty-nine passengers reaching Norway, together with 117 tons of stores. Fifty-six refugees and six agents made the return journey back to Shetland.

Mitchell stayed in Scotland until mid-1942, when he was replaced by Colonel Arthur Sclater RM. By then SIS's networks were well established and an alternative route to Norway had been opened up: the special duties squadron began flying sorties across the North Sea, and during the year twenty-one agents were parachuted into enemy-occupied territory in eleven operations. As SOE's activities escalated, so the Norwegian government-in-exile raised objections to the organisation's tactics. In January 1942, in an effort to reduce the tension, John Wilson, previously head of SOE's Training Section, took command of the newly separated Norwegian Section, which had established itself in Chiltern Court, Baker Street. The following month he attended a new liaison body, the Anglo-Norwegian Collaboration Committee, which had been set up to improve relations between the Norwegian authorities and SOE. At the end of the year there was a further structural change inside the organisation, and General Sir James Marshall-Cornwall was appointed to a new post of Regional Director.[7] However, just before he appeared, SOE's Norwegian Section experienced a major catastrophe, Operation FRESHMAN.

FRESHMAN had been inspired by SIS's Norwegian Section, headed by

Commander Eric Welsh, and it was based on the knowledge that the Germans were planning to develop an atomic weapon. The plan called for the destruction of a hydro-electric complex at Vemork, which had been identified as a source of a particular commodity known as 'heavy water', which was regarded as essential to the enemy's research. Gubbins, who was then SOE's director of operations, recalls that 'the target, in the War Cabinet's view, was the highest possible priority and its destruction was first entrusted to Combined Operations'.[8] The objective was to deliver a group of glider-borne commandos to the plant and to blow up all the sensitive electrolysis equipment. It was SOE's responsibility to receive the planes, guide the troops to Vemork and provide the communications. In October 1942, after two attempts had been frustrated by bad weather, a four-man team, code-named SWALLOW, parachuted into the area and made contact with the raiding party as it approached the coast on 3 November. However, tragedy struck and the two gliders plunged into a mountainside, as did one of the Halifax towing aircraft. The few men that survived the crash were captured and later murdered.

This disaster caused much gloom in London, but SOE took the opportunity to press its own case. 'SOE then told the Chiefs of Staff that the operation was still feasible, if entirely entrusted to us and done by our methods,' recalls Gubbins.[9] Accordingly, a second less ambitious operation, codenamed GUNNERSIDE, was launched, which involved four saboteurs linking up with the SWALLOW team. On this occasion the mission succeeded and, on 16/17 February 1943, GUNNERSIDE landed safely and attacked its target ten days later. Its members then made an epic journey overland to Sweden on skis, leaving SWALLOW to report the demolition of the installation's vital equipment.

GUNNERSIDE's success, where FRESHMAN had failed, was to transform SOE's flagging fortunes. 'We received the thanks of the Chiefs of Staff and the congratulations of the Prime Minister in a personal note,' says Gubbins,[10] but the real achievement was in the political sphere. SOE's status within the Allied military command structure was still ambiguous, and certainly not understood by the various émigré governments which were also liaising with SIS. The existence of a second, parallel branch of 'British Intelligence', which appeared to have little in common with its rival, understandably baffled those who came into contact with it. Some governments-in-exile, no doubt on SIS advice, chose to ignore SOE or keep co-operation to a minimum. Therefore, SOE had pressed the Chiefs of Staff to regularise its position and, within a fortnight of GUNNERSIDE's success, the Chiefs of Staff acquiesced. Dated 20 March 1943 a memorandum confirmed that SOE was

the authority responsible for co-ordinating sabotage and other subversive activities including the organisation of Resistance Groups, and for providing advice and liaison on all matters in connection with Patriot Forces up to the time of their embodiment into the regular forces.[11]

This was a major coup for SOE, which wasted no time in circulating this part of the document to the Allied governments-in-exile, thus establishing SOE's status and authority in the most unambiguous terms. However, the fact that SOE had been at loggerheads with SIS did not escape the notice of the Chiefs of Staff, who added a significant condition to the memorandum headed 'Intelligence':

You should maintain close contact with the Joint Intelligence Sub-Committee. You will continue to pass on all intelligence you may collect to SIS. You may undertake the collection of intelligence for SIS in any areas should SIS request you to do so.

The requirements of SIS should in general be accorded priority over your own operations in Norway, Sweden, France and the Low Countries, and, if the appropriate Commanders-in-Chief agree, on the mainland of Italy and in Sicily. In other areas care should be taken that your activities do not clash with SIS and that the latter's sources of information are not imperilled.[12]

Before leaving the Scandinavian region, we should consider two other composite sub-sections which, though relatively small in size, did valuable work. The first, run by George Wiskeman from Baker Street, employed a large office in Stockholm, surrounded by the diplomatic protection of the British Legation, and was headed successively by William Montagu-Pollock (from November 1941), George Larden, Thomas O'Reilly and then Ronald Turnbull. Two SOE stay-behind networks were raised by Peter Tennant, who was in Sweden continuously, then operating under press attaché cover. One was semi-independent and based upon an anti-German group known as the Tuesday Club headed by the Countess Emelie Posse. The other was more widespread and consisted of members of the Syndicalist Party. Unfortunately, the British Minister, Sir Victor Mallet, strongly disapproved of SOE's activities in Sweden and categorically refused to pursue SOE's initiative to sabotage German shipping. SOE wanted the Swedish Government to participate in CLARIBEL, but Mallet would hear none of it. When Turnbull arrived at the Legation in March 1941 to head the SOE mission, he had no better success at persuading Mallet to involve the Swedes, but the contingency plans were pursued by various assistant military attachés, including Malcolm Munthe (who was expelled in July 1941), Andrew Croft (who had survived the CLAYMORE raid on the Lofotens) and Hugh Marks. In addition, some of these officers had dual responsibilities. Munthe and Croft, for example, represented SOE's Norwegian country section, just as Tennant looked after Germany and Denmark. Later there were to be different SOE personnel in Stockholm representing the interests of other country sections, such as Henry Threlfall of the German Section.

CLARIBEL was eventually called off in March 1942, when even Stewart Menzies began to question its value. He cast doubt on the wisdom of diverting resources to the unlikely prospect of a German occupation of Sweden when what he considered to be more important operations into Norway and Denmark were largely dependent upon clandestine support from neutral Sweden. In a characteristically barbed memorandum to Sir Frank Nelson he asked:

Does it advance the war effort to risk our and your valuable communications through Sweden to existing agents in order to make preparations to meet a German invasion of Sweden, a contingency which the Joint Planners declared to be remote? Personally, I feel quite sure it is not; and in this connection it will be remembered that post-occupational schemes have never so far operated when the time came, and that agents who have promised so much in the comparative security of peace have not fulfilled their promises in war.[13]

Menzies was drawing attention to the undeniable fact that, for all the elaborate preparations for German occupation in the Balkans, there had been precious little to show for it. If Nelson had known exactly how vulnerable SIS had been in the pre-war years, and the extent of its negligence in cultivating viable stay-behind networks on the Continent, he might have given a suitably trenchant reply, but even he must have conceded that a Nazi invasion was, by then, becoming increasingly improbable.

That SOE relied upon Stockholm for assistance in mounting operations into Denmark was undeniable. It was also true that SIS had a direct interest in their success. A unique agreement had been reached in mid-1941, which limited SIS to its existing network in Denmark, leaving SOE a free hand to run sabotage operations and recruit intelligence circuits. The situation had been forced on Menzies reluctantly by the quality of information being gathered by Ralph Hollingworth's Danish Section. Its origin was Ebbe Munck, an explorer and agent of the Danish military intelligence service who operated under journalistic cover, as a correspondent for a Copenhagen daily newspaper, the *Berlingske Tidende*. Munck worked in Stockholm and maintained close contact with SOE's Ronald Turnbull, claiming to be the link with a fully equipped resistance movement in the Danish army known as 'the Princes'. Turnbull's arrangement with Munck, which SIS endorsed, was that intelligence would be traded for a ban on sabotage, which, it was feared, would bring reprisals but very little lasting damage to the German military machine.

This controversial arrangement was accepted by SOE because it had nobody else to deal with in Denmark, and by SIS because it had no realistic prospect of recruiting new agents. Of course, it also accorded with SIS's philosophy that subversion and espionage were mutually incompatible. Gradually, SOE began to suspect that the so-called Princes had exaggerated their own strength just to impress London and had their own motives for discouraging operations. As Gubbins commented in October 1942, the Danes 'wish to keep their country absolutely free of any sabotage or anti-German action until the Germans break up altogether and begin to leave the country and then in point of fact we shall not need them.'[14] Although a harsh judgment, Gubbins was proved correct when, in August the following year, the Danish puppet government fell and the Nazis imposed their own administration. This was the opportunity for the Princes to act, but instead they fled. One of the four leading Princes was arrested, but two others escaped to Sweden. The fourth surrendered but was freed, thus allowing him to make his way to Stockholm and contact SOE, which, by now, was rather less enthusiastic.

SOE's Danish Section had not succeeded in getting an agent into Denmark until 27/28 December 1941, when Mogens Hammer and Dr Carl Buhn were dropped near Haslev. It was an inauspicious start, as the newly qualified doctor's parachute failed to open properly and he was killed. As he had been carrying the team's radio, Hammer was left for four months with no means of contacting London. Eventually, Munck was able to smuggle a replacement to him via Stockholm and he resumed contact on 26 April 1942. Hammer was to become a key SOE organiser and, in the same month, he welcomed three newcomers, Christain Rottboll, and a pair of former ships' radiomen, Poul Johannessen and Max Mikkelsen. On 1 August three more SOE agents, Knud Petersen, Hans Hansen and Peter Nielsen, joined them, but the network was broken up the following month after German radio direction-finders located Johannesen, who committed suicide to avoid arrest. Rottboll also died, this time in a shoot-out with police, and the remainder of the group went underground, with Hammer escaping to London. Hammer returned to Denmark on 20 October 1942 and linked up with Nielsen, who had stayed on, to find the other remaining agents, Hansen, Petersen and Mikkelsen. However, when the three men were assembled and tried to get to Sweden by boat, they were captured by the police and handed over to the Germans. On this occasion a promise was extracted that they would not be executed, and they survived the war in concentration camps.

SIS, however, did not honour its agreement to leave Denmark to SOE and not to recruit new circuits, as is demonstrated by an operation mounted in September 1941 to drop Thomas Sneum and a wireless operator named Christoffersen near Brofelde. Sneum was a young officer in the Danish army, who had made his escape to England in June 1941 by the rather improbable means of a home-made aircraft, which he had flown across the North Sea with a friend. It was only after MI5 had been satisfied that Sneum's odyssey had been authentic that he had been passed to SIS for recruitment. Upon their return to Denmark Christoffersen and Sneum landed safely, and a Danish police inspector, Roland Olsen, was recruited to improve the flow of intelligence. This proved timely because Olsen was able to warn Sneum of his imminent arrest and allow him to escape to Sweden. However, the news that SIS had been extending its activities in Denmark, in a blatant breach of its understanding with SOE, eventually reached Baker Street – not least because Olsen subsequently joined SOE – and inevitably generated further ill-will between the two rival organisations. Frank Stagg of SOE's Scandinavian Section later observed that SIS 'had jealously kept [Sneum] away from SOE and despatched him back to Denmark with regrettable consequences, not merely for Sneum but for at least two other Danes'.[15]

By mid-1942 SOE's record in Scandinavia was, by any standards, somewhat mixed. SIS and SOE had established a highly successful shuttle to Norway, but in Sweden their relations had been damaged by Alexander Rickman's amateurism, which had left him serving a lengthy prison sentence, and SIS's determination to maintain secrecy. In Denmark, the extraordinary appearance of the self-proclaimed Princes was to lead, according to the official historian of British Intelligence, 'to especially bitter rivalry' between SOE and SIS, which 'remained in the somewhat humiliating position of having to pass on intelligence obtained by its younger competitor from areas which it had failed to penetrate its own agents'.[16]

Part of the mutual distrust exhibited between the two secret departments undoubtedly stemmed from the embarrassment of the Rickman affair, which had tainted Anglo-Swedish relations at a very early stage, not to mention its malign impact on SOE. Ingram Fraser, the former advertising executive who had been the head of Section D's Scandinavian sub-section and had been one of the key players in the drama, had been transferred away from London in July 1940 when the opportunity presented itself. He was to represent SOE in a major new undertaking, a joint SIS/SOE enterprise in New York, which was to become known as British Security Co-ordination (BSC).

• • • • • •

Much has been written about the exploits of Sir William Stephenson, the 'Little Bill' who headed BSC from its inception in mid-1940 until it was dismantled in 1945, but few of the accounts have borne much relation to reality.[17] The fact is that Stephenson, a wealthy industrialist, had been a frequent contributor of commercial information to Desmond Morton's Industrial Intelligence Centre, a semi-official body which had collated data concerning Germany's rearmament programme in the late 1930s. As a director of Pressed Steel Limited, Stephenson visited Stockholm regularly and was knowledgeable about Sweden's iron-ore deposits and its exports to Germany. It was his idea to sabotage the docks at Oxelösund so as to deny this important commodity to the Nazis, but, having discussed various alternatives with Ingram Fraser in February 1940, had left the execution of the plan, codenamed STRIKE OX, to Rickman. As we have already seen, the operation ended in disaster with the arrest and conviction of Rickman and his fellow-conspirators. Stephenson returned to the intelligence scene in June 1940, when he was appointed head of the SIS station in New York, which, like most SIS posts abroad, operated under the transparent cover of the British Passport Control Office. He took up his appointment on 1 July 1940, in succession to Captain Sir James Paget RN, and proceeded to take responsibility for the security of a number of separate British missions already in the United States, such as those purchasing war *matériel* and the Imperial Censorship, which maintained unofficial premises in Manhattan.

SIS was, by treaty with the FBI, banned from indulging in espionage on American territory, but SOE was anxious to recruit French and Serbo-Croat speaking agents and needed a base from which to operate in North America. Accordingly, Fraser travelled to New York to join Stephenson and establish a Special Operations branch to his organisation, which, in January 1941, formally registered with the State Department under the title British Security Co-ordination. In the months that followed Fraser started a recruitment programme, assisted by Richard Coit and Ivar Bryce, which was to train fifty-three agents for action in South America, operating under 'Industrial Security Officer' cover, where Mostyn Davies was to develop a sub-section of BSC/SO. Not much is known about its activities except that, until the section was wound down on Louis Franck's recommendation in April 1943, so as to avoid offending American sensibilities, it employed more than three hundred personnel. Nor did BSC limit itself to the Western hemisphere. Ivar Bryce recalls recruiting

twenty such volunteers. About half never made it and for one reason or another were rejected, or even imprisoned to prevent any possible dangerous contact. Several succeeded and returned safely after completing their hair-raising missions. One, Jan van Schrelle, a young Dutch friend of mine from Brazil, was parachuted into Holland after his underground group was blown. He landed among a reception committee composed of Gestapo, and was never seen again.[18]

Among the senior SOE personnel to be sent to BSC was Bill Deakin, who was also attached, briefly, to the Latin American Section during 1941, before he moved on to Cairo. Other visitors seeking volunteers for hazardous work in enemy-occupied territory included Sweet-Escott and Bill Bailey, who together found twenty-two Yugoslavs willing to return to their country. During the following months BSC/SO sent representatives to Canada (Charles Vining, followed by Tommy Drew-Brook) and Washington (Bartholomew Pleydell-Bouverie). Later, in September 1941, a property was purchased on the north shore of Lake Ontario, near Oshawa, which was to become SOE's Special Training School 103. This acquisition was made at the instigation of Tommy Davies, the Section D veteran from Courtauld's who had become one of Nelson's two Chiefs of Staff, with responsibility for training and logistical support. Since a proportion of SOE's early volunteers came from Canada, it was logical that Davies would open a facility in North America and save having to transport every candidate across the Atlantic. When he came to select a commandant for STS 103 in September 1941, he chose Colonel Tommy Lindsay of the Irish Guards, who was then running Fawley Court. Lindsay made a preliminary inspection, but then dropped out without explanation, leaving Colonel Terence Roper-Caldbeck to take charge. Among his instructors, all with previous experience at schools in England, were Bill Brooker; Fred Milner, who was later to parachute into Burma; Cuthbert Skilbeck, who would return to command STS 31 at Beaulieu; Dan Fairbairn, a master of close-quarters fighting and, with his colleague from the Shanghai Police, Bill Sykes, the inventor of the lethal eponymous commando knife.

STS 103 was to attain a unique position in SOE's training directorate, chiefly because of its convenient geographical proximity to the United States. Of the 273 trainees who graduated, forty were to come from the American Office of Strategic Services, including sixteen instructors; ten were FBI Special Agents; and six originated from the US War Department's psychological operations department. Eventually, SOE established a second North American base in Okanagan Valley, British Columbia, under the direction of Hamish Pelham-Burn, which was to train agents for operations in the Far East.

•   •   •   •   •   •

By the time Oshawa opened for business, in November 1941, Davies had already masterminded an impressive network of training schools stretching right across England and Scotland. After their initial recruitment interviews, which were usually conducted in War Office premises, candidates underwent a month's intensive training at the Group A schools, mainly centred around Arisaig House and six neighbouring properties in the inhospitable and rugged Highlands terrain surrounding Loch Morar in Inverness-shire. Here Colonel Pat Anderson and Captain James Young taught the basic rules of survival and unarmed combat, as well as some of the more arcane arts, such as sabotage, silent killing and weapon handling. Others teaching on this preliminary, paramilitary course were Gavin Maxwell, later the author of *Ring of Bright Water*, and Matthew Hodgart, a Cambridge don. Local residents, of whom there were few, were told that the area had been allocated to training commandos. Graduates from Group A moved south to the Group B 'finishing schools', each linked to George Taylor's country sections, which put the finishing touches to the agents' skills and prepared them for undercover work in the field. Thereafter, the agents were either dispersed to holding centres to await deployment, or to other courses run by Group C operational schools. (A comprehensive list of all SOE's Special Training Schools appears in Appendix 2.) Parachute training was given under the guidance of Wing-Commander Maurice Newnham at Dunham House, Dunham Massey (STS 51a) in Cheshire, and later at two houses close to RAF Ringway, Manchester. A staff officers' course was run from Stodham Park near Petersfield (STS 3), and George Rheam, formerly of the Central Electricity Board, headed a specialist industrial demolition course at Brickendonbury (originally designated Station XVII) near Hertford, the commandant of which, Captain Frederic Peters RN, won the VC at Oran but died in an aircrash in Devon on the way home. Those with an aptitude for radio work did a wireless operator's course at Thame Park (STS 52). Finally, agents who passed a four-day test, requiring them to reconnoitre a target somewhere in England where the local police had been alerted to possible saboteurs, spent their last few nights before a mission at Brockhall in Northamptonshire, not too distant from Tempsford, or from 'Farewell House', which was actually Hassells Hall in Sandy.

Each of the country sections had their own separate schools. The Czechs went to Chicheley Hall (STS 46) near Newport Pagnell, while the Poles were concentrated at Hatherop Castle (STS 45), Gloucestershire, and Audley End House near Saffron Walden, with the Danes at Gumley Hall (STS 41), Market Harborough, and the Norwegians at Gaynes Hall, St Neots (STS 61). As well as Wanborough Manor, F Section was accommodated at Bellasis near Dorking (STS 2), Chorley Wood in Hertfordshire and eleven secluded houses on Lord Montagu's estate at Beaulieu in the New Forest, while RF Section was based at Inchmery, near Southampton.

•   •   •   •   •   •

Before returning to the main narrative of SOE's progress during 1941–2, we should consider some of the unpublicised operations that were conducted with a degree of success, untainted by inter-service rivalry. The first, undertaken by H Section, in Spain, was from the start a low-key affair to avoid antagonising Franco and, for that matter, Sir Samuel Hoare. A team of saboteurs codenamed RELATOR had been sent to Gibraltar in March 1941 to prepare for a Nazi invasion of Spain. As we have already seen, this mission was eventually abandoned, only to be replaced in November 1942 by a second mission, SKIDDAW, designed to coincide with the Allied invasion of North Africa. That, too, proved unnecessary and was added to the list of rather impractical contingency plans which SOE had been obliged to abandon.

In a period when SOE was preparing for much, but not actually achieving anything to impress either SIS or the increasingly sceptical Chiefs of Staff, Operation POSTMASTER was a splendid example of allowing some SOE enthusiasts an opportunity to score some points. It may well be that Julius Hanau, the former Vickers representative in Belgrade who had been evacuated from the Balkans and placed in charge of SOE's West African desk, may have been anxious to demonstrate that SOE did, contrary to all reports, have the ability to pull off clandestine coups. The plan involved Gus March-Phillipps, Anders Lassen and Geoffrey Appleyard sailing a Brixham trawler, the *Maid Honor*, to Freetown. Crewed by six volunteers and skippered by Graham Hayes, formerly the captain of a Finnish grain ship, the *Maid Honor* reached the Gold Coast in February 1942 and made contact with Philip Leake and Leonard Guise, then working under Louis Franck in SOE's West African operations section. With the benefit of local intelligence provided by Leopold Manderstam[19] and Hedley Vincent, they then proceeded to hijack two Italian vessels, a freighter, the *Duchessa d'Aosta*, and a tanker, the *Likomba*, which were sheltering off the neutral islands of

Fernando Po, which were then part of Spanish Guinea. Meanwhile, an undercover SOE officer, Captain Lippett, visited Fernando Po and threw a tremendous party for the Spanish port officials in Santa Isabel. This diversionary tactic worked admirably and the two ships were towed into international waters, where the Royal Navy boarded them. POSTMASTER was hailed as a great and timely success, one that was much needed in Baker Street.

4 · 'Der Englandspiel': SOE in Holland, Belgium and Czechoslovakia

In the Secret Service you must discount all your unhatched chickens in advance.

Commandant François van't Sant, Chief of the Dutch Central Intelligence Bureau until August 1941[1]

The year 1942 was to prove a momentous one for SOE, when the first major strategic advances of the war were to be gained, with the organisation making a useful contribution. To date, certainly in Europe, little had gone SOE's way apart from the establishment of N Section's clandestine route from Shetland to the Norwegian coast. A brief review of SOE's achievements in the north-west reveals a paucity of activity. The first Belgian agent had not been parachuted home by Claude Knight's section until May 1941, and then had been dropped straight into a prisoner-of-war camp on the German side of the Belgian frontier. Despite this mishap two agents were operational, and a further eight were to be inserted before the end of January 1942, by which time SOE's relations with the two rival Belgian intelligence organisations had reached breaking-point.

Contact had also been established with networks in Poland and Czecho-slovakia, and between September 1941 and January 1942 Harold Perkins's Polish Section, designated MP, had despatched fifteen agents. However, Peter Wilkinson's Czech Section, MY, had not fared so well. On 16 April 1941 its first agent, Otmar Riedl, had been dropped into Austria by mistake on Operation BENJAMIN and had been arrested for crossing the frontier illegally. Luckily, at the time of his capture, Riedl had already abandoned his equipment, so he was charged with nothing more serious than illicit border crossing, a relatively minor offence considering the penalties for espionage. Following the failure of BENJAMIN, Operation PERCENTAGE followed on 4 October, with Corporal Frantisek Pavelka being parachuted near Caslav with ciphers and a transmitter for the Czech resistance. He was arrested in Prague just three weeks later. In December another seven agents had gone on Operations SILVER A, SILVER B and ANTHROPOID, all of which had flown in the same aircraft from Tangmere on 28 December 1941. A further seventeen men followed between March and April 1942.

ANTHROPOID's objective was the assassination of the hated *SS-Obergruppenführer* Reinhard Heydrich in Prague, which was planned to take place on the Czech National Day, 28 October 1941. However, bad weather forced two postponements, so the team did not assemble in Czechoslovakia until late December. Eventually, after further delays, a new date was set for 27 May 1942 and an ambush was prepared as the Nazi was being driven into Prague from the country mansion he occupied. When his chauffeur-driven Mercedes approached a sharp bend on the outskirts of the city, it slowed to negotiate the corner; as it did so, two SOE men stepped into the road and attacked the open-topped limousine. The two SOE assassins were a pair of Czech paratroopers, Jan Kubis and Josef Gabcik, from ANTHRO-POID, with support from Josef Valcik from SILVER A and Adolf Opalka from OUT DISTANCE, two members of a three-man team which had arrived on 28 March. Gabcik's Sten gun jammed at the vital moment, but Heydrich was mortally wounded by a Mills grenade thrown by Kubis. Without waiting to see the results of their handiwork, the men escaped from the scene, only to be betrayed soon afterwards to the Gestapo by another member of OUT DISTANCE, Karel Curda, who identified his comrades and their hiding-place in return for a reward. Curda alone survived the war, to be hanged for treachery.[2]

ANTHROPOID was to prove controversial because of the appalling civilian reprisals taken by the Nazi occupation forces. Thousands perished in a wave of executions, and the population of whole villages were deported to concentration camps. One village, Lidice, was systematically reduced to rubble, the site remaining untouched to this day as a memorial to those who were murdered. Over thirteen thousand people suffered arrest in the aftermath of Heydrich's assassination, prompting many to wonder whether SOE's Czech Section had been wise to launch such a provocative operation. In fact, there is considerable doubt that SOE did anything more than give logistical support to ANTHROPOID, for the plan was certainly Czech in origin, having been hatched by the Czech government-in-exile in London, initially with *SS-Gruppenführer* Karl Hermann Frank, the Protektor's hated State Secretary, as the target. The assassins Kubis and Gabcek, who had transferred to the Free Czech Army from the French Foreign Legion, had been trained by SOE in Scotland and at Bellasis (STS 2), and had undergone their parachute course at RAF Ringway, but throughout were still officially attached to the Czech 1st Brigade at Cholmondeley Castle, near Whitchurch in Cheshire. SIS was also a party to ANTHROPOID, as confirmed by the then head of the Czech *Deuxième Bureau*, Colonel Frantisek Moravec, who recalled that the scheme 'was necessarily shared with several officials of the British MI6, who worked with us on the technical side'.[3] Whoever was behind ANTHROPOID, its effect was to decimate the number of potential resisters in Czechoslovakia, reduce the willingness of the inhabitants to help parachutists, and ensure that SOE's Czech Section would play only a peripheral role in the eventual liberation of that country. The chart opposite which lists SOE's Czech operations indicates that most of those sent to organise anti-Nazi resistance were soon captured by the enemy.

●   ●   ●   ●   ●   ●

SOE had also been active in Holland, where four Dutch agents had been parachuted home by Richard V. Laming's N Section. Laming himself had spent many years in Holland running a shipping company on the Rhine and, as he had never previously had any intelligence experience, apart from a period in the Ministry of Blockade during the First World War, he had not been compromised by the Venlo affair in November 1939. Thus, he was an unknown quantity to the Germans, who, following the Venlo incident, had acquired an encyclopaedic knowledge of Britain's pre-war intelligence personalities. Indeed, being a newcomer to the scene was an added virtue for Laming as the Dutch still harboured grave reservations about SIS's behaviour during the Venlo crisis, which had led to the death of a young Dutch intelligence officer.

One officer intimately involved in the Venlo affair had been Laming's deputy, Major Lionel Loewe, the SIS deputy Head of Station in The Hague, who had been conferring with the Dutch Director of Military Intelligence at the very moment that the news had come through that his superior, Major Stevens, had been kidnapped at the German frontier, and that his Dutch escort, Lieutenant Dirk Klop, had been killed by German gunfire. In March 1941, following his hasty evacuation to England, Loewe had been transferred to N Section, where he remained until January 1942.

Whether Loewe's presence in N Section inspired the Dutch intelligence authorities with confidence is unknown, but Dutch sensibilities had not been assuaged by SIS's record in Holland after the occupation. Their first agent, Lieutenant Lodo van Hamel of the Royal Netherlands Navy, had been dropped 'blind' near Sassenheim on 27 August 1940 and had

Czech Operations 1941-2

Date	Codename	Personnel	Conclusion
16 April 1941	BENJAMIN	Otmar Riedl	Arrested on minor charge
4 October 1941	PERCENTAGE	Frantisek Pavelka	Arrested three weeks after landing
28 December 1941	ANTHROPOID	Josef Gabcik Jan Kubis	Suicide in Prague, 18 June 1942 Suicide in Prague, 18 June 1942
28 December 1941	SILVER A	Josef Valcik Alfred Bartos Jiri Potucek	Suicide in Prague, 18 June 1942 Died of wounds, 22 June 1942 Killed, 2 August 1942
28 December 1941	SILVER B	Vladimir Skacha Jan Zemek	Abandoned mission Abandoned mission
27 March 1942	ZINC	Oldrich Pechal Arnost Miks Vilem Gerik	Killed in Prague, 18 June 1942 Killed, 30 April 1942 Surrendered, 4 April 1942
27 March 1942	OUT DISTANCE	Adolf Opalka Karel Curda Ivan Kolarik	Killed in Prague, 18 June 1942 Surrendered, 16 June 1942 Suicide on arrest, 1 April 1942
27 April 1942	BIVOUAC	Frantisek Pospisil Jindrich Coupek Libor Zapletal	Arrested 6 May 1942 Arrested 2 May 1942 Arrested 2 May 1942
27 April 1942	BIOSCOPE	Bohuslav Kouba Josef Bablik Jan Hruby	Suicide on arrest, 3 May 1942 Killed in Prague, 18 June 1942 Killed, 18 June 1942
27 April 1942	STEEL A	Oldrich Dvorak	Shot, 30 June 1942
29 April 1942	INTRANSITIVE	Vaclav Kindl Bohuslav Grabovsky Vojtech Lukastik	Arrested, March 1943 Arrested, March 1943 Shot, 8 January 1943
29 April 1942	TIN	Ludvik Cupal Jaroslav Svarc	Suicide, 15 January 1943 Killed in Prague, 18 June 1942
23 October 1942	ANTIMONY	Frantisek Zavorka Stanislav Srazil Lubomir Jasinek	Suicide, January 1943 Collaborated Suicide, January 1943

proceeded to develop a small circuit, including a radio operator, Johan van Hattem, who had built his own wireless set. However, six weeks later van Hamel had been arrested by Dutch police while on his way to a rendezvous with a Dutch amphibious aircraft, which was planning to land on the Tjeuke Lake. He was handed over to the Germans for interrogation, and an ambush was prepared for the seaplane. The Fokker T8, piloted by Commander Hidde Scappe, landed on 13/14 August, but just managed to escape the trap. Van Hamel was executed on 16 June 1941, but he had resisted the

Gestapo's interrogation, thus ensuring that van Hattem could remain at liberty and continue his activities for a further eighteen months. Three days earlier, on 13 June, a pair of SIS agents, a young naval cadet, Hans Zomer, and a former police inspector, Wiek Schrage, had been dropped and had established themselves in Bilthoven. Zomer was soon spotted by German radio direction-finding and was arrested on 31 August 1941 while transmitting a signal. After interrogation Zomer agreed to send a message to London under German control, but the ploy was detected. Thereafter, Zomer was tried for espionage and executed on 11 May 1942, leaving Schrage trying to find a means of escape to England.

While Euan Rabagliati's Dutch country section in SIS had actually achieved a successful insertion, it was to be some months before SOE managed to do the same. All of SOE's first attempts were failures, and Laming's first agent, a volunteer named van Driel, crossed the North Sea in August by a motor gunboat from Felixstowe, but an enemy patrol spotted him as he approached the beach. He promptly ditched his radio and pretended to be a deserter from a merchant ship, a ruse which saved him from arrest. The next two agents, Ab Homburg and Corre Sporre, were parachuted in on 6/7 September 1941, both intending to make a short reconnaissance before being picked up from the beach. The rendezvous never materialised, so both men established themselves in Haarlem, where Homburg was recognised and betrayed to the Gestapo on 6 October 1941. He was subsequently sentenced to death, but managed to escape from prison the night before his scheduled execution. He eventually made his way back to England by trawler from Ijmuiden, arriving in February 1942, and, after a lengthy debriefing, joined the RAF.[4] Meanwhile, Sporre had avoided arrest and made contact with Schrage. Together they tried to escape by boat in November, but they were never heard of again and were presumed lost at sea.

A month after Homburg and Sporre had gone missing, Laming parachuted in another two agents, Huub Lauwers and Thys Taconis, to look for them. The pair, who shared a background of having worked in the Far East until the outbreak of hostilities, landed safely, but their radio proved to be faulty so that their first message to London was not transmitted until 3 January 1942. Soon afterwards Taconis traced Homburg and reported his arrest and subsequent escape. London's reply was an instruction that Homburg should make his own way back to England and the news that, because there was still no sign of Sporre, it must be assumed that he had drowned while attempting to cross the North Sea by boat with Schrage. Lauwers and Taconis based themselves in The Hague and maintained a regular radio schedule with London. Using this channel they arranged a supply drop on 28 February, which went largely according to plan (except that one of the two containers was lost), but Lauwers was arrested a week later, on 6 March, when German direction-finding equipment isolated the address in The Hague from which he had been transmitting. The Germans also recovered his wireless and a quantity of his previous signals. Three days later, Taconis was taken into custody.

During intensive interrogation Lauwers was persuaded to use his radio to transmit, under German control, back to London. This he did on 12 March, confident that SOE would spot the tell-tale omission of his security check. Surprisingly, SOE not only acknowledged the signal, but announced the imminent arrival of another agent, Lieutenant Arnold Baatsen. This was strange because, although SOE might pretend to sustain a compromised radio link with the objective of keeping their captured agent alive, the despatch of an authentic agent, if carried out, would simply and unnecessarily endanger another. Furthermore, the act would provide absolute proof that the deception had not been detected. The only conclusion to be drawn was that N Section had failed to spot the lack of the security check in Lauwers's transmission. Baatsen, who had been a professional photographer before the war, duly landed on 27/28 March, marking the start of a long deception that netted the Germans more than fifty Dutch agents. On the question of whether SOE had registered Lauwers's missing security check, Robin Brook gave the following explanation in October 1949 to the Parliamentary Commission of Enquiry conducted by the Dutch: 'This fact was established and it was weighted against other arguments which testified to the conclusion that this agent was at liberty. In view of this consideration it was decided to continue the traffic.'[5]

Exactly who took the decision deliberately to ignore the significance of Lauwers's omission is not clear, but it was evidently spotted and someone must have chosen consciously to continue the contact. N Section's headquarters staff was itself quite small, consisting until October 1943 of just eighteen officers, seven secretaries and five FANY (First Aid Nursing Yeomanry) clerical assistants. None of the officers spent more than eighteen months continuously in N Section, although Lieutenants Kay and Parr did two tours of duty at Baker Street, both leaving in 1942 to return the following year. Accordingly, there was very little continuity among those directly dealing with N Section's operations, which contrasts with, for example, F Section, where Buckmaster remained in control from September 1941 onwards, right through to the Liberation. So what went wrong? Brigadier Brook's testimony, which is the only explanation available publicly, does not expand on the options available to SOE. If, for example, N Section suspected that it was in contact with an enemy-controlled circuit, SOE was under an obligation to hand over the entire case to SIS. The position is further complicated by the fact that in February 1942 Laming had been replaced as the head of SOE's N Section by Charles Blizard, a regular army officer who had himself only been attached to N Section the previous December. Although both must have had a knowledge of these events, neither Laming nor Blizard gave evidence to the post-war enquiry. Instead, Blizard made a statement to SIS's internal investigation, which was conducted by Colonel John Cordeaux, but has never been published. Cordeaux, of course, was himself later to become a leading advocate in the House of Commons of the principle that nothing whatever should be disclosed publicly about SOE's operations.

Whatever the reason for the blunder, it was to have tragic consequences. The *Abwehr*'s control over Lauwers, Taconis and Baatsen coincided with a dramatic escalation in N Section's activities. The night after Baatsen was dropped, two teams landed. The first, which landed safely, consisted of Han Jordaan, a student who had been studying in England, and Gosse Ras, a trader in textiles. Unfortunately, the second pair were not so lucky: their radio was smashed on impact and Jan Molenaar was mortally injured, leaving his companion, a twenty-eight-year-old student in holy orders named Leonard Andringa, to administer a suicide pill, the capsule of cyanide which was standard issue to all agents. Thereafter Andringa made his way to Amsterdam, where he lived rough for a while. A third team, consisting of Hendrik Sebes, who was a veteran of Dunkirk, and Barend Klooss, who had recently returned from South-East Asia, followed on 5/6 April and established itself in Hengelo without incident. The next arrival, on 8/9 April, was Jan de Haas, who was landed by a British motor torpedo-boat with the objective of linking up with Lauwers and Taconis, not realising that both were already in German custody. His search failed, but on 27 April Lauwers received a fatal message from London instructing him to go to Haarlem to meet de Haas. Instead, the Germans moved in and cornered both de Haas and Andringa, who had become increasingly desperate following the death of his partner and had been forced to seek help from his friends. If this breach of security was not bad enough, worse was to follow when Andringa was coerced into attending a rendezvous on 1 May in a café with Ras, Jordaan and Klooss. However, just before the Germans sprang their trap, Jordaan slipped away and was able to alert Baker Street to the arrest of his companions. His liberty lasted only a few hours, for both Jordaan and Sebes were caught using information extracted from the others.

Indeed, the German triumph was completed when they substituted their own operator for Jordaan and re-established contact with SOE. This had only been made possible because Jordaan had recently requested permission to recruit and train his own operator in the field, a highly unusual departure from the standard security procedures. N Section had granted the request, and this message had been discovered among Jordaan's effects.

Thus, the *Abwehr* was presented with an ideal opportunity to run and exploit a second captured radio. This in turn resulted in another parachute operation, on 29 May, which delivered two saboteurs, Antonius van Steen and Herman Parlevliet, both former Dutch gendarmes, straight into the hands of the enemy and provided the Germans with another two active wireless links with Baker Street. More were to follow. Jan van Rietschoten, a technical college student who had rowed to England the previous year, and his radio operator, Johannes Buizer, arrived near Assen on 23/24 June and were forced to send a 'safe landing' signal. Then, a month later, Gerard van Hamert dropped straight into an enemy reception committee and was obliged to hand over his radio. When they searched him, the Germans found some orders addressed to Taconis, whom they had imprisoned in March, which amounted to confirmation that N Section had no inkling of the extraordinary deception game now under way involving six separate wireless channels.

In van Hamert's case the Germans went to elaborate lengths to pretend that Taconis had at least attempted to complete the mission assigned to him by van Hamert, the destruction of a radio station mast at Kootwijk. Allied direction-finding had identified this location as one of the bases used to transmit signals to the U-boat fleet, so it was therefore considered a target of some strategic importance. An assault was planned for 8 August 1942, and Lauwers reported the day afterwards that the attackers had been beaten off by an unexpectedly large number of sentries. This bogus explanation, backed up by a fireworks' display at the appropriate moment, satisfied SOE that Taconis had mounted a daring raid. N Section sent its commiserations to Taconis and announced that he had been decorated with the Military Medal.

The Germans nearly achieved a seventh SOE transmitter when a South African named George Dessing was dropped accidentally into the middle of an SS training camp on 27/28 February 1942. He casually walked out, giving Nazi salutes to the guards, who assumed that he was authorised to be there. Later he had another lucky escape, when the Germans tried to use Andringa to entrap him in a café. Sensing that something was wrong, Dessing had casually walked out, straight past Andringa's German escort, thereby narrowly avoiding capture for the second time. Realising that his friend Andringa was under enemy control, Dessing decided to get out of Holland as soon as possible, but he was unable to warn Baker Street of what had happened because he had no independent means of communicating with London. Jan Molenaar, who had been killed on landing, was supposed to have become his radio operator and, without him, Dessing was powerless. He eventually made his way to Switzerland, but he did not reach London until the autumn of 1943.

In the meantime, the duplicity continued. On 26 June 1942 Professor George Jambroes, a senior and influential figure in the Dutch government-in-exile, and his wireless operator, Sjef Bukkens, were dropped straight into a German reception committee, and Bukkens's radio was used to report on the supposed low morale and security of the *Orde Dienst* resistance movement. These depressing messages merely served to exacerbate some of the prejudices that already existed within N Section against the government-in-exile's view of what was taking place in Holland, which was perceived as being unrealistically over-optimistic. On 4/5 September 1942 four more agents followed Jambroes: a young student, Knees Drooglever, and an engineer, Karel Beukema, were taken, and the former's transmitter became the eighth to join the game; Arie Mooy and Commander Jongelie were next, but the latter, a tough naval officer who had worked undercover in the Dutch East Indies, refused to co-operate, so the Germans sent a message to London indicating that he had been fatally injured during the landing. Once again, SOE raised no query. Indeed, N Section was so keen to hear from Professor Jambroes, who was supposed to be liaising with the *Orde Dienst*, that he was put in touch with a contact in Paris so that he could be exfiltrated down an escape line. This clue was pursued by the *Sicherheitsdienst* in France with ruthless efficiency and almost led to the collapse of SOE's F Section, as we shall see in Chapter 8.

Gradually, the Germans took control of a substantial part of SOE's network in Holland, but at least it had been operated in isolation from SIS's circuits, which were every bit as extensive, but had experienced their own difficulties. One handicap had been the loss in March 1942 of a British naval officer and a Dutch sailor.

Euan Rabagliati had been attempting to send over two agents, again by boat across the North Sea, but the first operation proved a complete disaster. On 11 March 1942 a brand new vessel, *MGB 325*, commanded by a peacetime solicitor, Peter Williams, was assigned the task of taking two agents to Holland. *MGB 325* was a 110-foot Fairmile 'C' Type, capable of twenty-seven knots and carrying a crew of sixteen. The two agents, one of whom was a Dutch sailor named Maessen, were accompanied by Angus Letty, a leading figure in SIS's private navy. Having reached the Dutch coast, the agents were rowed ashore by Charles Elwell, the *MGB 325*'s first lieutenant. Unfortunately, their craft capsized and a German patrol caught them. Maessen was subsequently shot, and Elwell went to a prisoner-of-war camp, ending up at Colditz, but not until he had been interrogated. He was later to comment that his chief inquisitor 'not only knew the actual numbers of his gunboat, but also the names of many of the officers' stationed at Great Yarmouth, where the 15th Motor Gunboat Flotilla was based. Indeed, he believed that the Germans knew more about SIS's clandestine operations than he did![6]

Rabagliati's principal asset in Holland was Aart Alblas, a twenty-one-year-old merchant seaman who had been operating independently in Holland since his arrival on 5/6 July 1941. After the arrest of Hans Zomer, the naval cadet who had been caught by direction-finders in Bilthoven, SIS had decided that Alblas's codes might have been compromised and had used a former naval signalman, Wim van der Reyden, to deliver a new set. This courier parachuted into north Holland in September 1941 and duly handed over the material, but in February the following year he was arrested in the company of another SIS agent, Johannes Ter Laak, whose radio had needed repairing. Van der Reyden had been delivered to Scheveningen by boat on 21 November 1941, but his wireless had fallen into the water. The arrest of van der Reyden and the courier was a chance encounter for the Gestapo and, although they tried to raise London on the radio, SIS spotted the absence of the all-important security check and declined to acknowledge the signal. However, under interrogation van der Reyden confirmed the existence of the third agent, Alblas, and his signals were monitored. Eventually, in early July 1942, he too was trapped, but, when the Germans tried to exploit his transmitter, SIS spotted the ruse and signed off instantly.

In the coming months more SIS agents were swept up. Ernst de Jonge, who had been landed by boat in February 1942, was caught with ten other members of the Ijmuiden resistance on 18 May 1942. Once again, SIS refused to respond to de Jonge's transmitter when it was operated under enemy control. Soon afterwards three more SIS agents, Jan Emmer, Evert Radema and Felix Ortt, were arrested.

SIS responded to these losses by dropping Willem Niermayer in the spring of 1942, but by October the former journalist had run short of funds and Rabagliati had to ask SOE to deliver a roll of banknotes to his agent. The courier was a Dutch naval officer, Aat van der Giessen, who was also handed a set of emergency identity papers for Niermayer which contained his photograph. Accordingly, when van der Giessen was received by the Gestapo, it did not take them long to trace Niermayer. He was promptly arrested, but SIS would not respond to his radio signals, realising from his faulty security check that he had come under enemy control. This, however, was not to be the last of the game.

SOE still had no clue as to the tragedy unfolding around it and stepped up the number of agents being dropped into Holland. Nine went in October, with a further four in November. By December 1942 the Germans had captured forty-three British agents and were controlling fourteen different radio channels. In the New Year of 1943 little changed. SOE continued to despatch agents and, by April, another thirteen SOE men had arrived, as well as a woman from MI9, Beatrix Terwindt, whose mission had been to build an escape line like those that had developed in Belgium and France. She too was accommodated at the seminary in Haaren, which the *Abwehr* and Gestapo had acquired to isolate their prisoners. However, the German policy of securing all their captives in the same place led to a leak, which eventually reached the British Embassy in Berne in June 1943. For the first time Baker Street received word that eight British parachutists, including Pieter Dourlein who had arrived on 1/2 March, were in German custody.

Quite why the head of the Dutch Section chose to ignore this warning is unknown, but he certainly authorised an operation in May, which sent Anton Mink, Laurens Punt and Oscar de Brey to the cells in Haaren and gave an eighteenth radio link to the Germans. Ingeniously, it was one of these channels that the *Abwehr* used to smear two of the agents, Pieter Dourlein and Johan Ubbink, when they escaped from Haaren on 30 August 1943. Realising that the entire deception was threatened by this resourceful pair, the Germans reported to Baker Street that they had actually been captured by the Gestapo and allowed to escape, having been turned. Dourlein and Ubbink eventually reached Berne on 22 November 1943 and gave a detailed account of their experiences, most of which they blamed on Blizard's successor at N Section, Seymour Bingham, who had taken over in February 1943 and had supervised Dourlein's mission the following month (but not that of Ubbink, which had taken place on the last night of the previous November). The full text of the historic telegram, transmitted by the SIS Head of Station in Berne, Count Frederick Vanden Heuvel (and not, significantly, by his SOE counterpart), reads:

Lieutenant Johan Bernhard Ubbink, cover-name Edema and codeletters CEN, para-chuted into Holland during the night of 1 December 1942, and Sergeant Pieter Dourlein, cover-name Diepenbroek, code letters ACO, dropped during the night of

10 March 1943, have both arrived here. Both report that they were met by a reception committee who knew their cover-names yet turned out to consist of Dutch Nazis and German SD, who immediately arrested them. During their interrogations it became clear that the Germans were completely aware of the whole organisation with its codes and passwords. For a long time the Germans have been transmitting to England pretending to be agents. They guess that at least 130 men have been arrested in this way so that the whole organisation is in German hands. During the night of 30 August 1943 they escaped from prison. They suspect Major Bingham of treachery without daring to accuse him outright and press for the utmost caution with this message. On 25 November I can send them to Spain using our normal route, but arrangements have to be made to ensure that they spend as little time as possible in Spain, in view of the importance, in my opinion, of their information. Do you agree with this or do MI6 want to give them a new assignment? Please let me know immediately if they really are who they say they are. Description of first mentioned. Height 1.82m, face long and thin, hair blond, blue grey eyes, quite a large nose and somewhat crooked, scar on left knee. Of the second, height 1.78m, face thin and somewhat triangular shaped heavy chin, prominent jaw, dark blond hair, eyes green grey, heavy eyebrows, nose long and thin, damaged middle finger left hand, on right arm tattooed anchor.[7]

This signal, with its grave accusation, caused chaos in Baker Street, and prompted SIS to circulate a damning message to all its agents warning of SOE's insecurity. It read: 'Sister service totally infiltrated by Germans. We therefore urge you to break off all contact with their agents and keep clear of them. Please warn OD [*Orde Dienst*] and other organisations.'[8] This, of course, was intercepted and read by the Germans, who finally realised that the game was up.

Ironically, the two agents who conveyed the bad news to SOE, Ubbink and Dourlein, received harsh treatment when they finally reached England, via Gibraltar, on 1 February 1944. They were interrogated at length in London and then moved under open arrest to Guildford. In May they were transferred to Brixton prison and then released, to be told that one of those who had helped them to escape from Holland, a former police inspector from Tilberg named van Bilsen, had been assassinated by the resistance.[9]

At the end of the war an investigation was launched to discover the fate of the agents sent to Holland by SIS and SOE during the twenty months of what had become known as '*der Englandspiel*'. It was revealed that virtually all of them had perished in the Nazi concentration camp at Mauthausen early in September 1944. Of the SOE agents, only Lauwers, Dessing and the two escapees lived through the experience.

The Dutch authorities were understandably bitter about what had happened, especially as their own intelligence service had never been allowed any operational control, and their communications had always been in the hands of SIS. Two key facts emerged: that SIS had learned of the German penetration in May 1943 and had warned SOE immediately; and that several assessments had been made by SOE following irregularities in the security checks, but, 'after taking into consideration the personalities and characters of the agents', the decision had been taken by SOE to maintain contact. In SOE's view, the security check was not the sole arbiter of the continued integrity of a particular agent. In difficult field conditions, under constant stress and with the fatigue of hours spent encoding messages, agents invariably made mistakes in their procedures. As Dourlein himself later admitted, 'agents who were at liberty forgot their check or used it incorrectly'.[10]

At the end of hostilities much time was spent in determining whether or not, as the Germans had mischievously suggested at the time, their intelligence had been supplied by a traitor within SOE's headquarters in London. The truth was that the Germans were very inventive and devoted considerable resources to exploiting the system. It was also an unusual example of close co-ordination between the military intelligence service, the *Abwehr*, and its rival, the Gestapo. Both were adept at mounting quite sophisticated penetration schemes and, quite apart from this manipulation of SOE's operations, proved themselves skilled at infiltrating and eliminating other resistance groups. In May 1942 seventy-two members of the *Orde Dienst* had been executed, and a further twenty members were shot in July 1943. In addition, the enemy's deception had only been made possible by the activities of enthusiastic Dutch *agents provocateurs*. After the surrender the principal enemy counter-espionage personnel were brought to London for detailed interrogation and an intensive study was made of captured documents. One in particular made damning reading. Dated 6 December 1943, the paper listed forty-six agents who had been taken prisoner during the *spiel*, of whom only seventeen were described as not having collaborated in any way.

One still unexplained aspect to the entire affair is the curious way in which SIS was never duped. Many attempts were made to establish contact with it over captured radios, but on each occasion the link was terminated almost instantly. Was this a reflection of the relative professionalism of the older service? This was not the prevailing view at the time, for Rabagliati suffered much the same fate as Laming and had been retired. Blizard, in contrast, had been transferred in February 1943 to head SOE's Italian (J) Section and had been succeeded by his ineffectual deputy, Seymour Bingham. The latter's antecedents were not impressive. He had been a director of a Dutch commercial enterprise before the war and had been transferred to SOE in mid-November 1941 from a security screening post at the Royal Victoria Patriotic School in Wandsworth. Allegedly the move had been prompted by a complaint from MI5 about his drinking. He was to be replaced by Major Ivor Dobson in March 1944.

The disaster that befell N Section was not limited to Holland. Hardy Amies's Belgian (T) Section, permanently at odds with the Belgian authorities, was also contaminated. The problem lay in the political differences between the *Sûreté de l'État*, which co-ordinated the government-in-exile's resistance groups, and the Ministry of National Defence, which worked with SOE to run the military resistance networks of the *Légion Belge*. The *Sûreté* was headed by Baron Fernand Lepage, and Philip Johns, an SIS officer, recalls the atmosphere:

Jealousies and rivalries invariably exist amongst the various intelligence agencies of any nation, not only owing to the pressures operating from the top level of government insisting on results, but also from the conflicting personalities of the heads of these services. Thus Fernand Lepage, a most intelligent administrator in his own field, had had no previous experience in regard to the aggressive and explosive activities controlled and executed by SOE. He was consequently perhaps not the easiest official to get along with in the latter domain, and was more at home and in sympathy with the less dangerous operations of SIS.[11]

The situation was further exacerbated by SIS, which had failed to leave a stay-behind organisation. The Head of Station in pre-war Brussels, Colonel Edward Calthrop, had been confined to a wheelchair and had fulfilled a liaison role with the *Sûreté* before moving into Baker Street as SIS's liaison officer with SOE. His successor as head of SIS's country section was Major F. J. Jempson, who managed in January 1941 to make contact with CLEVELAND, a home-grown network based upon members of a similar circuit known as the WHITE LADY, which had operated during the First World War. CLEVELAND was run by Walther Dewe, a senior telephone executive who had developed a very efficient escape line for Allied airmen. Another veteran of the WHITE LADY was Adrien Marquet, who parachuted home on 12 August 1941, made contact with CLEVELAND and its successor, CLARENCE, and started another intelligence-gathering group, codenamed MILL. It was through these circuits that SIS was able to maintain a direct link with Belgium, while SOE's enforced relationship with the exiled Prime Minister Pierlot's administration virtually precluded it from developing any useful contact for a long period.

The isolation of the émigrés undermined SOE's relationship with the

Belgian government-in-exile, which evidently did not share all of SOE's objectives. On the subject of sabotage, for example, the Belgians took the view that large-scale disruption would not damage the German war effort, but might handicap Belgium's post-war economic recovery. So, instead of a strategy of wholesale sabotage, a campaign of minor pinpricks was adopted, albeit reluctantly. On 20 February 1942 an agreement had been reached with Pierlot for SOE to liaise directly with *Action*, a sub-section of the *Deuxième Direction* of the Ministry of Defence, headed by Major Bernard. This arrangement broke down almost immediately, and it was not until October 1942, when Bernard had been replaced by Colonel Jean Marissal, that a new treaty of co-operation could be negotiated. Even then, the personalities still jarred, with Philip Johns observing that Marissal 'had been too orthodox for him to adapt to this relatively newly constituted SOE'.[12] The new document was signed on 30 October 1942 and heralded a two-phase approach: a preparatory stage in which arms would be stockpiled and a 'secret army' recruited, followed by a co-ordinated and disciplined general insurrection after the Allied invasion. This ambitious plan was never fully realised, partly because of political infighting and 'the paranoiac suspicion and jealousy which existed between Lepage and his staff on the one hand and Marissal and the *Deuxième Direction* on the other . . . The internecine struggle, though understandable up to a point, was deplorable.'[13]

However, in spite of the internal conflict, the difficulties experienced by T Section were mainly due to German penetration of its networks. As well as running a large number of Belgian collaborators, the Germans also exploited the few links which existed between the compromised Dutch networks and the Belgian escape lines. In one lengthy undercover operation in the spring of 1942 the *Abwehr* actually took control of SIS's circuits, infiltrating its own surrogates into key positions, and rounded up all the related resistance groups, including an extensive one run by Major van Serveyt.

During the course of the war 250 agents were despatched to Belgium, of whom 105 were arrested. Only forty-five of those taken into German custody survived the experience. Part of the blame for this lies with SIS, which requested Gerard van Os, from the GOLF team which parachuted into German hands on 18/19 February 1943, to contact Gaston van der Meerssche, the SIS agent who ran the RINUS network. Van der Meerssche had been parachuted home in 1942 and had built up an important organisation, which smuggled intelligence via couriers on coastal freighters to Sweden for onward transmission to London. Baker Street's disastrous signal to van Os alerted the Germans for the first time to the existence of RINUS and they were able, through the use of skilled impersonators, to destroy the network. Van der Meerssche himself initially avoided capture, but was later arrested in Paris, en route to Spain.

Enemy manipulation of RINUS was so complete that the German who had infiltrated the network had negotiated with SOE in London to receive N Section agents in Belgium, because the Dutch networks had been so comprehensively penetrated. The German agents in RINUS had shown enthusiasm for the idea, but fortunately SOE decided to drop its remaining agents 'blind', without the benefit of a reception committee, and on 22 July 1943 Captain Zembsch-Schreve was landed near Mechelen. He was followed two months later by A. J. Cnoops, and on 18 October a further pair, Hans Gruen and J. D. van Schelle, arrived safely. Of these four, only Gruen was entrapped by the *Abwehr* and he survived captivity. Once the bitter truth had sunk in, SOE resumed drops into Holland, and two radio operators, Peter Gerbrands and Captain Tonnet, landed during 1943 and avoided arrest.

Paradoxically, SOE's determination to insulate their latest agents from those tainted by '*der Englandspiel*' proved in one case to be counterproductive. In November 1943 three more prisoners followed the example set by Dourlein and Ubbink and escaped from Haaren: Anton Wegner, Jan van Rietschoten and Aat van der Giessen rejoined the resistance and eventually tried to contact London via Peter Gerbrands, the agent who had managed to avoid arrest. However, Dobson was by this time so wary of people claiming to be escapees that none was returned to England. On this occasion at least the trio were genuine, and their version of what was happening at Haaren would have been invaluable to N Section's damage control exercise, then fully under way.

During the course of '*der Englandspiel*' more than four thousand signals were exchanged, unwittingly, by Baker Street with the enemy. After the war the Dutch military intelligence service claimed that of this total, the messages in less than two hundred had been shared with them. When the full scale of the disaster became known in February 1944, Seymour Bingham was shifted to Australia and his place was taken by Dobson, with Philip Johns acting as controller for a new Low Countries Section formed in November 1943 combining Belgium and the Netherlands. This development should not be interpreted to mean that blame for the tragedy was exclusively SOE's. On the contrary, SIS had supplied all the original ciphers which SOE had used and, initially at least, controlled its wireless circuits. Indeed, the breakthrough into SIS's cipher system, which was at that time shared by SOE and which had made the whole deception feasible, had been the capture of a single SIS agent, Wim van der Reyden, together with some of his past messages.

The full impact of what had happened to N Section under the leadership of Laming, Blizard and Bingham only became apparent when the *Abwehr*, in recognition that '*der Englandspiel*' had come to an end, on 31 March 1944 sent an identical message on ten separate channels, in plain language, addressed to Bingham and, significantly, to Blizard, using his nom de guerre, 'Blunt':

To Messrs Blunt Bingham and Successors Ltd. You are trying to make business in the Netherlands without our assistance. We think this is rather unfair in view our long and successful cooperation as your sole agent. But never mind whenever you will come to pay a visit to the Continent you may be assured you will be received with same care and result as those you sent us before. So long.[14]

This signal was routinely acknowledged by six of the ten SOE circuits used.

In hindsight SOE might have been well advised to have suspended all their operations in May 1943, when SIS gave the first warning that SOE's Dutch networks had been penetrated, and to have sent an independent team in 'blind' to double check on their bona fides. This procedure had been adopted by the *Abwehr* unsuccessfully to confirm their agents in England were not operating under control, so it was by no means foolproof. Nevertheless, it is a fact that three agents, Mink, Punt and de Brey, were all despatched on 21 May 1943, straight to a German reception committee, and all three were later executed. They at least might have been saved if SOE had exercised even a minimum of caution.

5 · A Deep and Abiding Jealousy: French Operations

There was, and still is, a deep and abiding jealousy of the F Section or Buckmaster circuits, and a deep interest in the doings of everyone connected with them both on the part of the *Deuxième Bureau* and also on the part of the Communists ... There is considerable irony in this attitude of the Communists. During the Resistance period the most frequent clashes of opinion arose precisely over the question of supplies to the Communists.

Colonel Bourne-Paterson, deputy Head of F Section, in the still classified *British Circuits in France 1941–4*, a summary of F Section's wartime work written for the Foreign Office and dated 30 June 1946

SOE is probably best known for its operations conducted in Nazi-occupied France, and certainly more books have been written about its activities in this theatre than any other. Individual accounts were released quite soon after the end of hostilities, and the first government-sponsored history was published in 1966, almost coinciding with E. H. Cookridge's controversial book, *Inside SOE*, which aroused much interest in F and RF Sections, especially among the survivors.

While SOE was never far from contention, interest centred on what had occurred in France for three reasons. Firstly, the very large number of casualties suffered there during the occupation. Exact statistics are hard to come by, but there is broad agreement on the numbers of those despatched to France by SOE. Professor Foot maintains that F Section's attrition rate was an acceptable twenty-five per cent and states that F Section sent over about 'four hundred-odd' agents, which amount to about a quarter of the total number despatched by SOE to France.[1] Cookridge refers to a total of 480 agents sent to France, with 130 captured, of whom twenty-six survived the experience.[2] The French historian, Henri Michel, uses larger numbers, but agrees that 1,600 agents in all were infiltrated.[3] These figures coincide with Bourne-Paterson's official ledger, which states that 'F Section in all sent 393 officers to France. 119 of these were arrested or killed by the Germans. Of those arrested only seventeen came back.' According to more recent research, all these figures are underestimates, and 152 SOE-trained agents and their fates are detailed on pages 126–30.

Given the paucity of records, it is almost impossible to determine exactly how many agents were sent to France and how many were captured. However, what is certain is that the number of casualties suffered by SOE circuits (rather than simply the agents who had undergone training in England and had been despatched) was far higher than the figures used by Foot or Cookridge. SOE personnel primarily fulfilled the role of organisers, recruiters, instructors and wireless operators, leaving the tasks of couriers, safe-house minders, quartermasters, target surveyors and saboteurs to other members of the nearly one hundred independent circuits of *réseaux* set up before the Liberation. Although most of the networks were quite small, some had several thousand members. And when they collapsed through enemy activity, there were invariably dozens, if not hundreds, of arrests as a consequence. Thus, ordinary members of the resistance, who had not been to England but had volunteered their services and had participated in SOE-run operations, using weapons and equipment supplied by the organisation, often fell victim to enemy action one way or another, but appear to have been omitted from the calculation of official SOE casualties. The best example is that of PROSPER, a huge organisation which expanded with great rapidity and, as we shall see, collapsed with the loss of twelve SOE agents. By June 1943 this enormous circuit covered twelve *départements*, boasted thirty-three landing grounds and had received no less than 254 containers of stores. It reached a peak of activity in mid-June 1943, when it broke all records and received a further 190 containers in a period of nine days, and thereby attracted the enemy's attention. Some of those directly involved estimate that, apart from the SOE-trained personnel, there were around fifteen hundred others implicated and arrested in this one tragic episode.

What makes the whole subject so sensitive is the performance of SOE itself, an organisation whose members were denigrated as mere amateurs by the self-styled professionals in SIS. Certainly the headquarters in Baker Street was staffed largely by enthusiastic volunteers, only a few of whom had any real knowledge, understanding or training in clandestine operations. Maurice Buckmaster, the third successive head of F Section, who took over from Henry Marriott in September 1941, had only been in SOE since

March and for part of that time had worked in the Belgian Section. Apart from having attended the standard War Office intelligence course at Minley Manor, he had no previous experience in secret operations, yet he was expected to recruit suitable French-speaking British subjects and train them to 'set Europe ablaze'. His transfer back to F Section had happened when the Section had been paralysed by the internal dissension that had seen the departure of Cadett, as well as Marriott and David Keswick.

When Buckmaster had first gone to work at Baker Street, he had expressed surprise to Hambro that as yet not a single agent had been sent into the field. In the six months which had elapsed since his recruitment he found that not much had changed in F Section. Recently four agents had been sent into the field, but in September there was still no news of them. His headquarters staff, initially at least, consisted of just seven officers and his personal assistant, of whom only one had actually seen France during the occupation, to handle recruiting, information, planning, operations, escorting, signals and briefing. Prior to Buckmaster's appointment they had succeeded in sending only about twenty agents into the unoccupied zone, with instructions to work their way north. A year later most of these agents were either in prison or on the run, and of the four who had been entrusted with wireless transmitters, only two had survived. No wonder then that Buckmaster found that 'questions were being asked by inquisitive generals about the usefulness of our organisation and the efficiency of its staff'.[4] Fortunately Ben Cowburn (*Benoit*, the Lancashire oil engineer who had been dropped near Châteauroux on 6/7 September) was to supply some useful information about oil storage depots, which Buckmaster was to circulate in an attempt to improve F Section's standing, but the acquisition of this type of target intelligence, though helpful to the RAF, was not really SOE's responsibility.

Buckmaster's task was not an easy one. As well as having to restore order to F Section's management in Baker Street, he had to endure obstruction from SIS and open hostility from the Free French RF Section. He recalls that

The conflict between de Gaulle's *réseaux* and ours was also a factor which had to be taken into account when we were planning operations in France. We did our best to turn these rivalries to good purpose and we hoped that the competitive element in our relations would lead each group to outdo the other. This may not have been the ideal way of running things, but it did make the best of conditions as they actually were. What liaison did exist between us at Baker Street and de Gaulle was conducted unofficially by individual officers whose tact and charm was the only weapon against jealousy and intransigence.[5]

Another cause of controversy in SOE's operations was the behaviour of the French, for the success achieved by the Germans in penetrating the resistance circuits was greatly enhanced by collaborators, who actively helped the *Abwehr* and the *Sicherheitsdienst*. This is another reason for the controversy surrounding SOE's performance in France. The sheer scale of the collaboration on the part of the French is breathtaking, as is the hypocrisy with which the subject is handled in France. As the Comte de Marenches remarked, having escaped the occupation and spent much of the war in de Gaulle's intelligence service in London, 'what most surprised me when I returned to France at the end of the war was to discover that forty-two million people had fought for the Resistance'.[6] In fact, after the war there were no less than 118,000 prosecutions for collaborating with the enemy, of which about 50,000 actually went to court; 38,000 Frenchmen and women were convicted, of whom no less than 791 were executed. A much greater number had their death sentences commuted. Even half a century after these events, the whole issue is still the cause of much bitterness in France. The Germans used collaborators on an individual basis, assigning them missions to infiltrate targeted *réseaux*, or deployed them as *agents provocateurs*, sending them down escape routes pretending to be agents or airmen on the run. Whole teams of collaborators, like the notorious Bony-Lafont gang in Paris, were signed up by the SD and put to work as paramilitaries, keeping suspects under surveillance, participating in arrests and even staffing the notorious SD interrogation centre at 82 Avenue Foch and the Gestapo's prison at 13 bis Place des Etats-Unis. Led by an ex-police inspector, Pierre Bony, and a notorious criminal, Henri Lafont, the gang penetrated several circuits and were responsible for entrapping hundreds of *résistants*.

The whole subject of French complicity with the occupation authorities, and the enthusiastic support given to them by the police and, most notoriously, the Vichy *Milice*, is still a sensitive topic in France. So too is the role of the Communist resistance cells, which, as we shall see, were to complicate the scene further. Buckmaster's deputy and Planning Officer, R. A. Bourne-Paterson, was to have some very trenchant remarks about 'the political distractions which tended to assail all purely French Resistance movements',[7] but political expediency ensured that they were never published.

Although sheer ineptitude played a part in some of SOE's disasters in France, penetration and betrayal were the more usual reasons for German success. One early loss was the CARTE network in the South of France, which was eliminated because a courier, André Marsac (*End*), fell asleep on a train in November 1942 and had his briefcase stolen by an *Abwehr* agent. When the Germans examined the contents, they discovered the names and addresses of hundreds of the circuit's members.

CARTE's origins lay in a small determined group of *résistants* centred on Antibes led by André Girard, an artist after whose field name the network was named. He and his friends were of interest to SOE partly because they were well organised, many of them having military backgrounds, but mainly because, being located in the South of France, they were within SOE's reach by *felucca* via Gibraltar. They also had the advantage that, apart from being anti-Nazi patriots, they were not politically aligned to de Gaulle or any other party or movement. Contact with CARTE had been established through a courier who visited Switzerland quite regularly on legitimate business. SOE's initial opinion of CARTE, a study undertaken by Peter Churchill (*Michel*),[8] who landed from a submarine in January 1942, was very favourable and, superficially at least, CARTE seemed ideal for F Section's purposes. A talented linguist and a former ice hockey player for England, Churchill had transferred to SOE from the commandos and had been sent to Cannes to assess CARTE. Since the *réseau* was essentially a home-grown organisation, it did not conform to SOE's established security procedures. On the question of cryptonyms, for example, F Section used the names of trees and then occupations as the codenames for operations, hence PLANE, CHESTNUT, ACROBAT, SALESMAN. The Free French (RF Section) used fish, such as ROACH and CARP, for operations, occupations for organisers and tribesmen for wireless operators. Inter-Allied missions tended to have herbs, and Air Liaison stuck to weapons.

Codenames were not the only area where CARTE diverged from the norm. *Carte* himself insisted on running all aspects of the organisation personally, but, as it turned out, had little idea of security. Instead, he relied on friends in the local administration to get his members out of trouble once they had been arrested. Fortunately, his helpers included two senior figures in the Vichy counter-espionage apparatus, Colonel Vautrin and General Cochet, both of whom were sympathetic to the cause. This arrangement did not suit the Germans, who learned of CARTE's existence when the network's courier was caught smuggling watches out of Geneva. Evidence found on him, combined with a substantial part of CARTE's complete membership roll, which was acquired in November 1942, ensured that the *Abwehr* had no difficulty in penetrating, and eventually rolling up, the entire network. *Carte* himself was successfully extracted by *Michel* in March 1943 and brought to London, where many of the simmering internal disputes which had characterised the network boiled over. The *réseau* collapsed into betrayal and recriminations, leaving a bitter *Carte* to resume his career as a painter in New York.

While many of CARTE's members were casualties, some of the key SOE figures regrouped in St Jorioz to form SPINDLE, but that circuit too was to be short-lived. The *Abwehr* manipulated the wretched Marsac to its advantage, and he actually fell for his interrogator's improbable tale of being a potential defector. The skilful German was Hugo Bleicher, who had already penetrated INTERALLIÉ and taken Mathilde Carré as his mistress.[9] Bleicher was put in touch with Roger Bardet (*Chaillan*) and Odette Sansom (*Lise*), supposedly to negotiate a Lysander flight to London, but instead he arrested Bardet and then, the following day, travelled to St Jorioz where *Lise* was based. Odette Sansom was the mother of three daughters and the widow of a British businessman, whom she had married in Boulogne. In June 1942 she had been recruited by Selwyn Jepson into F Section and the following October had been assigned to SPINDLE. Unfortunately, when after midnight Bleicher and his men burst into the Hôtel de la Poste, they found *Lise* and Peter Churchill. *Michel* had only just parachuted back into the Haute-Savoie after a four-week respite in London, and had landed that very evening to find *Lise* as a member of his reception committee. It was the fourth time he had been infiltrated into France, but, despite his orders to avoid *Lise* until she had shaken off Bleicher, whom SOE headquarters was rightly suspicious of, Churchill agreed to spend a few days at the same hotel. (They were later to marry in 1947.) His decision to stay in St Jorioz was to prove disastrous for SPINDLE and CARTE. He survived his subsequent imprisonment by encouraging his captors to believe, falsely, that he was the Prime Minister's nephew.

Worse was to follow for F Section when *Chaillan* opted to work for the *Abwehr* as a double agent and proceeded to identify the remains of CARTE, including a contact, Germaine Tambour (*Annette*), who had so far avoided capture. This single clue was in turn to have profound implications for PROSPER.

Some collaborators, particularly Raoul Kiffer and René Lefebvre, masqueraded as evaders and skilfully entrapped dozens of their fellow Frenchmen. However, such activity was not restricted to the French. A British renegade, Harold Cole,[10] inflicted great damage on MI9's escape lines, and Helen James, an attractive Irish girl living in Paris, proved herself as adept at exposing SOE circuits as her *Abwehr* lover, Robert Kayser. Together the latter pair moved in on PROSPER, using *Chaillan*'s identification of *Annette* as a starting-point, and thereby initiated one of SOE's worst losses.

The origins of the PROSPER débâcle is still a matter of debate, for it is not known exactly when *Annette* had come under *Abwehr* surveillance. That she did so is not in dispute for she and her sister Anne were arrested at the end of April 1943, following *Chaillan*'s treachery. Nor do we know the exact method Helen James employed to introduce another *Abwehr* agent into the circuit. What is confirmed is a fatal meeting which took place at the end of May 1943 while the SOE organiser, Francis Suttill, was away in London conferring with Buckmaster on, among other issues, the implications of *Annette*'s arrest. Quite apart from her own importance as a key agent of long standing, her apartment had been used as a letterbox for PROSPER and a rendezvous for its members. In addition, another apartment in the same building had also been employed as a safe-house.

The PROSPER *réseau*, which took its name from Suttill's own field name, was a direct attempt by SOE to rebuild an organisation in Paris following the disappointment of AUTOGIRO. Suttill, a young barrister who had been born in Lille to a French mother and an English father, had been parachuted into the Touraine in October 1942 to take over MONKEYPUZZLE, an existing *réseau* based round Tours, which was experiencing some difficulties. Led by a British chef born and trained in Paris, Raymond Flower (*Gaspard*), the MONKEYPUZZLE circuit consisted of Marcel Clech (*Bastien*), a former cab driver and Section D veteran who had been brought in from Gibraltar by submarine; an ex-prisoner of war named Pierre Culioli; and SOE's first woman agent to be parachuted into enemy-occupied territory, Andrée Borrel (*Denise*). She was a twenty-two-year-old nurse, who had already cut her teeth in the resistance with the MI9 escape line known as PAT. When the route had been betrayed, after two years of operations which repatriated nearly six hundred Allied airmen, she had made her way to London, where she had been accepted into F Section, despite her strong political commitment to the Left and her French nationality. MONKEYPUZZLE had been handicapped by personality differences between Flower and his wireless operator, Clech, who thought him insecure.

SOE's use of women agents is the third reason for the French theatre to attract so much attention. A few women agents were employed in other areas, but the overwhelming majority of SOE's female agents were sent to France, with tragic results. Of the fifty-two who went, seventeen were arrested and twelve died in concentration camps. The use of women in ungentlemanly warfare was not universally accepted in 1940, and it was widely believed that SIS ought not to have employed Edith Cavell twenty-five years earlier. Certainly the Germans did not use women on quite the same scale, although two *Abwehr* agents, Mathilde Krafft and Vera de Cottani-Chalbur, were arrested and interned in England. In addition, four other agents, Lily Sergueiev, Friedle Gaertner, *Bronx* and *The Snark*, were 'turned' by the Security Service.

Yvonne Rudelatt adopted the field name *Jacqueline* and was the third woman agent to go to France for SOE, the first to arrive by clandestine means. She had been preceded by Giliana Balmaceda, a Chilean actress, and Virginia Hall, the American journalist with the wooden leg, both of whom had official permission to be in the Vichy zone. Separated from her Italian husband, in civilian life *Jacqueline* had been a receptionist in a West End hotel. In July 1942 she was put ashore from a *felucca* and went to work as a courier for the PHYSICIAN network. She subsequently moved north to join Suttill upon his arrival and *Denise*, the first of SOE's women agents to be landed by parachute on 24/25 September 1942. A month later *Prosper* took command and was followed on 1 November by a wireless operator, Gilbert Norman (*Archambaud*), and then in December by Jack Agazarian (*Marcel*), a second radio man.

As well as taking over the troubled MONKEYPUZZLE from *Gaspard*, *Prosper* was given the objective of re-establishing contact with Ben Cowburn's *réseau*, which had miraculously survived the German penetration of INTERALLIÉ. Having achieved this, and having developed what was to become SOE's largest network to date in France, *Prosper* returned to London to confer with F Section. During his temporary absence between 14 May and 12 June 1943, *Archambaud* made a catastrophic mistake, which was to prove absolutely fatal for PROSPER. He not only attended a rendez-vous with two men purporting to be SOE agents from Holland, but was accompanied by three other key members of PROSPER: *Denise*, *Marcel* and his wife Francine, who had taken the field name *Marguerite* and had arrived to join him by Lysander on 17 March. What none of the four realised was that the two supposed agents, who had taken on the identities of '*Arnaud*', a Belgian resistance leader, and 'Captain John Kist' ('*Anton*'), an N Section agent on the run, were really both Germans who had been exceptionally well-briefed by Helen James on DF escape routes and were following up leads made through the Dutch *funkspiel*. Surprisingly, the Germans did not arrest the four immediately, but merely placed them under surveillance so that they could compromise other members of the circuit.

Whilst this meeting, held at the Café Lorraine in Montmartre, was the first definite moment that the Germans achieved access into PROSPER, considerable doubt surrounds another extraordinary figure in SOE's hierarchy who was a self-confessed double agent for the *Sicherheitsdienst*. Henri Dericourt (*Gilbert*) has been the subject of at least two biographies and remains one of the most enigmatic characters of the war. As F Section's air movements officer in the field, he arranged fifteen clandestine flights in and out of occupied France between his arrival, by parachute on 22/23 January 1943, and his return to England in April 1944. During this period *Gilbert* headed FARRIER and, as a former Moon Squadron pilot himself, was exceptionally well-qualified to select sites and supervise air operations. However, on his own admission, he was also in constant contact with the SD in the person of *Sturmbannführer* Karl Boemelburg, with whom he had been acquainted in Paris before the war while he had been an Air France pilot and the latter had been attached to the German Embassy. *Gilbert* only said that he had known Boemelburg before the war and never elaborated on the nature of their relationship. One of his biographers, an Australian journalist named Robert Marshall,[11] claimed, citing no evidence, that the two men had been introduced by the Reuters correspondent in Paris, Nicholas Bodington, who was later to become Buckmaster's deputy in F Section and to play a crucial role in the PROSPER fiasco. *Gilbert* himself acknowledged having maintained contact with the enemy since 'the late spring of 1943' because he was anxious about his wife Jeannot, who had continued to live at their apartment at 58 rue Pergolese. Curiously, Hugo Bleicher was her next-door neighbour at number 56. In the absence of *Gilbert* himself, who is alleged to have been killed in an aircrash in Laos on 21 November 1962, the authoress Jean Overton Fuller is his principal defender, and she is emphatic that Dericourt admitted only to having known Boemelburg before the war.[12] Unfortunately, Boemelburg himself died in December 1946 after an accident near his home in Germany, where he lived as a fugitive, so he never gave evidence concerning *l'affaire Dericourt*.

The Dericourt controversy centres on his astonishing success in ferrying SOE's agents in and out of France on each full moon. This was no easy matter in enemy-occupied territory and involved finding suitable landing strips, recruiting reliable helpers, maintaining radio contact with London and signalling to the aircraft as they approached the designated airfield. That Dericourt enlisted the SD's help to accomplish his mission either demonstrates his undeniably resourceful nature, or his treachery, depending upon one's viewpoint. As might be expected, SOE's own opinion on the issue, both then and after the war, was thoroughly ambiguous.

The fact that *Gilbert* had been in touch with the enemy had been disclosed to Bodington by 23 June 1943, the date of a scribbled memorandum by the latter to Buckmaster. Others, including Harry Sporborg, have proposed an earlier date for the admission, suggesting that the link had been regarded as an asset, but the truth of the matter is difficult to fathom. *Gilbert* definitely supplied the SD with details of his operations and copies of the regular handwritten agent reports that supplemented their signals to London. He also held clandestine meetings with Boemelburg and the architect of the Paris SD's *funkspiel*, Dr Josef Goetz. But was his motive to protect his wife and his agents, or simply his own hide? When challenged during his trial in Paris after the war, Bodington gave crucial testimony for Dericourt and ensured his acquittal, confirming that all *Gilbert*'s contacts with the SD had been made with the full knowledge and authority of London. This assertion surprised not a few old Baker Street hands, who had not been told of Bodington's intention to appear as a witness for the defence. Bodington gave no explanation for his behaviour, took up a career at UNESCO and died in 1974.

There are still many unexplained loose ends in *Gilbert*'s story, but, from F Section's position, there was a single denunciation by Henri Frager (*Paul*), who had grave suspicions about *Gilbert*: he had strong reason, based on what was admittedly circumstantial evidence, to believe that *Gilbert* had been copying the contents of his courier satchels to the Germans. Frager was an architect who ran the DONKEYMAN circuit, having originally been returned to France in a submarine in July 1941 to found CARTE. He had endured numerous scrapes with the enemy and had even survived an encounter with Bleicher, but had always managed to avoid arrest. Yet DONKEYMAN seemed beset with German interference and Frager ascribed this to Dericourt, whom he disliked, rather than to his own close friend Roger Bardet, who was, of course, also in league with the enemy. When Frager voiced his anxiety about *Gilbert* to Baker Street, SOE responded by recalling Dericourt for 'consultations'. In addition there were three further, separate allegations against him which had required answers. However, the source of these charges may have mitigated in Dericourt's favour as they were themselves all hostile to F Section. One came from Forest Yeo-Thomas, of RF Section, who reported that one of his agents had alleged that whoever had been in charge of operations in Angers had 'caused the arrest of two men and a woman whom he had received'. An almost identical charge had been laid by the *Deuxième Bureau*. Finally, there was a claim by a returned SIS agent that *Gilbert* had been guilty of indiscretion upon his return to France, a lapse which had brought him into contact with the Gestapo, which 'had consequently sought an interview with a view to using him as an agent'. Not only could SOE dismiss these charges as being based on jealousy of F Section's success, but there was some lingering doubt about Frager himself. Shortly before he had been arrested, *Prosper* had remarked that 'anyone in contact with Frager sooner or later found himself in trouble'. This was true, but not because of Frager's treachery, but rather that of his trusted deputy, Bardet.

Whether *Gilbert* was responsible for betraying PROSPER, or whether the fault lies with *Archambaud* for entertaining the two *Abwehr* stooges '*Arnaud*' and '*Anton*', is unclear. No doubt F Section itself should shoulder some of the blame for its poor security procedures. *Prosper* himself had felt so strongly about the loss of the Tambour sisters that he had incriminated himself in attempting to engineer their escape from Fresnes by bribery. No doubt he had felt compelled to do so because they had been among his first contacts. Indeed, *Annette* had originally worked for Section D and been a common link between several supposedly strictly compartmented circuits over a long period. However well-intentioned, *Prosper*'s behaviour only endangered the network further. Jean Worms (*Robin*), the agent he selected to negotiate their release from prison, supplied the Germans with a million French francs, the notes having been torn in half with the rest promised once the Tambours were free. The Germans responded by turning two elderly prostitutes loose and demanding even more cash. As well as having compromised *Robin*, who was to be arrested on 1 July, the episode exposed other members of the *réseau* who had been standing by to receive the escapees. Nor was this kind of appalling lapse in security very unusual. Because of the shortage of wireless operators, *Marcel* had found himself transmitting messages for twenty-four SOE agents, all of whom were under instructions to isolate themselves from each other.

The bitter truth is that the Germans could have obtained their initial leads into PROSPER from several other sources besides *Gilbert* and *Chaillan*. The controversy has been made more complicated by the knowledge that Dericourt's field name, *Gilbert*, was identical to Major Norman's Christian name, the name he habitually used in preference to his field name within PROSPER. This was bound to lead to confusion, especially as *Archambaud*'s radio was later to be played back by the SD in a *funkspiel*.

The collapse of his organisation was already well under way when *Prosper* returned to Paris on 14 June 1943. Ernest Wilkinson (*Alexandre*), an RAF officer who headed the sub-group PRIVET around Angers, walked into a Gestapo trap in Paris on 6 June, but he resisted his interrogators. However, the catalyst occurred on 18 June, just two days after a pair of Canadians, Frank Pickersgill (*Bertrand*)[13] and John Macalister (*Valentin*), had parachuted north of Valençay to start another PROSPER sub-group, ARCHDEACON. Pickersgill, originally a Left-orientated intellectual from Winnipeg, had already spent two years in France, having been interned as an enemy alien in Paris in 1940, and had escaped to England via Portugal. His French was perfect, but the same could not be said for his companion, the wireless operator *Valentin*, himself a Rhodes Scholar married to a

French wife. They had teamed up with Culioli and *Jacqueline*, but all four were arrested during a random spot check while driving to Paris. The latter pair tried to escape, but both were wounded in the attempt. When the Gestapo searched their belongings, a series of messages from London were discovered, written in English and addressed to various PROSPER agents, each identified by his authentic field name. Furthermore, the Canadians were found to be carrying a wireless crystal for *Archambaud*, together with detailed instructions for him on how to use it. Of the four, only Culioli emerged from the concentration camps, to face two prosecutions for collaboration with the enemy, charges he was acquitted of. However, the real damage to SOE was to be inflicted unintentionally by Pickersgill and Macalister, for F Section took months to realise that they had been captured.

Indeed, in his 1958 memoirs *They Fought Alone*, Buckmaster was to describe Pickersgill as one of F Section's 'principal agents' (see page 117), evidently not realising that in fact *Bertrand* had been arrested two days after his arrival in France. The Germans were to manipulate ARCHDEACON skilfully for the following ten months, during which time F Section made fifteen airdrops to it and despatched a sabotage instructor, François Michel (*Dispenser*), to the bogus circuit in September 1943.

The really devastating arrest for the network followed four days after the capture of the ARCHDEACON team, on 24 June 1943, when *Prosper* himself was caught at the small hotel he had moved to in Paris. Only a very limited number of his subordinates knew the exact address, so treachery probably played a part here too. In any event, once in the hands of the Gestapo, *Prosper* made a pact with his captors, who offered to treat his circuit as prisoners of war in return for a complete membership roll and details of all their arms caches. Within twenty-four hours of his capture, *Prosper* had given them a letter of introduction to Captain Georges Darling, a Frenchman of English extraction who ran a safe-house in Triechâteaux near Gisors, instructing him to disclose the exact location of his arms dumps. Two SD agents adopted the identities of *Bertrand* and *Valentin*, and Darling only realised the deception too late when he had already started his guided tour of the locality and helped the two Germans load weapons from a cache hidden in a wood on to their lorry. He was shot while trying to escape on his motorcycle and died the following day in hospital. By then *Archambaud* and *Denise* had also been arrested in Paris, in circumstances that allowed the latter's radio and codes to be used to continue the *spiel*.

Although London had been informed of *Prosper*'s arrest, F Section was confused about how much damage to the circuit had been sustained and

Map from *They Fought Alone*

A map from Buckmaster's *They Fought Alone*, published in 1958 and reproduced by kind permission of Colonel Buckmaster, which suggests that F Section never realised that Frank Pickersgill operated under German control. He is described as one of F Section's 'principal agents', although he had been caught by the SD within forty-eight hours of landing. His entire network was subsequently rounded up by the Germans and his place was taken by a skilful impostor.

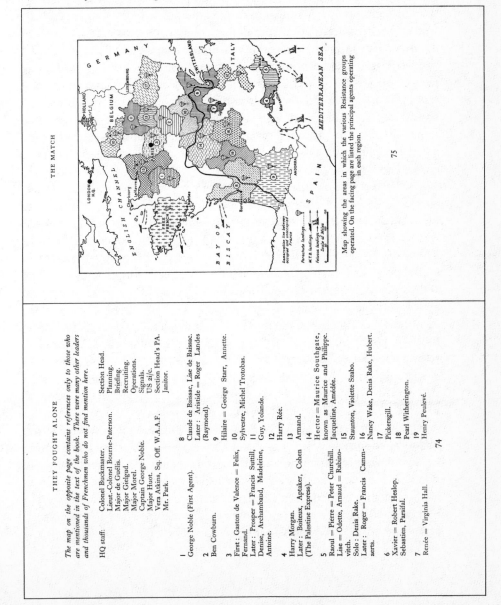

continued to respond to *Valentin*'s radio, which had come under SD control. This was to prompt yet more arrests, for *Valentin* had been instructed to link up with Noor Inayat Khan (*Madeleine*), who had landed by Lysander on 16 June to operate a wireless for CINEMA. She occupies a special place in SOE's story, not least because of her bravery after capture and her apparent unsuitability as a secret agent. She was gentle and breathtakingly attractive, and so hardly conformed to the conventional inconspicuous ideal for someone operating undercover in enemy territory. Temperamentally she seemed unprepared for her ordeal on a clandestine mission, having been brought up by her Indian parents in the Sufi sect, and had previously worked in Paris translating stories for children. One of her trainers had reported that, in his opinion, she was unfit for operational duties, but he had been overruled because of the enthusiasm she had manifested. Having been implicated by *Valentin*, *Madeleine* was placed under surveillance and was eventually arrested on 13 October. However, in the meantime she had held several meetings with the undercover Gestapo agents and had unintentionally compromised several other members of PROSPER. After her arrest her radio was also used to communicate with London, which, even at this late stage, appeared to be unsure of the situation in the field.

The level of confusion at Baker Street was partly understandable, especially as *Valentin* and *Archambaud* were still playing the *spiel*. The rather unsatisfactory solution was to send Bodington to Paris to see for himself who was still at liberty. He went on 22/23 July, accompanied by *Marcel*, in a Hudson organised by *Gilbert*. They arrived safely, oblivious to the German surveillance, and tossed for who should investigate *Archambaud*'s contact address, as supplied to London over his suspect wireless link. *Marcel* lost and was arrested as soon as he entered the SD's 'mousetrap'. This development finally persuaded Bodington that what was left of PROSPER had come under enemy control and, having reported to London via *Madeleine*, he returned to England on *Gilbert*'s flight at the next full moon, on 15/16 August. Surprisingly, instead of resuming his job in Baker Street, Bodington was detached from SOE for six months, lecturing Allied troops destined to invade France on the intricacies of French politics.

Nothing approaching a full *post-mortem* was possible until *Gilbert* himself was recalled to Baker Street on 7/8 February 1944. Once back in London he was obliged to submit to an interrogation conducted by John Senter in order to determine the extent of his collaboration with the SD. *Gilbert* confirmed that he had been in regular contact with the Germans for the best part of the year and justified this by pointing out that his unusual arrangement had enabled his air operations to be completed without any enemy interference. The statistics tended to bear out the assertion. Under his auspices, forty-three agents had arrived and sixty-seven people had left on twenty-one separate aircraft. None had experienced the slightest difficulty with enemy fighters or hostile reception committees. Accordingly the security enquiry, which was chaired by Harry Sporborg, found in favour of *Gilbert*, but banned him from any further participation in clandestine operations. *Gilbert* was transferred to the Free French and, six months later, was nearly killed when his reconnaissance aircraft crashed near Châteauroux. He spent the rest of the war in hospital recuperating.

What seems astonishing is that, even after Bodington's return to Baker Street with the news that PROSPER had effectively come to an end, F Section did not withdraw *Madeleine*. Although never officially notified of her arrest in October, SOE did realise that her radio had come under control. However, after she had responded correctly to a series of check questions designed to test whether she was still free, F Section revised its opinion and began to treat her as though she was operating independently. This led to the SURVEYOR drop near Poitiers on 7/8 February 1944, which sent four young men straight into the arms of the Gestapo. Raoul Alexandre, François Deniset and Jacques Ledoux were all arrested on arrival, and their wireless operator, an American named Robert Byerly, was forced to transmit a safe-arrival signal. However, it was quickly realised that Byerly must be sending under duress as none of his messages included the special security checks he had been issued with before his departure.

Perhaps more incredibly, the SURVEYOR disaster was followed on 28/29 February 1944 by a further drop, of Madeleine Damerment (*Solange*), a young *résistant* who had previously worked on the PAT escape line with Andrée Borrel, France Antelme and his wireless operator, Lionel Lee. Their tragic mission was to investigate PARSON in Brittany, which had been run by the enemy for some time. All three landed directly into a German reception committee, a full three weeks after *Gilbert*'s interrogation had begun in London. Worse still, Lee's radio was to be played back by the SD, and F Section failed to notice that his security checks, whilst technically correct, had been inserted into the wrong places in his messages. Thus, it was not until the end of April that Baker Street finally realised that Antelme and his two assistants had fallen under enemy control.

The PROSPER débâcle was to be the worst of its kind. Estimates of those involved in the wave of arrests that followed vary, but Professor Foot acknowledges that a figure of 400 would be 'conservative'.[14] Others suggest 1,500, and it is certainly the case that PROSPER boasted 144 fully accredited agents, and a total of 1,015 helpers. Exactly how many perished in German camps is unknown, but the full toll was considerable.

It is not unreasonable to ask how, given the British reputation for assiduous secret service work, F Section fared so badly. The explanation is by no means simple. One fundamental flaw was the policy of tight compartmentation carried out at Baker Street, if nowhere else. Thus, when RF Section experienced an enemy playback on OVERCLOUD in December 1941, none of the lessons was learned by, or circulated to, N or F Sections. In that particular case the Comte de Kergolay (*Joew*) had been captured with his wireless set in December 1941 and had operated it under enemy control until early 1943. As soon as *Joew* omitted his security check, which he never disclosed to the *Abwehr*, RF recognised the traffic as a playback *spiel* and handled it accordingly, designating the double deception SEALING WAX. After the war the French authorities convicted de Kergolay of collaboration, but Yeo-Thomas was able to clear him of the charges relating to OVER-CLOUD and get his life sentence reduced.[15] F was not as astute with ARCH-DEACON. Frank Pickersgill's wireless was used for ten months before it was realised belatedly in London that it had fallen into German hands. In consequence, the SD received fifteen arms drops and seven SOE agents. Nor was this an isolated incident. BUTLER and PHONO were also penetrated by the enemy and manipulated to entrap unsuspecting agents despatched from London. All were to die in extermination camps.

It is certainly a paradox that whilst there was deliberate separation of SOE's French sections, with Hutchison's RF at a house in Dorset Square and Buckmaster's F at 6 Orchard Court, individual agents socialised with each other at their respective training schools, allowing the suspicion to arise that some operations had been compromised before they had really had a chance to get going.

One lapse in security adopted by SOE which broke all the accepted norms was the apparent acceptance by the management of the principle that senior officers could put themselves at risk by going on operations. Whilst it is often an advantage to give successful agents staff posts after their return from the field, so that they can capitalise on their own experience and pass on tips to their subordinates, it should be a cardinal rule that personnel who have had access to classified data should never be placed in a situation that might compromise it. F Section undoubtedly benefited from the experiences of Gerard Morel, Georges Begué and the others at headquarters who had worked in the field and, in the example of Jean Le Harival, seen the inside of a Vichy prison. Le Harival had been part of the CORSICAN mission in October 1941 which had fallen into Vichy hands, but had succeeded in escaping to Spain ten months later. It was the practice of sending men into occupied territory *after* they had learned so much about SOE that seems so dangerous. Bodington was a prime offender: while Buckmaster's deputy, he had accompanied an MTB to the coast of Brittany in February 1942 to deliver and collect agents, and had undertaken three missions to France, the first to CARTE in August 1942, then to PROSPER in July the following year, and finally to organise PEDLAR on the Marne in July 1944. RF Section was in a similar position and was equally guilty. Bodington's counterpart in RF, Yeo-Thomas, was captured in March 1944 after just a month at liberty. Fortunately, the Germans never realised his true identity. His immediate superior, James Hutchison, also parachuted into enemy territory, as a member of a JEDBURGH team (see page 230). Such behaviour seems really at odds with a determination to run safe, security conscious operations. Nor were these risks limited to the headquarters staff. Even training personnel, like Harry Peulevé from Beaulieu, were to go into the field and be caught.

Another curious aspect to F Section's approach was the paucity of counter-intelligence briefing material available to either the management or the agents. During training agents were told to expect the worst at the hands of their German captors, and they were requested to maintain their silence for forty-eight hours if they decided not to avail themselves of their 'L' pill. This delay, so it was confidently stated, would be sufficient for the remainder of the circuit to undertake a damage-limitation exercise. In reality, this advice was poor. The Germans were extraordinarily well-informed about almost everything to do with F Section (not to mention N Section) and the SD interrogators at 82–6 Avenue Foch and their Gestapo counterparts at 11 rue des Saussaies exploited the fear and expectation of torture quite subtly; in fact, some of the key figures on the German side, such as the resourceful Hugo Bleicher or Ernest Vogt, were never accused of having maltreated any of their prisoners. In most cases, physical abuse was not necessary to obtain co-operation, and John Starr, who was present for much of the time, testified after the war that he was not aware of any prisoners having been manhandled in the Avenue Foch while he was resident there.

Bleicher, who had so successfully penetrated the INTERALLIÉ network, thus ensnaring Pierre de Vomécourt, and then had stage-managed the coup in Haute-Savoie which had led to the capture of Odette Sansom and Peter Churchill, co-operated with the Allied authorities after his arrest in Holland in 1945 and attempted to piece together what had gone wrong with F Section. After he had given enough evidence to convict his former agents Raoul Kiffer and Roger Bardet, he returned to Germany and later opened a tobacconist in Tettnang in Württemberg. He was to remain on such good terms with his former prisoners that on one occasion he went to stay in England with Odette and Peter Churchill.

The unpalatable fact that an untrained myopic non-commissioned officer, whose peacetime occupation had been that of a clerk in a shipping company, and whose only advantage was his skill as a linguist, had been able to dupe the combined experience of the F Section headquarters staff, highlighted some of the latter's shortcomings. The lack of counter-intelligence data put F Section at a disadvantage, and allowed Bleicher and his associates to use the same tricks several times over, masquerading at least twice as a politically disenchanted *Luftwaffe* officer to gain the confidence of different circuit organisers. Nor were agents well prepared for the very large number of collaborators recruited by the enemy, and there were numerous instances of indiscretion, with even experienced *résistants* supplying complete strangers with incriminating information, purely on the grounds that a German trying to speak French was widely thought to be instantly detectable. In fact this was not always the case and a high proportion of *Abwehr* personnel spoke the language like natives. The PROSPER circuit for one was decimated by Lucien Prévost, René Lefebvre, Roger Dupré and Jacques d'Arcangues, who acted as *agents provocateurs* for the *Abwehr*. Another consequence of SOE's poor counter-intelligence capability was its inability to understand and exploit the many weaknesses displayed by the *Sicherheitsdienst* and the *Abwehr*. The two organisations were mutually hostile and rarely co-ordinated their overlapping operations. Curiously, no effort was directed to the penetration of the offices of either, and no attempt was made to turn any of their collaborators. When Colonel André Grandclément, once the head of SCIENTIST, was finally unmasked in July 1944 as a key Gestapo source, he was killed, along with his wife and his aide, Marc Duluguet. All three had been tricked into believing that they had been ordered to London, and willingly followed a group from ACTOR to what they thought was to be a rendezvous with a Lysander. Instead, they were led into some woods near Léognan and shot.

As we have already seen, only a couple of very senior SOE management were privy to ULTRA summaries, and one can only speculate about the quality of information relevant to the *Abwehr*'s and the *Sicherheitsdienst*'s activities in France that was accumulated by other services through GCHQ's interception work. MI5 for one knew a great deal about the *Abwehr* in Paris, not least because several of its double agents were controlled by leading *Abstelle* personalities. MI5 and SIS had acquired sufficient information about the German intelligence apparatus by August 1942 to produce a detailed report, which 'described the *Abwehr*'s organisation and its deployment in the Reich, in occupied Europe and in neutral countries'. This remarkable document was later to be the foundation of a handbook dated July 1944 prepared for use by specialist counter-intelligence teams on the Continent.[16] Where did the information come from? The Radio Security Service's early successes at monitoring and decrypting the *Abwehr*'s prodigious radio traffic suggests that there may well have been a concentrated effort on Paris. The evidence comes chiefly from the Security Service, which has implicitly confirmed an impressively detailed knowledge of contemporary *Abwehr* preparations for espionage targeted against Britain. In the case of the double agent, Eddie Chapman, who underwent lengthy training in France before he was despatched to England in December 1942, the official historian admits that Chapman's progress was under constant surveillance through GCHQ's Sigint programme.[17] Indeed, MI5 was so well briefed when Chapman eventually dropped into Cambridgeshire that its case officers even knew the state of his dentures. Two other German spies, Lily Sergueiev (*Treasure*)[18] and Hans George (*Dragonfly*), shared the same *Abwehr* controller, Major Kliemann, who was based at the Hôtel Lutetia, the *Abstelle* headquarters in Paris. Not far away was the *Abstelle*'s radio training centre in the rue de l'Assomption, where several agents underwent training given by another *Luftwaffe* officer, Gerard Jacobi. Since these individuals and the location of their offices were known to British Intelligence, it is not improbable to assume that their signals came under scrutiny. And since it is known that Colonel Oscar Reile referred all decisions concerning deals with SOE personnel to his immediate superior in Berlin, it is equally likely that, if some of those exchanges took the form of encrypted radio traffic (as opposed to landline cable communications), they would have been intercepted and decrypted.

The same, however, cannot be said of the *Sicherheitsdienst*'s signals, for though the *Abwehr*'s main Enigma key, designated ISK by GCHQ, was read fairly consistently from December 1941 onwards, the Gestapo's equivalent, known as TGD, remained unbroken throughout the war. Thus, whatever Boemelburg confided to his senior in Berlin, Horst Kopkow, it would stay secret. Whatever the material that passed between Paris and Berlin, none of it has been released officially, and certainly none was disclosed at the relevant time to F Section. In fact, F Section only really had an opportunity to piece together its own story when SOE established an office after the Liberation at the Hôtel Cecil in Paris (and later at 37 Boulevard des Capucines). Buckmaster's principal assistant, Vera Atkins, also travelled to Germany to interview the survivors and interrogate the Germans involved.

According to some ex-prisoners, they were discouraged from asking questions about German penetration. Whether Buckmaster himself was fully aware of what had happened is open to doubt. As late as 1954 he was still insisting that only one circuit ever came under enemy control, despite the volume of damning evidence which had been produced in the French courts after the war, including, of course, Roger Bardet's trial in December 1949. Bardet was sentenced to death for collaboration, reprieved and released from prison in 1955.

As well as the operational miscalculations, F Section experienced difficulty in the area of policy and hardly demonstrated much political acumen when dealing with the Gaullists, Communists and others allied against the Nazis. Relations with the Free French were needlessly exacerbated by what appeared to be SOE's meddling in French internal politics. There were several incidents which heightened French suspicions, few more potent than F Section's persistent but futile attempts to persuade influential politicians to come to London. In September 1941 George Langelaan parachuted near Argenton-sur-Creuse to find Edouard Herriot, the former French Premier, and persuade him to come to London to lead a government-in-exile. Herriot refused, and Langelaan was arrested by the Vichy police soon afterwards. He was followed by Georges Dubourdin. Another equally frustrating attempt was made by France Antelme in June 1943. Then there was the embarrassing episode of *Radio Patrie*, a short-wave station which began broadcasting to France under the auspices of the Political Warfare Executive (PWE) in October 1942 and was forced to close down soon afterwards under pressure from de Gaulle, who complained that the bulletins were replete with propaganda hostile to him. Once again, F Section's fingerprints were all over the case. Two of the volunteer staff, and the principal offenders, had been recommended by *Carte* and had been escorted to London by Bodington after his inspection tour of CARTE in September. As we shall see, many more similar incidents were to mar SOE's delicate relations with the Free French.

The question arises that if F Section demonstrated such naïveté with the French, how did they fare against SIS? Accusations flew thick and fast after the war, especially from those who had been dropped straight into the hands of the Gestapo, but a more complex scenario emerged later which suggested that PROSPER had been deliberately sacrificed, either to enhance a deception plan linked to the invasion of Europe, or that the circuit had simply been the victim of a complicated feud between SOE and the ruthless head of SIS's French sections, Claude Dansey. Professor Foot was aware of the first proposition when he prepared his official history, *SOE in France*, and he took the opportunity to confirm that 'no use was made of SOE's work in France for any purposes of deception'.[19] The latter point, canvassed most recently by Robert Marshall in *All The King's Men* and James Rusbridger in *The Intelligence Game*, is harder to disprove because they portray *Gilbert* as having been the chief instrument of PROSPER's demise and insist that, as well as working for SOE and the *Sicherheitsdienst*, he was also a double agent under MI6's control. The evidence for this is thin to the point of being non-existent, apart from a few ambiguous remarks attributed to Dericourt about his working for what he termed the 'British Intelligence Service'. That foreigners failed to discriminate between the different branches of the British secret establishment during the war is understandable, especially when the initials SOE were rarely spoken. The *cognoscenti* sometimes referred to 'the racket', but few outsiders really understood the differing responsibilities of SOE and MI6, not to mention the numerous other parallel departments such as PWE, MI5, Security Intelligence Middle East (SIME) and the rest.

As F Section's survivors emerged from imprisonment and exchanged horror stories on their experiences, blame was directed at headquarters by some of the agents who had been caught; this was reciprocated by allegations from the Baker Street staff of breaches of elementary security. Since SOE was to be closed down in 1946, and most of the participants dispersed to their peacetime occupations, there was little opportunity for those with grievances to pursue them except through the medium of publication. Accordingly, a series of personal accounts has been published describing, with varying degrees of accuracy, how F Section prosecuted the war. Some, like the two volumes written by Buckmaster, pay full tribute to the bravery of the agents, while others have concentrated on the critical failures of INTERALLIÉ and PROSPER, and the unspeakably horrendous fates suffered by agents like Andrée Borrel and Noor Inayat Knan in the Nazi death camps at Natzweiler and Dachau.

The sad fact is that for all the sacrifices of 1942 and 1943, F Section approached the critical New Year of 1944 with the prospect of an Allied invasion, in a state of disarray, having seen most of its circuits wound up or penetrated by the enemy, and many of its key organisers in touch with the Germans, if not actually working for them, as can be seen in the list that follows of SOE-trained agents arrested in France.

SOE-trained Agents Arrested in France

*An asterisk indicates survived imprisonment.

Name	Codename	Circuit	Date of Arrival	Date of Arrest	Fate
G. W. Abbott			11 Feb. 1942	12 Feb. 1942	Colditz*
Jack Agazarian	*Marcel*	PROSPER	Dec. 1942	30 July 1943	Flossenbürg
Raoul Alexandre		SURVEYOR	7 Feb. 1944	7 Feb. 1944	
E. A. L. Allard		LABOURER	5 April 1944	April 1944	Buchenwald
Jean Amps	*Tomas*	PROSPER	1 Oct. 1943		
P. J. Aphlett			16 Aug. 1943		Flossenbürg
France Antelme	*Antoine*	DONKEYMAN	29 Feb. 1944	29 Feb. 1944	Gross Rosen
J. M. Aron	*Joseph*	AUTOGIRO		Nov. 1942	
Denis Barrett	*Honoré*	MINISTER	3 March 1943	July 1944	Buchenwald
Yvonne Baseden	*Odette*	SCHOLAR	18 March 1944	July 1944	Ravensbrück*
Francis Basin	*Laurent*	CARTE	21 Sep. 1942	18 Aug. 1943	Escaped
Alcide Beauregard		LACKEY	8 Feb. 1944	15 July 1944	Montluc
P. E. Bec		HEADMASTER	May 1944	16 June 1944	Killed in action
Yolande Beekman	*Mariette*	MUSICIAN	18 Sep. 1943	13 Dec. 1943	Dachau
Georges Begué	*George One*	AUTOGIRO	5 May 1941	24 Oct. 1941	
Robert Benoist	*Lionel*	CLERGYMAN	March 1944	18 June 1944	Buchenwald
Gustave Bieler	*Guy*	MUSICIAN	1 Nov. 1942	13 Dec. 1943	Shot
Denise Bloch	*Ambroise*	CLERGYMAN	2 March 1944	19 June 1944	Ravensbrück
Pierre Bloch	*Draftsman*	CORSICAN	6 Sep. 1941	Oct. 1941	Shot
Marcus Bloom	*Bishop*	PIMENTO	Nov. 1942	April 1943	
Andrée Borrel	*Denise*	PROSPER	25 Sep. 1942	24 June 1943	Natzweiler
André Bouchardon	*Narcisse*	SACRISTAN	19 Aug. 1943	23 Dec. 1943	Escaped
Noel Burdeyron	*Gaston*		9 July 1941	April 1942	Colditz*
Christopher Burney		AUTOGIRO	31 May 1942	Aug. 1942	Buchenwald*
Muriel Byck	*Violette*	VENTRILOQUIST	8 April 1944	May 1944	Died[1]
Robert Byerly		SURVEYOR	7 Feb. 1944	7 Feb. 1944	Gross Rosen
Bruce Cadogan			Sep. 1941	Oct. 1941	
Eric Cauchi	*Pedro*	STOCKBROKER	Aug. 1943	6 Feb. 1944	Shot
Blanche Charlet	*Christiane*	VENTRILOQUIST	1 Sep. 1942	24 Oct. 1942	Escaped
Peter Churchill	*Michel*	SPINDLE	27 Aug. 1942	April 1943	Survived
Marcel Clech	*Bastien*	INVENTOR	13 May 1943	19 Dec. 1943	
Georges Clement	*Edouard*	PARSON	July 1943	28 Nov. 1943	
Edward Coppin	*Oliver*	URCHIN	May 1943	23 April 1944	Executed

Name	Codename	Circuit	Date of Arrival	Date of Arrest	Fate
Roger Cottin	*Albert*	AUTOGIRO	13 May 1941	21 April 1942	Survived
Madeleine Damerment	*Solange*	BRICKLAYER	29 Feb. 1944	29 Feb. 1944	Dachau
Jean Dandicolle		VERGER	May 1944	7 July 1944	Shot
Georges Darling		PROSPER		25 June 1943	Shot
Marcel Défence	*Dédé*	SATIRIST	7 March 1944	7 March 1944	Gross Rosen
Alphonse Defendini		PRIEST	March 1944	March 1944	
François Deniset		SURVEYOR	7 Feb. 1944	7 Feb. 1944	Gross Rosen
Baron de St Genies	*Lucien*	SCHOLAR	18 March 1944	July 1944	Shot
J. T. J. Detal		DELEGATE	29 Feb. 1944	29 Feb. 1944	
Pierre de Vomécourt	*Lucas*	AUTOGIRO	13 May 1941	25 April 1942	Colditz*
Robert Dowlen	*Richard*	CHESTNUT	17 March 1942	31 July 1943	
Albert Dubois	*Hercule*	DONKEYMAN	14 April 1943	Nov. 1943	Buchenwald
Georges Dubourdin	*Alain*	DONKEYMAN	22 March 1943	March 1943	Executed
P. F. Duclos		DELEGATE	29 Feb. 1944	29 Feb. 1944	Gross Rosen
Comte du Puy		AUTOGIRO	6 Sep. 1941	April 1942	Colditz*
M. Escoute			Jan. 1944	Jan. 1944	Faulty drop
Jack Fincken		AUTOGIRO	Jan. 1942	25 April 1942	Colditz*
D. Finlayson	*Guillaume*	LIONTAMER	March 1944	March 1944	
Ernest Floege	*Alfred*	SACRISTAN	14 June 1943	Dec. 1943	Escaped
Marcel Fox	*Ernest*	BUTLER	23 March 1943	7 Sep. 1943	
Henri Frager	*Louba*	ARCHDEACON	March 1944	8 Aug. 1944	Buchenwald
H. H. Gaillot	*Ignace*	PARSON	July 1943	3 Feb. 1944	
François Garel	*Max*	BUTLER	23 March 1943	7 Sep. 1943	Buchenwald
P. A. H. Geelen		LABOURER	5 April 1944	April 1944	Buchenwald
C. Grover-Williams	*Sébastien*	CHESTNUT	31 May 1942	2 Aug. 1943	
Lt Guiraud	*André*	GLOVER	1944	1944	
J. T. Hamilton		SPRUCE	29 Dec. 1942	31 Dec. 1942	Gross Rosen
Charles Hayes	*Yves*	SCIENTIST	Nov. 1942	Oct. 1943	
Jack B. Hayes	*Victor*	CORSICAN	10 Oct. 1941	1941	Escaped
Mary Herbert	*Claudine*	SCIENTIST	31 Oct. 1942		Survived
Richard Héritier					Survived
Desmond Hubble		BENJOIN?	8 May 1944		Buchenwald
Charles Hudson	*Simon*	HEADMASTER	24 Sep. 1942	8 Oct. 1942	
Noor Inayat Khan	*Madeleine*	CINEMA	16 June 1943	8 Oct. 1943	Dachau
C. Janyk		JOCKEY		April 1944	Survived
George Jones	*Isadore*	HEADMASTER	24 Sep. 1942	23 May 1943	Escaped
Sydney Jones	*Félix/Elie*	INVENTOR	13 May 1943	19 Nov. 1943	

Name	Codename	Circuit	Date of Arrival	Date of Arrest	Fate
Claude Jumeau Kane[2]		CORSICAN	April 1943	April 1943	Died
Comte de Kergolay	*Joew*	OVERCLOUD	15 Oct. 1941	Dec. 1941	Survived
Peggy Knight	*Nicole*	DONKEYMAN	6 May 1944	1944	Survived
Henri Labit	*Leroy*	BASS	2 May 1942	May 1942	Suicide
E. Langard	*Dimu*	VAR	27 Feb. 1944	26 June 1944	Buchenwald
George Langelaan	*Langdon*		6 Sep. 1941	6 Oct. 1941	Survived
Maurice Lanis	*Colin*	LIONTAMER	2 March 1944	2 March 1944	
M. L. Larcher		VERGER	May 1944	8 July 1944	Shot
Jacques Latour		JOCKEY		April 1944	Survived
M. Leccia		LABOURER	5 April 1944	April 1944	Buchenwald
Marie Le Chene	*Adèle*	PLANE	Aug. 1943		Survived
P. L. Le Chene	*Grégoire*	PLANE	1 May 1942	Dec. 1942	Survived
Georges Ledoux	*Tir*				Survived
Jacques Ledoux		ORATOR	Feb. 1944	Feb. 1944	
Lionel Lee	*Mechanic*	PHONO	29 Feb. 1944	29 Feb. 1944	
L. Lee Graham			April 1943	April 1943	Survived
Cicely Lefort	*Alice*	JOCKEY	16 June 1943	Sep. 1943	Ravensbrück
Jean Le Harival		CORSICAN	10 Oct. 1941	1941	
Vera Leigh	*Simone*	INVENTOR	13 May 1943	30 Oct. 1943	Natzweiler
R. Lencement		TROMBONE	29 Aug. 1941		Survived
M. Lepage		LIONTAMER	March 1944	March 1944	
E. Lesout	*Tristan*	LIONTAMER	2 March 1944	2 March 1944	
Joel Letac	*Joe*	OVERCLOUD	15 Oct. 1941		Survived
Yves Letac			3 Feb. 1942		Survived
Edward Levine		DONKEYMAN	16 Nov. 1943	26 Nov. 1943	
Robert Lyon		ACOLYTE	10 May 1944		Escaped
John Macalister	*Valentin*	PROSPER	16 June 1943	18 June 1943	Buchenwald
G. McBain		LIONTAMER	March 1944	March 1944	
John McKenzie					
Claude Malraux	*Cicero*	SALESMAN	1943	25 Feb. 1944	
Jean Manesson		CONJURER	16 Nov. 1943	16 Nov. 1943	
P. M. Martinot		JOCKEY		April 1944	Survived
René Mathieu	*Aimé*	STATIONER	12 April 1944	1 May 1944	
Pierre Mattei	*Gaétan*	STATIONER	1944	Feb. 1944	
Albert Maugenet	*Benoit*	CONJURER	16 Nov. 1943	16 Nov. 1943	Collaborated
John A. Mayer		ROVER		25 May 1944	Buchenwald
François Michel	*Dispenser*	ARCHDEACON	Sep. 1943	Sep. 1943	Gross Rosen

Name	Codename	Circuit	Date of Arrival	Date of Arrest	Fate
Roger Milhaud	*Aimé*	STATIONER	1944	1944	
Gerry Morel			4 Sep. 1941	Oct. 1941	Escaped
Pierre Mulsant		MINISTER	3 March 1944	July 1944	Buchenwald
Eileen Nearne	*Rose*	WIZARD	2 March 1944	1944	Escaped
Isadore Newman	*Pépé*	SALESMAN	July 1943	25 Feb. 1944	
Alfred Newton	*Arthur*	GREENHEART	1 July 1942	April 1943	Survived
Harry Newton	*Hubert*	GREENHEART	1 July 1942	April 1943	Survived
Gilbert Norman	*Archambaud*	PROSPER	1 Nov. 1942	24 June 1943	Mauthausen
Orabona³			July 1942	July 1942	Faulty drop
Paul Pardi		CONJURER	16 Nov. 1943	16 Nov. 1943	
D. M. Pearson		PEDAGOGUE	Aug. 1944	1944	Gross Rosen
Marcel Pellay	*Paquebot*	COMBAT	22 July 1943	1943	Survived
Maurice Pertschuk	*Eugène*	PRUNUS	April 1942	April 1943	Buchenwald
Harry Peulevé	*Paul*	AUTHOR	17 Sep. 1943	21 Mar. 1944	Buchenwald*
Frank Pickersgill	*Bertrand*	PROSPER	16 June 1943	18 June 1943	Buchenwald
Eliane Plewman	*Gaby*	MONK	13 Aug. 1943	May 1944	Dachau
Alec Rabinovitch	*Arnaud*	BARGEE	2 March 1944	2 March 1944	
Brian Rafferty	*Dominique*	HEADMASTER	24 Sep. 1942	June 1943	Flossenbürg
Charles Rechermann					Buchenwald
Claude Redding			11 Feb. 1942	12 Feb. 1942	Colditz*
Lt Reeves⁴	*Olivier*	FARMER	13 June 1943	28 Nov. 1943	Collaborated
Elizabeth Reynolds	*Elizabeth*	MARKSMAN	18 Oct. 1943		Survived
Raymond Roche			19 Sep. 1941	Oct. 1941	Escaped
Lilian Rolfe	*Nadine*	HISTORIAN	5 April 1944	July 1944	Ravensbruck
Marcel Rousset	*Léopold*	BUTLER	23 March 1943	1943	Escaped
Diana Rowden	*Paulette*	ACROBAT	16 June 1943	Nov. 1943	Natzweiler
Yvonne Rudelatt	*Jacqueline*	PROSPER	July 1942	18 June 1943	Ravensbrück

According to official records, F Section sent 393 officers to France, of whom 119 were killed or arrested, and only seventeen survived German captivity. A total of 104 names appear on the F Section memorial at Valençay, but this list includes Lieutenants L. E. D. Bertheau (of AUTHOR) and J. Renaud (of DITCHER), who were locally recruited and commissioned in the field, and therefore strictly do not qualify for entry above which is limited to SOE personnel trained in Britain. In addition to the 173 named above should be added two unknown participants of SCULLION II who were captured but survived.

¹ Muriel Byck died of meningitis.

² No further details of Kane are available. For the sole reference to him see Cookridge's *Inside SOE* (p. 385).

³ Orabona was a wireless operator attached to RF Section.

⁴ Lieutenant Reeves 'is strongly suspected locally of having betrayed his commanding officer (Michael Trotobas) although he has been officially cleared in England of the charge of having wilfully done so' (Bourne-Paterson, *British Circuits in France 1941–4*, p. 50). Forty-five people were arrested when Trotobas was shot. By the Liberation, FARMER had lost fifty members shot by the enemy, eighty-five deported and assumed dead, and 200 killed in action, out of an estimated total membership of 8,000.

Name	Codename	Circuit	Date of Arrival	Date of Arrest	Fate
Roger Sabourin		PRIEST	2 March 1944	2 March 1944	Buchenwald
Odette Sansom	*Lise*	SPINDLE	31 Oct. 1942	April 1943	Survived
P. Sarrette		GONDOLIER	May 1944	5 Sep. 1944	Accident
A. L. Schock					Survived
A. Schwatschko		SHIPWRIGHT	Feb. 1944	7 June 1944	Killed in action
Henri Sevenet	*Rodolphe*	DETECTIVE		20 July 1944	Shot
A. P. Shaw	*Olive*	HECTOR	1944	1944	
Robert Sheppard	*Patrice*		June 1942	June 1942	Survived
Jean Simon	*Pedro*	TREASURER	June 1943	Feb. 1944	Shot
Octave Simon	*Badois*	SATIRIST	7 March 1944	7 March 1944	Gross Rosen
Jack Sinclair		MONK	6 March 1944	6 March 1944	
Charles Skepper	*Bernard*	MONK	May 1943	23 May 1944	Buchenwald
Maurice Southgate	*Hector*	STATIONER	Oct. 1943	1 May 1944	Survived
Albert Staggs		FARMER	18 Nov. 1942	Dec. 1943	Released
John Starr	*Bob*		May 1943	Nov. 1943	Survived
Arthur Steele	*Laurent*	MONK	19 June 1943	May 1944	Buchenwald
Brian Stonehouse	*Célestin*	DETECTIVE	1 July 1942	24 Oct. 1942	Survived
André Studler		HISTORIAN	1944	July 1944	Escaped
Francis Suttill	*Prosper*	PROSPER	2 Oct. 1942	23 June 1943	Saschenhaus
Violette Szabo	*Louise*	SALESMAN	5 April 1944	10 June 1944	Ravensbrück
P. R. Tessier		MUSICIAN	Dec. 1943	12 Dec. 1943	
Michael Trotobas	*Sylvestre*	FARMER	18 Nov. 1942	27 Nov. 1943	Shot
Denis Turberville	*Daniel*	CORSICAN	10 Oct. 1941	11 Oct. 1941	
Georges Turck	*Christophe*	CORSICAN	6 Aug. 1941	Oct. 1941	
P. S. Ullmann	*Alceste*	STOCKBROKER	14 April 1944	April 1944	Shot
François Vallee			1943	1943	
Ernest Wilkinson	*Alexandre*	PROSPER	6 June 1942	May 1943	Released
George Wilkinson	*Etienne*	HISTORIAN	1944	June 1944	Buchenwald
T. Winter		AQUATINT	12 Sep. 1942	12 Sept. 1942	Escaped
A. V. Woerther		WOODCUTTER	Aug. 1944	1944	Gross Rosen
Jean Worms	*Robin*	JUGGLER	12 Jan. 1943	1 July 1943	
Forest Yeo-Thomas	*Seahorse*	ASYMPTOTE	24 Feb. 1943	21 Mar. 1944	Buchenwald*
John C. Young	*Gabriel*	ACROBAT	May 1943	Nov. 1943	
Edward Zeff	*Georges 53*	HECKLER	April 1942		Survived
Zembsch-Schreve	*Pierre*	PIERRE-JACQUES		April 1944	Ravensbrück

6 · A Hot Humid Summer: SOE in North Africa and the Balkans

One of his tasks was to keep the peace between the intelligence departments – SOE, SIS, PWE – which were all quarrelling among themselves with the service departments and with the Foreign Office. Cairo – particularly in the hot humid summer – seemed to act as a catalyst to interdepartmental jealousies.

Ivor Porter, on the appointment of Oliver Lyttelton as Resident Minister of State at Cairo in 1941[1]

In the run-up to TORCH, the Allied invasion of North Africa in November 1942, SOE was given an opportunity to play a key role. After two years of retreat and defeat, Britain was finally ready to take the offensive and re-establish a presence in the Mediterranean in anticipation of a return to Europe. Strategically the undertaking made great sense, opening up the coast for operations against Italy and the Balkans; it also had the added advantage of demonstrating that the Allies could co-operate together and mount a really large-scale amphibious landing against a defended beach. It was to be a joint operation, under the command of Generals Eisenhower and Alexander, with the Americans playing the lead role, and would involve close liaison with the French, who, following their heavy naval losses at Oran and Dakar after the Royal Navy's ultimatum and bombardment, were naturally sensitive about British activities in this sector of the Mediterranean. In return, the British were conscious of French insecurity, especially after a courier from de Gaulle's headquarters, carrying highly secret documents relating to TORCH, was killed in September 1942. His Coastal Command Catalina aircraft had crashed off the Spanish coast near Cádiz and, according to the *Abwehr*'s messages intercepted at Bletchley, strenuous efforts had been made by the enemy to recover his papers. Fortunately the attempt failed, but the incident highlighted the rather casual attitude of the

Free French to a category of classified material which should never have left London.

Apart from the troubled relations with the Free French, there was another important obstacle to the Allied objective of making an amphibious landing in North Africa. GCHQ had reported the existence of a German infra-red device designed to spot shipping in the Straits of Gibraltar. Since more than eight hundred ships were to be used to transport 100,000 men to the beaches, including a British assault in the Mediterranean at Algiers and Oran, removal of the enemy's apparatus, which they had codenamed *Bodden*,[2] was deemed essential to the execution of TORCH. Accordingly, SOE was given the task of eliminating the transmitting station which had been established in a clifftop villa outside Tangier. This operation, code-named FALAISE, was executed by Edward Wharton-Tigar, a young accountant who had worked for Chester Beatty at the Trepca Mine but had not joined Section D,[3] and a locally recruited SOE agent, James Ponsonby, in the face of disapproval from Sir Samuel Hoare, the British Ambassador in Madrid. Hoare had set a high priority on his relations with Franco and was always determined that Major Richardson's H Section should not jeopardise them. Despite Hoare's objections, thirty-eight pounds of judiciously placed explosive eliminated the offending *Bodden* station, which happened to be located at 4 rue de Falaise, together with its German operators. Another scheme, to sabotage a French dredger destined for Brest, was less successful. The limpet mine, which had been carried to Tangier on 5 February 1942 by a diplomatic courier, exploded prematurely on the ferry and killed thirty-nine people, including eight Britons. Unlike FALAISE, when the Spanish authorities assumed that the Germans had been casualties of their own dangerous experiments, on this occasion the SIS Head of Station, Toby Ellis, had to take the blame and experienced a damaging round-up of his local agents. This did little to enhance the already strained relations between SOE and SIS.

SOE's principal office in the region was the Villa Lourdes in Gibraltar, run by Hugh Quennell, one of the many partners of the City solicitors Slaughter & May who had been recruited into SOE, with an undercover officer, P. J. Greensleeves, operating from Britain's only diplomatic premises in North Africa, inside Tangier's International Zone. In June 1941 he was replaced by Wharton-Tigar and (Dame) Barbara Salt, who was later to become a senior British diplomat. However, their task in North Africa was to be far from easy for, following the destruction of the French fleet at Mers-el-Kebir in July 1940 and the Vichy regime's subsequent refusal to deal with Britain, the movements of SOE's representatives had been somewhat restricted. This prompted Wharton-Tigar to take control of a network of twelve American vice-consuls, which covered Casablanca (LINCOLN), Algiers (YANKEE), Oran (FRANKLIN) and Tunis (PILGRIM), and which reported from March 1942 onwards to a base station in Tangier (MIDWAY). He also arranged for two OSS officers, the noted anthropologist Carleton Coon and Gordon Browne, to be trained in sabotage techniques by Charles MacIntosh[4] of H Section in Gibraltar, and to carry over quantities of arms and ammunition in the US Consul's diplomatic pouch. Browne was an archaeologist, who had spent much time in Morocco and had compiled a military dictionary for the army. Before their arrival in North Africa, under consular cover, Browne and Coon had been approached by Reginald Teague-Jones (operating under his usual alias of Major Ronald Sinclair) on behalf of BSC in the hope that they would work in Tangier for SIS under commercial cover. Both had rejected the offer, only to find themselves in OSS and undergoing training at the hands of the British. For Coon much of MacIntosh's tuition would have been superfluous as he had been one of the first graduates of STS 103, at Oshawa on Lake Ontario. Their radio personnel, mainly locally recruited Frenchmen, were also sent over to Gibraltar to be indoctrinated into the techniques of operating clandestine transmitters. Coon was later to reflect on the inter-agency rivalries he witnessed in North Africa before the invasion:

All in all I may say that I have never met anywhere a finer group of men than the SOE outfit, and that I would consider it a privilege and a pleasure to go anywhere and take on any job with them. Unfortunately I cannot say the same for SIS. This British intelligence service holds itself aloof from the SOE as from us, and it is a question whether the worst enemy of the SOE is the German or the SIS. In Tangier the SIS was headed by Colonel Ellis, a man of no scruples, universally detested by the British, Americans, Arabs and everyone else. There would be no point in my listing his malefactions here, all I need say for the record is that our relations with him were formal, aloof, mistrustful. He tried on several occasions to impede our operations, and if he had succeeded he might have completely ruined our preparations for the landing and given the show away.[5]

The US involvement in the preparation of TORCH was to be the key to the entire operation, for the Americans managed twelve consulates along the coast and were enthusiastic novices in the field of secret intelligence. An Office of the Co-ordination of Information had been created by President Roosevelt in June 1941 and had opened a branch in Grosvenor Square five months later. In the summer of 1942 the OCI acquired a new title, the Office of Strategic Services, but had remained under the leadership of

Colonel 'Wild Bill' Donovan. A noted trial lawyer by training and a much decorated war hero from his experiences in France in 1917, Donovan was close to the President. Reflecting the British division of responsibilities, OSS was divided into Special Operations (SO) and Secret Intelligence (SI). Both were to cut their teeth in North Africa, where a US marine, Colonel William Eddy, had taken up residence as naval attaché at the American Legation in Tangier. Eddy, who sported a wooden leg after having been wounded in the First World War in France, was a remarkable character, having once been head of the English Department at Cairo University. He spoke French and Arabic fluently, was a distinguished author and scholar, and harboured an innate distrust of SIS. However, he suppressed his anti-British sentiments long enough to install a wireless set in a sumptuous mountain-top villa, the Jama el-Mokhra, borrowed from a former British consul-general in Zanzibar, John Sinclair. From this strategic site Eddy was able to relay signals across the Straits and supervise the rest of the network with Wharton-Tigar.

The origins of SOE/OSS co-operation dated back only to June 1942, when Hambro had thrashed out a blueprint for future collaboration with Donovan and his Deputy Director of Operations, Preston Goodfellow. The Americans had stayed in London for a week and the resulting document, dated 26 June 1942, had clearly divided the world into two separate spheres of influence.[6] In areas where there was an overlap of British and American interests, such as North Africa, a compromise had been reached. This meant that Eddy would be appointed Chief of Special Operations in North Africa 'to co-ordinate the activities of SOE and SO'. This treaty was confirmed during the summer by the Chiefs of Staff on both sides of the Atlantic and finalised in Washington in October, when George Taylor flew to Washington to negotiate the details with Donovan. The outcome was an arrangement whereby the two organisations would collaborate on TORCH and, thereafter, would run training, radio and headquarters facilities on a joint basis. Unfortunately, owing to an administrative lapse, Taylor's report failed to get circulated in Baker Street. Worse still, SO's senior officer in London, Colonel John Gunther, had initiated plans for separate headquarters in North Africa for the French and Mediterranean theatres. It was the latter that prevailed, which led to the creation of an exclusively OSS headquarters at the Villa Rosa, a palatial building in Algiers, and OSS training camps at Ain Taya and Djebel Hallouf.

Accompanying TORCH, albeit discreetly so as not to inflame French sensibilities, were to be two SOE contingents. The first, codenamed BRANDON, was destined for Tunisia and led by Colonel Alexander Anstruther, with Francis Brooks Richards (from the Helford River) as his assistant. The other, MASSINGHAM, was headed by John Munn from the Training Section, accompanied by an operations officer, (Sir) Douglas Dodds-Parker (from AL),[7] who was to succeed him in January 1943, and two former merchant bankers, David Keswick and (Sir) Francis Glyn. This was followed by a larger team despatched soon afterwards to act as a forward base for the Mediterranean theatre's new section, designated AMF. Also known under the cover title of 'Inter-Service Signal Unit 6', it established itself in a comfortable villa at Cap Matifou, ten miles east of Algiers. A training camp was then constructed by Major Rucker on a 100-acre beach resort, the Club des Pins, fifteen miles west of Algiers near Staoueli at Sidi Ferruch. Close by, on an airfield located at Blida, Ray Wooler, a former Canadian car salesman, who had been Chief Instructor at Dunham Massey (STS 51a) and had devised the parachute course for SOE at RAF Ringway, set up a similar scheme which was to teach the rudiments to several hundred agents. At Baker Street, the London end of MASSINGHAM was to be handled by Major E. H. Sherren.

MASSINGHAM's delicate existence, scarcely tolerated by the local French regime under Admiral Jean Darlan, was transformed on Christmas Eve 1942 when the latter was assassinated by an SOE weapons instructor, Lieutenant Fernand Bonnier de la Chapelle, who had been seconded to Ain Taya. The pro-Nazi Darlan had been Vice-Premier of the Vichy Government and had subsequently been put in command of the Vichy forces by Pierre Laval. Darlan happened to have been in Algiers when the invasion had occurred and had quickly decided to co-operate with the Allies. His previous politics, however, made him an awkward supporter for the British and American Governments to deal with, and he certainly complicated their relations with de Gaulle, who was deeply suspicious of him. His assassin, de la Chapelle, and his accomplice, Captain Gilbert Sabatier, had been assigned to MASSINGHAM and had been issued with revolvers on David Keswick's authority. It was one of these that de la Chapelle had used to shoot the hated Darlan. A summary court-martial was held almost immediately and a French firing squad shot de la Chapelle two days later. Even as he was led to his execution, before dawn on Boxing Day, the twenty year old refused to say where he had obtained the gun or to name his co-conspirators. Sabatier, who went missing after the murder, was arrested on 4 January 1943 and charged with supplying de la Chapelle with his gun and plotting to overthrow the state. Somehow the British negotiated his release and the entire matter was discreetly dropped. For its part OSS closed the camp at Ain Taya and was unable to operate any independent training facility until January 1944, when Station P opened near Algiers. This was to expand three months later and move to Chrea, where several dozen French recruits were to undergo Special Operations training in parachuting and associated tradecraft.

SOE complicity in the assassination has never been established, but the incident certainly did not conflict with British policy and actually helped the Allies in their dealings with the Vichy Government.[8] According to Sir Alexander Cadogan's diaries, he noted on 14 November 1942, 'We shall do no good till we've killed Darlan'; and six days after the assassination, he 'went to see Pound to arrange telegram to Cunningham to deny charges that the Secret Service was in any way connected with Darlan murder'.[9] The first entry demonstrates a willingness to contemplate drastic action against Darlan, whose right-wing politics were alienating the Communist resistance cells, even if the second appears to show that there was no British involvement. However, one unexplained aspect to the affair was the unusual appearance of Stewart Menzies in Algiers over the Christmas period. Fred Winterbotham recalls that he lunched with Georges Ronin and Louis Rivet, of the *Deuxième Bureau* and the *Service de Renseignements* respectively, in a villa only 'a few hundred yards away' from the scene. 'With the coffee came the news that Darlan had been shot,' he wrote. 'They could not have cared less.'[10]

Whether this is evidence of genuine indifference or traces of a plot is unclear, but this is the only moment that Menzies is known to have travelled abroad throughout the entire war. Whatever brought him to Algiers must have been more compelling than the prospect of being reunited with two senior French intelligence officers who had escaped from the German occupation of the Vichy zone. Both were to fly to London soon anyway. And whilst SIS would have been very unlikely to conduct an operation of such political sensitivity in conjunction with SOE, it is the case that the relationship between the two organisations was never better than in North Africa. Dodds-Parker got on well with Colonel Trevor-Wilson, his SIS counterpart, and confirms the level of co-operation that was achieved:

A welcome development in those weeks was the spontaneous agreement by the British Special Service heads in Algiers to hold a weekly meeting. We had all seen the difficulties flowing from interdepartmental jealousies in London and Cairo. None of us had professional careers to advance. Agreed approaches to our Allies were vital, first to the Americans, then to the French, and later to all the others. So SOE's voluminous Intelligence was made over to MI6. Priorities over use of aircraft were agreed between us.[11]

Dodds-Parker was certainly never intimidated by SIS. In fact, he had been asked to join two years earlier, but, on Peter Fleming's advice, had 'politely declined the invitation, saying [he] wished to do something active'.[12]

MASSINGHAM's main role was as a means of facilitating access to southern France and, accordingly, it accommodated a sub-branch of F Section, under the command of Jacques de Guélis, Buckmaster's briefing officer, who had himself already completed a successful mission into occupied France. Transport to France was provided by 138 Squadron, which flew out a Flight for every period of the full moon, and Gerald Holdsworth arrived with his crew of unconventional sailors from Cornwall. In addition, the Free French navy provided Captain L'Herminier and his submarine *Casabianca* for clandestine landings and the Royal Navy supplied Captain Fawkes and a depot ship, HMS *Maidstone*, together with the occasional use of a submarine, HMS *Clyde*. De Guélis stayed at MASSINGHAM's headquarters until October 1943, when Francis Brooks Richards took over the Mediterranean Section, AMF, and transformed it from a mirror image of F Section to one of RF, staffed entirely by Gaullists, with John Anstey running MASSINGHAM's administration and Michael Mason, a former Section D hand in the Balkans, supervising operations. Communications, in the capable hands of Bill Corbett, maintained a radio link both to London and to some of the circuits in southern France. Later another forward base, codenamed RING-LET, was established by Donald Hamilton-Hill near the French colonial airfield at Protville in Tunisia.[13]

In December 1943 the wasteful duplication of dual SOE–OSS activities was reduced by the introduction of Special Operations Mediterranean, designated SO/M, a joint co-ordinating section under the skilful leadership of Dodds-Parker, who, after the war, was to be elected to Parliament. SO/M was later to move from Algiers to Caserta, via Mola di Bari, as the war progressed. Dodds-Parker went to Brindisi, leaving Bartholomew Pleydell-Bouverie at Algiers, where he was later succeeded by Lord Harcourt.

One of MASSINGHAM's most impressive achievements was the liberation of Corsica, which was brought about with the aid of *Cesari*, a gendarme named Colonna d'Istria who organised the local resistance, known after the local undergrowth as the *maquis*, a term that was to become synonymous with anti-Nazi guerrillas. Corsica also accommodated one of SOE's several forward operating centres. The BALACLAVA mission, led by Andrew Croft, who had previously distinguished himself in the rather colder climes of the Scandinavian Section, consisted of a training camp, set up at Calvi, and an agent-holding facility which was established in a citadel overlooking the Gulf of St Florent, a few miles from Bastia. SOE's role was to infiltrate agents on to the island in advance of the main Allied forces and to undertake the kind of reconnaissance missions that SIS might have expected to conduct.

Following success in Corsica, MASSINGHAM acted as a co-ordinating centre for operations conducted during the invasion of Sicily, in which Italian Americans recruited by OSS played an important role. Algiers was also to be the base for a first, apparently disastrous, infiltration of northern Italy. SOE's Italian (J) Section, run by Major Roseberry in London, had depended largely upon the energy of Jock McCaffery, then under diplomatic cover in the British Legation in Berne. He had established contact with anti-Fascist Italian partisans in the north, but clearly Switzerland could not be used as a jumping-off point for operations. Indeed, it was suspected, correctly, that the efficient Italian military intelligence service, SIM, had penetrated some of the circuits and run its members as double agents. Although the Italians had not made much of a reputation for themselves on the battlefield, their security apparatus had proved itself to be ruthlessly efficient, both at home and in occupied France.

Unable to operate from the north, SOE attempted to initiate operations from North Africa and started with Richard Mallaby, who was parachuted into Lake Maggiore, only to be arrested immediately by the *Carabinieri*, the Italian police. This was a disappointing start for J Section, but, despite his maltreatment, Mallaby was to enable the Italians to switch sides. In July 1943 Marshal Pietro Badoglio, the fiercely anti-Nazi Chief of Staff, succeeded Mussolini as Premier and made the first overtures to the Allies to negotiate a surrender. He sent an emissary, General Guiseppe Castellano, to make contact with the British in Madrid, which led to a secret meeting in Lisbon in mid-August where terms were discussed. Kenneth Strong and Major Roseberry represented the British at this initial gathering, with Walter Bedell Smith looking after American interests. A further secret meeting took place at MASSINGHAM's headquarters, where matters were finalised and a direct channel of communications was opened to Badoglio via Mallaby's wireless set. Mallaby was released from prison in Milan, reunited with his transmitter and escorted to the Quirinale in Rome, where he maintained a radio link with SOE Algiers, thus ensuring that Badoglio had advance warning of the Allied invasion at Salerno on 9 September 1943 and could time his announcement of the Italian armistice to have maximum effect. Codenamed MONKEY, the plan worked to perfection, and the day after the landings Badoglio and King Victor Emmanuel made their way to

Brindisi to form a new government. Three days later it declared war on Germany and passed command of some 350 aircraft belonging to the Italian air force over to the Allies.

● ● ● ● ● ●

After the invasion of Italy, MASSINGHAM sent a detachment, codenamed MARYLAND, to Monopoli on the Adriatic, while Cairo, now under the overall command of General William A. Stawell, formerly the Deputy Director of Intelligence at the War Office, despatched a unit to Bari, just down the coast. Both of these centres were to play an important part not just in the liberation of German-occupied Italy, but in Northern and Eastern Europe as well. Polish and Czech operations were conducted from Monopoli by Henry Threlfall's Force 139, which established an operational base at Latiano and a training school at Ostuni. Also at Monopoli was No. 1 Special Force, commanded by Gerald Holdsworth, which was later to move north to Siena.[14] Logistics were handled by Brigadier Miles's Force 333, another offshoot of SOE Cairo, now renamed Force 133. Located at Torre di Mare, it was conveniently close to the RAF airfields at Apulia and Brindisi, which were also used as supply routes to Albania, Yugoslavia and points east. The small harbour at Monopoli also accommodated the Adriatic flotilla of SOE's private navy, under the command of (Sir) Morgan Morgan-Giles, which was later to operate from Naples as well. Previously, Eastern Mediterranean naval operations had been centred at Haifa, the headquarters of the innocent-sounding Levant Fishing Patrol. As well as a fleet of inshore fishing vessels, SOE also had the use of fast MTBs, which could race across to the Albanian coast to collect agents. It was on this route that (Sir) Anthony Quayle, an actor in later life, distinguished himself. He recalled that 'no one at HQ could tell us much about Albania – chiefly because no one at HQ knew much about the situation themselves'.[15]

MARYLAND was to be exceptionally industrious, considering its limited foundations, which, for the first few months, consisted of a single liaison with the resistance in Rome, codenamed RUDDER. By November 1943 this had been transformed into six separate missions and, within a year, No. 1 Special Force had despatched thirty-seven British officers and seventeen J Section missions behind enemy lines in the northern half of the country.

In addition to the above, the German Section's Austrian sub-section, run by Miss Graham-Stamper, operated from Italy under cover of 'No. 6 Special Force', and 'Force 266' concealed the activities of SOE Cairo's Albanian sub-section at Bari, then headed by Captain Watrous and John Eyre. The situation in Albania was, as Quayle has said, virtually unknown to the Allies. The country had been under Axis occupation since Easter 1939, when Mussolini had invaded, forcing King Zog and his family to flee to Greece. Since then Julian Amery had plotted from Belgrade for Section D, and Fanny Hasluck had formed the nucleus of an Albanian Section by teaching a handful of volunteers about the country and its fiercely tribal people. Since the invasion of Yugoslavia, and the loss of the SIS station in the British Legation in Belgrade, there had been no news from the capital Tirana. Amery recalls that, in preparing for a reconnaissance mission, SOE

were wholly in the dark as to the situation in Albania, and did not even know for certain whether an Albanian resistance movement existed at all. Thus, to the sufficient dangers of an incursion into enemy territory would be added the anxieties of a journey into the unknown.[16]

SOE's first mission to Albania was CONSENSUS, when Billy McLean and David Smiley parachuted into northern Greece on 17 April 1943 intending to walk across the frontier. With them was a small team which included Lieutenant Garry Duffy of the Royal Engineers, who was a demolition expert, and a wireless operator, Corporal Williamson. Their interpreter, an Albanian named Elmaz, decided at the last minute to abandon the mission, so he was interned at a special camp in the Sudan. Despite this setback CONSENSUS landed safely in Epirus, linked up with John Cook of SOE's Greek Section and set up a base at the headquarters of the nearest British Military Mission, headed by Major Guy Micklethwaite. CONSENSUS then undertook a hazardous trek across the mountains into Albania, where, on the second attempt late in June 1943, contact was made with Enver Hoxha, the French-educated Communist guerrilla leader. Once relations had been established with him, by a series of air drops to equip his men, permission was granted by Hoxha for the installation of a British Military Mission. Smiley remembers that he

got on well with Hoxha, even though he was inclined to bluster and lose his temper at our endless meetings. I took delight in teasing him about his politics, and the more Communist propaganda he aimed at me, the more right-wing, capitalist and imperialist I became.[17]

The main British Military Liaison Officer, Brigadier 'Trotsky' Davies, parachuted into Albania with a full headquarters team, dropped from two aircraft based at Benina, to a reception committee organised by CONSENSUS. A couple of nights later Alan Hare arrived with the remainder of the contingent. In July two RAF officers, Tony Neel and Andy Hands, were dropped and then, in August 1943, four teams were launched in two Halifaxes on the same day from Derna: SCULPTOR, led by Major Bill Tilman; SCONCE, headed by Major George Seymour; SAPLING, commanded by Major Gerry Field; and STEPMOTHER, consisting of Peter Kemp.[18] Together these missions, attached to large mixed bands of Communist irregulars, Italian deserters and Bulgarian stragglers, harried the occupying forces by setting ambushes and organising raids on local enemy garrisons. Although none of the actions by themselves led to any general collapse of the occupation, the Germans were obliged to waste precious resources at a critical time by strengthening an area that had virtually no strategic value.

By the time McLean and Smiley had been extracted in November 1943, by MTB from the Albanian coast to Bari, SOE's presence in Albania was quite considerable. Richard Riddell and Anthony Simcox were flown in to replace them, and by the end of April the following year Smiley was back, on CONSENSUS II, this time accompanied by Amery. In addition, John Hibberdine had been dropped in December with Lieutenants Merritt and Hibbert. Unfortunately, none of these operations was achieved without casualties. Two Halifaxes crashed in Albania while approaching their drop zones, killing all their crews and two entire SOE missions. Gerry Field blew himself up with high explosives while fishing, and Colonel Arthur Nicholls died of gangrene. SCONCE's wireless operator, Bombardier Hill, was killed by enemy action and Trooper Roberts of STEPMOTHER died of exposure after he had been captured and had managed to escape. Brigadier Davies was also captured, on 8 January 1944, along with Jim Chesshire, Captain F. Trayhorn and his RAF sergeant, a former rear gunner named Smith. Another significant loss was Philip Leake, killed in a German air raid six weeks after he had landed in May 1944.

Although Davies was the most senior SOE officer to be captured in the Balkans, his knowledge of SOE's operations was very limited. A regular officer, he had been mystified by his selection for clandestine work and, until he had arrived in Cairo, he had believed that he was destined for Yugoslavia. However, the same could not be said of Nicholls, who had been Gubbins's Chief of Staff in London and had been destined to take over SOE Cairo from Keble. Davies recalls that Nicholls 'was anxious not to be taken prisoner, as he had been in the organisation in London, and knew much of the secret side of Special Forces. He knew what the German Gestapo were capable of doing to captured SOE officers, and to what limits they went in interrogating prisoners.'[19] Davies himself, though badly wounded, endured Mauthausen concentration camp and Colditz to be liberated in 1945. The question arises as to whether Nicholls was even remotely suited to his task. He had no previous knowledge of the Balkans and, until he had been to SOE's Special Training School at Ramat David near Nazareth, had no parachute experience.

In comparison to the three other brigadiers leading British Military Missions in the region, Myers (in Greece) and Maclean and Armstrong (in Yugoslavia), Davies was also a novice. Nor did he inspire confidence among his subordinates. When he dropped into Albania, where ammunition and all the basic necessities of life such as food were at a premium, he arrived complete with all the bureaucratic paraphernalia needed to run a regular battalion, including a clerk equipped with a typewriter. Moreover, his diplomatic skills were not all they might have been. Two veterans of his command, David Smiley and Peter Kemp, recall an awkward discussion led by Davies with a bemused Enver Hoxha regarding British regimental connections. The Communist guerrilla chief could not understand why officers from units with obvious royal connections, such as the Royal Horse Guards and the Royal Scots Greys, were fighting to preserve Socialism. Davies went through the list of his officers' embarrassingly smart regiments and ended by reassuring Hoxha that his own, the Manchester Regiment, was thoroughly plebeian.

SOE personnel sent to Albania endured appalling privations and, whatever else, perpetuated the strategic fiction that the Balkans was the probable target for an Allied thrust straight into Germany. This scenario, ever popular with Churchill, was never a likely prospect, but the German High Command failed to appreciate the strength of instinctive opposition articulated by the British Chiefs of Staff and the Americans, based on their unhappy experience in the First World War. In consequence a disproportionate number of Axis units were kept tied up in South-East Europe by what amounted to a tiny group of Allied liaison officers attached to a rather larger number of guerrillas, who, it must be recognised, spent almost as much of their time fighting each other as engaging the common enemy. On the political front SOE failed to dissuade the disparate factions involved from participating in what amounted to a civil war in Albania and Yugoslavia, and in both cases abandoned the respective monarchs, King Zog and King Peter, having initially appeared to have backed the royalist governments-in-exile. In Albania and Yugoslavia, which had both been created after the chaos of the First World War, SOE's logistical support contributed to eventual Communist supremacy; the same nearly happened in Italy and Greece. In Hungary, Bulgaria and Romania the outcome was the establishment of totalitarian regimes, although SOE participation in those countries was on a much more limited scale.

Predictably, SOE's experience in Albania included friction with both

SIS and OSS. Smiley and McLean fell out with a representative of the former, a Greek who called himself Tony Corsair, when one of their supply drops was hijacked. Perhaps unwisely they had confided their signal system to Corsair, who intercepted the containers 'and used the weapons for his own purposes'.[20] Relations with the Americans were strained because SOE 'had refused to co-operate with OSS agents unless they accepted British command and used British communications'.[21] OSS was unwilling to accept these conditions, so no SO teams were ever despatched to Albania. Instead, some five SIS missions were sent, the first of which, TANK, arrived on 17 November 1943 by an SIS-sponsored motorboat from Italy and based itself in a cave by the sea. This was obliged to withdraw three months later following enemy activity in the area and the ill-health of the group's three members. They were replaced by BIRD in March, which provided a reception committee for three further Secret Intelligence teams, all of which remained with the Communist guerrillas until Tirana was liberated. OSS's official historian, Kermit Roosevelt, had some hard words for the lack of British enthusiasm for the SI Division's efforts:

The principal difficulty encountered by SI/Albania was its lack of control over transportation ... Support of US teams by the Balkan Air Force (British) was unreliable throughout. After months of waiting had beset several missions, the head of the Albanian desk unsuccessfully proposed, as had sections chiefs in other areas, the establishment of an OSS air unit to obviate such delays.[22]

Several of those who emerged from Albania subsequently wrote about their experiences: Julian Amery in *Sons of the Eagle*, Peter Kemp in *No Colours or Crest*, David Smiley in *Albanian Assignment*, 'Trotsky' Davies in *Illyrian Adventure* and Anthony Quayle in *A Time to Speak*, and Xan Fielding, himself a member of SOE's Greek Section, has recounted Billy McLean's adventures in *One Man in His Time*. Squadron Leader Neel's memoirs, though written, have yet to be published. All have the common theme of mismanagement at SOE headquarters in Cairo and Bari, and display great affection for the guerrilla bands with whom they lived and fought.

After the war SIS misinterpreted the loyalty expressed by some former comrades-in-arms and employed some previous members of SOE's Albanian sub-section to subvert Hoxha. Alan Hare, John Hibberdine, David Smiley, Dayrell Oakley-Hill, Anthony Northrop, Peter Kemp and Julian Amery all played active parts in mounting an ill-fated clandestine offensive against Tirana in 1949. Blame for the débâcle has often been attributed to Kim Philby's duplicity, but the reality is that SIS's post-war planners underestimated the determination of the Albanians to defend themselves, and even a despotic government, from external interferences. The first three missions sent into Albania by SIS overland from Greece or across the Adriatic suffered only minimal casualties, and it was not until the CIA embarked upon large-scale air drops, employing émigrés trained at a major camp in Germany, that the Communists inflicted a really heavy toll on the infiltrators. Most were captured and then subjected to a show trial in Tirana, which ended in executions or long terms of imprisonment. The prospects of those that completed their mission and tried to leave the country were not much better. Both the Yugoslav and Greek authorities were hostile to the scheme and refused to co-operate with SIS or the CIA. The whole project was finally abandoned late in 1951, leaving Albania to Hoxha, who ensured that it remained a political and economic backwater for the next half century.

•   •   •   •   •   •

In Yugoslavia SOE's controversial decision to abandon Mihailovic in favour of Tito's partisans had led to almost total Communist domination of the anti-Axis guerrilla forces. Politically the country encompassed several quite distinct religions, ethnic and nationalist groups, the largest being the Serbs, but the Axis had exploited local nationalism by granting Croatia its nominal independence. By concentrating Allied aid on Tito's men, his forces grew, at Mihailovic's expense, into a formidable army. The very last British presence with Mihailovic's forces was Brigadier Armstrong's mission, which was finally extracted in May 1944 by 267 Squadron, leaving liaison with the Cetniks entirely in the hands of a small OSS team, which was itself withdrawn in October 1944.

Of the SOE personnel sent to help the anti-Communist Cetniks, relatively few were around to catch the flight to Italy because of the extraordinarily high attrition rate. The first mission to arrive, DISCLAIM, on 5 February 1942 was handed over to the Germans three days later. Captain Morgan's mission, dropped 'blind' on 15 April 1943, suffered a similar fate, having been captured by Bulgarian troops as soon as it had landed. None of its members was ever heard of again. A monocled New Zealander, Lieutenant Micky Hargreaves, and his Polish companion, Captain 'Nash', also came to grief. The Pole had been killed instantly by a hand-grenade, but Hargreaves was to survive the Gestapo's brutality after his capture and was liberated from Oflag 4C by the Americans in April 1945. Captain Hawksworth, who had landed on 20 May 1943, and his entire mission of five British personnel had been wiped out by Bulgarians. Terence Atherton, the leader of HYDRA, had been murdered for his gold bullion in April 1942;

Paul Pavlic was killed in a German ambush; Major Neil Selby had been captured and then shot while attempting to escape; and Bill Stuart, the SIS representative on TYPICAL, SOE's pathfinding mission to Tito in May 1943, had died in an air raid which wounded Deakin and Tito. In addition, several of the wireless operators had died, including Sergeant Blackmore, Lieutenant Smith and Leading Aircraftman Thompson from FUGUE. Captain Vercoe, who had been severely injured in a bad parachute landing in September 1943, was captured the following March and then repatriated while still on crutches in January 1945. Three other prisoners survived the war: Captain Watts of the Royal Tank Corps and his two sergeants, Cornwall and Robinson, were caught by Bulgarian troops as they landed and received harsh treatment from the Gestapo, but they emerged alive. Thus, in comparison to the missions sent to Tito's partisans, very few SOE liaison officers lived to commend Mihailovic.

The American involvement in Yugoslavia was quite substantial and much greater than the effort put into Albania. This in part was due to OSS's determination not to be stifled by SOE, which insisted that it 'use SOE communications and SOE code'.[23] Furthermore, the British 'opposed any independent SI operations in Yugoslavia',[24] and this manifested itself in the difficulties SI had in obtaining flights into the country, compared to the minimal delays experienced by their SO colleagues. In fact, the first two SI missions, ALUM and AMAZON, did not get off the ground until 26/27 December 1943 and were then delivered to the wrong place. A navigational error left three of the seven OSS personnel to drop into a camp of pro-Axis Croatian White Guards. Fortunately, they were able to escape and complete their mission without further incident, even if ALUM's leader, who was himself of Yugoslav descent, demonstrated a strong pro-partisan bias.

Exasperated by the British obstruction, and particularly SOE's negative attitude to an independent OSS wireless net, OSS resorted to the simple expedient of redesignating SO missions to the SI division, and thereby excluding them from the SOE/OSS agreement of June 1942.

The first OSS teams were parachuted to Mihailovic and Tito respectively on 18 and 22 August 1943; by October the following year this figure had escalated to forty OSS officers in fifteen different missions. However, it soon became apparent to them all that both the partisans and the Cetniks were only interested in American weapons, and not in US leadership or advice, thus obliging the OSS men in the field to adopt an entirely different role:

The SO men became in effect intelligence officers and were instructed to send in enemy battle order, economic information, and political and military intelligence on the resistance. Lack of SI training was evident on political and economic reporting. In general, the SO officers had little conception of economic intelligence, and sent none. Their political appreciations compared unfavourably with those prepared by their British colleagues. Understandably, they usually supported the groups they were living and fighting with. Liaison officers with the Cetniks favoured the Cetniks, while those with the Partisans supported the Partisans. Even more unreliable were agents of Yugoslav descent, who usually were predisposed to one side or the other and reported the situation in moral black and white.[25]

Some who survived the Yugoslav mountain battles were not to see the end of the war. John Sehmer was shot by the Germans during a mission in Czechoslovakia, and Anthony Hunter was killed in Normandy. Major Slim Farrish of OSS was later to die in Albania, and David Russell was to disappear in Romania.

These appalling casualties were insignificant compared to those inflicted upon the civilian population in reprisals, and the internecine feuds. Jasper Rootham, of EXCERPT, recalls the consequences of an attack on the Danube in October 1943, which had left the German skipper of the *Centaur* shot dead and the river traffic temporarily disrupted: 150 of Mihailovic's sympathisers were executed in Belgrade. 'For this sacrifice of innocent lives no military objective of comparable importance had been achieved and we knew well that it was we ourselves who forced the action.'[26]

The campaign in Yugoslavia was one of contradictions. Most of the missions, particularly to Mihailovic's liaison officers, were dreadfully ill-equipped and ill-prepared, and the choice of personnel was quite eccentric. When, for example, there was a determined effort to send in reinforcements during the spring of 1943, the majority of SOE's Serbo-Croat speakers were Canadians and members of the Communist Party.[27] Two of FUNGUS's three agents had fought in the Spanish Civil War, and HOATHLEY I consisted entirely of miners from Quebec. About twenty-eight Canadian or American immigrants returned to fight in their homeland, of whom five disappeared, and at least three chose to remain in Yugoslavia after the war, taking jobs in the Communist regime, evidently undeterred by the appalling massacres that followed Tito's take-over.

Even William Jones, the one-eyed Canadian veteran of the First World War, who parachuted into Slovenia with no knowledge of the language or country and little experience apart from a course at STS 102, at Ramat David, was smitten by the Communists. He spent a year with the partisans before being brought back to Bari, where he got to work on 'a rather outspoken book on the political manoeuvrings of the British in Yugoslavia', according to Major Lindsay Rogers, who completed three SOE missions with the partisans as a surgeon. 'I heard a year afterwards that he was still trying to get his book published and still trying to get home to Canada, but unfortunately a passage at that time "could not be given".'[28] Jones eventually made his way to Edinburgh, where he campaigned for the Labour Party during the 1945 general election, and then returned to Ontario, where he continued to maintain contact with Belgrade, and published *Twelve Months with Tito's Partisans*.[29]

Several of those who fought with the Cetniks and the partisans have written accounts of their experiences, with varying degrees of bitterness. Certainly many of the SOE personnel who managed to return to Bari held strong views on what was perceived to be mismanagement in Cairo, if not ruthless political manipulation. Understandably, men in the field could not keep up with the bewildering changes which took place back at headquarters. In April 1944 General Stawell had arrived in Bari as head of Special Operations Mediterranean, of which the Yugoslav and Albanian sub-sections became part, under the cover title Force 266. The Polish and Czech sub-section was referred to as Force 139. Such bureaucratic complications were unappreciated by the guerrillas, who had acquired a jaundiced view of politics in the highly-charged atmosphere in Yugoslavia. Occasionally these high feelings reached Castellani, where Force 266 was accommodated, and sometimes those who had backed the Cetniks, and thought they had been betrayed, had to be separated from the rest.

In the books recounting their adventures, Jasper Rootham (*Miss Fire*), Bill Deakin (*The Embattled Mountain*),[30] Donald Hamilton-Hill (*SOE Assignment*), Lindsay Rogers (*Guerrilla Surgeon*), Michael Lees (*The Rape of Serbia*)[31] and Basil Davidson (*Partisan Picture*)[32] all provide an epic picture of disjointed supplies, atrocious weather, inadequate shelter and poor food, but emphasise the indomitable spirit of the native population, which, regrettably, rarely set aside the complexities of local politics to combine against the common enemy. Against a backdrop of spasmodic communications, insufficient air support and a headquarters staff that could never be completely up to date with the latest developments in the field, the liaison personnel often felt isolated if not ignored. All those who experienced the Yugoslav scene at first hand found it both harrowing and rewarding. Another common strand, highlighted by Deakin, and based on his own acute observation while leading TYPICAL, was the 'lack of vital and accurate intelligence of events within Yugoslavia at crucial moments'. The fact that TYPICAL's mission was officially concluded in September 1943, but its survivors were unable to reach Italy until early December, is itself evidence of some of the other difficulties encountered by SOE's men in the field which they regarded as avoidable.

It was the arrival in September 1943 of Sir Fitzroy Maclean that marked the turning-point for SOE in Yugoslavia, in both military and political terms. He instantly took to Tito, later gave an account of events as he saw them in *Eastern Approaches*[33] and subsequently wrote Tito's biography. He came with the status of Winston Churchill's personal representative and, in so doing, gave *de facto* recognition to Tito's ascent over Mihailovic. Unlike the ramshackle headquarters run by Brigadier Armstrong, Colonel Hudson and Major Jack, Maclean's organisation boasted an astonishing elite of the British military establishment, complete with experienced SAS officers, expert sappers and commandos, separate lines of communications and a network of sub-missions spread across the country. Maclean's staff had direct access to the very highest levels in Cairo and London and also included, at one moment in 1944, Evelyn Waugh and Randolph Churchill. Whether the latter pair really assisted the Allied effort in Yugoslavia is doubtful. On their first visit, on 16 July 1944, their plane crashed on landing in Croatia and they were both evacuated to hospital in Bari the following day. Waugh recorded in his diary: 'Force 399 absolutely useless in giving us any help.' Their second tour lasted longer, from 16 September to 6 December, but was scarcely more successful. According to Waugh, Churchill was rarely sober and spent much of his time arguing with equally drunken Communist functionaries at Tito's headquarters. Waugh concluded that the Yugoslavs

have no interest in fighting the Germans but are engrossed in their civil war. All their vengeful motives are concentrated on the *Ustase* who are reputedly blood-thirsty. They make slightly ingenuous attempts to deceive us into thinking their motive in various tiny campaigns is to break German retreat routes. They want the Germans out so they can settle down to civil war.

Waugh also witnessed the lack of logistical support given to the British Military Missions and noted that in Glina the local British liaison officer was 'in a rage about the miscarriage of his supplies . . . It was plain from the figures he gave us that supplies are sent haphazard as they become available without reference to the laboriously prepared tables of priority.'[34]

The accident experienced by Waugh and Churchill was not the only mishap to occur at Tito's base. Two SOE officers, Robin Weatherly and Donald Knight, were killed on 27 November 1944, when their captured Dornier was caught on the ground shortly before take-off and strafed by a German aircraft.

After the Liberation Maclean took up residence in Belgrade, his Military Mission having been transformed into more of a diplomatic one with his staff, fresh from the mountains, turning their hands to more mundane, administrative matters. For its part, OSS reduced its field detachments from fifteen to eight, and established a thirteen-strong unit in Belgrade. Co-operation with Tito was, however, to be short-lived. Permission for OSS to remain in Yugoslavia was rescinded in March 1945, and the last remaining unit was transferred to Trieste, under the jurisdiction of SI/Italy in July.

Yugoslav Operations

Date	Mission	Personnel	W/t Operator	Conclusion
20 Sep. 1941	BULLSEYE	Col D. T. Hudson Major Zaharije Ostojic Major Miro Lalatovic	Veljko Dragicevic	Extricated
27 Jan. 1942	HENNA	Lt Rapotec	Sgt Stevan Shinko	
4 Feb. 1942	HYDRA	Major Terence Atherton	Sgt P. O'Donovan	Murdered
5 Feb. 1942	DISCLAIM	Major Kavan Elliott Lt Pavle Crnjanski Sgt Miljkovic	Sgt R. Chapman	Captured
Sep. 1942		Captain Charles Robertson		
24 Dec. 1942	RAPIER	Col S. W. Bailey Major Kenneth Greenlees		
15 April 1943		Captain Morgan	Corp. Small	Captured
18 April 1943	ENAMEL	Major Erik Greenwood Captain 'Arlo'	Sgt W. Anderson	
19 April 1943	ROUGHSHOD	Captain John Sehmer Captain Robert Purvis Sgt Leban Sgt Harvey	Sgt Blackmore	Captured
19 April 1943	NERONIAN	Col Bill Cope Major Rupert Raw		
20 April 1943	FUNGUS	Petar Erdeljach Paul Pavlic	Alexander Simic	Killed
20 April 1943	HOATHLEY I	Steven Serdar Milan Druzic George Diklic		
20 April 1943	ANGELICA	Captain Robert Wade Lt George More	Roberts	
18 May 1943		Major William Jones Captain Anthony Hunter	Ronald Jephson	

Date	Mission	Personnel	W/t Operator	Conclusion
20 May 1943		Captain Hawksworth	Sgt Lindstrom	Captured/ Executed
21 May 1943	EXCERPT	Captain Jasper Rootham Lt Micky Hargreaves	Sgt C. E. Hall	Captured
23 May 1943	REPARTEE	Major Neil Selby		Shot, Aug. 1943
27 May 1943	TYPICAL	Major Bill Deakin Captain Bill Stuart Ivan Starceviv	Sgt W. Wroughton	
May 1943	FUGUE	Michael Lees Lt Smith	Lt Tommy Tomlinson L A/c Thompson	Shot
June 1943		Sgt Johnson Sgt Faithfull	Sgt Lesar	
15 June 1943	RANJI	Captain David Russell Captain 'Nash'	Nicolae Turcanu	Murdered Killed
		Major Dugmore Sgt Monroe Sgt Walker	Sgt Rogers	Killed Killed
3 July 1943		Nikola Kombol		Evacuated
15 Aug. 1943		F/Lt Kenneth Syers Major Ian Mackenzie		
16 Aug. 1943	SAVANNA	Major Basil Davidson		
Sep. 1943		Major Peter Solly-Flood		
Sep. 1943		Captain Vercoe Captain Patterson	Sgt Scott	Captured
25 Sep. 1943	SERBONIAN	Brig. C. D. Armstrong Col Archie Jack Col Howard		
15 Oct. 1943		Captain Scorgie		
12 May 1944		Dr Colin Dafoe		
Sep. 1944		Nikola Kombol		

●　　●　　●　　●　　●　　●

Elsewhere in the Balkans similar events were taking place, but not quite with the Yugoslav campaign's unique degree of divisive drama. In Bulgaria SOE's man was Mostyn Davies, who had parachuted into Macedonia with a Canadian Croat interpreter in September 1943 and then crossed into Bulgaria on 27 January 1944, accompanied by Tito's deputy, Vetozar Vukmanovic, known as *Tempo*, to receive Frank Thompson. This was a late start to operations in Bulgaria, but the country had been entirely isolated, as far as SIS and SOE were concerned, since the British Legation in Sofia had been evacuated. The pro-Nazi Bulgarian Government, led by Professor Filov, had joined the Axis in March 1941 and therefore did not strictly qualify as enemy-occupied territory in SOE's definition, even though Bulgaria's new borders now included what had been Yugoslavia. In April 1942 the situation had changed somewhat when the Germans had demanded that the Bulgarians send troops to the Russian front. The assassination of King Boris III had led to further political instability, because his heir, Simeon II, was just six years old. Three regents had therefore taken control of the monarchy, and SOE had seized the opportunity to unite the many groups of stragglers, deserters and anti-Fascists that roamed the countryside. This ambitious task was assigned to Davies and Thompson.

Davies, an Oxford-educated civil servant, who had been Lord Llewellyn's private secretary at the Ministry of Transport and Shipping before joining SOE, had worked for Louis Franck in Lagos and had then moved with him to New York to take control of BSC's South American operations. This had led to a posting to Force 133 in Cairo. Thompson was also an Oxford man, but a committed Communist too. He had been recruited into Force 133 by James Klugmann in September 1943 and, after a spell at STS 102, had volunteered to use his knowledge of Russian to assist Davies, whose only foreign language was Spanish. Their combined mission, code-named MULLIGATAWNY, was disrupted at the end of March, when they were caught in a watermill by a Bulgarian patrol. Davies and his sergeant wireless operator were killed, but Thompson managed to escape.

The nearest British Liaison Officer, Major Dugmore, signalled Bari from Macedonia, and a replacement team was arranged by SIS. However, on the night of the intended drop the head of SIS's Yugoslav Section, John Ennals, and the wireless operator were injured in a motor accident in Italy, so Flight Lieutenant Kenneth Syers was obliged to drop alone. This was not the first time that he had had to do so. The previous August he had joined TYPICAL as Bill Stuart's replacement. On this second occasion he was to lead CLARIDGES, a new team to organise the Bulgarian partisans, assisted by a wireless operator, Sergeant Kenneth Scott of the Royal Signals, who was dropped in on 7 April 1944. They were joined by Sergeants Monroe and Walker from Dugmore's headquarters, and together they made their way deep into Bulgaria, leaving Syers to undertake a separate reconnaissance mission for SIS. On 1 June 1944 Monroe and Walker were killed in an ambush, and Thompson and Scott were taken prisoner by Bulgarian troops and handed over to the Gestapo in Sofia. Four days later Thompson, who boasted of his Communism, was shot by a firing squad, supposedly for the crimes of learning the Bulgarian language and being a self-confessed political activist. Scott was forced to transmit messages to SOE using CLARIDGES's surviving wireless set, but his traffic was instantly recognised as being under enemy control because he had deliberately omitted his security check. By established convention the case then had to be handed for analysis and possible exploitation to SIS, which operated from Cairo under ISLD cover. The radio link was maintained successfully by SIS, thereby preserving Scott's life, until September, when he was moved to a prison and then released in anticipation of the Red Army's imminent arrival. Bickham Sweet-Escott recalls one of the many difficulties in keeping up the charade:

Each message we received from Scott had to be passed to [SIS], which in due course handed to us the reply it thought should be sent. Sometimes we did not agree that the reply altogether met the case and we had many anxious days. The Gestapo were evidently keen to score an easy success by shooting down one of our aircraft, for they were always asking for a sortie. We, of course, had to think of all the possible reasons for not sending one.[35]

Scott was subsequently taken to Turkey by the Russians and then flown to Cairo by the Americans, who had made a determined effort to reach Sofia to free a group of 325 US Army Air Force prisoners of war. A two-man OSS team had trekked across the Greek frontier, having landed on 23 August, but, when they arrived in the capital on 17 September, they were met by four OSS officers who had taken a shorter route by driving overland from Istanbul. However, both missions, and a newly arrived SIS contingent, were beaten by the Red Army, which had entered Bulgaria on 7 September. The British and Americans were ordered to leave the country on 24 September and, when they refused, the Soviets promptly threatened to imprison them. All then left without further encouragement.

When Scott arrived in Egypt he found SOE had changed out of all recognition. General Stawell had left SOM, leaving Louis Franck at Bari and Henry Threlfall in overall command of Force 133.

In Romania SOE's activities got off to a rather slower start even though the British Legation in Bucharest had provided both SIS and SOE with a base of operations until its evacuation in mid-February 1941. The pro-Axis dictatorship, led by Marshal Ion Antonescu since September 1940, asserted a grip on the entire country and effectively excluded Allied intervention until 1943. The SIS station had been a one-man office with undercover help from the local *Times* correspondent (and former Z agent) Archie Gibson. SOE, in contrast, had been a rather larger undertaking, with the ex-*Daily Mirror* journalist David Walker heading an impressive team, which had included Bill Harris-Burland and Gardyne de Chastelain. The latter had organised the JOCKEY circuit, a stay-behind network headed by one of his friends, Rica Georgescu, a petroleum executive who had worked for the same oil company. Following the Iron Gates sabotage fiasco, in which they had both played key roles, Harris-Burland and de Chastelain had moved quickly to Istanbul, establishing a SOE sub-office in the palatial surroundings of what had once been the British Embassy. Unfortunately, Georgescu had been arrested on 15 August 1941, leaving SOE's principal agent in Bucharest, an opposition politician named Juliu Maniu, without any means of communicating with Cairo. This gap was supposed to have been bridged by a young Scots Guards officer, David Russell of RANJI, who was flown into Yugoslavia on 15 June 1943. Unfortunately, as we have seen, a few weeks after it had crossed the Romanian frontier the RANJI mission fell foul of bandits out for Russell's gold sovereigns. His last signal was received on 13 August and he is thought to have been murdered on 4 September 1943. However, his wireless operator Nicolae Turcanu, a former signalman from the Goeland Shipping Company, escaped the same fate and successfully re-established contact with Maniu, thereby ensuring that at least one of RANJI's objectives was accomplished. A reception committee was prepared and AUTONOMOUS was launched, initially with limited success. As Ivor Porter, a former English teacher in pre-war Bucharest, who was recruited into SOE's Romanian Section, recalls:

Some misunderstanding almost always creeps into communications between an intelligence headquarters and its agents in the field. In the case of SOE Cairo and the Romanian Resistance it was made worse by the two-year break in their radio link. At the end of 1943, during the run-up to the AUTONOMOUS operation, Cairo had little idea of the operational set-up in Romania.[36]

The first attempt, by Gardyne de Chastelain on 22 November, ended when he bailed out over Italy. His Liberator had taken off from Tocra, near Benghazi, but had failed to find the dropping zone. It had then got lost above Albania, suffered a signals failure and run out of fuel over the Adriatic. A second AUTONOMOUS mission with Porter and de Chastelain was launched on 5 December, briefed by Charles Maydwell, but that too failed when contact could not be made with the reception committee. Finally, on 21/22 December 1943, de Chastelain, Porter and a Romanian agent, Silviu Metianu, dropped into Romania, only to be arrested by the local gendarmerie before they could find RANJI. Within days they were under the *Abwehr*'s control in Bucharest, which extracted the maximum propaganda value out of their capture. Mischievous press reports began to circulate that

AUTONOMOUS had been authorised to negotiate a separate peace with Antonescu's pro-Axis regime, thereby infuriating the Kremlin. This in turn irritated Churchill, who had not been fully briefed about AUTONOMOUS. Perhaps confusing Tom Masterson, the head of SOE's Romanian Section in Cairo, who had played an active part in sabotaging the Romanian oilfields during the First World War, with Ivor Porter, Churchill minuted Eden on 7 May:

Why were these two . . . important oil men picked? It does seem to me that SOE barges in in an ignorant manner into all sorts of delicate situations . . . It is a very dangerous thing that the relations of two mighty forces like the British Empire and the USSR should be disturbed by these little pinpricks interchanged by obscure persons playing the fool below the surface.[37]

Clearly AUTONOMOUS had become a major embarrassment to the Government at a very delicate moment. Matters were all the more sensitive because Eddie Boxshall's father-in-law, Prince Barbu Stirbey, had arrived in Cairo to negotiate secretly an armistice on behalf of Antonescu, another development which was bound to alienate the Soviets. The solution was to invite the Russians to participate in the secret discussions, and Ambassador Novikov helped settle the terms of the Romanian surrender. These were conveyed to Bucharest over the AUTONOMOUS wireless link, but when Antonescu read the Soviet conditions he rejected them. De Chastelain dutifully reported this to Cairo, but unwisely used rather undiplomatic language, not realising that SOE's telegrams were being shown to the Russians as a belated demonstration of good faith. De Chastelain's candour in supporting Romanian objections to what amounted to a Soviet occupation was not appreciated by the Kremlin, and once again Molotov berated Churchill, who responded by suspending all of SOE's operations into the Balkans. On 12 May the Foreign Office instructed de Chastelain to cease transmitting. The impasse continued until the end of August 1944, when a royalist coup swept Antonescu from power and the AUTONOMOUS mission found itself released from captivity, and the only British representation in Bucharest. In the absence of any working radio transmitters, de Chastelain was flown to Istanbul by the new regime, of which Rica Georgescu happened to be a leading member, to explain the situation, leaving Porter as the sole British representative in the capital. He was later absorbed into the new British diplomatic staff attached to the Allied High Commission in Bucharest, as was Turcanu. However, it did not take long for SIS to appear on the scene, in the person of Archie Gibson (still operating under what must by now have been a semi-transparent *Times* cover), who flew in from

Istanbul with the first group of Western journalists. He had worked for ISLD throughout the war, as had his brother Harold, who had been the SIS Head of Station in Bucharest for eight years during the 1920s and was now SIS Head of Station in Istanbul.

Although AUTONOMOUS never quite achieved what was expected, and most of its members experienced a lengthy period of imprisonment, never certain whether they would be handed over to the Gestapo, it was nearly instrumental in organising a separate channel to the Allies, but, for whatever reasons, the link was to prove disastrous. It was also to lead to a further clash between SOE and the Foreign Office, with Lord Selborne accusing Eden, in a memorandum dated 19 May 1944, of being too weak in dealing with the Russians, and even of following a policy of appeasement. This stinging criticism led the Foreign Secretary to rebuke him for a 'gross impertinence'.[38]

A similar episode occurred in Hungary, where Section D's man in Budapest, Basil Davidson, had been forced to decamp to Belgrade following the German invasion on 3 April 1941 before there was time to recruit a stay-behind network. Anyway, the British Minister, Sir Ronald Campbell, thoroughly disapproved of covert operations and had ordered his military attaché to throw Section D's cache of sabotage *matériel*, stored in the Legation's basement, into the Danube, threatening to denounce Davidson to the pro-Nazi Hungarian authorities if he created a diplomatic incident. Hungary's dictator, Miklós Horthy, had ruled his country since 1920 and, though not formally a member of the Axis, had conspired with Mussolini to invade Yugoslavia. From this unpromising start it is not surprising that SOE had considerable difficulty in re-establishing a presence in the country after Britain declared war on Hungary in December 1941, and it was not until Lazlo Veress appeared in Turkey, apparently on a semi-official mission to negotiate a surrender to the Allies, that a radio was successfully infiltrated into Budapest. Veress was a young diplomat, who, having had his overtures rejected by Harold Gibson, found the Section D veteran Bill Bailey more accommodating. Two transmitters were handed over to Veress, who returned home on 10 September 1943 and managed to maintain contact until the German invasion on 19 March 1944. He then made his way to Zagreb, where he found some partisans and talked his way on to a flight to Bari. With Varess out of the country, SOE was again at a disadvantage, so Peter Boughey, head of the Hungarian sub-section in Baker Street, whose own staff had been depleted by the prosecution and imprisonment of the Soviet agent Ormond Uren, volunteered to lead a 'blind' mission. His team was caught within a few hours of landing near Lake Balaton, and Boughey was delivered to the Gestapo. Only Boughey survived the war, having escaped from a prisoner-of-war camp in Silesia, where he had been sent as an NCO. He eventually made his way back to England via Odessa. Another mission, dropped 'blind' into southern Hungary, was also eliminated, and an OSS attempt, led by Florimond Duke, resulted in his being imprisoned at Colditz. Basil Davidson, who had parachuted into Yugoslavia in September 1943 with the intention of reaching Hungary, was never able to do so.

SOE's record in the Balkans was to be one of bitter disappointment, especially for those who participated in the British Military Missions, and for the royalist forces who trusted SOE to restore their monarchs to the thrones of their respective countries. In almost every case the idealists were betrayed and the Left-orientated pragmatists reached accommodations with Stalinist regimes, which, with hindsight, were scarcely more attractive than the Nazi dictatorships they replaced.

7 · Pass Down the Blame: SOE in Greece

The Brigadier loved blood, the Colonel cared
For rank, red tabs, his liquor and his chair
Of idle office where in high arrear
Mounted unread reports from those who dared
Attempt the projects their superiors aired.
For victory? No; planned I rather fear,
To earn promotion for the Brigadier,
With his complaisant Colonel smugly paired
In Cairo where intrigue is the road to glory;
To lick the lolling buttocks of the great,
Snub all initiative, pass down the blame
For their own faults (the old, the dirty story).
Such were the chiefs we left to undertake
A mission which might magnify their fame.

Arthur Reade (Head of Administration, SOE Cairo, and an agent in Crete) in a sonnet written about Brigadier Keble and Colonel Tamplin

Traditionally the British Foreign Office had always been sensitive to Soviet ambitions and, during much of the war, there was a very real fear that Greece might fall into Stalin's sphere of influence. For as well as fighting the hated German occupiers, the Greeks often seemed almost more determined to fight each other, thus creating an unstable situation which the Communists were well placed to exploit. At the heart of the conflict was King George II's endorsement of the regime installed by General Ioannis Metaxas in 1936, which was distinctly Fascist-orientated. When, somewhat unexpectedly, Metaxas rejected the Axis ultimatum in 1940 and resisted the subsequent German invasion, both SIS and SOE had been taken by surprise. Certainly SOE had already started to develop an embryonic stay-behind network in mainland Greece, but its efforts had been doomed because a complete Nazi take-over had never been contemplated. Both SIS and SOE had been working to the prevalent Foreign Office political analysis of the region, which suggested that the Metaxas regime would find an accommodation with the Axis. With this in mind Peter Fleming and Nicholas Hammond, the Cambridge don who had been studying the archaeology of southern Albania and north-east Greece since 1930,[1] had made a start at preparing a stay-behind organisation, training local Communists in wireless techniques, but the Axis onslaught of April 1941 had brought their meagre efforts to an abrupt end, forcing the senior SOE officer in Athens, (Sir) John Stevens, to withdraw his staff of Ian Pirie and Bill Barbrook to Crete at short notice just as the Germans entered the capital. There they found John Pendlebury, the distinguished archaeologist with a glass eye and swordstick, who had previously been the curator of Knossos and had been active on the island for Section D. His embryonic organisation, which included two academics, Terence Bruce-Mitford from St Andrew's and Jack Hamson from Cambridge,[2] was to disintegrate after he had been killed by German paratroopers on 22 May. Thereafter, effectively starting from scratch, SOE's Greek sub-section sent three resourceful officers to the STS at Haifa to instruct agents for clandestine insertion back into Greece. They were Hammond; the Hon. Monty Woodhouse, who had just come down from Oxford with a Classics double first and was to be elected a Tory MP in 1959;[3] and the travel writer Paddy Leigh Fermor, who had transferred to SOE from the Irish Guards. All were to play key roles in SOE's Greek operations.

While SOE had opted to associate itself with the Greek Left, SIS had concentrated its efforts in Athens on liaison with the Greek intelligence services, run collectively by General Demetrius Xenos. The local British Passport Control Officer, Albert Crawford, was responsible for cultivating this overt contact, but when the Legation was evacuated the PCO was closed, leaving its assets unsupported and its few individual agents to fend for themselves. A parallel SIS network, run under commercial cover by Roland Gale from a shipping office, was also obliged to abandon its sources, thus leaving the field to SOE, which, in the short time available, had established good links with the Communists and other anti-monarchists, not realising that there was even the remotest prospect of a Greek government-in-exile being established under King George. This miscalculation was to have profound implications later in the war, when SOE and SIS found themselves backing opposing political factions. However, before tackling the mainland, SOE began its operations in Crete. As the island served as a useful microcosm of SOE's practical experience of Greek politics, it is worth first examining exactly what occurred there.

After General Karl Student's paratroopers had soundly beaten the British and Anzac defence force deployed in Crete in May 1941, hundreds of stragglers had been left to find their own way back to Egypt. The constant trickle of survivors who had trekked south in the hope of being picked up off the beaches provided SIS's regional headquarters in Cairo (operating under ISLD cover) with a useful supply of intelligence about conditions on the island, and gave SOE and MI9 a pool of experienced escapees from which they could select volunteers willing to return. In accordance with their separate evolvement elsewhere in Europe, SIS and SOE operated entirely independently, with Edward Dillon running ISLD's Greek Section and John Stevens heading SOE's Greek sub-section in Cairo, with Eddie Boxshall taking a supervisory role over a combined Romanian, Greek, Cretan and Albanian desk back at Baker Street.

At first there was an element of co-operation between the two rivals and, indeed, the very first clandestine mission to Crete, a joint SIS/ SOE operation which landed from HMS *Thunderbolt* on 9 October 1941, was led by Jack Smith-Hughes, a barrister in peacetime who had only recently been evacuated. Formerly in charge of the RASC field bakery in Canea, Smith-Hughes had been captured and placed in a camp at Galatas, from which he quickly escaped with a group of friends. Together they had formed a band of irregulars and had lived with Cretan sympath- isers until being collected from the Preveli coast by a British submarine in August 1941. On his mission, to re-establish contact with the Cretans who had helped him and his companions, Smith-Hughes was accom- panied by an ISLD wireless operator, Ralph Stockbridge, a Royal Signals NCO and Cambridge graduate who had also successfully evaded the enemy before being evacuated to Egypt. They were followed the following month, on 23 October, by Monty Woodhouse. Upon his return to Cairo after ten weeks in the field, Smith-Hughes was placed in charge of SOE's Cretan sub-section. Although nominally under the command of John Stevens (and later Tony Simonds), 'the Greek office and the Cretan office were completely independent of one another' and were respectively designated B6 and B5.

A sea route to Crete was maintained by 'Skipper' Pool, a former Section D member and ex-Merchant Navy officer who had previously managed the local Imperial Airways seaplane terminal. Equipped with two *caiques*, the *Escampador* and the *Hedgehog*, manned by Michael Cumberlege and John Campbell, SOE initiated and maintained a regular link from Mersa Matruh, near Alexandria, to the secluded beaches scattered along Crete's southern coastline. Xan Fielding, an important figure in SOE's Cretan sub-section, who had been editing a newspaper in Cyprus when war broke out, attempted to use this method late in December when he was infiltrated into western Crete with a seven-man team – which consisted of a wireless operator, Reg Everson; an Australian sergeant, Guy Delaney; a First World War veteran named Guy Turrell; and four Cretan graduates of the Haifa STS – but bad weather dictated the employment of a submarine, HMS *Torbay*. By the middle of 1942 Crete had been divided into three sectors, each commanded by an SOE officer. Paddy Leigh Fermor, Fielding and an Australian, Tom Dunbabin, the former assistant director of the British School of Archaeology in Athens, were to join Fielding, together with another wireless operator, Sergeant Alec Starves. Later Fielding was to be replaced by Smith-Hughes's staff officer, Dennis Circlitira, and a New Zealander, Sergeant Dudley (Kiwi) Perkins, who was to be killed in a German ambush in February 1944.

Despite establishing a presence on Crete at a relatively early stage, SOE was to find that it was by no means universally welcome. The Germans had adopted a ruthless policy of hostage-taking and burning down villages in reprisal for assistance given by the local population to Allied personnel engaged on covert operations, or offered to the scattered groups of 'bandits' operating in the mountains. The situation was further complicated by the hostility of the self-styled national resistance front, known as EAM, which was actually nothing more than a convenient instrument of the Greek Communist Party. However, the fact that EAM and its guerrilla wing, ELAS, were under Communist control was not fully appreciated by either SIS or SOE for some time and their relationship was to develop into an issue of considerable controversy for both organisations.

The kind of political problems that were to hamper SIS and SOE were manifested at an early stage when a three-man, all-Greek SIS team led by Stelio Papaderos abandoned its mission to set up a radio in the White Mountains because of what were politely termed irreconcilable differences. Papaderos was evacuated to Cairo, leaving in the field his two ISLD colleagues who had insisted on limiting their local recruits to only EAM/ELAS supporters.

It soon became clear that the island's ELAS commanders were determined to thwart SIS and SOE, partly because of the reprisals inflicted upon the local civilians, which made the British-sponsored resistance groups unpopular, but also because of the declared official British policy of supporting the eventual establishment of a democratic form of government, headed by a constitutional monarch. The Communists not only opposed the King's return, but capitalised off other, more moderate republicans. Nor was opposition to the King's return limited to the Communists. The rival National Liberation Front was equally unenthusiastic about the prospect, but this was practically the only matter on which the two resistance organisations agreed. Xan Fielding, who transferred to SOE from the Cyprus Regiment in December 1941, admits to having been 'naïve enough to imagine that the two parties would co-operate in perfect amity',[4] but he was to be disappointed. He recalls going

out of my way to meet and hold discussions with the rival leaders whenever I could. But every conference ended in the same way with the EAM supporters demanding that I arrange for arms to be dropped to them while at the same time refusing to accept my suggestions as to how those arms should be distributed and used.[5]

In consequence, betrayals were frequent and ELAS often deliberately wrecked plans by threatening to denounce the whereabouts of British personnel to the enemy. At least one SOE wireless operator, a Cretan named Manoli, was sold to the Germans, and the feuding probably accounted for the deaths of several others, including two sergeant-majors, a Coldstreamer and a New Zealander attached to an SOE mission led by Dennis Circlitira. This perpetual conflict, combined with a complete disregard for security, 'where careless talk was the rule rather than the exception', and the very high proportion of airdropped supplies lost, made Crete extremely dangerous. Much of these losses were accounted for by the inhospitable terrain, but theft was also a significant factor. Mission leaders, who naturally were obliged to organise reception committees, found it difficult to persuade their more enthusiastic recruits to be discreet, and the majority of parachuted containers routinely went missing after each drop. These constant problems made operations difficult if not actually impossible.

Yet another obstacle was the continuing rivalry in Cairo between Edward Dillon's SIS desk in the GHQ Middle East compound and SOE, which was accommodated nearby in Rustum Buildings. Relations between the missions on the ground were always good, chiefly because the chronic shortage of wireless operators and sets obliged each organisation to rely to some extent on co-operation from the other. At one moment, in September 1942, communications became so desperate that Flight Sergeant Joe Bradley, a radio man who had bailed out over Crete from a stricken bomber during a raid on the Kastelli airfield, was co-opted by an SOE mission and retained as its wireless operator, rather than passed on down an MI9 line for repatriation. Yet in spite of the necessity of sharing these valuable resources, attempts were made to extend Cairo's inter-agency feuds to the island. In at least one instance an SOE officer was cautioned during his briefing not to trust the SIS team with whom he was about to go on a joint operation, and since

it belonged to our rival organisation which was concerned exclusively with intelligence and had nothing to do with subversive activity, I was quite seriously advised, in the interests of security, not to let my own team fraternise with them during the journey – even though we were to travel cheek-by-jowl for over a week in the close confinement of a submarine.[6]

SOE responded to SIS's challenge by attempting some unorthodox missions which would raise the organisation's prestige. The first, dreamed up in 1942, was designed to wreck German plans to repair HMS *York*, which was lying damaged in Suda Bay. The enemy was rumoured to be about to refloat the battleship, and the Royal Navy was especially anxious to prevent this from happening. The selection of Arthur Reade as the saboteur gives credence to Xan Fielding's belief that the entire operation had been accepted by Brigadier Keble, SOE Cairo's unpopular Chief of Staff, merely to remove a troublesome staff officer from Cairo, as he happened to be entirely unsuited for the task, being forty years old, 'a poor swimmer and ignorant of the technicalities of marine sabotage'. In addition, Reade's responsibilities at Rustum Buildings were particularly sensitive, for he was the head of the section dealing with the recruitment, welfare and accommodation of agents, and therefore had enjoyed access to the most secret categories of information, including the true identities of individual agents. A more unsuitable candidate for a risky mission would be hard to find.

The Brigadier must have known that the suicidal enterprise was doomed in advance to failure, so I could only conclude that he was less interested in destroying a top-priority target than in getting rid of a junior officer with whom he was on bad terms.[7]

Reade was landed 'blind' in Crete by Greek submarine, the *Papanicholis*, on 27 November 1942, but his mission proved quite impossible and he was withdrawn six months later, 'dismissed the service and sent back in ignominy to England'. Instead, HMS *York* was left to the attention of the RAF, an altogether more practical remedy.

Another ambitious scheme, undertaken in 1944 by Paddy Leigh Fermor and another inveterate traveller, W. Stanley Moss, was the abduction from Crete of a senior German officer. The target was General Müller, commander of the 22nd Sevastopol (Bremen) Division, but, by the time the team had flown separately from Tocra and assembled on 4 April, he had been replaced by Major-General Karl-Heinrich Kreipe of the 22nd Panzer Division, recently arrived from the Russian front.[8] The operation was delayed further by ELAS, which, according to Moss, threatened that 'if we persisted in carrying out our intentions they would not only betray us to the Germans, but would also expose every person who had helped us or was in any way concerned with the operation'.[9]

Moss and Leigh Fermor were typical of the young adventurers who naturally gravitated towards SOE and undertook extraordinarily risky operations, which, on paper at least, appeared to have virtually no chance of success. Moss had been born in Japan, lived in Latvia, spoke Russian fluently and had sailed to England across the Baltic and North Sea from Stockholm to join the Coldstream Guards in 1939. Posted to the Libyan desert, he had volunteered to go to Crete for SOE and, as his friend Sir Ian Moncreiffe commented wryly, 'it was natural that he should have been chosen to go there for he spoke little Greek and no German'.[10] Leigh Fermor had also led a peripatetic life, wandering across Europe for four years in preference to attending university, before being posted to the short-lived British Military Mission to Greece in 1940.

Neither Moss nor Leigh Fermor was daunted by the intimidation from ELAS, and they succeeded in stopping Kreipe's unescorted Opel outside Heraklion on the night of 26 April 1944, while the General was on his way home to his villa at Knossos[11] after a night of bridge in the German officers' mess at Ano Arkhanais. Dressed as German military policemen, Moss and Leigh Fermor signalled the General's driver to stop near a road junction and climbed in, coshing the driver. They then drove the limousine into the mountains and spent the next three weeks moving from one hideout to another, evading the numerous German search parties, until 15 May, when they were picked up by a motor launch piloted by Brian Coleman and returned to Mersa Matruh. Kreipe, who, despite his unpopularity among his brother officers, had been promoted to the rank of lieutenant-general the day after his capture, remained a prisoner of war in Sheffield and then Canada until 1947.

Apart from demonstrating that SOE was capable of pulling off quite impressive coups in enemy-occupied territory, the operation achieved little else, for Kreipe had not participated in any of the atrocities that so characterised the German occupation. On this occasion SOE went to considerable lengths to inform the German garrison, through the medium of leaflets dropped from aircraft, that there had not been any local participation in the abduction. However, this did not prevent the Germans from persisting with their policy of reprisals, taking ten Cretan lives for each German soldier lost. Every house in Anoyia was dynamited and dive-bombed in August 1944, and the villages of Lokhria, Saktouria, Magarikari and Kamares were razed to the ground in retaliation for British-inspired operations. Altogether several thousand Cretans were massacred as a result of Axis reprisals for Allied raids. It was an effective policy which was pursued throughout the rest of Greece, albeit on a much larger scale. Indeed, political turmoil, theft of supplies and inter-organisational rivalry were all to be components of the much larger canvas of mainland Greece.

By the time the Germans withdrew in December 1944, SOE had established eight missions in Crete under Dunbabin's command, headed by Sandy Rendell, Dennis Circlitira, Dick Barnes, Terence Bruce-Mitford, John Houseman, Hugh Fraser from the 7th Hussars and Matthew White, who had originally landed in June 1942 as Leigh Fermor's wireless operator. The only casualty was Geoffrey Barkham, who was taken prisoner on 17 October by the Germans whilst prematurely celebrating the collapse of the occupation in Canea. He subsequently escaped from a prison train in Yugoslavia en route to a concentration camp in Germany.

SOE's first mission to the Greek mainland, codenamed HARLING, was initiated in September 1942 and led by Brigadier Edmund Myers of the Royal Engineers. It resulted in contact with both the EDES and ELAS resistance movements and the demolition of the Gorgopotamos viaduct on 25/26 November. Myers was an unlikely candidate for the mission, his only tenuous connection with SOE being that he was courting, and was later to marry, Bickham Sweet-Escott's sister Louisa. A professional soldier who had recently been through the Middle East Staff College in Haifa and the Combined Operations parachute course at Suez, in September 1942 he had been scheduled to return to England. Instead an acquaintance, Colonel William Hamilton, a senior member of SOE Cairo's staff, persuaded him to volunteer for HARLING. He spoke no Greek and his local knowledge was 'limited to a few hours in Athens and Dubrovnik'.[12] Hamilton assured him that this was plenty of experience by SOE's standards and told him that he had four days in which to prepare himself for his mission. His objective was one of three viaducts which carried the main railway through Greece to the port of Piraeus. The Afrika Korps was heavily dependent upon this supply route, and the RAF had been unable to prevent its supply ships from dashing across from Crete to Tobruk and Benghazi under cover of darkness. Having failed to sink Rommel's ships, GHQ Middle East had asked SOE to destroy the vital railway link somewhere between Salonika and Athens. General Alexander's request, in anticipation of the Eighth Army's offensive at El Alamein scheduled for mid-October, was relayed to

SOE's main source in Athens, Captain Koutsoyiannopoulos of the Royal Hellenic Navy, known as *Prometheus II*, who was operating a radio left by SOE during the evacuation of Athens. His reply, received in Turkey and couriered to Cairo on 21 September, confirmed that such an operation was possible and recommended that about ten parachutists equipped with sabotage *matériel* be dropped between 28 September and 6 October.

Of the twelve SOE men due to land on the appointed evening from three Liberators, only eight actually parachuted on the last night of September, and of them only four could speak any Greek. The third aircraft failed to find the dropping zone and returned to Egypt. Two further attempts were abandoned because of bad weather and eventually, some six weeks later, the last contingent landed in the Karpenisi valley, miles away from the rest of the group and on the outskirts of a town under Italian occupation. The garrison opened fire and the SOE parachutists fled, abandoning their containers to the Italians. Despite the fact that plans of their target had been packed in one of the containers and must have fallen into enemy hands, the operation went ahead, but without the expected support of dozens of local guerrillas, who simply failed to materialise. Clearly *Prometheus II* had exaggerated the number of pro-Allied guerrillas in the area and SOE Cairo had been unable to double-check his information. Once Myers had assembled his party and established contact with a band of local guerrillas known as *Andartes*, he led an assault on the Italian garrison guarding the bridge and engaged the enemy for an hour, while Tom Barnes, 'a delightfully bluff and direct New Zealander',[13] and John Cook laid their demolition charges. When the raiders eventually withdrew, having suffered only four wounded, several of the bridge's steel spans had been dropped into the gorge forty feet below. The operation had taken place about a month late, long after the big armoured push at El Alamein, but, says Woodhouse, 'it showed for the first time in occupied Europe that guerrillas, with the support of Allied officers, could carry out a major tactical operation co-ordinated with Allied strategic plans'.[14]

Despite the apparent belated success of HARLING, which cut the vital rail link to Germany for a crucial six weeks, the rest of the operation was not to go well. No submarine turned up to collect Myers at the appointed time, and Cairo sent a signal explaining that, owing to the loss of another submarine in the vicinity, it was too risky to collect his team, which, because of the appearance of a pair of escaped Cypriot prisoners of war, had grown to more than a dozen. Whilst this did not matter to Woodhouse and his two wireless operators, Sergeants Len Wilmott and Doug Phillips, who had always intended to remain in Greece as liaison officers with the local guerrillas, Myers had not bargained for this extended undertaking. Nor, for that matter, had he been briefed for it. Even from what Myers had witnessed during the three months he had spent involuntarily in the mountains, 'it was apparent that the authorities in the Middle East knew little about the military strength and composition'[15] of the local resistance movements.

Moreover, although we had one or two agents in Athens who were in touch by runner with some of the *Andarte* bands in the field and by wireless with the Middle East, SOE Cairo had obviously been told little about the political aspects of the Greek resistance movements. The Greek government in London ... probably knew little more than SOE and the Middle East Command.[16]

One significant problem confronting SOE was the contradiction within the reports received from *Prometheus II* which suggested that ELAS enjoyed greater local popularity and constituted a better organised resistance movement than its more right-wing rival, the anti-monarchist EDES. Accordingly, SOE sent two missions into north-west Greece to liaise with EDES, led respectively by Nicholas Hammond and Rufus Sheppard, a lecturer at Cairo University who had fought in the Abyssinian campaign. Sheppard's group of two Greeks and an English wireless operator dropped during the first full moon of 1943 and was followed the next month by Hammond and three Greeks, all of whom Hammond had trained at Haifa and then accompanied on a parachute course at Kabrit. Sheppard's task was primarily political, to liaise with ELAS and report on them, whereas Hammond was given a military objective by Brigadier Keble: the destruction of the strategically important railway bridge over the River Peneus at the Temple Pass.

The insertion of this second and third mission into Greece caused complications for Myers, who had not been consulted in advance and was anxious not to give support inadvertently to an unknown guerrilla group. Therefore, he established himself as the senior British Liaison Officer, taking Woodhouse as his second in command, and divided up the country into four regions, to which he assigned the two Royal New Zealand Engineers, Tom Barnes and Arthur Edmonds, and the two academics, Sheppard and Hammond. Under these new arrangements a second operation was launched to sabotage the key north–south rail link, which had been repaired. A mission consisting of Major P. Wingate and two sappers, Captains Scott and McIntyre, was dropped into the territory controlled by a tough ex-commando, Geoffrey Gordon-Creed, and together they mounted an attack on the heavily defended bridge at Asopos. Having been joined by another commando, Donald Stott from New Zealand, and an escaped prisoner of war, Lance-Corporal Chester Lockwood, they finally succeeded at the second attempt on 20/21 June 1943. The structure was almost unapproachable as it spanned a deep chasm between two long tunnels, with forty German sentries armed with machine-guns posted at both entrances. The only possible approach was a near-suicidal frontal attack up the gulley with the saboteurs climbing the ironwork to attach their charges. Gordon-Creed's team, unarmed apart from rubber coshes, braved a torrent of floodwater to carry five packages of high explosive to the base of the canti-levered bridge. One inquisitive enemy picket was despatched silently, and the party placed their charges on a guard platform directly under the main span and retired. An hour and a half later the delayed-action charges detonated, transforming the fortified viaduct into a mass of useless iron-work. It was later reported that the Germans were so convinced that only treachery could have enabled the saboteurs to destroy the viaduct that they executed the entire guard detachment.

News of Gordon-Creed's success was well received in Cairo, but the celebrations were to be short-lived. Soon afterwards Donald Stott made his way into Athens on a sabotage mission and found himself negotiating with the German occupiers through the offices of the Mayor of Athens. When word of his initiative spread, SOE was denounced for colluding with the enemy, and Cairo ordered him to extricate himself immediately without compromising SOE any further.

Relations between SOE's men in the field and the desk men in Cairo were always strained, sometimes unnecessarily so. Staff officers who had never served in the field had little idea of the tension under which men in the field worked. For them there was no prospect of cocktails in the bar of Shepheard's Hotel or a dinner party at a villa overlooking the Nile after the office closed. The pressure of operating in enemy territory, constantly at risk from betrayal and ambush, made the agents hyper-sensitive to the need for security. A signal addressed to Denys Hamson, a former Section D adventurer in the Balkans, once asked the true names of himself and the rest of his team, which consisted of Tom Barnes and an engineer from New Zealand, Arthur Edmonds, five months after they had landed. Cairo explained, less than tactfully, that 'owing to reorganisation, previous records had been mislaid' and headquarters needed to know with whom it was communicating.[17] Apparently, Colonel William Hamilton and Major Derek Lang, the two SOE officers responsible for mounting the operation, had been transferred soon after Hamson and his men had been despatched and SOE had been unable to establish the mission's composition. Not surprisingly, they were bitter at their treatment. Nor were all the British

Liaison Officers prepared to tolerate ELAS's ruthless tactics and Nicholas Hammond requested to be withdrawn from the field. Of this episode, prompted by a fleeting visit to his mission by Karl Barker-Benfield, Keble's successor at SOE Cairo, when the latter countermanded Hammond's instructions and gave concessions to ELAS, Hammond says,

> It was thought in military circles that [Woodhouse] and I had become embittered by too long an experience in the field, and that our view of ELAS had grown distorted and biased. [Woodhouse] had fought against this attitude in the Middle East and in London but without success.[18]

Once in Italy Hammond had been to see General Stawell, but found him 'a tired man with little fight in him, and he made it clear that he adhered to Barker-Benfield's views and to those of the higher command'.[19] Nor did he have much confidence in the head of SOE's Greek sub-section, John Stevens (who was later to become Chairman of the City of London merchant bankers Morgan Grenfell), whom he believed to be 'unduly favourable in his opinion of ELAS, partly as a result of an initial prejudice, and mainly from the very brief experience he had had in Greece . . . he was a clever, quick-witted man of eager temperament and quick enthusiasms'.[20]

Although SOE was never able to disentangle itself from the complexities of Greek politics, it did achieve some limited strategic success in distracting the enemy in the run-up to the invasion of Sicily in July 1943. Prior to that momentous event there was a certain amount of harassment of Axis supplies using the single rail route south into Greece, but it was never cut for long, much to the consternation and frustration of the Allied commanders in North Africa. However, German units amounting to six divisions were kept tied down by a wave of sabotage, which helped convince them that an Allied assault somewhere in the Balkans was imminent. Telephone communications were cut, convoys ambushed and trains derailed, all in an impressive (and unique) display of unity. However, as soon as the landings in Sicily were announced officially, the old rivalries re-emerged and once again SOE found itself at odds with individual bands of guerrillas, as well as the Foreign Office. The original paucity of information experienced by SOE was intended to be rectified by a tour of inspection undertaken by John Stevens, and a similar mission completed by Major David Wallace of 60th Rifles in July 1943 on behalf of the Foreign Office. Wallace had been sent as Anthony Eden's personal emissary to see what was happening on the ground and, according to Myers, he was quite surprised by what he found during his fortnight with ELAS, which was equally obviously a great shock to him. It seemed that neither he nor the political authorities in either Cairo or London had any idea that EAM and its armed forces, ELAS, had such an extensive grip on the people in the mountains, and such extreme left-wing political control. He appeared surprised at the way that, time and again, I had turned a blind eye to their behaviour, when it had not critically affected operational plans, in order to remain in their confidence and to get the best value militarily.[21]

Despite his naïveté, Myers was so impressed by Wallace, 'not more than thirty years old, keen and straightforward',[22] that he retained him at the end of his inspection as his political adviser. Wallace also accompanied Myers to Cairo when he was withdrawn in August 1943, but his second mission, in July 1944, ended in disaster when he was killed during a raid on Menina a month after his arrival.

When Myers and Wallace arrived in Egypt on 9/10 August 1943, they discovered that they were the first members of the British Military Mission in Greece to return from the field. John Stevens, who had been dropped in the previous March, had left by *caique* and had been delayed in Turkey. This caused considerable difficulties because both SOE Cairo and the Foreign Office still seemed to be backing the Greek government-in-exile, led by the King, which was completely out of touch and out of favour with the men in the mountains. Worse, Myers had been accompanied to Cairo by Communist-backed ELAS delegates, who did not know what to make of the ambiguity of the British position and were as keen to be rid of the King as they were of the Axis. Cairo, however, had not been given advance warning of the arrival of the Leftist delegates and a political row ensued, which went right to the top. Woodhouse recalls that 'both sides accused each other, and both suspected the British authorities of bad faith and ulterior motives. The atmosphere of Greek politics in an Egyptian summer made it easy to believe almost anything of almost anybody.'[23]

SIS's role in all this is hard to fathom. The key ISLD officers with responsibility for the Greeks were Edward Dillon and his assistant, David Balfour, a brilliant linguist who had graduated from the University of Athens and is reputed to have undertaken a mission into occupied Greece disguised as an Orthodox priest before being assigned to ISLD's Greek desk in Cairo in September 1943, with responsibility for liaising with the Greek government-in-exile and the diplomatic rank of second secretary.[24] By adhering so closely to the expatriates SIS effectively threw in its lot with the King's supporters, who included a group of six equal ranking officers in Athens, led by Colonel Spiliotopoulos, and another shadowy royalist organisation based in Salonika, headed by Colonel Argyropoulos and known as the defenders of northern Greece. This also put SIS in direct conflict with SOE, which had, perhaps inadvertently at first, given its support to the Communists. This contradictory policy, which so baffled the Greeks themselves, was later referred to as 'inconceivably unco-ordinated activities' by Pan Kanellopoulos, the Greek deputy Prime Minister.[25] He had reason to be bitter. Not only was he SIS's conduit to the six colonels, but he had been obliged to flee Athens after a British officer had been captured in March 1942 with his name on a list of SIS contacts still in Greece.

While the Greek factions fought among themselves, Lord Glenconner (who had been appointed as Terence Maxwell's successor as head of SOE Cairo the previous year) and Myers were flown to London, and the latter was rebuked by the Foreign Office for straying into political matters. He recalls that

the Foreign Office still would not take me into their confidence. It was clear they considered SOE had exceeded its charter in that it had, so they believed, pursued a dangerous political policy of its own without keeping the Foreign Office informed. At the same time they obviously thought that I was to no small extent responsible for the political crisis which had recently arisen in Cairo. As a result any recommendations I was permitted to make were regarded with suspicion and I could make no progress.[26]

Worse was to follow. Instead of returning to Greece, Myers was posted to the STS at Haifa. While Myers had been in London the King of the Hellenes had issued an ultimatum: if Myers was sent back to Greece, the King would abdicate. This was proof enough for London that SOE had been meddling in local politics, and Lord Glenconner was replaced as head of SOE Cairo by Major-General William Stawell. In addition, the head of Cairo's country sections, Colonel Guy Tamplin, was to be removed, and Glenconner's Chief of Staff, Brigadier Keble, replaced by Brigadier Karl Barker-Benfield. Tamplin died at his desk, of a stroke, before he heard the news and his loss was not mourned. As a long-time resident of Estonia he had developed an expertise on the Baltic states that never extended to the Balkans. As for Keble, he was universally disliked for his ruthless internal politicking. Xan Fielding, an SOE agent in Crete, France and Saigon, who subsequently joined SIS in post-war Germany, and is therefore well-qualified to criticise, called him 'a globe-shaped choleric little militarist', who 'did his best to conceal his natural and professional shortcomings by a show of blood-thirsty activity and total disregard for the agents in the field, whom he treated like so many expendable commodities'.[27]

Stawell's appointment was to be one of significance for SOE Cairo, not least because, unlike his four predecessors, he was an experienced Near East hand, having fought in Greece, Serbia and Bulgaria, winning a Military Cross in Turkey during the last war where he had been wounded. Stawell's other distinguishing characteristic was that he was to keep the post for two years, longer than anyone else. He was later to run the United Nations Relief and Rehabilitation Administration's operations before becoming Deputy Chief of the Intelligence Division of the post-war Control Commission for Germany in 1947.

SOE's losses, in terms of personnel, were also part of the political problems experienced in Greece. Altogether about four hundred British officers and other ranks went to Greece, but a proportion of the casualties were the victims of internecine strife rather than enemy action. An SOE officer in charge of a stay-behind network had been captured early on, soon after the evacuation from Athens; a second, Mark Ogilvie-Grant, was caught after a clandestine landing by submarine in the Peloponnese; another was arrested on Antiparos 'in conditions that brought disaster on several Greek agents in Athens'.[28] A hundred and twenty partisans were transported to concentration camps following the discovery of an arms dump on Andicythira, and another large cache fell into enemy hands on Samothrace, near the Turkish coast. Later Michael Cumberlege was captured while preparing to block the Corinth Canal,[29] but it was the death of a New Zealander, Lieutenant Hubbard, shot by ELAS forces at Triklinos at the beginning of the civil war, that really created a furore, both locally and in the House of Commons.[30] Hubbard had apparently been shot accidentally by an ELAS gunman but, according to Monty Woodhouse, he had been killed 'by criminal negligence'. Rufus Sheppard was blown up when he stepped on one of his own mines, also at the outbreak of the civil war, soon after he had firmly given his support to the Communists.

Casualties among the Greek civilian population were, of course, much greater than those sustained by SOE. The scene had been set following HARLING, when the Germans had taken 300 Greek army reserve officers hostage and shot fifty of them. In Crete the occupation forces had wiped out whole villages, including Kandanos, Lochria, Kamares, Magarikari and Skines.

SOE's Greek mission also provided a convenient base for launching teams into neighbouring territory. Billy McLean and David Smiley's CONSENSUS mission, the first to venture into Albania, had originally been received by Myers before trekking across the frontier, and John Cook also used Greece as a useful jumping-off point for his own contacts with the Albanian partisans.

When the Germans finally withdrew from Greece in the autumn of 1944, ELAS launched an offensive, not against the retreating *Wehrmacht* columns, but on EDES. Using weapons and money largely supplied by SOE, ELAS tracked down numerous EDES groups and engaged them in battle, thereby sparking off the Greek civil war, which, only narrowly, prevented post-war Greece from becoming a Communist state and a Soviet satellite.

In retrospect it is astonishing that there should have been so little information available in Cairo about events taking place in such a sensitive area as Greece. SIS evidently had no assets left after the Axis invasion and SOE was to pay dearly for placing so much reliance on a single source, *Prometheus II*. Nevertheless, Myers achieved the impossible by disrupting the German railway traffic, and Woodhouse succeeded, against the odds, in persuading sworn political enemies to bury their differences occasionally in the interests of harrying the Nazis. Both men not only accomplished much of a military and strategic value in Greece, but they helped restore SOE's dwindling reputation in Cairo and London. Before their despatch on HARLING in September 1942, it is clear that SOE had not the slightest comprehension of the political minefield that awaited its personnel in Greece. The very first reference to EAM appeared in an SOE signal to Myers dated 21 December 1942, but it was not until 24 February 1943 that he stated, for the first time, 'I believe Communists control EAM unknownst to most members.'[31] By then the whole of the HARLING mission had been transformed reluctantly and unintentionally, by SOE's inability to extract their men, into the first British Military Mission, thereby giving *de facto* official British support to the Communists. This was to be compounded by Rufus Sheppard, who initially failed to realise that the guerrillas around Mount Olympus, to whom he had been parachuted, were led by covert Communists. Indeed, they duped him into reporting that ELAS was 'purely a military resistance movement' with 'no political aims whatsoever'.[32] Perhaps the last word on the controversy should be left to Woodhouse, who concluded that

the staff of SOE, in contrast with those of SIS, were amateurs who had to learn on the job: there could naturally be no trained professionals, as in espionage, for a task which only existed in wartime. The main handicap of SOE in Greece was faulty direction, not practical incompetence.[33]

8 · Exorbitant Cost: The Oriental Mission

It is clear that the British Colonial administration in the Far East, and the British Secret Service had failed to make adequate preparation in time of peace for internal organisation in time of war, e.g. Fifth Column activities in enemy territory, communications and intelligence on anything approaching the scale accomplished by Japan.

Sir George Moss, SOE Adviser[1]

The decision to send an SOE mission to the Far East was taken in the autumn of 1940 by Sir Frank Nelson, together with his Director of Overseas Groups and Missions, Colonel Brian Clarke. Their deliberations resulted in a document outlining its terms of reference dated 26 November 1940. This was followed by a directive to the Commander-in-Chief and the colonial governors, which was transmitted on 24 January 1941 and timed to coincide with the arrival of two senior SOE officers, Valentine Killery and Basil Goodfellow, both former Imperial Chemical Industries executives, who were to establish SOE's Oriental Mission in the Cathay Building in central Singapore. Almost simultaneously a former MI(R) officer, and veteran of the Auxiliary Units, Major Alan Warren RM, arrived in Malaya with instructions to co-ordinate special operations in the region. Warren's previous claim to fame had been his leadership of MI(R)'s ill-fated raid on France in August with a group of French-speaking officer cadets from Woolwich. The operation had ended in fiasco, with Warren and his men rowing home across the Channel and being picked up by the Dungeness Lightship, a pantomime which had attracted Churchill's anger.

SOE, of course, was not the only British clandestine organisation to be active in the Far East. SIS, in the person of Wing-Commander Pile of the ISLD, was already on the scene, but SOE took the initiative and began work on a Special Training School, designated STS 101, which was constructed at Tanjong Balai, a large private estate on an island at the mouth of the River Jurong, and connected to Singapore by an easily defended causeway. Placed in charge of the STS, which opened for business on 26 June 1941, was Major Jim Gavin, a veteran Section D officer, who had participated in the Oxelösund fiasco in Sweden, with a recent recruit from England, Steven Cummins, as Chief Instructor with responsibility for the Burmese and Chinese country sections. Cummins was to prove a good choice, having worked in the region for the British merchants Butterfield & Swire. Siam and Indo-China were left to a former Gordonstoun house-master, Lochailort instructor and intrepid mountaineer, Freddie Spencer Chapman. Together these colourful enthusiasts set to work training saboteurs and making contact with people they deemed to be potentially useful allies.

It was not long before the Oriental Mission was in trouble with the Foreign Office, the Royal Navy and the local military garrison. The first sign of discord had occurred when the British Minister in Bangkok, Sir Josiah Crosby, complained that SOE had been undermining his diplomacy by fomenting rebellion among the hill tribes of Burma. These fiercely independent people effectively controlled the eastern approaches to the Indian sub-continent and had nothing in common with the lowland Bur-mese, whom they despised. SOE's first plan had been to cultivate the hill people and turn them into a well-armed force capable of slowing up any Japanese advance through their territory. The prospect of the comparatively primitive inhabitants of the north acquiring modern weapons alarmed the Burmese authorities, as was reflected in Crosby's telegrams.

SOE also managed to tread on toes in South-East Asia, where the organisation had made contact with opponents of the Vichy regime which controlled all the French colonies. The senior British figure in the region was the Commander-in-Chief China Station, Admiral Sir Geoffrey Layton, who denounced the efforts of Baron François de Langlade, a Free French officer operating in tandem with SOE, to subvert the Vichyites with whom the Admiral was attempting to parley. Perhaps a more serious complaint was one rather closer to the Oriental Mission's headquarters, from GHQ itself. It insisted that SOE's training exercises, which showed up the deplor-able security at British military camps and airfields around Singapore, were unhelpful and a waste of precious resources.

Nor did SOE receive much comfort from those who were intended to be its beneficiaries. In Malaya there was a marked reluctance from the British civilian and military authorities to arm and organise stay-behind networks. To do so, they argued, would appear to the Oriental mind as admitting defeat before the battle had even begun. But apart from the psychological impact, there were other, more serious objections of principle to SOE's proposals. It was pointed out that it was inherently impractical to expect Europeans to blend in to a local native population and escape detection. There was also the question of limited manpower. The intransigent GOC, General A. E. Percival, claimed that any large-scale SOE plan would be bound to reduce the number of men with a detailed knowledge of the country and its languages, a precious commodity, available to the army. In addition, there was the thorny issue of the Malayan Communist Party (MCP), whose overtures had already been rejected by the Governor, Sir Shenton Thomas.

Malaya was Britain's most valuable overseas possession, rich in strategically important raw materials like tin and rubber, and home to the Royal Navy's principal base in the Far East. Economically it was the most prosperous country in Asia, but British rule was not unchallenged and there had for years been a gradually escalating internal threat from the Chinese, who, though numerically only a small proportion of the total population, which included Tamil Indians and aboriginals as well as the native Malays, were sophisticated, well educated and very active in commerce. The predominantly Chinese MCP had always been opposed to British colonial rule, almost as much as it was against the Japanese, and its ringleaders, operating underground, had been adept at fomenting labour trouble across the country. However, the MCP was about the only organised element of Malayan society that could be relied upon to resist a Japanese invasion and had volunteered its help. SOE also pointed out that the Chinese had been engaging the Japanese with guerrilla tactics elsewhere in the Far East for the past four years, with quite impressive results. Accordingly, the administration was persuaded to come to an unpalatable accommodation with its implacable peacetime foe, which had done so much to create strikes and civil disturbances. This was more complicated than it sounds, for the ubiquitous Malay Special Branch had penetrated the MCP at a very high level, and even had the MCP's Russian-trained General Secretary, Loi Teck, on its payroll. However, once the Japanese onslaught had begun, Thomas was obliged to reverse his position.

The preliminary to the extraordinary arrangement which subsequently materialised was hammered out at a secret meeting on 18 December 1941, held in Singapore and attended by two Special Branch officers, G. E. Devonshire and Innes Tremlett, with Freddie Spencer Chapman representing SOE.[2] This initial contact was followed by a similar, but higher level, rendezvous between John Dalley, the Special Branch's head of counter-espionage at Kuala Lumpur, Chapman and the Communist leadership on the last day of 1941. The agreement reached on that occasion committed the British authorities to release their MCP detainees and send them to SIS's Special Training School, designated STS 102, in requisitioned premises at the Chunjin Chinese School near Kuala Lumpur, under the direction of Major Rosher, to train and equip MCP cadres. Ironically, among SIS's early recruits was John Davis, a Chinese-speaking Special Branch officer who found himself dealing with the newly recruited Communists he had only recently had imprisoned.

In fact, when the Japanese did sweep into South-East Asia, SOE played practically no useful role whatever. By the time the Governor had given his reluctant consent to SOE's plans, at the end of December 1941, half of Malaya had been occupied by the Japanese. The first enemy forces ashore had landed at Khota Baru in Siam, where Sir Josiah Crosby had 'done all he could to prevent' SOE from operating, on the grounds that any such preparations 'were unnecessary and would merely upset the people'.[3] In fact, SOE had ignored the ban, and several clandestine teams had been infiltrated into the country with contingency plans for just such an eventuality. Owing to the chronic lack of radio equipment, most had been issued with ordinary receivers, with instructions to listen for a particular news item broadcast which would order the missions into action. The main story was to be the loss of valuable documents by a careless British officer and the announcement of the serial numbers printed on the papers. Each set of digits would identify a different group and indicate to them their particular prearranged targets. In the event, the very first European casualty of the offensive was an SOE sergeant, who was shot while attempting to raise the British army signals centre at Kranji, outside Singapore, on his wireless transmitter, in a vain attempt to alert SOE to the invasion. The special broadcast was eventually made, but much too late, by which time the highly efficient *Kempei'tai*, the Japanese security apparatus, had arrested and interned most of SOE's agents, including ten in and around Bangkok. Among them was SOE's first prisoner in the Far East, Sergeant Wright, who was arrested before he could undertake his mission proper. He survived the war, having persuaded his captors that he was nothing more dangerous than the deputy manager of a local mine. The net result of SOE's activities was, therefore, disappointing. Sergeant Misselbrook reported that the airport at Phuket had been seized back from the Japanese, but it was denied to them for just two days; Vic Wemyss, aboard the aptly named minesweeper *Mata Hari*, launched BETTY, a raid on Tonkah, where three Italian freighters were scuttled; and of the thirty-four mines earmarked for sabotage, only three were put out of action. At the conclusion of these operations the personnel involved made their way north, towards the Indian frontier.

Prompted by such a poor performance, Chapman turned his attention to Malaya and abandoned an ambitious but largely fanciful plan for the deployment of SOE raiding parties to launch covert operations behind the Japanese lines. The fact was that he simply did not have the personnel available, chiefly because of the Government's prohibition on the use of Asiatic agents. Instead, Brian Passmore, Captain Trappes-Lomax and ten other ranks were sent up-country to Penang in a futile attempt to stem the Japanese advance. Simultaneously, Chapman hastily prepared a makeshift stay-behind network of eight teams, each led by a graduate of STS 101. Almost all were to come to grief. Of the forty-five Europeans in the network, only four evaded death or capture.

The first party, led by Chapman himself, who left Innes Tremlett to head the Malayan country section in his absence, consisted of three rubber planters, Boris Hembry, Richard Graham and Bill Harvey; a demolition instructor from the Royal Engineers, Sergeant John Sartin; and a Mandarin-speaking Chinese wireless operator, Ah Lam. This group established itself deep in the jungle in mid-January 1942, but its relative success was not to be characteristic of the operation as a whole. Party No. 2, headed by a surveyor, W. H. Stubbington, was more typical. It consisted of G. W. Rand, C. W. Pearson, O. Darby, E. F. Elkin and Shika Bin Liba. Of this group, only Pearson and Elkin survived, but as prisoners.[4] However, Party No. 1 could not be regarded as a complete success for it did not emerge from the jungle for another three years, and for much of that period was regarded by SOE's headquarters as probably having been captured, because Chapman's radio had been stolen and so no contact had been made with his group. It was not until another team, an ISLD mission led by a rubber planter, Maurice Cotterill, and a tin miner from New Zealand, Bryan Tyson, stumbled across it accidentally on 1 January 1943 that SOE was informed of its survival. Unfortunately, this did not improve the situation much as Tyson was very ill and was to die soon afterwards, and the ISLD Chinese wireless operator had been robbed and murdered by bandits a year earlier. In reality Party No. 1 achieved very little in military terms, but to have endured the appalling hardship of living unsupported in the jungle was itself quite an accomplishment. Boris Hembry extracted himself much sooner and eventually hitched a ride on a sampan to Sumatra in the Dutch East Indies, managing to return to Singapore while it was still in British hands.[5]

When SOE failed to raise Chapman's callsign, DJJ, it had good reason to believe that his party had perished. Most of the others had been rounded up quickly by the Japanese, and several of his own team had fallen into enemy hands. Harvey, Hembry and Graham had split up and been evacuated when Singapore fell in February 1942, and a second team sent to find Chapman, consisting of Frank Vanrennan and Graham, had been captured on 15 March. The resourceful pair managed to escape, but were recaught and then beheaded on 18 September.

After the loss of his radio, Chapman's main problem was one of communications. The remaining staff left at STS 101 was exfiltrated to Dutch Sumatra on 12 February and Kranji was closed down three days later. Most made their way to Ceylon and eventually to India, but by then they had lost touch with the few surviving teams left in the jungle. An SIS escape route, via some of the offshore islands to a small camp at Bagan Si Api on Sumatra's east coast, was built by John Davis and a former civil servant, Richard Broome, but it was soon overwhelmed by civilians and deserters. Only Colonel Warren, who organised SOE's escape line from Singapore, delayed his departure, and he was captured by the Japanese. Adopting the identity of a naval officer, he was never discovered by the *Kempei'tai* and was among the first to be sent to work on the notorious Burma railway. Meanwhile, on 5 February 1942, STS 101 was abandoned and its staff transferred temporarily to Rangoon, and then to an SOE camp at Lashio, close to the Chinese border.

Apart from the chaos of the evacuation, there were technical reasons for the lapse in communications. Firstly, the equipment carried into the jungle by the stay-behind parties was woefully inadequate for the conditions there. Chapman's set was an ancient wireless with a limited range, which could only just raise Kranji. Secondly, there were not enough radios available, so the other sub-missions had to make do with receiving coded messages broadcast after the regular news bulletins by the BBC. If Chapman wanted to communicate with his colleagues, he was obliged to signal Singapore, which would then relay the message over the airwaves, a most unsatisfactory and insecure procedure. He recalls that

Communication was a serious problem. At the time there was practically no suitable light-weight equipment in the Far East . . . in fact the only available set capable of working from the field to Singapore, much less India, was a cumbersome, antiquated apparatus which, with its petrol generator, fuel and batteries, needed six men to carry it.[6]

The problem over radios, which was to dog SOE throughout the Far East, stemmed from the arrival in July 1941 of Jack Knott, from the organisation's Signals Directorate in London. His original supplies, which depended upon mains electricity, were quite unsuited to the humidity and rainfall of the tropics, and it was not until the end of 1942 that the B2 wireless was introduced. However, this was no solution, for, although it was less bulky, it was an integrated system, which meant that a malfunction of either the power unit, receiver or transmitter would put the entire set out of action. A Mark III version was eventually perfected by Knott, but even then charging the batteries remained a problem. The choice lay between a noisy generator of doubtful reliability or a charger on a bicycle-like contraption. The difficulty with the latter was that it had been built for European legs, and the frame was much too big for the natives to use.

SIS's experience in Malaya, under its ISLD guise, was about as bleak as SOE's, but, without a ban on the recruitment of Asiatics, it was able to concentrate on the MCP and deploy an impressive number of Chinese intelligence agents very quickly. Exact figures vary, but it is believed that John Davis and Richard Broome alone supervised the insertion of 163 MCP members into Japanese-held territory before the final British collapse. But their rate of survival was no greater than SOE's teams, with eleven being captured and executed after one engagement at Kuala Pilah. A team led by an agent named Cole disappeared entirely, and Major Cauvin's mission of Sergeants Meldrum and Regan ended when, in September 1942, the latter, who was the wireless operator, died in the jungle of an infection and Cauvin himself committed suicide. For a while following the chaos in Singapore the one remaining link with the outside world was a certain Captain McMillan, who had run a radio interception unit at Kranji. He was moved to Java, where he maintained a link with some SIS NCOs, organised by Major James Barry, a former counter-espionage expert from the Malayan–Siamese border, who himself survived for two years behind enemy lines with some evaders, Privates Brian O. Smith and Jim Wright. Barry eventually went mad and slashed his wrists in July 1944, and most of his companions succumbed to illness and festering wounds. Perhaps the best-known ISLD agent among them was Sergeant John Cross, who subsequently spent just over three harrowing years in the jungle, together with Lance Corporal Fred Wagstaff and Signalman Douglas Morter. Cross had been recruited from the Royal Signals by ISLD's Major Rosher and had undergone the STS 101 treatment with a team of Chinese nominated by the MCP. Their mission, to organise a stay-behind network, was evidently not considered very secret because Cross recalls that, as they set out, 'we were spotted by some of our old friends in the 3rd Indian Corps of Signals and greeted with a derisive shout of – "Here comes the Secret Service!" '[7]

By the time Cross and his party were in position, Rosher had abandoned Kuala Lumpur and only his second in command, a Captain Knott, remained. Their wireless contact was with McMillan in Java and they stayed in the rain forest under the continuous protection of the MCP, suffering appalling weather, health and food. Cross recalls:

Our position was quite different from that of British agents working in occupied France where Frenchmen, regardless of their politics, were basically concerned with ousting the Germans, and, I would imagine, fully co-operated with the agents knowing that the British would withdraw from the country after liberation. We were with Chinese communists whose over-riding aspiration was a Malayan republic.[8]

Cross's mission eventually linked up in April 1945 with John Hart of MINT. They were collected off the beach by HMS *Thule* on 31 May 1945 and taken to Perth, Australia, where they were welcomed home by Boris Hembry. Looking back on his ordeal Cross marvelled at how ill-equipped he had been, compared to the kit supplied to Force 136 later in the war:

Now, instead of the charging-engines requiring to be carried by at least two men and necessitating an unlimited supply of petrol and oil, we have light generators which could be strapped on a tree, anytime, anywhere, and operated manually. And instead of rifles, which gave out a tell-tale click of the bolt when reloaded in the silence of the jungle and Tommy-guns with their numerous projections which cut into the skin of their bearer on the march, were carbines which reloaded automatically, and lay snug and flat across one's body. Instead of heavy studded leather boots, which made foot-tracks advertising the presence of the British Army and which filled with swamp-water and rotted apart, were green, rubber and canvas light knee-length boots, tongued and laced to keep out leeches. And instead of the khaki-drill, which made the wearer a sitting-duck against the vivid green undergrowth, were the green uniforms which made the wearer indistinguishable from his background.[9]

•   •   •   •   •   •

Elsewhere in the Oriental Mission's operating area, precious little was ever accomplished by either SOE or ISLD. In Burma Steven Cummins ran an advance camp at Lashio, in the north of the country and close to China, with an airfield which proved a useful staging-post halfway to Chungking. A network of stay-behind groups was organised on the initiative of H. N. C. Stephenson, an STS 101 graduate and member of the Burmese Frontier Force. He recruited the hill tribesmen, and by the time of the British retreat to India, there were some 1,500 Karens in the forests to cover the withdrawal, as well as numerous Shans, Chins and Kachins. A few parties, like those led by Major Seagrim and Lieutenant Heath, made a limited attempt to implement a scorched-earth policy to deny the enemy any British assets, and they were assisted by some of the senior members of the timber industry. However, most were forced to make their way northwards, and then continue a long and arduous trek across the Chaukkan Pass to India. It was during this forced march, which was the first time that the route had ever been used in the rainy season, that SOE's Burma Section suffered its only casualty, Corporal Sawyer, who was swept away and drowned while fording a flooded river.

SOE India was so concerned about the lack of communications with the Oriental Mission's Burma Section that Peter Lindsey was sent to Lashio, in March 1942, to determine the situation on the ground. He was soon participating in the rearguard action against the Japanese, so Colin Mac-kenzie, head of the India Mission, was obliged to fly in to see the situation for himself. By the time he arrived, the rout was almost complete and the Oriental Mission had effectively ceased to exist. The Burma Section had abandoned Rangoon and had long since lost touch with Singapore. Worse, the Chinese had closed the frontier to the British, thus sealing off a potential line of escape. (Sir) John Keswick, of the famous merchant family that ran Jardine Matheson's commercial empire in the Far East, who was also the Oriental Mission's representative in Chungking, had been negotiating with Chiang Kai-shek for SOE to develop some training facilities on his territory and Valentine Killery had flown to complete the arrangements in January 1942. An embryonic STS had been opened near Chungking in March, but thereafter the relationship had faltered, principally because of the head of the Generalissimo's intelligence service, General Tai Li, who, among other demands, insisted that a Chinese officer should head the STS. Instead of finding a compromise, Keswick and his White Russian deputy, Vladimir Petropavlovsky, were ordered to leave the country forthwith. The British Ambassador, Sir Alexander Clark-Kerr, reported this unfortunate episode in the following terms:

SOE got into such bad odour with the Chinese because its personnel were almost exclusively representatives of British interests and their tactless and misguided activities, that Chiang Kai-Shek himself ordered them out of China and refused them permission to operate.[10]

This setback could hardly have come at a worse time for the hard-pressed remnants of the Burma Section that limped back into India after a harrowing ordeal in the jungle. Both Keswick and Petropavlovsky were redeployed, the former to London, where he was appointed Director of Missions, Area

C, covering India, the Far East and the Americas; the latter to the Balkans.

In Shanghai SOE's efforts were effectively nullified by the Foreign Office, which, anxious as ever not to offend local sensibilities, vetoed the only proposal the organisation came up with, the sabotage of the *Eritrea*, an Italian warship anchored just off the International Settlement. W. J. Gande, SOE's local representative, headed a team of six untrained volunteers, but their ambitions were thwarted by the Ambassador, who prohibited any action which would arouse anti-British feeling, provoke a Japanese occupation or compromise the Settlement's neutrality. Thus nothing was undertaken, and the entire group was eventually arrested by the Japanese acting on information from a *Kempei'tai* agent planted in Gande's office. Gande himself was sentenced to four years' imprisonment at the Ward Road Gaol, but most of his team were later repatriated in an exchange of prisoners.

In Hong Kong the position was only marginally better. A local resident, F. W. Kendall, had been recruited by Jim Gavin when he had visited the colony, and Kendall had subsequently gone on an STS 101 course in July 1941. He had returned to form the Reconnaissance Unit, a small stay-behind group centred on some custom-built hides in the New Territories. When the Japanese did sweep down into Hong Kong, Kendall's men continued to harass the enemy and undertake the occasional act of sabotage, but when it became clear that the position was hopeless, they either surrendered or trekked north-west to Chungking. Kendall managed to escape, as did (Sir) Robert Thompson, (Sir) Ronald Holmes and E. B. Teesdale.

The only other Oriental Mission section that needs to be mentioned is de Langlade's, covering French Indo-China. However, it too was a victim of administration-inspired opposition. One project, an operation designed to land a group of Free French from a Yangtse river boat, the *Wuchan*, on to Japanese-held territory, ended in abject failure. Led by Chapman, and assisted by Jack Knott and Sergeant Shufflebotham, a wireless instructor from STS 101, the mission was cancelled just as the steamer was approaching the Vietnamese coast. Bitterly disappointed and highly indignant, the Free French reluctantly agreed to return to Singapore. It later transpired that the recall signal had been ordered by Admiral Layton, who was at that very moment conducting secret negotiations for the defection of the local French governor. A raid at this juncture would have wrecked his scheme, so SOE's plans had had to be shelved. Unimpressed by this explanation, the Free French chose to switch their regional base to Kunming, where they could operate without any further British interference.

If the French Indo-China Section accomplished little, even less was achieved by liaison with the Dutch. General Wavell, the British Allied commander, 'made no attempt to conceal his distrust of SOE' and appointed his own nominee, the South African writer and explorer, (Sir) Laurens van der Post, to organise guerrillas and prepare escape routes. Valentine Killery, who arrived in Java after the fall of Singapore, also attempted to do much the same, but once again it was a case of too little, too late. Seven wireless transmitters were supplied to stay-behind groups by the Oriental Mission, but none of the parties survived long. Van der Post himself was caught by the Japanese towards the end of June and his wireless operator, Lieutenant Cooper, a volunteer from the Royal Navy, surrendered to prevent the Japanese from carrying out a threat of reprisals against the local native population, which was itself not entirely sympathetic to its former Dutch colonial masters.

That the Oriental Mission was going to be a catastrophe had been widely predicted. In August 1941 Christopher Hudson had been appointed SOE's first Head of Far East Branch in London, and he had sent Major A. B. O'Dwyer to Singapore in November to carry out an inspection. His subsequent report to Sir Frank Nelson had made dismal reading, almost as depressing as Killery's final report, submitted after the evacuation of Singapore.[11] When Nelson gave a copy to his minister, Hugh Dalton, he observed: 'It is most tantalising to see in the report how His Majesty's representatives have vetoed any preparatory work, cried for help from SOE the moment trouble started, and then complained if we did not deliver the goods.'[12] Dalton was so amazed by the document that he commented that 'the story ought to be written at length like a novel and printed for private circulation'.[13]

9 · Too Many Plans: The India Mission

The unconditional surrender of Singapore on 15 February 1941, with 80,000 prisoners falling into Japanese hands, cast a terrible shadow across British military confidence all over the globe. In India there was an uncomfortable feeling that the Japanese were quite unstoppable, and for the first time politicians and staff officers began to contemplate the likelihood of an attack on the eastern states neighbouring Burma. At some point in April the Secretary of State for India, Leo Amery, asked for an SOE mission; however, the request did not receive an entirely favourable response in India itself, probably because of the personalities involved. General Wavell, after all, had not formed a very high opinion of the organisation in the Middle East, and the person chosen to lead what was to become known as the India Mission, Colin Hercules Mackenzie, was not drawn from SOE, but was a personal friend of the Viceroy, Lord Linlithgow. They were both Etonians and had served as directors of the same textile company in England, J. & P. Coats. Mackenzie, formerly a Classics scholar at King's College, Cambridge, where he had won a First in Economics, had lost a leg while fighting in France during the First World War with the Scots Guards. The son of a general, he was highly intelligent, something of a poet, and was still only forty-two years old. Accompanying him as his deputy was Gavin Stewart, another newcomer to SOE.

Despite Mackenzie's connections with the Viceroy, the India Mission got off to a poor start, as Mackenzie himself was to remark in a report to London: 'Gavin Stewart and I have now been in this country for ten months and it must be admitted that to date we have very little to show for it.'[2] The reason for the lack of performance was the vague nature of the Mission's objectives, which, initially at least, were entirely defensive and therefore contrary to SOE's *raison d'être*. Mackenzie had established his headquarters at Meerut, a cantonment some forty miles north-east of Delhi, leaving a small office in the capital to liaise with the Viceroy; he also opened an STS at Kharakvasla near Poona. He had minimal contact with his SIS counterpart, Colin Tooke, and concentrated on the preparation of a stay-behind network which could operate if the Japanese overran Assam, Madras and Calcutta. This was no easy task as SOE's most obvious allies, the Communist Party, had long been in conflict with the police. Much to the consternation of the local Special Branch, 150 Communists were selected for post-occupational sabotage work and put through a special course at Kohima.

SOE India was run by Mackenzie and Stewart along business lines, employing mainly merchants with experience of trading in the Far East. There was a board of four controllers, one for each of the divisions: Finance and Administration, Operations and Training, Political Warfare and the Country Sections. Of the latter, there were three separate groups. The first, based at Calcutta and designated A, included Burma (R. E. Forrester), Siam (Peter Pointon) and French Indo-China (François de Langlade). The B Group at Colombo ran missions into Malaya and Sumatra (Basil Good-fellow), Anglo-Dutch territory (Frits Mollinger) and the Islands. When SOE was allowed back into China, Group C was formed in Chungking and Kunming. All operated under British army cover, using the military designation GSI(k). This was to be the cause of considerable misunder-standing about the India Mission's exact role, which often seemed in danger of being blurred into SIS's exclusive parish of intelligence-gathering. London certainly knew what it was, and at one point sent an emphatic reminder that 'we must never forget the "O" in Special Operations Executive'.[3]

This unrealistic attitude ignored the India Mission's relative remoteness from the Japanese front line and the uncertainty of what had befallen SOE's stay-behind networks. Only at the extreme limit of the twin-engined Hudson's range could aircraft from Ceylon, for example, reach occupied Malaya, and given the extreme climatic conditions prevalent in the region, especially during the monsoon season which stretched from May to October, it is hardly surprising that no clandestine flights were made until May 1942. The first took two agents, who were dropped into Siam from

Jessore, but only ten other flights were made during the following eighteen months. Nor was there any significant radio contact with SOE's units in the jungle. Few had been equipped with transmitters of sufficient power to pick up SOE's remaining bases, and in reality none of them was to survive the Japanese occupation. Of all the target countries in the India Mission's region, only Indo-China and Burma could be reached overland, from China and India respectively, but hostile bandits along the infiltration routes prevented SOE from trying either. Instead, it had to rely on the RAF's Special Duties squadrons and the occasional submarine. As we shall see, the Royal Navy proved very reluctant to risk its craft on hazardous missions of doubtful import.

The few survivors of the ill-fated Oriental Mission in Singapore congregated in Ceylon or Calcutta. John Davis and Richard Broome took a junk on an epic voyage of thirty-four days across the Indian Ocean before their party of SOE stragglers was rescued. Jim Gavin made Trincomalee with a second group aboard the SS *Krain*, and arrived just in time to learn that the island was under threat from an enemy carrier force. A third party, consisting of Valentine Killery, G. Egerton Mott and Boris Hembry, headed south and reached Australia. At some stage virtually all were reunited at Meerut, determined to salvage SOE's honour and reputation.

Having experienced hostility from the Indian police, and in particular the Director of its Intelligence Bureau, Sir Denys Pilditch, SOE was anxious to shrug off its passive reputation and engage the enemy. Its first opportunity, Operation LONGSHANKS, was seen as an ideal chance to demonstrate just what SOE could do when it was allowed to flex its muscles. Unfortunately, the episode degenerated into a classic SOE farce, causing much embarrassment to all concerned. The idea was to repeat the exercise undertaken in West Africa in which SOE had covered itself with glory, seized some enemy shipping and ingratiated itself with the Navy. But, unlike in Fernando Po, very little went according to plan. The objective was four ships which had taken refuge in neutral Goa: the Italian *Anfora*, and the German *Braunfels*, *Druchenfels* and *Ehrenfels*. SOE was to bribe the Portuguese Governor, Colonel Jose Cabral, who would throw a party to entertain the masters of the four Axis ships, and then lead boarding parties which would quietly overpower the skeleton crews and sail to a prearranged rendezvous just outside the territorial limit. Mackenzie's deputy, Gavin Stewart, made a preliminary visit to Goa in November and endorsed the scheme. A further reconnaissance was completed in December 1942 by Lewis Pugh and, on 13 February 1943, the operation was sanctioned, on the understanding that the Italian and German seamen had already indicated their willingness to surrender, so no violence would be necessary. Unfortunately, SOE miscalculated on almost every score. Far from welcoming the raid, which took place in the early hours of 9 March, the Germans had set a trap on the *Ehrenfels*. When Pugh's men climbed aboard from a barge borrowed from the Calcutta Port Commissioners, they were met by gunfire. The brief battle that followed left five of the German crew dead and all four ships on the bottom, having been scuttled.

The hopper barge managed to withdraw, taking three prisoners, but that was insufficient prize to placate the Foreign Office, which pointed out, with some justification, that SOE had broken every promise it had made. Portuguese neutrality had been compromised, enemy nationals had been killed, and there was plenty of evidence that the culprits had been the British. Mackenzie promptly offered his resignation to Gubbins, but the latter, having previously urged the India Mission to take the initiative and engage the enemy, felt that he could not accept it. Lord Selborne was outraged and thought Mackenzie ought to be recalled, but instead settled for a severe reprimand. Meanwhile George Taylor, who had succeeded Brian Clarke as Director of SOE's Overseas Groups and Missions in March 1942, constructed an entirely bogus report, which purported to demonstrate that the débâcle had been the result of a series of misunderstandings and not the deliberate disregard of instructions from Major Leonard Guise, the head of the Far East Branch in London. Whilst this impressed no one, it did coincide with a *post-mortem* from the British Consul in Goa, Colonel Bremner, who disclosed that the Portuguese authorities had investigated the entire affair and, with a little prompting, had drawn the bizarre conclusion that the Germans had manufactured their improbable tale of a British attack so as to conceal what had really taken place – a Communist-inspired mutiny! As Lord Selborne commented, 'This is the most amazing piece of luck SOE has ever had.'[4]

Having survived LONGSHANKS, SOE acquired the confidence to start operations in earnest and Christopher Hudson, Major Guise's predecessor as head of SOE's Far East Branch in London, flew out to Ceylon in September 1942 to organise a local base for the India Mission. There he found Innes Tremlett, a survivor of the Oriental Mission, who had already begun to make the necessary preparations. The main headquarters at Kandy was in a purpose-built compound 'with basha huts to live in and a huge restaurant-cum-lounge-cum-dance-hall stuck up high in the middle'.[5] A training facility was accommodated in a splendid beachside mansion at Mount Lavinia (now Galkissa), eight miles south of Colombo and once the home of a former governor, Sir Edward Barnes. Holding camps were constructed at Horona, near Kandy, and on an island in China Bay, not far from Trincomalee. A final acquisition, which proved very popular, was a bungalow at Yawalatene, twelve miles from Kandy and deep in a tea plantation.

The first operation launched from Ceylon was BUNKUM, a reconnaissance of the sparsely populated Andaman Islands, which had been evacuated by the Dutch in mid-March 1942 and occupied by the Japanese soon afterwards. The officer chosen to lead the mission was Denis McCarthy, a former District Superintendent of Police in the islands, who had served there for five years before the war. Four NCOs had been selected for him by the operation's briefing officer, Bill Beyts, and Sergeant Dickens of the Royal Signals was assigned as his wireless operator. The question then arose of how to transport the group to their target. There were no aircraft available and, as we have already seen, the Commander-in-Chief, Admiral Layton, had no time for SOE. He believed that submarines were better employed sinking Japanese shipping than undertaking high-risk clandestine schemes of doubtful value. This was a view shared by many of his staff, who preferred to attack Japan's long sea routes than have to forgo tempting targets just to protect the integrity of a secret mission, which may or may not achieve anything of comparable strategic value. In face of this lack of confidence the Dutch country section, now headed by Major Pel, arranged for a submarine of the Royal Netherlands Navy, the *O 24*, to accept the task. Accordingly, the party embarked on 14 January 1943 and made their landfall four days later after an uneventful crossing. McCarthy stayed in the Andamans for the next nine weeks and suffered only one casualty: Jemadar Habib Singh, a former military policeman from the islands, who accidentally shot himself with his sten gun and was killed almost instantly.

Although McCarthy lost three stone in weight while ashore, and suffered such ill-health that he was eventually repatriated to England, the operation was judged a partial success. The original intention had been to leave BUNKUM in place and to reinforce it with BALDHEAD II, led by Colonel Beyts, but the loss of Habib Singh and McCarthy's poor condition mitigated against following the plan. Instead, Beyts landed on 24 March to clear up all traces of BUNKUM and buried the remaining stores for later use. In fact the follow-up, BALDHEAD III, was not initiated until late in December 1943, when Major Greig took a group of fifteen back to the Andamans on HMS *Taurus*.

Whatever else, BUNKUM provided conclusive evidence that it was possible to insert agents by submarine, and demonstrated that wireless contact could be maintained with Calcutta from Japanese-occupied territory. These two factors were enough to justify an escalation of SOE's effort in Ceylon.

Innes Tremlett took over the Malay country section from Basil Good-fellow and supervised its first mission to Japanese-occupied Malaya under the auspices of the India Mission. Codenamed GUSTAVUS I, it was led by John Davis and was delivered to the Malacca Straits by the *O 24*, together with five Chinese agents, on 24 May 1943. This was followed on 25 June by GUSTAVUS II, consisting of a former Straits Settlement police officer, (Sir) Claude Fenner, with Richard Broome. These landings were to become the foundations for the development of a fully fledged resistance movement in the region, supported entirely by the MCP under the overall direction of John Davis. Submarines bringing supplies kept to a regular monthly sched-ule, and the GUSTAVUS network even made contact with Freddie Spencer Chapman, who was subsequently evacuated from the jungle. Although GUS-TAVUS was always to be handicapped by wireless difficulties, and contact was not established fully until 1 February 1945, ten months after Davis had last landed, a link with Ceylon was maintained on an intermittent basis through another mission, CARPENTER, which relayed two reports from Davis in December 1944 and January 1945. CARPENTER was itself a sig-nificant development because it was the first team to be delivered to Malaya's east coast from Australia. The Royal Navy had been reluctant to send a submarine from Ceylon through the Straits of Malacca, where the Japanese were known to have been particularly active. The alternative was a lengthy circuitous voyage around Sumatra, which made the shorter Aus-tralian route much more attractive.

•   •   •   •   •   •

Since the fall of Singapore SOE had been operating in Australia from what appeared to be a quiet suburban house in Melbourne under 'Inter-Services Reconnaissance Department' (later Force 137) cover and the leadership of Major G. Egerton Mott. Assisted by Jack Finlay, Egerton Mott had built training facilities near Brisbane and at Darwin. Before Spencer Chapman had been posted to STS 101, he had laid the groundwork for a similar establishment at Wilson's Promontory, at the most southern tip of Australia in Victoria, and since then Egerton Mott and John Chapman-Walker had greatly expanded SOE's presence in anticipation of operations in the south-west Pacific. It subsequently transpired that the Commander-in-Chief, General Douglas MacArthur, was not prepared to accept SOE – he felt much the same about OSS – which left SOE Australia looking north. Accordingly, an operational base was constructed at Morotai in the Moluccas, and two advance camps were placed on Lubuan Island and

Balikpapan Bay to support operations in South-East Asia and, in particular, Malaya. In March 1944 Egerton Mott was transferred to London to head SOE's Far East Branch.

Commanded by Major W. B. Martin, CARPENTER disembarked from HMS *Telemachus* on 5 October 1944. As well as being the first team to Malaya to originate from Australia, CARPENTER also set a record by raising Colombo in its radio. It continued to operate until the end of the war, despite the loss of Martin, who was killed by the Japanese in January 1945 while running a reception committee for a supply drop. He was replaced early the following month by Major Hart, of CARPENTER II, and a group of sixteen in CARPENTER III, which arrived in May 1945.

SOE Australia was to initiate several missions to Japanese-occupied Malaya, including two led by Ivan Lyon, who had been part of the Oriental Mission and had helped set up Experimental Station Z, an STS at Cairns in northern Queensland. In September 1943 he returned to Singapore with three Australians on Operation JAYWICK, one of the most successful and daring missions to be undertaken in the Far East. Lyon and his companions sailed a small fishing boat some two thousand miles, from Exmouth on the north-west cape of Australia to enemy-held Singapore, sank seven Japanese ships with limpet mines, and then made it back home without sustaining a single casualty. However, Operation RIMAU, an attempt to repeat JAYWICK a year later with a party of twenty-four aboard the Australian submarine *Porpoise*, ended in failure.[6] Lyon and several of his men were killed in a fierce gun battle, and the few that managed to escape were later captured and executed.

GUSTAVUS, the mission which formed the basis of SOE's Malayan operations, was to be reinforced by a further series of landings, codenamed REMARKABLE. These placed further teams into Malaya, but the situation was to become complicated by the unannounced 'blind' arrivals of some ISLD teams, which inadvertently stirred up the enemy. In September 1943 this was to be the subject of a protest from Davis, who complained that GUSTAVUS was in danger of being compromised by MAY and MUD, two ISLD parties which had been inserted in April and May 1943. Up until this incident SOE had co-operated well with ISLD, the relevant country section of which was headed by Boris Hembry, himself a survivor of the Oriental Mission. The conflict had arisen because the pressure on submarine availability had obliged SOE and ISLD to share transport. On this occasion P. E. Young and the three other Chinese members of MUD had joined REMARKABLE I on HMS *Tally-Ho*, which also had orders to pick up men from GUSTAVUS EMERGENCY. The first phase of the operation,

disembarking REMARKABLE 1's single Chinese agent, equipped with a transmitter and 1,000 pounds of stores, went according to plan, but the rest did
not go quite so smoothly. After they had been collected, the men in the
GUSTAVUS party refused to allow MUD ashore, insisting that SOE's agreement with ISLD prohibited this type of joint operation. Consequently,
MUD was returned to Trincomalee. Utterly exasperated, the submarine
commander, Lieutenant-Commander Bennington, later reported:

> The GUSTAVUS party in Malaya considered it too dangerous to land other personnel
> or stores. The co-operation between the authorities responsible is not very apparent.
> It is considered the personnel of Operation MUD could have made their way ashore
> by folboat without prejudice to Operation GUSTAVUS. The senior army officer said
> that this procedure would be contrary to an agreement that exists between the two
> organisations.[7]

When these remarks were read in Ceylon, Captain R. M. Gambier, in
command of the 4th Submarine Flotilla, minuted that 'whilst I fully understand the object of the agreement between ISLD and SOE and the necessity to prevent either party compromising the other, in this particular case I
feel a more accommodating view could have been adopted.'[8]

As well as straining SOE's relations with ISLD, MUD's postponement
put more pressure on the navy's limited resources and caused a delay in
sending other missions. This aggravated matters further, so that when
Major J. P. Hannah was ready to join GUSTAVUS, his mission, codenamed
FUNNEL, was obliged to wait until an ISLD operation, codenamed EVI-
DENCE, had been completed. This mission was intended to drop an
intelligence-gathering team into a rubber plantation close to where Hembry
had worked before the war; coincidentally, it also happened to be where
Davis was believed to be waiting patiently for a working radio. ISLD therefore offered to carry an extra one and deliver it to him, and the Burma
Section gratefully accepted. However, just before EVIDENCE actually
arrived, Davis's operator jerry-rigged a transmitter and, after a delay of a
year, finally made contact with Ceylon. Thus, when EVIDENCE's courier
reached Davis's camp with news of a radio, it was explained that none was
now needed. The curt tone of Davis's brief message in reply, 'Thank you
but we don't want your wares', was entirely misunderstood by the ISLD
team, which misinterpreted Davis's reluctance to use the word 'radio' in an
insecure plaintext message that might be read by the *Kempei'tai* as a rude
and ungrateful rebuff.[9]

EVIDENCE was later to complain that GUSTAVUS had persuaded local
guerrillas not to help ISLD, an accusation which was denied vehemently

by SOE. As SOE's official historian, Charles Cruickshank, was later to comment, this was 'not untypical of the relationship between the two organisations'. According to an eyewitness, Squadron Leader Terence O'Brien, who flew dozens of air missions for SOE and ISLD,

There was little contact between senior staff officers of the clandestine groups. Tremlett of 136 Malayan section and Hembry of ISLD did exchange information occasionally down in Ceylon but this was unusual, and there was no 136–ISLD contact in Calcutta.[10]

Nor was ISLD's standing with the navy especially high, for whereas SOE's operations involved the relatively straightforward infiltration of agents on a deserted beach, SIS engaged in much more complicated and dangerous undertakings. MULLET is just one example, a mission led by Hembry in February 1944 with four stated objectives: to establish an ISLD base camp on a remote island; to carry out a reconnaissance; to pick up an agent codenamed *Keat* from Penang; and to capture a junk. In the event, through sheer bad luck, none of these was accomplished and Hembry's seven agents were returned to Ceylon by HMS *Tactician*, its entire patrol having been wasted. Moreover, this was not an isolated occurrence. Operation RESIDENCY, a reconnaissance of Sumatra mounted in April 1944 by Major J. G. Lowe and Captains Wright and Annan from the Royal Engineers, ended in disaster. The plan called for Lowe's group to be dropped ashore and then collected from a prearranged rendezvous a few hours later, and it was this latter part that distinguished ISLD operations from SOE's and made them so much more risky. The submarine was required to approach close inshore, stand off for a while and then repeat the exercise, a formula for a significant naval loss if anything went wrong. RESIDENCY's shore party ran into some unexpectedly well-prepared Japanese defences, and Lowe and Annan were killed by machine-gun fire. HMS *Templar* managed to withdraw safely and even signalled Ceylon, so that *Truculent*, which was operating in the same area, could be alerted to the increased level of enemy activity. On this occasion both submarines escaped unscathed, but it highlighted the dangers inherent in most ISLD schemes and explains why they were regarded as so unpopular by those expected to support them.

Despite a few arrests by the *Kempei'tai* in March 1944, the GUSTAVUS network and its MCP members were to be the key to SOE's success in Malaya, an achievement made possible by John Davis. No doubt the fact that he knew that the MCP's General Secretary, Loi Teck, had been a Special Branch mole since his recruitment in 1938 strengthened his hand considerably and made the organisation more compliant towards SOE's wishes.[11]

The Malaya country section's story would not be complete without mention of OATMEAL, one of the more remarkable, not to say unique, examples of SOE/ISLD co-operation. The plan was for an all-Malay team, led by Ibrahim bin Ismail, to be landed from a pair of Consolidated Catalina amphibious aircraft at Kelantan on the north-east coast of Malaya. Ismail had been an officer cadet at the Indian Military Academy at Dehra Dun at the time of the fall of Singapore and upon his graduation had been posted to the Hyderabad Regiment at Agra in the North-West Frontier province. As soon as he heard about special operations, he obtained a transfer and underwent training at Avisawella in Ceylon, then operated by a former rubber planter, Jack Tovey, of the Malaya country section. Ismail's first operation, LIKEWISE I, was an attempt to infiltrate an SOE team into Malaya from HMS *Severn*, but the mission had been postponed because of bad weather and then abandoned on 13 August 1944 after a mechanical failure.

The first OATMEAL mission, on 28 October, was cancelled when a Japanese patrol surprised the planes after they had landed. The four agents were eventually delivered safely, albeit to the Perhentian Islands close to the original target area, on the second attempt on 31 October 1944. Having survived an epic flight lasting thirty-one hours, the entire team was betrayed to the *Kempei'tai* within hours of its landfall and, worse still, was captured with its transmitter, codes, radio schedule and security check intact. That the latter was carried into the field written on paper, and not committed to memory, was the most elementary breach of security, and may have been decisive in persuading the *Kempei'tai* to try playing back OATMEAL as a double agent.

Although OATMEAL had no way of knowing it, news of its members' arrests had been reported to the Malaya Section by APPRECIATION (see pages 204–5) and CARPENTER, so that when its first signal was received on 13 November, it was actually acknowledged by an ISLD unit to whom the case had been handed as a potential triple-agent radio game. Despite being under Japanese control, Ismail skilfully persuaded his captors that his safe arrival and security check responses ought to be reversed, thereby confirming to Ceylon that he was transmitting under duress. From that moment ISLD ran the *spiel* as a classic conduit for deception, even to the extent of dropping a consignment of requested supplies on 7 August 1945. Communications were maintained until the surrender, by which time Ismail had been awarded a Japanese decoration for his duplicity and offered advice by the *Kempei'tai* on how to evade the advancing enemy! He and all the

OATMEAL team thus survived Japanese captivity in some comfort, having been set up in a villa near Taiping.[12]

Opinion differs as to OATMEAL's strategic value. Squadron Leader Brookes, who flew one of the mission's Catalinas, considers the case to have been 'one of the finest spoof operations of the whole of the last war',[13] while the official historian of wartime deception, Professor Sir Michael Howard, with only the surviving documents to rely on, suggests that the 'honours rested very much more even' between the two protagonists.[14] However, Charles Cruickshank states that 'neither side profited from OAT-MEAL'.[15] In any event, the OATMEAL affair demonstrated that, even if it was a very rare occurrence, ISLD and SOE could sometimes co-operate.

Whatever OATMEAL's significance, SOE played a major role in the liberation of Malaya, although, it must be admitted, few of the many tons of arms supplied to the MCP were returned to the authorities after the Japanese surrender of Singapore on 12 September 1945. A total of ninety British officers had been infiltrated into enemy-occupied territory, forty-eight illicit wireless stations had been established, and an unknown quantity of arms and ammunition dropped into the jungle.[16] Indeed, many of the weapons used by the MCP during the Emergency later in the decade were found to have come from SOE originally. Paradoxically, the close connection between Force 136 and the MCP was to handicap the police when counter-insurgency operations began. Many European residents were bitterly resentful of the adventurers, who had escaped, as they saw it, to fight a glamorous war in the jungle, while the majority obeyed General Percival's order to surrender and, thereby, endured the appalling privations of Japanese capture.[17]

10 · Bitter and Unfruitful Arguments: SOE in South-East Asia

Where SOE in Europe had achieved particular success had been in establishing liaison through secret agents with numerous small independent units in Western Europe in preparation for widespread acts of sabotage and guerrilla activity on D-Day. Where they had – unavoidably – acted on a different plan, dealing with the top leadership of a country, they had got themselves involved in the most frightful political trouble and had been engaged in bitter and unfruitful arguments with the Foreign Office and Churchill himself. Fishing for sprats in Yugoslavia they had caught a man-eating shark (Tito) which rapidly swallowed their pet mackerel (Mihailovic); while in Greece the political parties with which SOE was in liaison might be likened to a bathful of barracudas. The thought of getting involved through Siam in another such contention gave SOE a fit of the vapours. Hence their instructions to the Siam Country Section to keep politics out of it.

Sir Andrew Gilchrist, Siam Section's Intelligence Officer, *Bangkok Top Secret*[1]

Although Malaya was a major preoccupation for SOE's India Mission, it was by no means the only one, for the country sections of Groups A (Burma, Siam and French Indo-China) and C (China) remained based on the subcontinent. From a skeleton, defensively orientated organisation headquartered in Meerut, with a sub-branch in Calcutta, the India Mission was transformed gradually into an aggressive fighting unit dedicated to SOE's original purpose of harrying the enemy, which, from 16 March 1944, became known as Force 136. This evolution was the consequence of the availability of greater resources and logistical support, and a reluctant recognition on the part of the military establishment that SOE was capable of doing more than simply plan for the worst by preparing stay-behind networks in territory expected to fall to the enemy. The unpalatable fact was that the swift Japanese advance across South-East Asia had left the British army in no position to engage the enemy or mount offensive operations, and the only hope of undermining the Emperor's forces was to adopt unconventional tactics. In practical terms this meant giving SOE priority on sea and air operations, and granting its personnel the training and logistical support needed to harass the Japanese. However, as SOE was bound to rely on locally recruited guerrillas in the field, it was to encounter the kind of complex political hazards which had so disadvantaged it in other theatres. Indeed, those complications were to be exacerbated not only by the usual hostility from SIS, but also by conflict with American regional interests.

As head of the India Mission, Colin Mackenzie's chain of command extended through his deputy, Gavin Stewart, to his Chief of Staff, Robert Guinness, who was a regular soldier seconded from the Royal Engineers. Agents were managed through a useful front or cut-out, the School for Eastern Interpreters (SEI), centred on a large house in Bombay owned by Mohammed Ali Jinnah, the founder of Pakistan. In Calcutta, where Gavin Stewart was based as Station Commander from May 1943, the SEI was accommodated in a mansion beside the River Hooghli at Alam Bazaar, which belonged to the poet Rabindranath Tagore.

Once the immediate threat of a Japanese invasion of India had passed, the country sections run by Steven Cummins were encouraged to plan their return to enemy-occupied territory. This, however, was easier said than done, because SOE's training facilities were spread far and wide. The average agent candidate was obliged to travel more than four thousand miles and attend three different camps before he had qualified in the required skills of signals (at the wireless training centre at Meerut), parachuting (at the RAF's Air Landing School at Chaklala, and then at Jessore) and demolition (Poona). Many of those who served in the India Mission were convinced that SOE London had little grasp of the sheer size of India and the enormous distances involved. For example, the train journey from Calcutta to Delhi took thirty hours. When George Taylor undertook an inspection tour early in 1944, he commented on this upon his return:

When the internal distances between one establishment and another, combined with wartime transport deficiencies, are taken into account it seems almost as if the administrative difficulties behind the lines equalled in complexity and demand for clear leadership those of the men operating in the jungle against the Japanese.[2]

For the Burma Section, headed by Ritchie Gardiner,[3] the young Scots manager of a timber company, who had walked out of Burma through the

Force 136 (Meerut and Kandy)

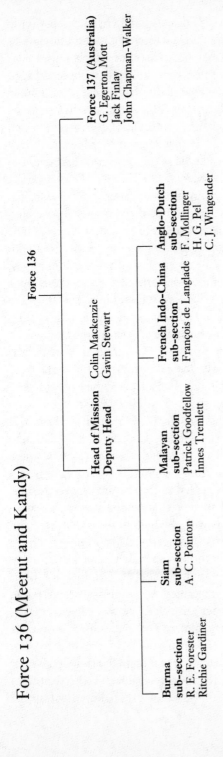

Force 136

Head of Mission   Colin Mackenzie
Deputy Head   Gavin Stewart

Force 137 (Australia)
G. Egerton Mott
Jack Finlay
John Chapman-Walker

Burma
sub-section
R. E. Forester
Ritchie Gardiner

Siam
sub-section
A. C. Pointon

Malayan
sub-section
Patrick Goodfellow
Innes Tremlett

French Indo-China
sub-section
François de Langlade

Anglo-Dutch
sub-section
F. Mollinger
H. G. Pel
C. J. Wingender

Chaukkan Pass with the remnants of SOE's ill-fated Oriental Mission in Singapore, active operations meant building on the very modest foundations left by the Oriental Mission's stay-behind parties, of which only Major Hugh Seagrim and his Shan supporters were believed to have escaped capture. Gardiner, who had originally intended to have a career in mining before joining the teak business of Macgregor & Co. in Burma, had replaced Major Forrester in July 1943, by which time contact had been re-established with the tribesmen in the Karen Hills. Before the war Gardiner had lived and worked in the jungle for eight months of the year and had come to know the rain forests and their inhabitants, the Karens. These warlike people, who are still fighting for autonomy fifty years after these events, had much to fear from being ruled from Rangoon by their traditional enemies, the lowland Burmese, who were inclined to collaborate with their occupiers. The Japanese invasion of Burma had been completed by early 1942 with Rangoon falling on 8 March, leaving the enemy firmly in control of almost all the country, with the exception of the northern hills where the Karens commanded the jungle. Since these tribes were the only native Burmese likely to welcome a return of British colonial rule, they made natural allies for SOE, which put several groups through the special training schools.

Operation HARLINGTON, consisting of four SOE-trained Karens, was the pathfinder in February 1943. Over the following months there were twenty attempts to supply it with a radio, but all failed because of poor weather or mechanical problems with the ancient Hudsons; eventually, on 12 October 1943, Major Jimmy Nimmo parachuted in and linked up with Seagrim. Two months later they were joined by Captain Eric McCrindle, but his arrival was to mark the end of what had been a long and quite successful campaign. Ignoring pleas from Force 136 regarding wasteful duplication and poor security, ISLD decided to drop a team of three Karens 'blind' into Seagrim's area. One of their agents landed badly and could only be extricated from some bamboo with the help of local villagers, who immediately alerted the Japanese garrisoned nearby. This prompted a huge sweep by the enemy to find ISLD's three parachutists, but in the event they succeeded in capturing SOE's Nimmo and McCrindle. Reprisals against the Karen villagers were then instituted, so Seagrim surrendered in March 1944 in order to prevent further atrocities. He was gaoled in Rangoon and then executed with his companions. A later attempt to revive the Karens, FLIMWELL, failed when a two-man team was arrested as they landed, one of them actually having been dropped on to the roof of a house. With some justification SOE held ISLD responsible for the deaths of Seagrim and his SOE companions, and it was widely believed within the

Burma Section 'that all three would have been safe had ISLD not blundered into the area and aroused the Japanese'.[4]

While HARLINGTON was under way, the Burma Section launched several other operations. DILWYN I, in March 1943, was the first of a series to arm the Kachins, and on 5 March 1944 Major L. V. Lovett-Campbell was successfully parachuted into the area, in time to assist in the preparation of reception committees used by General Orde Wingate's own private army, the Chindits. An exponent of irregular warfare, the eccentric Wingate had applied his unorthodox ideas to great effect in Palestine and Abyssinia, but he had little time for Force 136. Although his glider-borne troops were to operate behind enemy lines, in exactly the same territory as SOE, there was only minimal consultation, and Guinness only learned of Wingate's expedition by accident. This was an extraordinary duplication of effort, which led to some angry exchanges between GHQ and Force 136. The explanation was that Wingate 'disliked and suspected' SOE,[5] but none the less the two organisations co-operated to good effect once they were on the ground together.

The Burma Section's main handicap, apart from only minimal contact with its target country, was an almost complete lack of knowledge about conditions in the capital or the southern provinces. SIS, masquerading as ISLD, was in much the same predicament: it had almost no assets left to supply even the most basic intelligence. Therefore, SOE was obliged to work in the dark. As a result of this relative ignorance, SOE almost lost what was to prove a vital link with Rangoon, Thein Pe, codenamed *Merlin*. Thein Pe was a supporter of the local Communist Party, which, like the MCP, was thought to be only marginally more opposed to the Japanese than to the British. Accordingly, he got a hostile reception when he arrived in India in July 1942 with tales of a home-grown resistance organisation in Burma. Instead of being welcomed as a much-needed ally, he was nearly thrown into gaol as a dangerous subversive. Eventually, he was accepted for training and was taken back to Burma by motor-launch with a companion, Tin Shwei (*Lancelot*). There was then a considerable delay in opening wireless communications with the resistance, a breakthrough that was not achieved until November 1944, when a Burmese wireless operator, DONKEY, was dropped successfully. Thereafter, about seventy recruits sponsored by the Communists were exfiltrated and prepared for missions home.

ISLD's absence from Burma placed a greater burden on SOE, although this was a role that Force 136 accepted with reluctance. Its personnel had been trained to raise guerrillas and conduct clandestine sabotage operations

against the enemy, not gather intelligence. This distinction was not appreciated by General Slim, who constantly complained about the lack of quality
intelligence emanating from SOE, to such a degree that he even advocated
that it be replaced by 101 OSS or that, alternatively, it be amalgamated
with Z Force, the special unit co-ordinating the 14th Army's reconnaissance
patrols. SOE opposed both proposals and managed to maintain its independence, but only just. Certainly the Burma Section's reputation was never
to be very high.

This was not entirely SOE's fault. Several agents, on whom SOE had
pinned high hopes, had proved a disappointment. A member of the Indian
Communist Party was parachuted close to Rangoon in June 1943 in Operation MAHOUT with the hope that he would make contact with other Indians
in the area, but he had achieved little apart from some minor sabotage
before his arrest in September 1944. A similar attempt to infiltrate some
Chinese, known as the Pandas and volunteered by the Chinese Nationalists,
also came to nought. Some of them turned out to have had no knowledge
of Burma, and of the eighteen selected for Force 136, only seven were
considered suitable for training. Of this number, only two or three were
ever deployed, usually as wireless operators. The single agent sent to Man-
dalay was not heard of until 1945, when he turned up with completely
out-of-date information. In fact, SOE subsequently discovered that these
agents' main objective was to learn about SOE and report back to Chungking in China, rather than actively to participate in Burma Section operations.

SOE's difficulties in Burma were compounded by the presence of 101
and 404 OSS, for whom Slim had a high regard, as did the local American
commander, General Joseph Stilwell. It was under pressure from the latter
that SOE was eventually withdrawn from the Kachin Hills in northern
Burma, much to the dismay of the 3,000 tribesmen who had been armed
and trained by the British. This left the field open to 101 OSS, commanded
by Dr Carl Eifler, and the prospect of much inter-agency rivalry.

Another problem for SOE, highlighted by the experience of a self-
contained, three-man JEDBURGH team from Europe, was the organisation's
willingness to accept assistance from all comers, whatever their previous
allegiances and behaviour. Major T. A. Carew led the JEDBURGH CAMEL,
which was dropped to reinforce HOUND in December 1944. HOUND was
one of a series of missions dropped 'blind' into the jungle to establish
wireless stations and reception committees for subsequent teams. Its wireless operator, a tribesman from the Chin Hills, also had a highly developed
sense of humour. When signalled instructions from headquarters on how to

handle potentially hostile villagers in his area, he replied with commendable brevity: 'Natives friendly.'

CAMEL's objective was to gather intelligence and call in air strikes by wireless on the retreating Japanese. This they did with the enthusiastic help of the Anti-Fascist Organisation (AFO), a disciplined group of self-styled resistance fighters, who only turned on the Japanese in 1945. Prior to that most had been active collaborators and members of the notorious Burmese National Army (BNA), which, despite its misleading name, had been under Japanese command. Having subjugated the country, Japan had gone through the pretence of granting Burma independence, a sham which was never taken seriously by the Allies regardless of the BNA's complicity. However, Force 136 soon became aware of some uncomfortable political realities, when Carew was eventually overrun by the advancing Allies and his erstwhile comrades were taken into custody and charged with terrible war crimes. Once news of this episode filtered up to the India Mission's headquarters, a furious debate took place. SOE insisted that it needed help on the ground and that its liaison personnel could not be expected to examine the credentials of every volunteer guerrilla. The Burmese government-in-exile insisted that SOE was arming Communist terrorists, who would demand a stake in the post-war administration, a development which was considered quite unthinkable. Mackenzie disagreed. He knew that Seagrim's helpers had paid a terrible price, but had remained loyal and had maintained their silence under tremendous pressure. Not to arm them, he insisted, would 'condemn them to death',[6] and Force 136 would rather cease all operations into Burma. As the row progressed the Burma Section was instructed to suspend its activities, and then directed to avoid contact with the AFO. These orders were then countermanded, and confusion reigned while the decision was passed to London. In the meantime, SOE continued to supply the AFO and came to regard the Burmese civil authorities in India as 'hostile'. The Foreign Office learned of the controversy when Lord Louis Mountbatten, as Supreme Commander, sent a signal to London announcing his decision to back SOE. Eden was horrified and minuted the Prime Minister: 'The tone of this telegram is reminiscent of too much we have had from SOE in the past. Surely we should not boost these people so much. They will give great trouble hereafter.'[7]

Despite the opposition of the Foreign Office, SOE persisted with its policy of arming the politically unreliable AFO and thereby did great damage to the Japanese, who incurred thousands of casualties. Railway lines were cut, bridges sabotaged, roads mined and convoys ambushed. Certainly Slim, somewhat belatedly, recognised the strategic importance of SOE's contribution, which included tying down an estimated fifty thousand enemy troops in the Karen Hills alone. With his consent two major operations, codenamed NATION and CHARACTER, were launched to assist the 14th Army's advance into South-East Asia. Both involved Force 136 personnel (see table on page 197) linking up with some fairly unsavoury members of the BNA and the AFO, but this was the price exacted for engaging the enemy at minimal cost. DONKEY was the first in the NATION series, landing 'blind' in November 1944, preparing the way for TERRIER, ELK, WEASEL and REINDEER a few months later. Together they were to take control of a sizeable area and to identify dozens of enemy transport, storage depots, ammunition dumps and troop concentrations so that they could be attacked from the air by the RAF. The India Mission was later to claim that NATION killed 3,381 Japanese troops and wounded 201, for an Allied loss of thirteen killed and fifty-two wounded, a very acceptable ratio by any standards.

What made NATION possible was the arrival of 357 Special Duty Squadron with ten B-24 Liberators and ten C-47 Dakotas. Operating from Jessore, they flew more missions during the December 1944 moon period than the total number undertaken during the previous year, when the RAF had been obliged to rely upon borrowed Hudsons. A month later 358 (SD) Squadron, with a further sixteen Liberators, was transferred to Jessore, allowing nearly fifty missions to be flown during January 1945. These dramatically improved air-supply facilities were quickly translated into more effective results on the ground, both in terms of intelligence relayed to the regular forces and the number of natives (and defectors) volunteering for enlistment. Air superiority allowed more missions to be undertaken, which meant more supply drops and a realisation by the native population that the harassed Japanese were headed for defeat.

The story was much the same with CHARACTER, which, using experienced JEDBURGH teams released from the European theatre, succeeded in inflicting more casualties on the retreating enemy than the regulars. CHARACTER was a series of co-ordinated missions, based in the Karen Hills, which intended to prevent the occupiers from moving south into central Burma. The target was the Japanese 15th Division and what was left of the 28th Army, and both beleaguered units faced sustained guerrilla and air attacks at every river crossing. The pressure was maintained until mid-September 1945, when news of Japan's capitulation was finally believed by the local commanders.

Even SOE's sternest critics were forced to admit that the Burma Section had acquitted itself well in action, regardless of the political complexities encountered. Altogether 270 Burmese, drawn more or less equally from the hills and the lowlands, were trained in India and sent on operations, and they had taken a heavy toll of the Japanese. What tarnished their performance, however, were the bitter rear echelon disputes, which, as we shall see, were to engulf the Americans as well as SOE's other country sections.

•   •   •   •   •   •

SOE's Siam Section was headed from its inception in June 1943 by Peter Pointon, a Cambridge-educated businessman who, having won an MC in the First World War, had spent most of his career in the timber trade of Burma and Siam. He spoke Siamese and ran the country section from Calcutta with the assistance of N. F. Nicholson, formerly the head of Lever Brothers in Bangkok. Together they only just managed to avoid the political controversy which had been generated in neighbouring Burma. The difficulty arose over the exact status of the pro-Japanese regime in Bangkok, which, by virtue of its declaration of war on Britain and America in January 1942, was technically categorised as a belligerent. Was it a puppet administration that deserved to be helped to rid itself of its unwelcome occupiers, as SOE maintained, or was it simply a compliant member of the Axis, as defined by the Foreign Office? Either interpretation had implications for the treatment and formation of a post-war government and, as usual, the professional diplomats took what they regarded to be a long-term view.

For SOE, expediency was the watchword, and when an opportunity presented itself in September 1943 to establish contact with what purported to be a dissident faction within the Siamese Government, in the form of an Oxford-educated messenger from the Finance Minister, Luang Pridi, it was seized. Pridi had always been anti-Japanese, but his influence within the administration had been reduced when he had been appointed as one of the two Regents selected to represent the monarchy while the young King was in Switzerland. His approach to the British came in a roundabout fashion, via a refugee in China who had been interviewed by Major J. McMullen, an SOE officer attached to the British Embassy in Chungking. This initial contact persuaded SOE to launch PRICHARD, an attempt to exfiltrate Pridi in response to a favourable coded signal from him broadcast over Radio Bangkok. This was a crucial breakthrough for the Siam Section because it already boasted a sizeable pool of expatriate agents from which to draw, but not the means to arrange the all-important reception committees that SOE had learned were an essential component of successful operations. Most of the candidates had been studying in England at the time of the Japanese take-over, and thirty-five had volunteered to fight and had been accepted into the Pioneer Corps even though they had been officially classified as enemy aliens. However, SOE knew to its cost that before taking the next logical step, of infiltrating them back into Siam, secure arrangements would have to be made for their safe arrival. The details were to be contained in the coded message on Radio Bangkok.

Whether the correct, prearranged text was ever really transmitted remains a matter of doubt. Nevertheless, the country section sent three Siamese students, all recruited from colleges in England, to Ceylon, where they boarded HMS *Tactician* for a rendezvous off the coast of Siam. Unfortunately the operation, scheduled for 6 December 1943, was delayed for three days by MISSIVE II, an unsuccessful ISLD pick-up in Malaya, which meant that no reception committee was found when the party finally arrived at the prearranged spot. The submarine waited a week and then returned to Trincomalee with the disappointed agents. A further 'blind' attempt by Liberator, APPRECIATION I, was made on 14 March 1944 and on this occasion the three landed safely, but in the wrong place. The agents were promptly arrested, but Pridi intervened before they could come to any harm. A similar fate befell APPRECIATION II, which landed 'blind' three weeks later, on 4 April. SOE's third mission, BILLOW, fared even worse: its leader, Captain Ngit Yin Kok, was killed and his three companions captured. It was not until 17 August that SOE in Calcutta learned of what had happened through a letter delivered to the British Embassy in Kunming. A duplicate also found its way to Baker Street, via the Siamese Legation in Berne. In them Pridi revealed that, apart from the six SOE men from the two APPRECIATION missions now in his hands, ten other agents to his knowledge had been intercepted by the Siamese authorities, of whom six had been killed. These deaths could have been avoided, he observed, if he had been consulted before their despatch, a comment which was conveyed to OSS and ISLD, who had sponsored some of the missions concerned. Pridi went on to suggest a radio rendezvous, and wireless contact was established with APPRECIATION on 22 August, when the correct call-signs of both missions, JBJ and SDK, were transmitted. Thus, after a delay of nearly five months, the Siam country section could finally boast a single (amalgamated) station in enemy territory. Whilst this was, on the face of it, a welcome development, it also bore some weighty implications, not the least being its reliability. Tony Fearfield, the section's signals officer, cautioned that there was good reason to believe that APPRECIATION's operator was working under duress, which in turn suggested that Pridi himself might be part of a sophisticated Japanese-controlled deception ploy.

This direct link with a government which was supposedly part of the Axis caused the Foreign Office considerable grief, but on 25 September the War Cabinet ignored Eden's recommendation that SOE should terminate the contact and authorised Mountbatten to send Pridi an encouraging letter, on condition that it did not make any commitments regarding the composition of a post-war government in Rangoon. All this proved exceptionally convenient for SOE, which had already made arrangements for just such a message, in the form of a directive and questionnaire in the Supreme Commander's name. During the period that anguished messages were exchanged between Kandy and London on the topic of the British Government's attitude to the Siamese, ISLD started to prepare for a take-over of the case on the basis that APPRECIATION had come under enemy control. The Siam country section's Intelligence Officer, Andrew Gilchrist, remembers being told

that a special unit was being formed for double-playing the Japs and that Major Smith, Intelligence Corps, was already on his way to Calcutta, and would take over all our contacts; we were to hand over to him all relevant records, codes and equipment on a date which would be notified to us by signal. This was extremely depressing for both Peter [Pointon] and myself. Remember that we both believed firmly in the authenticity of the contact.[8]

SOE's solution was to use an ingenious scheme devised by Gilchrist, who, up until his internment by the Japanese in December 1941, had been a junior diplomat at the British Embassy in Bangkok. After his release in September 1942, through an exchange of detainees in Lourenco Marques, he had volunteered for SOE and had been posted to Calcutta, where he had arrived in August 1944, just in time to participate in the deliberations over what should be done to exploit APPRECIATION's unexpected radio link. Fortunately, Gilchrist had been acquainted with Pridi in Bangkok and had the means to ensure that it really was the Minister who was in control of APPRECIATION, and not the ubiquitous *Kempei'tai*. He simply asked for his own home address in Scotland, knowing that Pridi either possessed it or had the means to find it through Gilchrist's friends. The reply, which was correct in every respect, even confused SOE's cipher staff, who assumed that, even after decoding, the five-figure groups of text had been corrupted: KERSE LESMA HAGOW LANAR KSHIR ESTOP HOPET HISIS OK.

Once SOE was satisfied with APPRECIATION's bona fides, it decided to send in a further team to maintain independent contact with the anti-Japanese activists who had formed the Free Siamese Movement (FSM). Reports from Bangkok made it clear that, although APPRECIATION might be operating for Pridi, the Japanese were fully aware of the situation and there was a persistent danger that the *Kempei'tai* might intervene at any moment. Experience elsewhere had demonstrated that the *Kempei'tai* was a sufficiently sophisticated practitioner of the art of counter-intelligence to mount quite impressive deception operations and run double agents. Operation BRILLIG was designed to remedy the problem and was despatched on 6 September 1944. This was a two-man team, consisting of Captains Kris Tosayanonda (*Kong*) and Prasert Padumananda (*Pau*), both qualified wireless operators. Within two days BRILLIG was firmly established in Bangkok and had made contact with Pridi. This was regarded as a major breakthrough because, although SOE was not told at the time, ISLD and OSS had both tried to infiltrate missions, a total of five in all, but none had survived. Certainly there were never any doubts about BRILLIG's credentials. Shortly before his departure Tosayanonda had engaged in a furious row with Jack Balharry, the country section's administration officer, because a request to take some high value articles on his mission, such as gold chains, had been denied. BRILLIG's third signal from the field contained a detailed list of every item Balharry had previously vetoed.

Pridi's response to BRILLIG was Operation SEQUENCE, a secret delegation which was sent to Ceylon by Catalina and which arrived on 22 February 1945. While SOE was delighted with this progress, the Foreign Office remained deeply suspicious about what it perceived as political meddling, and was especially anxious that Mountbatten should not be drawn into any discussions that in turn might compromise the British Government's official policy on Siam. Those with a knowledge of the subject were dubious about all of this, for in reality *there was no official policy*. The issue was a difficult one because Colin Mackenzie, following Mountbatten, had moved his headquarters to Kandy in December 1944, which meant that Ceylon had been transformed strategically from a relative backwater, a mere operations sub-branch of the India Mission, into Force 136's main base. Perhaps surprisingly, given the organisation's past performance, SOE succeeded in manoeuvring the SEQUENCE group through the political minefields in Ceylon, and returned its members safely to Rangoon having noted, but not actually accepted, Pridi's suggestions about Siam's post-war independence. Nevertheless, the way had been paved for a series of airdrops to FSM guerrillas sympathetic to Pridi.

First among these was COUPLING, which put a three-man team led by Major Snoh Nilkamhaeng into the north-east on 5 December 1944. This meant that the Siam country section was running short of recruits, so INFLUX was mounted to collect a group of FSM volunteers. Vic Wemyss and Ben Bathurst negotiated for a Catalina from 240 Squadron to undertake the mission, and this was arranged by Frank Godber, the section's Air Liaison Officer, who had recently transferred to SOE from that very unit. The plan was to take off from the Red Hills Reservoir in Madras, fly to a rendezvous off Terutao Island on Siam's west coast, pick up eight potential agents and then deliver them to Ceylon. Apart from some anxious moments when, three hours after landing, all the Siamese had still not managed the difficult journey from the beach through treacherous surf, the operation was completed without any loss, apart from two rubber boats. It was subsequently repeated, with INFLUX II, to collect a further seven volunteers, and again with INFLUX III.

Once these volunteers had been trained in Ceylon, they were returned to Siam as part of PRIEST, SOE's contribution to support Mountbatten's plan to capture Phuket and then use the island as a base from which to mount air strikes against the mainland.[9] PRIEST required no less than six separate sub-missions, so APPRECIATION and one of BRILLIG's sub-agents were ordered south to the target area. This reduced the number of new teams needed to just four, which were to be infiltrated from Ceylon by Catalina, with only one dropping by parachute.

All that remained were some direct talks with Pridi to alert him to Mountbatten's intentions, a task that for security reasons could not be entrusted to any of the Siamese already in the field. Indeed, headquarters decreed that this called for the infiltration of a high-powered official British military liaison mission. Codenamed PANICLE, it was ready for despatch by Catalina at the end of April, once the inclement weather had settled. The man chosen to lead it was Brigadier Victor Jaques, a much decorated veteran of the First World War, who, as one of the leading lawyers in pre-war Bangkok, was a well-known and much respected figure in the capital. Jaques was joined on PANICLE by Tom Hobbs and Prince Subha Svasti (*Arun*). After five days of talks with Pridi, Jaques returned with an enthusiastic report, which allowed SOE to confirm that PRIEST was ready for action. It was at this moment that Mountbatten changed his mind and opted for another, bolder plan, which would exploit the growing weakness of the Japanese and reach Singapore quicker.

The cancellation of PRIEST was a bitter disappointment for those involved, but it did allow the Siam country section to return to the business of organising the FSM. After a brief respite in Ceylon, Jaques returned to Siam, where he remained until the end of hostilities. In May the FSM was to be joined by some of SOE's experienced personnel, like Peter Kemp and Rowland Winn, who had been released from the European theatre. Among them were Christopher Hudson, who went to COUPLING; David

Smiley and Tom Hobbs to CANDLE; Philip Oliver to PHUKEO; and John Hibberdine, Stanley Moss and Kenneth Scott to SONGKLA. By August no less than thirty wireless units had been linked to the country section in Calcutta, which itself had grown to include Bryce Smith, Paul Ashwell, Harry Small and John Warrell. At this late stage very little Siamese territory was left in Japanese hands and the final surrender came too soon for Pridi's resistance groups to be put to the ultimate test, a large-scale rising. Such an event had been planned to occur in around January 1946, but the atomic bomb brought hostilities to a swift and, as far as SOE was concerned, an unexpected conclusion.

●   ●   ●   ●   ●   ●

Group A's third remaining country section, Indo-China, stayed largely unchanged when it transferred in July 1943 from the Oriental Mission to the India Mission. Baron François de Langlade continued in command, supported by a small group of French rubber planters, Pierre Boulle among them, who had been trained by STS 102.[10] After the fall of Singapore they had dispersed, a few to India via Batavia, some to Kunming, but most had simply disappeared.

Quite apart from being hampered by a severe shortage of agents, de Langlade's freedom of movement was somewhat limited by the difficult political situation in his region. Chief among them was President Roosevelt's determined opposition to French colonialism. While lukewarm about British and Dutch colonial ambitions in the Far East, the President was adamant that the French should not be allowed to return to re-establish themselves as a colonial power. Churchill disagreed with this policy, but he was unwilling to challenge Roosevelt on the issue, which left the French isolated. Meanwhile, de Gaulle's supporters were keen to send a military mission to liaise with Mountbatten's staff, but the War Cabinet was not prepared to let it leave Algiers if its reception in Kandy was to be interpreted as a commitment to a continued post-war French presence in South-East Asia.

This stalemate was discussed by Colin Gubbins when he visited North Africa in June 1944, where he met General Blaizot, de Gaulle's nominee to head the Free French Military Mission to the Far East. Exactly what they talked about is unknown, but an invitation was extended to Blaizot to make an informal visit to Ceylon. This resulted in his arrival in October 1944. In January 1945 his troops followed, much to the dismay of the Americans and the Foreign Office. SOE was accused of having misled Mountbatten about the Foreign Office's hostility to the unwelcome appearance of the French, but Gubbins replied, disingenuously, that Mount-batten's permission must have been endorsed by his political adviser, (Sir) Esler Dening. When the Chairman of the Joint Intelligence Committee, Victor Cavendish-Bentinck, read of the furore that followed, he simply closed the file with the apposite comment, 'Typical of SOE!'[11] Once again, SOE had been caught meddling in politics and interfering with Foreign Office policy.

One curious aspect to this particular row, which once again demonstrated the kind of trouble that could be stirred up when SOE strayed into the political arena, was the involvement of Major Peter Murphy, Mountbatten's very close friend and a former member of the Communist Party of Great Britain.[12] Quite how Gubbins learned of their relationship is unclear, although he may have been briefed by Colin Mackenzie, who had known Murphy when they were both up at Cambridge. In any event, when Gubbins and Mountbatten met in Cairo at a regional conference in 1944, they had discussed the possibility of Murphy being transferred from his post with the Ministry of Economic Warfare in Algiers (where he was in contact with Blaizot) to Mountbatten's staff as CD's liaison officer and the Supreme Commander's 'Personal Staff Officer'. This appointment undoubtedly gave SOE an advantage over its rivals in the clandestine field, and Murphy's timely negotiations with Blaizot may be an explanation for Mountbatten's willingness to back SOE on the issue of the Free French, in defiance of the Foreign Office. Certainly Murphy enjoyed considerable influence over Mountbatten, and it may well be that Gubbins used his appointment as a means to counter the recent introduction of P Division, a co-ordinating body headed by Captain Garnons-Williams RN (working with an American deputy, Captain Taylor USN), which had been created to supervise the various clandestine groups operating in South-East Asia Command and adjudicate in disputes between them. When explaining his new post to Murphy, Mountbatten wrote, 'You would not in fact be specifically employed on SOE duties on my staff, but would keep in touch with Captain Garnons-Williams who is my co-ordinator for SOE, SIS and OSS.'[13] In reality P Division was a committee chaired by Garnons-Williams, which met weekly and included representatives of OSS, SOE, SIS, Psychological Warfare, Deception, the RAF, the Royal Navy and various specialist staff branches. Once cleared by P, a proposal was forwarded to the transport liaison officers to determine whether a particular suggestion was feasible. The French, by virtue of their ambiguous status in the region, were naturally excluded from this machinery except, of course, through SOE and de Langlade's country section.

Long before Blaizot's arrival, de Langlade had been making overtures to the French resistance in Indo-China using the single remaining radio link between Hanoi and Chungking, and in the summer of 1944 he decided to make a personal inspection, Operation BELIEF. Weather and mechanical problems delayed his departure until July, when he was infiltrated into the north of the country from China. The tour was completed without incident, but upon his return de Langlade discovered that Force 136 had been thrown into turmoil for sponsoring the visit. When the Americans had learned that de Langlade had been briefed by de Gaulle before his departure, and that he had carried a letter of introduction from the General, they accused Mackenzie of deliberately undermining the stated American policy of preventing the French from recolonising the region. Angry telegrams were exchanged between the India Mission and London, which led Mountbatten to ask for Robert Guinness's dismissal. Guinness's infraction had been his approval of de Langlade's mission, and the consent he had given in his capacity as acting commander of Force 136 while Colin Mackenzie was on a visit to England. Such a head of steam built up on this issue that SOE had to pay the price demanded. On 15 November 1944 Guinness was recalled to London and replaced by John Anstey from North Africa. Mackenzie's view of all this can be judged by the fact that, on the day of Guinness's departure, de Langlade made a second visit to Hanoi to negotiate with the pro-Japanese French administration there. The results were a commitment to de Gaulle and the development of a large resistance network, which, by the end of December, amounted to no less than thirteen transmitters linked to Calcutta.

The number of airdrops to the Free French resistance increased dramatically during January and February 1945, and this escalation may have played a part in the Japanese decision to mount a ferocious coup on 9 March. The outcome was a complete Japanese take-over of the country and the loss of most of SOE's wireless units. The suddenness of the French collapse, just as SOE had been building up the strength of its networks, caused ructions for the India Mission. Mackenzie blamed the Foreign Office for having prevented the transfer of more French at an earlier stage, and the latter insisted that judicious caution had been exercised because of SOE's record of political mayhem. As Charles Cruickshank succinctly put it, 'Force 136's efforts in Indo-China were totally wasted.'[14] Once again, SOE had attempted to mix politics and warfare, and had come out the loser.

●   ●   ●   ●   ●   ●

The last remaining area of Force 136's operations that requires study is the Anglo-Dutch country section, which, based in Ceylon, concentrated its attention on Sumatra. Although no stay-behind networks had been prepared, the Dutch had pursued a scorched-earth policy so as to deny the island's many natural assets to the enemy. When the last Allied forces were evacuated, the oilfields were torched and the plantations wrecked, but few believed that the Dutch would ever be welcomed back. The fact was that, as colonial powers went, the Dutch had a poor record, and their reputation was so bad that they had been obliged to disarm even their own native police shortly before the evacuation because they could not trust them. The only group considered likely to oppose the Japanese were the Chinese, but, given the Dutch record of ruthless suppression, they were hardly good prospects. It is therefore not surprising that the first Anglo-Dutch operation, MATRIARCH, was an abject failure. The section, headed by Christopher Hudson with Frits Mollinger as his second-in-command, had intended for a submarine to put a team ashore on Sumatra and then collect it after a short reconnaissance. The mission, led by Jan Scheepens and consisting of five Dutchmen and two SOE officers, landed from the *O 24* in March 1943, but, after a fruitless encounter with unco-operative villagers, ran into a Japanese ambush. Following this narrow escape, the remainder of the plan was abandoned.

ISLD did not have any greater success. RESIDENCY and SUGARLOAF followed at the end of April 1944, both with limited military objectives, none of which was really achieved. The plan was for the capture and interrogation of a few locals, and a survey to locate some potential landing sites for future airborne operations. Once again disaster struck. HMS *Templar* dropped a party led by Major J. G. D. Lowe on Sumatra's southern coast. The others were Jan Scheepens, Lieutenant Sisselaar and Captains A. F. Wright and W. R. Annan from the Royal Engineers, together with fourteen Indian and Dutch soldiers. Once ashore the group split into two, but Lowe, Annan and their Pathan guide were killed when they stumbled across a Japanese machine-gun post. The rest of the operation was promptly cancelled and *Templar* evacuated the survivors.

It was the combination of Japanese vigilance and a reluctance to co-operate on the part of the native population that effectively prevented Hudson's section from making any headway. A series of operations codenamed RETALIATE was launched to gather potential agents off Chinese junks in Sumatran waters, but again the parties returned home with little to show for their efforts. Nor was abduction generally regarded as the best way of recruiting committed helpers. Thus, by January 1945 Sumatra was the only territory in Force 136's theatre without a single SOE agent. This depressing position did not improve much in the months that followed, and it was not until the end of June 1945 that TETHER, a four-man team led by Sisselaar, was dropped 'blind' into the north of the island to find some other suitable landing sites. Once TETHER had been established, more operations followed: Commander Lefrandt arrived with SWEEP on 1 July, and on 3 July HMS *Torbay* landed Major Lodge's STEEL. All were still on the island in November 1945 when SOE's Far East branch was disbanded, leaving ISLD in the field alone. Thus, the Anglo-Dutch country section 'had had little chance to distinguish itself in the three years of its existence'.[15]

●　　●　　●　　●　　●　　●

If the India Mission needed a single country section to restore its prestige in London, it might easily be claimed that, perhaps for all the wrong reasons, Force 136's Group C under Colonel Gill-Davies did so. As we have already seen, the China Section got off to an unpromising start when John Keswick fell out with Chiang Kai-shek's intelligence service. Thereafter, SOE's efforts to work from China were somewhat fragmented. Finlay Andrew and Jim Galvin tried to build bridges by offering financial support to one of Chungking's many local clandestine agencies, the Institute for International Relations, which operated a useful network of agents across the Far East, including two in Shanghai, and all equipped with radios. Once this relationship had been able to prosper, the Chinese allowed Colonel P. H. Munro Faure to open an office in Kunming under assistant military attaché cover, and consented in principle to participate in a joint wireless training scheme: SOE was to provide the sets and signals personnel, with the Chinese supplying the operators. This plan never developed because of the Japanese surrender.

SOE's other attempts to operate in China were stymied by the American commander, General Wedemeyer, who distrusted the organisation and had already crossed swords with Mountbatten over SOE's activities in Indo-China. He insisted that all plans be cleared through him personally, and his power of veto was exercised on political, rather than practical, lines. Group C quickly realised that at the heart of American objections was a broad antipathy to collaborating with Chinese Communists, who were actually the most active anti-Japanese guerrillas. Recognising that Wedemeyer could not be persuaded, and that the risks of outflanking the Americans were too great, Group C was obliged to divert its Chinese agents, recruited in Canada and trained at the Okaganan Valley STS in British Columbia, to the Malayan country section, where they were eventually put to good use.

Although the Americans conspired to 'keep Force 136 inactive for the rest of the war in China',[16] there was one highly secret operation undertaken in the area which was to have far-reaching consequences. Its origin was MICKLEHAM, run by (Sir) Walter Fletcher, a commodity trader of immense proportions, who had drawn up a scheme for the illicit purchase of rubber. According to his calculations the producers in South-East Asia had created a large surplus, which was too great even for the Japanese to handle. His solution was to build a network of buyers, who would persuade local entre-preneurs to smuggle rubber out of enemy-held territory and sell it to his agents. The project floundered for the lack of willing purchasing agents and working capital, but Fletcher, a future Labour MP, was undaunted. He turned his attention to other strategic materials, identifying quinine, tungsten, silk and mercury as markets which could be usefully exploited to the advantage of the Allies.

In practice Fletcher's proposals never quite worked, although the econ-omic intelligence he generated was considered valuable. However, during the course of his negotiations he discovered a highly profitable method of dealing in the black market and raising very large sums of money in China. The basis of the wholly illegal transactions that followed, codenamed REMORSE, was the artificially high rates of exchange for the Chinese National Dollar in Kunming, and the restrictions on foreign currency by the Indian Exchange Control. What took place was, quite simply, 'the biggest currency black market in history'.[17] Fletcher smuggled diamonds, rubies, Swiss watches and gold into China and sold them for local dollars, which were then exchanged at the official rate for hard currency. This hugely lucrative scheme was run for Fletcher by Edward Wharton-Tigar, formerly SOE's representative in Tangier, who had already acquired some considerable knowledge of how to exploit the currency markets for the benefit of the Treasury. Not only was the Bank of England a willing partner in this enterprise, but so was the Chinese intelligence service. Its head, General Tai Li, was invited to participate at an early stage, thereby ensuring that REMORSE's couriers were not bothered by customs controls. Estimates of the operation's total profit vary, but around £80 million is reasonable.

•   •   •   •   •   •

Before drawing to a close on SOE's activities in the Far East, we should turn for a moment to OSS, which operated in the area and played a significant role in Burma in particular. By virtue of OSS's original treaty with SOE, China was designated as being within the US's sphere of influ-ence, leaving OSS to co-operate with SOE in Malaya, Burma, Siam and

Indo-China. However, as has already been seen, the Americans were ideo-logically opposed to a restoration of the British Empire and were, therefore, regarded with a measure of circumspection by the British. Nevertheless, OSS was encouraged to develop its presence in the region, albeit under Mackenzie's supervision, and this was eventually translated into the estab-lishment of several OSS detachments, the first being designated 101 in September 1942 and located at Nazira in Assam.

The first signs of inter-Allied conflict emerged when a 101 advance team of fifteen was attached to SOE's Kachins at Sumprabum in north Burma in December 1942. The British officer in command 'demanded that OSS operate according to his instructions, which not only conflicted with OSS policy but were apt to be changed drastically according to his personal whim'.[18] This particular dispute was settled diplomatically when SOE advised its mission that OSS was to be 'assisted not directed'.[19] This unpromising start was followed by a drop of six Anglo-Burmese into the jungle near Lashio in February 1943. No 'safe arrival' signal was heard, but shortly afterwards Radio Tokyo announced the discovery of 'six British spies', of whom three had been killed and three captured.

By the end of the year 101 had created two advance bases, FORWARD and KNOTHEAD, in Burma and was in touch with eleven different teams behind enemy lines. An office was opened in Calcutta to facilitate communi-cations and the head of OSS, General Donovan, made a whistle-stop tour to inspect his organisation's progress. This latter excursion was later to be the cause of criticism, for he had flown deep into enemy territory to reach 101's camp, in direct contravention of the rules governing the conduct of senior Allied personnel with knowledge of advance operations. This, how-ever, was only a minor episode in the deteriorating Anglo-American relationship. On 7/8 March 1943 the Royal Navy landed a six-man party that had been requested to assist Wingate's attack on Akyab. The party landed intact, but was left on the beach by the detachment's commander, who returned to Chittagong, having told his men, all Anglo-Burmese, 'not to be taken alive'. He then 'said goodbye and pushed off'. None of the team survived the mission.[20]

By 1 July 1945, when 101 formally handed over to the British and with-drew, eighty-seven Americans had been parachuted into Burma and had enlisted the support of an estimated ten thousand natives. It was a remark-able achievement, for the loss of only twenty-seven Americans, 350 Kachins and forty agents out of a total of 162 missions launched, but not one that was without its share of political controversy. Kermit Roosevelt, who wrote OSS's classified official history, was to comment:

The hostility directed toward OSS manifested by the Indian government, the Headquarters of the Indian Army, and the British clandestine organisations operating in the area – particularly British SOE – led Donovan to establish a new operational unit in the Theatre rather than expand the basic one which already existed.[21]

Matters came to a head in November 1943, when Donovan announced his intention to deploy his organisation throughout Mountbatten's area of command. This brought utter dismay to the American commander, General Stilwell, because he believed OSS to be in grave danger of falling under British domination. Nor were the British wholly enthusiastic. They were worried about American expansion in a region that was intended to be strictly a British theatre. Despite his reservations, Mountbatten was persuaded by Donovan to authorise several new OSS units: 404 in Ceylon, 303 in New Delhi and 505 in Calcutta. Indeed, there is some evidence to believe that Mountbatten used OSS as an alternative source of strategic information about the Japanese, maybe because 'the claims of British intelligence . . . consistently tended to overestimate enemy capabilities'.[22]

Whether this was a wise development is doubtful. General Peters, who succeeded Carl Eifler as the Detachment's commanding officer, secured the Supreme Commander's consent for a dramatic escalation, which led to training camps being built at Galle, Clodagh and Trincomalee in Ceylon, in addition to the headquarters unit at Kandy and a supply depot at Colombo. This increase in activity, which brought 101 OSS to a strength of 250 officers and 750 enlisted men, only heightened tensions between OSS and SOE. The fact was that without complete integration there would be strife, an inevitable reflection of the difference in political policy between the two Allies. In short, Britain had imperial interests which America wanted to frustrate. The result was that, apart from Burma, where 101 overcame the obstacles placed in its path and was credited with killing 5,500 Japanese, the destruction of fifty-seven bridges and the derailment of nine trains, OSS achieved very little at all in the rest of South-East Asia. Several missions were sent to the Dutch islands, but little was accomplished. In Siam, OSS obtained Stilwell's permission to drop two agents close to Bangkok late in 1944 without consulting SOE. Their (entirely political) task was to make an approach to the Regent and convey a secret message from the US State Department, which implied sympathy with the Government's ambiguous position. This of course contradicted the agreed Allied policy and also served to undermine SOE's contacts with the FSM. Fortunately, the operation went undiscovered, and when the Chief of Special

Operations went to Bangkok in January 1945, courtesy of a British flying-boat, SOE believed that this was OSS's first tenuous contact in the country. In fact, OSS was working with the FSM to frustrate what was seen as sinister British ambitions in Siam. OSS's official historian was remarkably candid about this episode, no doubt confident that the files would not be released for many years:

The best political card OSS could play in Siam was to hold out hope of official American support to Siam in her struggle to maintain her independence and territorial integrity against suspected British designs. This was a most delicate matter, for not only had care to be taken not to embarrass the US Government, but it was also necessary to avoid stirring up the Siamese against the British. Military considerations required that Siam co-operate with the British clandestine services as well as OSS, and in the interests of the Siamese themselves it was essential to discourage any behaviour that might be interpreted as obstructionism by the British.[23]

In fact, despite OSS's manoeuvres in Bangkok, it ended up with little to show for its efforts. The two-man OSS mission made contact with the Regent and was accommodated close to his palace, but when one returned to India for secret consultations, his companion suffered a mental breakdown. The strain of being left on his own in a shuttered room during the daylight hours took a toll on his stability and he had to be evacuated for psychiatric treatment. And while OSS continued to negotiate with the Regent, SOE was building up its own camps in the jungle. Thus, by August 1945 Force 136 had put several thousand Siamese under arms, while OSS had only managed to construct seven guerrilla bases and, since December 1944, had only put twenty-three Americans into the field in ten missions.

Ironically, once the Japanese had surrendered, OSS remained in Siam to gather intelligence about the British. This behaviour was not appreciated and some acrimonious disputes followed as measures were taken to prevent the Americans from staying in South-East Asia a day longer than necessary. The US 'blocked all British efforts to curtail OSS activities'[24] and never entirely accepted that the British and French had been reinstalled in the region.

'Relations with the British naturally deteriorated, at least on the highest levels,'[25] and this was particularly evident in SOE, which had shouldered the lion's share of clandestine operations in the area. Of course SOE was also at war with ISLD, and it is interesting to note that, whilst the Group A country sections had very poor relations with their ISLD opposite numbers, even the Group B sections in Ceylon were similarly afflicted by an apparent inability to co-operate. Obviously the conflicting priorities that arose over the allocation of limited transport facilities aggravated the situation, but one might have thought that in Ceylon, isolated from the highly charged political atmosphere prevalent in Delhi, more of an effort would have been made to discourage the morale-sapping interdepartmental rivalries.

By the end of the war Force 136 had established some ninety British officers in the field and had no less than forty-eight separate wireless sets operating. Although figures for the casualties inflicted on the enemy vary, there is agreement about SOE's losses, which amounted to just sixty-eight Europeans.

II · Clandestine Bodies: SOE in 1944

> The question of relations between SOE and more, rather than less, clandestine bodies is delicate. Various secret services were trying to do different things, but sometimes had to do them in the same places; rivalry was the inevitable result.
>
> M. R. D. Foot, *SOE in France*[1]

Even if SOE's overseas missions experienced difficulty in accommodating the Americans, the London headquarters was to become a model of integration, and nowhere was the level of co-operation greater than in France, where the creation on 10 January 1944 of the Special Forces Headquarters (SFHQ) was to prove a milestone on the path to the Liberation.

The initiation of General Donovan's American OSS into what was euphemistically termed 'Special Operations' had taken place back in July 1942. At that time SOE had already established itself in France and the Americans, eager to learn the arcane arts, had arrived in England in some strength and established relations with both SIS and SOE. Following the British example, they had divided their single organisation into two separate disciplines, Special Intelligence (OSS/SI) and Special Operations (OSS/SO). This compartmentation directly reflected the evolution of the British intelligence structure into SIS and SOE. However, for all their enthusiasm, OSS's SO branch was really very slow to get its agents into the field. The first, a former French Legionnaire named Peter J. Ortiz, had been dropped by SOE from Algiers in June 1943. However, the very first mission to be wholly controlled by SO London was not despatched to France until 13 June 1943, when Ernest Floege (*Alfred*) arrived to start SACRISTAN in the Le Mans area. Floege had been born in Chicago and, therefore, had American citizenship, but much of his life had been spent running a bus company in Algiers, where he had many friends. He was joined on 20 August by a

218

younger man, André Bouchardon (*Narcisse*), a former government employee, but their circuit came to an abrupt halt on 23 December when one of their couriers, Floege's son, was arrested routinely by the Gestapo and found to be carrying highly incriminating messages. The young prisoner broke under interrogation and within a couple of days forty-five members of the network had been arrested. *Alfred* only just evaded capture and went on the run, but *Narcisse* was not so lucky. He was shot when the Germans raided a café and bundled into the back of a car. Despite a bullet lodged in his chest, Bouchardon pulled his revolver from his pocket, shot his three escorts and threw himself from the vehicle as it crashed. He eventually made contact with an escape line in Paris and reached England, via Spain, on 31 March 1944. Undaunted, both *Alfred* and *Narcisse* volunteered to go back, and their offer was to be accepted soon afterwards.

The second OSS operation, perhaps more accurately described as participation, by two Americans, Lieutenants G. Demand and Victor Soskice (*Solway*), was a sabotage mission to blow up a shale oil refinery near Le Creusot. Codenamed SCULLION II, it was planned in two parts, with Demand parachuting in first, alone, on 12 August 1943 in order to prepare a suitable landing site for his six companions, led by Hugh Dormer of the Irish Guards, who followed four days later. Dormer had already tried, but failed, to destroy the plant the previous April on SCULLION I, and had walked out of France through Spain. His second mission, HOUSEKEEPER, to wreck the lock gates of the St Quentin canal, had to be abandoned at the last moment because of a breach of security. Thus, SCULLION II was his third attempt and it proved a success. The refinery, located near Autun, was forced to suspend production, but the team itself was not so lucky. Most of the team were arrested, and only Dormer and his wireless operator, Sergeant Birch, managed to get away to Paris and thence to London. Dormer returned to his regiment, 2nd Battalion Irish Guards, and was killed in a tank outside Caen on 1 July 1944.

OSS/SO London also provided personnel for two SOE circuits. On 18 October 1943 Owen Johnson (*Gael*) joined *Xavier* as MARKSMAN's wireless operator, and on 4 January Claude Arnault (*Néron*) was dropped to WHEELWRIGHT to act as lieutenant to its organiser, George Starr.

Thus, by the time SFHQ was instituted in January 1944, SO London had sent five agents to France, of whom only three were still at liberty. SOE, on the other hand, was running twenty-one fully fledged circuits and was in the process of building a further five. This would certainly appear, superficially at least, to be an impressive amount of activity, but, like almost everything to do with SOE, matters were really rather more complicated.

To begin with, there was the true state of the *réseaux* in France. A closer look reveals that F Section was in a state of crisis. Many of its circuits had been decimated during 1942–3 and the combined forces of the *Abwehr* and *Sicherheitsdienst* had done much to eliminate the biggest networks. Then there were the intractable French political disputes: the differences between the Gaullists and the Giraudists, and the ever-shifting Communists. Some observers were inclined to the view, with some justification, that many Frenchmen were more interested in preparing for seizing power after the war than actually fighting the Germans.

There was also a matter of strategy to be considered. SOE had been planning for D-Day since the end of August 1943, when the subject of its participation in NEPTUNE, the long-awaited invasion, had been discussed at a senior level for the first time. It had been widely agreed that security considerations would prevent SOE's circuits in the field from being given much advance warning of the date of the offensive, or of where the landings were to take place. Virtually every one of its *réseaux* had come under a degree of enemy control at some stage, and the planners were determined not to allow such an important undertaking to be jeopardised by enemy penetration. There was, it had been conceded, simply too much at stake. But there was also some lingering doubt about the role SOE had adopted in France following TORCH in November 1942, when the Germans had proved themselves to be adept at penetrating SOE's circuits. Whether clandestine networks would really have a major contribution to make in the eventual Liberation was open to serious question. The only experience of freeing French territory from the Germans to date upon which to rely suggested otherwise. The last occupiers had been withdrawn from Corsica in October 1943, but at no moment in the short campaign had it appeared that the local resistance had been the deciding factor, or even a significant component. However, there was good reason to believe that the local *maquis*, usually bands of young men who had opted to live in the forests rather than face conscription into forced labour groups, did represent a potentially powerful force if armed and organised properly. But this was much more of a paramilitary role than SOE had ever adopted previously in North-West Europe. Whilst of course it had embraced such tactics in the Balkans, the experience in that theatre was no particular recommendation for an attempt to replicate it. The very prospect of SOE indulging in highly charged political ventures of this kind must have caused severe anxiety in Whitehall. The French political scene was already quite delicate enough without SOE arming selected groups of Communists or, for that matter, others whose credentials had not been examined thoroughly. The potential for creating a political imbalance when France's democratic future would be on a knife edge was considerable. The fear of meddling clumsily, and thereby precipitating a civil war, as had occurred in Yugoslavia and Albania, was very real indeed. Of special concern was the influence of Soviet-orientated moles known to be influencing events behind the scenes. One, Captain Ormond Uren, had already been discovered passing SOE's secrets from the Hungarian sub-section to the Russians, and he and his contact had been convicted of espionage (see page 65), but others were suspected to be in place. A detailed study circulated in October 1943 listed

57 known Communists who had access to secret information, in some cases to information of the highest secrecy; they included 23 in the Ministry of Supply, 18 in the Army and 8 in the universities of whom 3 were employed on the Anglo-US atomic project.[2]

One measure taken to eliminate covert pro-Communist support from within British ranks was a secret investigation, conducted by the Security Service, to exclude CPGB members from important posts. However, even MI5's management had been obliged to acknowledge, albeit privately, that its own organisation had been compromised. One of its sources inside the CPGB, the homosexual writer Tom Driberg, had been exposed in such a way as to leave little doubt that his identity had been betrayed from within MI5 itself. Driberg had complained bitterly to his Security Service case officer, Max Knight, that he had been accused by the CPGB's Secretary-General, Harry Pollitt, of having informed for MI5 and used the acronym 'M8'. This information was proof to Knight, who had been circulating Driberg's reports internally for some years under the anonymous attribution M8, that his agent had been betrayed by a Soviet mole. That the culprit was Anthony Blunt was not to be confirmed for a further twenty years. Although the Prime Minister was never told of that particular embarrassment, Churchill had authorised the investigation into the CPGB's influence over Whitehall, which he termed a purge, and which he referred to in his memoirs in the context of de Gaulle's National Committee of Free French:

We are purging all our secret establishments of Communists because we know they owe no allegiance to us or our cause and will always betray secrets to the Soviets, even while we are working together. The fact of the two Communists being on the French Committee requires extremely careful treatment of the question of imparting secret information to them.[3]

An uncharacteristic indiscretion in a decrypted Soviet signal had allowed the Security Service to put names to two moles working for Soviet military intelligence in de Gaulle's entourage. One was Jacques Soustelle, a Leftist academic and archaeologist who had been appointed in September 1943 to run the Free French BCRA from Algiers and was later to be a member of de Gaulle's cabinet. The other's identity remains a secret, and although de Gaulle was informed of MI5's discovery, he declined to take any action against them.[4] However, quite apart from this pair, there were plenty of other Communist activists in senior positions within the French resistance. In fact, two of the three members of the *Action* sub-committee of the *Conseil National de la Résistance* (CNR), M. Valrimont and its chairman, Pierre Ginzburger, were both members of the Party.

Finally, of course, there was the on-going problem of SOE's relations with SIS, whose hostility was undiminished. Claude Dansey continued to be very sceptical of SOE's efforts and, even after the formation of SFHQ, he circulated a minute, allegedly based upon a conversation with the BCRA's Dewavrin, which suggested that SOE had greatly exaggerated the scale of popular support it enjoyed in France. Dated 8 February 1944 the paper stated that, when called upon to do so, less than two thousand men were realistically likely to take up arms against the occupation. This heresy was in direct contradiction of SOE's own estimates of tens of thousands being willing to engage the enemy if supplied with sufficient logistics. In fact, SOE had called for a massive increase in transport facilities, pointing out that 138 and 161 Squadrons at Tempsford assigned to North and North-West Europe were only equipped with twenty-three Halifax bombers, scarcely enough to maintain an adequate level of drops to the existing circuits without taking account of any significant escalation in operations.

Whilst SIS and SOE must have realised the vast scope for overlap and misunderstandings during the invasion, with competing rival missions operating in the same territory, there was an added complication, namely SIS's responsibility for running all of SOE's double-agent operations. While this was a perfectly sensible arrangement, ensuring a single conduit for the dissemination of controlled information to the enemy, there were to be continuing suspicions concerning the sensitivity of the material being conveyed. This delineation was to provide yet another fertile source for inter-agency suspicion.

The question of tactics was central to the entire debate of how the different clandestine services were to prepare for D-Day. Was SOE to concentrate on building up its existing *réseaux* in the urban areas and conduct small-scale sabotage when called upon to do so, or should it develop its links with the *maquisards* in the countryside in the hope that they would emerge at the right moment and engage the enemy, thereby tying down the enemy far from the battlefront? The former strategy had a high nuisance value, but the destruction of power installations and the mining of roads, bridges and other minor enemy assets would be scarcely likely to influence the outcome of the greater conflict. It was criticism of this kind which had prompted Lord Selborne to circulate a review of SOE's sabotage coups in January 1944, in which he had listed thirty-seven instances where F Section had inflicted significant damage on the German war machine during the previous twelve months. Yet, beyond acts of sabotage, there were tremendous risks involved in developing and encouraging large bodies of ill-disciplined men who could hardly be expected to take on regular troops on equal terms. Even with the advantage of local knowledge and support, the guerrillas would be decimated by enemy armour and air power if drawn into any extended confrontation. It was a choice between pinpricks and potential massacres, which, with the uniquely complex elements of French politics and the active participation of American and British personnel, made such decisions concerning strategy all the more crucial.

The characteristically British compromise was the JEDBURGH, a concept promoted by Gubbins as early as July 1942, which attempted to square the circle, and was to meet most of the needs and objections of the clandestine agencies. The idea was to infiltrate dozens of three-man teams into enemy-held territory in uniform. Each team would have a multinational content, with an American, British and either French, Dutch or Belgian member, one of whom would be a fully trained wireless operator. Some JEDBURGHS would have intelligence-gathering roles, while others would be deployed to the *maquisards*, together with larger SAS units and the SAS's American counterparts, the Operational Groups (OG). The intention was to despatch the JEDBURGH teams once the invasion was under way, but in the meantime SFHQ would continue to develop SOE's more orthodox circuits, a list of which, and their deployment, appears below.

In fact, by the end of 1943 there were only a handful of really effective networks left. Only six *réseaux* from the 1942 vintage had survived: DONKEYMAN, which had experienced much attention from the *Abwehr*, had been put on ice while its leader, Henri Frager (*Louba*), visited London. A former aide to Giraud, he was to return to France in February 1944 to revive his circuit and move it north from the Auxerre region. PIMENTO was Tony Brooks's (*Alphonse*) remarkable sabotage organisation of railway workers, which had spread across the south from Toulouse. Aged only twenty when he had been dropped 'blind' on 1/2 July 1942, Brooks had gone on to develop a network which was to paralyse much of the mainline

SOE's Circuits Active on D-Day

Key	Codename	Date of Origin	Organiser/Codename	W/t Operator/Codename
1	VENTRILOQUIST	April 1944	Pierre de Vomécourt/*Antoine*	Emile Counasse/*Caton*
2	GARDENER	March 1944	Robert Boiteux/*Nicholas*	Gaston Cohen/*Justin*
3	DETECTIVE	Sep. 1943	Henri Sevenet/*Rodolphe*	Brian Stonehouse/*Célestin*
4	MARKSMAN	Sep. 1943	Richard Heslop/*Xavier*	Owen Johnson/*Gael*
5	DONKEYMAN	July 1942	Henri Frager/*Louba*	Henry Bouchard/*Noel*
6	PIMENTO	July 1942	Tony Brooks/*Alphonse*	Roger Caza/*Emanuel*
7	SCIENTIST	July 1942	Claude de Baissac/*David*	Roger Landes/*Aristide*
8	HEADMASTER	Sep. 1942	Brian Rafferty/*Dominique*	G. D. Jones
9	WHEELWRIGHT	Oct. 1942	George Starr/*Hilaire*	Yvonne Cormeau/*Annette*
10	FARMER	Nov. 1942	Pierre Seailles	
11	JOCKEY	March 1943	Francis Cammaerts/*Roger*	Auguste Floiras/*Albert*
12	STOCKBROKER	April 1943	Harry Ree/*César*	
13	SAINT	March 1944	Henri Lausucq/*Aramis*	Virginia Hall/*Diane*
14	ACOLYTE	June 1943	Robert Lyon	J. H. Coleman
15	AUTHOR/DIGGER	Sep. 1943	Harry Peulevé	*Camisole*

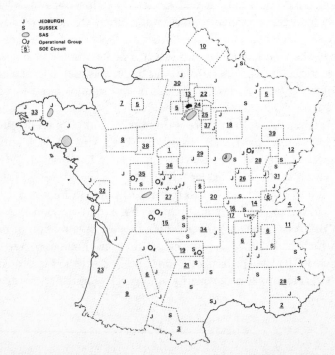

Key	Codename	Date of Origin	Organiser/Codename	W/t Operator/ Codename
16	DITCHER	Oct. 1943	A. Browne-Bartolli/*Tiburce*	Joseph Litalien/*Jacquot*
17	NEWSAGENT	Oct. 1943	Joseph Marchand	*Tweeds*
18	DIPLOMAT	Oct. 1943	Yvan Dupond/*Abélard*	James LaRosée/*Estèphe*
19	CLERGYMAN	Oct. 1943	Robert Benoist	Denise Bloch
20	GONDOLIER	Dec. 1943	Paul Sarrette	K. Mackenzie
21	FOOTMAN	Jan. 1944	George Hiller/*Maxime*	Cyril Watney/*Eustache*
22	SPIRITUALIST	Feb. 1944	René Dumont-Guillemet/*Armande*	H. L. A. Diancono/*Blaise*
23	ACTOR	March 1944	Roger Landes/*Aristide*	
24	WIZARD	March 1944	W. J. Savy	Eileen Nearne/*Rose*
25	MINISTER	March 1944	Pierre Mulsant	Denis Barrett/*Honoré*
26	MASON	March 1944	Jean Regnier	*Tailcoat*
27	FIREMAN	March 1944	P. E. Meyer	Paddy O'Sullivan/*Stocking*
28	SCHOLAR	March 1944	G. de St Genies/*Lucien*	Yvonne Baseden/*Odette*
29	HISTORIAN	May 1944	George Wilkinson/*Etienne*	Lilian Rolfe/*Nadine*
30	BEGGAR	April 1944	M. Bassett/*Ludovic*	Maurice Martin/*Adam*
31	TREASURER	May 1944	Comte de Brouville/*Théodule*	Edwin Poitras/*Paul*
32	CARVER	May 1944	Charles Corbin	A. Sirois/*Gustave*
33	RACKETEER	May 1944	M. Rouneau	None
34	FREELANCE	May 1944	John Farmer/*Hubert*	Denis Rake/*Justin*
35	SHIPWRIGHT	June 1944	René Maingard/*Dédé*	
36	WRESTLER	Sep. 1943	Pearl Witherington/*Marie*	*Wrestler*
37	DIETICIAN	May 1944	J. L. de Ganay	None
38	HERMIT	May 1944	Roger Henquet/*Robert*	Herbert Brucker/*Sacha*
39	GLOVER	June 1944	René Guiraud/*André*	Louis Hyde/*Fréderic*
40	CHANCELLOR	June 1944	George Millar/*Emile*	

OSS Operational Groups

	Codename	Date of Drop	Commander/ Codename	Area of Operations	JEDBURGH/ Circuit
1	PERCY RED	31 July/1 Aug.	William Larson/*Leander*	Limoges	SALESMAN
2	DONALD	5/6 Aug.	R. D. Hirtz	Finistère	HILARY
3	ANTAGONIST	13/14 Aug.	Fred Agee/*Antagonist*	Haute Vienne	SALESMAN
4	PERCY PINK	11/12 Aug.	Thomas Legare/*Sack*	Dordogne	DIGGER
5	PATRICK	14/15 Aug.	Serge Obolensky/*Butch*	Indre	HUGH
6	LINDSEY	16/17 Aug.	Pierce Earle/*Locker*	Cantal	BENJOIN
7	CHRISTOPHER	3/4 Sep.	Melvin Hjeltness	Poitiers	DESMOND
8	ADRIAN	9/10 Sep.	Wilbur Boemermann	Dijon	DESMOND

rail traffic after D-Day. His circuit placed explosive charges on dozens of locomotives and rolling-stock and effectively closed down most of the railway yards and switching points in their area, bringing the whole network in the Rhône Valley to a halt. Indeed, any train leaving Marseilles for Lyons after 5/6 June 1944 could guarantee that it would be derailed at least once during its journey. Then there was SCIENTIST in southern Normandy, headed by Claude de Baissac (*David*). A thirty-five-year-old Mauritian, he had been dropped 'blind' near Nimes on 30 July 1942 and only narrowly escaped being caught up in the PROSPER disaster. Two missions later he was back with a reformed SCIENTIST.

The three other surviving networks of 1942 were HEADMASTER, WHEELWRIGHT and FARMER. The first was run by Brian Rafferty (*Dominique*) following the arrest of its leader, Charles Hudson, in October 1942, just two weeks after he had landed in the Puy-de-Dôme. His radio operator, G. D. Jones, had been injured in a cycling accident, but had insisted on maintaining contact with Baker Street from his hospital bed, operating his transmitter with help from nurses and other patients. WHEELWRIGHT was quite the largest and most significant circuit of all with, at one moment, some twenty SOE-trained agents under the command of George Starr (*Hilaire*). It covered a huge territory in the south-west and was to be very effective at isolating the *Wehrmacht* Army Group G garrisoned near Toulouse by cutting its power and telephone lines. Starr had landed by *felucca* in November 1942 and had originally been intended for SPRUCE in Lyons, but that circuit collapsed just before his arrival. Instead, he had adopted the cover of a wealthy retired Belgian mining engineer from the Congo (which explained his awful accent) and had taken up residence in Castelnau-sous-l'Auvignon, where he was to be so popular that he was elected the town's deputy mayor.

FARMER's origins dated back to 18 November 1942, when Michael Trotobas (*Sylvestre*) and his operator, Albert Staggs, had been dropped by parachute and established a sabotage network in Lille. Their speciality was derailing trains with the enthusiastic help of local railway workers and the underworld, which handicapped the enemy's ability to move its troops. Trotobas, who had been born in Brighton, was to become a daring leader of the local resistance, renowned for walking into his sabotage targets in a well-cut suit, brandishing a Gestapo identity medallion. He was to be killed during a Gestapo raid on his safe-house in Lille in November 1943, but the circuit continued to be operated by his subordinates throughout the period of the invasion.

These six 1942 *réseaux* formed the basis of almost a dozen more networks built during 1943: JOCKEY was established by Francis Cammaerts (*Roger*) in March in the Alpes Maritimes on his second mission. A Cambridge-educated schoolmaster and former conscientious objector, Cammaerts was to be one of F Section's most successful and resourceful organisers. In April STOCKBROKER was created by another schoolmaster, Harry Ree (*César*), in Belfort, and a month later ACOLYTE was formed when Robert Lyon arrived by Lysander on his second mission. In September AUTHOR, MARKSMAN and DETECTIVE got under way. These were led, respectively, by Harry Peulevé (on his second mission, after having walked to Spain on a shattered leg after a bad parachute landing the first time around); Richard Heslop (*Xavier*, on his third mission, having been imprisoned in Vichy); and Henri Sevenet (*Rodolphe*, also on his second mission, who had climbed the Pyrenees into Andorra in winter to get back to England). A month later Elaine Plewman's brother, Albert Browne-Bartolli (*Tiburce*), was landed by Hudson in Burgundy to start DITCHER, together with a middle-aged *parfum-ier*, Joseph Marchand, of NEWSAGENT, and a landowner, Robert Benoist, of CLERGYMAN. DIPLOMAT's young Yvan Dupond (*Abélard*), originally from Paris, was dropped to Troyes, where he went to ground, ready to sabotage the locomotive yards when called upon to do so. The last circuit to be set up in 1943 which was to survive until D-Day was GONDOLIER, Paul Sarrette's network around Nevers.

In the new year of 1944 preparations for D-Day began slowly, perhaps too slowly for some, for they were to be placed in jeopardy by SFHQ's determination to establish a series of entirely new circuits as quickly as possible. The first went more or less according to plan, but then disaster struck. FOOTMAN, consisting of George Hiller (*Maxime*) and his wireless operator Cyril Watney (*Eustache*), was dropped on 7 January in the Lot with a political objective, to contact and mobilise the Leftist guerrillas known to be there. Instead of finding several hundred, as had been optimistically reported to London, there were less than fifty. The arrest of Jean Neunier (*Mesnard*) temporarily removed his DIRECTOR circuit in the Camargue from the scene and, although there was a delay in the news reaching SFHQ, MUSICIAN had been eliminated by the arrest in St Quentin of Gustave Bieler (*Guy*) and his operator, Yolande Beekman (*Mariette*). Early the following month René Dumont-Guillemet (*Armande*) on his second mission dropped 'blind' near to his home in Touraine and organised SPIRITUALIST with his operator, H. L. A. Diancono (*Blaise*). This was the first operation to be mounted by SFHQ and concentrated on the discreet rebuilding of an organisation in Paris, where, to SOE's lasting cost, the Germans had already proved themselves to be resourceful opponents.

Following amalgamation there was more activity during the March moon period, when Pierre Martinot (*Ulysses*) was dropped to JOCKEY from Algiers on 2 March, and Henri Lausucq (*Aramis*) accompanied Virginia Hall (*Diane*)[5] by boat to Brittany to form SAINT, the first entirely OSS circuit. Both of these operations were successful, but LIONTAMER proved to be the disaster that put all of F Section's D-Day preparations at risk. LIONTAMER had been founded on MUSICIAN, which, unbeknownst to Baker Street, had fallen into enemy hands. The operation was a three-man team, consisting of Maurice Lanis (*Colin*), E. Lesout (*Tristan*) from OSS and an SOE wireless operator, *Guillaume*, who were to be received by *Tell*, supposedly MUSICIAN's new leader.[6] Although the trio were despatched on 2 March, nothing was heard from them for three weeks, when *Colin* signalled that he and *Guillaume* had arrived safely and had been met by *Théodore*, who had recently replaced *Tell* as MUSICIAN's head. This news was received with some scepticism in London because of the omission of any mention of *Tristan*, and the growing suspicion that ARCHDEACON, of which MUSICIAN was a sub-group, had been penetrated by the enemy. Furthermore, *Théodore* was known to have been arrested, and a report from SPIRITUALIST that he had engineered his escape from the Gestapo had been disbelieved. In short, it seemed that *Théodore* was a *funkspiel* and that the LIONTAMER mission had been dropped straight to the enemy. None the less, contact with *Colin* was maintained in the vain hope that it might keep him alive. Unfortunately, SFHQ's decision to use ARCHDEACON as a route for infiltrating new circuits into the field was to account for the lives of at least eighteen agents, as we shall see later.

But it was in March 1944 that SOE really made its commitment to OVERLORD and sent some of its most experienced men into the field. Robert Boiteux (*Nicholas*) was dropped near Marseilles on 6 March to form GARDENER, together with two other French Jews, both hardened F Section agents: Gaston Cohen (*Justin* of JUGGLER) and Bernard Aptaker. During the rest of the month ACTOR, WIZARD, MINISTER, MASON, FIREMAN and SCHOLAR were built. Philippe de Vomecourt's VENTRILOQUIST was revived by its leader's return by Lysander on 16/17 April, and in May HISTORIAN, BEGGAR, TREASURER, CARVER, RACKETEER and FREELANCE were dropped. Fortunately all these operations passed without incident, but there was a common strand running through most of them: their reception committees had been arranged by Maurice Southgate of STATIONER. Born in Paris of British parents, Southgate had to date led a charmed war. He had survived the fall of France, the sinking of the *Lancastria*, and his penchant for wearing alternate army and RAF uniforms while on leave in London after he had transferred to F Section. Apparently, Buckmaster had arranged a commission for him in the RAFVR even though he was still officially in the British army. According to SOE folklore, his mother's neighbour had remarked to her: 'I never see your two sons go out together.'

Considering what F Section ought to have known about the perils of relying on a single circuit to convey senior organisers, this was yet another extraordinary risk for SFHQ to have sanctioned. But the reality is that no one in F Section had been told of N Section's disasters. Accordingly, Buckmaster authorised a single conduit to be used in a concentrated period of time to deliver key personnel. Nor is this criticism entirely fanciful. In fact, Southgate himself was arrested in Montluçon by the Gestapo on 1 May 1944 and taken to the Avenue Foch, where he was recognised instantly by John Starr (*Bob*). Luckily for his contacts he, unlike *Bob*, resolutely refused to co-operate with his interrogators. In his absence Pearl Witherington (*Marie*), who had joined STATIONER as a wireless operator on 23 September 1943, took over as WRESTLER and accomplished all her circuit's D-Day objectives. Not all were so lucky. LABOURER, a three-man team dropped to STATIONER on 5 April, was promptly betrayed and its members arrested. And when ROVER's organiser, John Mayer, was arrested at the end of May, his recently arrived operator, *Singlet*, was without the stores needed to mount attacks on the enemy so he simply went to ground. Something not too dissimilar happened to LACKEY, consisting of J. E. Lesage (*Cosmo*) and his young Canadian operator, Alcide Beauregard. They were flown to France by Lysander on 8/9 February, but, owing to *Cosmo*'s unpopularity on a previous mission to Lyons, upon their arrival they failed to find anyone willing to work with them, so the team went into limbo. A journalist, Philippe Liewer (*Clement*, on his second mission, having already been imprisoned in Vichy), and his operator, a fierce young French widow who was reputed to be F Section's best shot, Violette Szabo (*Louise*), tried to start SALESMAN in Rouen in April, but were exfiltrated by Lysander after three weeks because of lack of local support and pressure from the Germans.

As well as the experienced teams being reinserted into enemy territory, there were a few novices deployed as well. Two OSS men of HERMIT went to organise a sub-group for VENTRILOQUIST on 27 May and were subsequently joined by their SOE colleague, *Abel*, on 13 June. A similar OSS team was GLOVER, which dropped near Chaumont on 1/2 June, the last night that missions were to be inserted before OVERLORD proper was initiated. Also despatched into eastern France that night was George Millar (*Emile*) of CHANCELLOR, a young French-speaking Scottish officer, who had joined SOE after having been a prisoner of war for twenty months in Italy, where he had been appalled by the futility and inaccuracy of Allied air raids. He had subsequently escaped and made his way to England, where he was trained as an expert saboteur for a mission in France, despite his distinctive Scottish accent.

These operations were supervised by F Section, which continued its activities as before, albeit under SFHQ's umbrella, with Maurice Buck-master as head and Bourne-Paterson as his deputy. However, an OSS officer was assigned to complement every F Section staff post, with a US marine, William G. Grell, leading them. Thus, Stephen Millett went to the training unit, Robert F. Cutting to logistics and Lieutenant G. Bally to the documentation centre. This duplication worked well, but was limited in scope. Plans, Stores (Q), Finance and Administration, Communications and Records all remained in the hands of SOE personnel. However, SFHQ was by no means to enjoy a monopoly of Anglo-American operations in France. Despite the close relationship of OSS's SO branch and SOE itself, it had been SIS that had laid the foundations of an entirely separate joint project, codenamed SUSSEX.

This parallel scheme, which had no SOE participation whatever, was intended to send sixty two-man teams into northern France in anticipation of the D-Day landings, each to complete a tactical intelligence mission just behind the battlefront and then wait to be overrun by the advancing Allied forces. The important distinction here was SUSSEX's role, which supposedly was an entirely intelligence-orientated one, thereby excluding SOE and, more specifically, F Section. The entire undertaking was divided into OSSEX, the American element, and BRISSEX, SIS's contribution. It was supervised by a senior intelligence officer drawn from the services of their respective countries: Kenneth Cohen from SIS, Francis P. Miller from OSS and Gilbert Renault from the BCRA. Initially SUSSEX got off to a poor start because OSS was unable to find any suitable candidates fluent in French. That shortfall was remedied with BCRA's help and the first team, sent as a pathfinder to locate landing zones, dropped into the Châteauroux area on 8 February 1944 to survey several sites. Two months later, on 9 April, the first SUSSEX missions were infiltrated into enemy-occupied territory and, by the end of August, fifty-two teams had been inserted, of which only three fell into enemy hands. All six Americans died, including OSSEX's only woman agent.

Unlike SUSSEX, the JEDBURGHS came under SOE's command and oper-ated under SFHQ's direct control, a reflection of the fact that the entire scheme had been an exclusively SOE idea. Very little has ever been written about the JEDBURGHS, which is surprising when one considers the very substantial contribution they made to D-Day's success and, perhaps more importantly for SOE, the part they played in the organisation's history. The initiative had come from Gubbins originally, in a note dated 6 July 1942 to SOE's Security Section, which was responsible for the allocation of all operational cryptonyms:

A project is under consideration for the dropping behind of enemy lines, in co-operation with an Allied invasion of the Continent, of small parties of officers and men to raise and arm the civilian population to carry out guerrilla activities against the enemy's lines of communication. These men are to be recruited and trained by SOE. It is requested that 'JUMPERS' or some other appropriate code name be allotted to this personnel.[7]

There is no record of any further memoranda on this topic until the idea was given a practical test, codenamed SPARTAN, on 11 March 1943, when eleven SOE-trained JEDBURGHS were deployed as a mythical bridgehead was secured on Salisbury Plain and an Allied invasion force moved north-wards towards Huntingdon. The exercise also included the infiltration of six SOE agents equipped with transmitters, all reporting to a receiving station in Scotland. The experience gained from SPARTAN formed the basis of a secret document circulated by the head of SOE's Planning Section, Colonel M. W. Rowlandson, on 6 April 1943. This in turn resulted in the basic JEDBURGH directive, which was issued on 20 December 1943 and formalised the arrangements that were to be implemented soon afterwards with the intention of producing 300 JEDBURGH teams by 1 April 1944.

As it turned out this optimistic ambition was never to be achieved. An OSS officer, Henry B. Coxe, and a recently escaped prisoner of war, Major Combe-Tennant, were placed in charge of the JEDBURGHS, and a training programme was devised by the head of SOE's Training Section, Colonel James Young, and his OSS counterpart, Major John Tyson. Together they prepared a three-part course for all the volunteers who survived an extended interview with three psychiatrists: preliminary training in Scotland, followed by technical courses at Hatherop Castle in Gloucestershire (STS 45), Gumley Hall, Leicestershire (STS 41), and West Court, Wokingham (STS 6). This stop-gap continued until 3 February 1944, when Milton Hall (designated ME 65) became the main JEDBURGH training centre. This beautiful seventeenth-century property was situated just seven miles from Peterborough and the surrounding estate provided ideal facilities for prepar-ing the agents for their tasks. The radio operators went on to STS 54 for intensive wireless instruction, and a parachute course was run at Altrincham, Manchester (STS 51a). Thereafter, the graduates were given a five-day field test under simulated conditions at Horsham in Sussex.

Milton Hall was to become the JEDBURGHS's principal home and was staffed almost entirely by SOE. The first Commandant was Frank Spooner, with Major O. H. Brown as Chief Instructor and Major H. L. Trebilcock as Adjutant and Transport Officer. Bill Sykes led a team of fifteen instructors, who were supplemented by eight Americans. The organisation was divided into three Companies, commanded by Majors H. A. Dorsey, M. C. M. Crosby and B. W. Gilmour. However, before the first JEDBURGH team could be formed, in mid-March 1944, SOE experienced further difficulty in gathering sufficient personnel, but found a remedy in the recruitment of seventy Free French officers from the Middle East.

Once the training phase had been completed, and the JEDBURGHS were ready to be deployed operationally, the overall management was changed, with Colonel Smith and Major Coxe replacing Frank Spooner in command at Milton Hall. The composition of each team was chosen by Milton Hall's new Commandant, Colonel Musgrove, in consultation with his Chief Instructor, Major McLallen. On 27 April the first teams were sent to North Africa accompanied by a US marine, Major Horace Fuller, in expectation of being dropped into southern France. Each team was allocated a cryptonym, usually an English first-name although the names of drugs were introduced latterly when the Security Section ran out of Christian names. The Algiers group was beaten into the field by HUGH, the first JEDBURGH into France, which was despatched from RAF Harrington on 5/6 June to the Châteauroux area, where it linked up with the local *maquis* leader, *Philippe* of SHIPWRIGHT, and acted as liaison between his men, which numbered some two thousand spread across the Department of Indre, and a 1st SAS mission codenamed BULBASKET. The latter was under the command of Major J. E. Tonkin and wreaked havoc among the enemy defenders, until it was itself decimated by a battalion of SS infantry on 4 July. HUGH was not a typical JEDBURGH because it consisted of two Frenchmen and one British officer, but this did reflect the relative shortage of OSS personnel available in mid-June. In fact, although more teams were to be dropped into enemy territory in the days following D-Day, the first American did not go into the field until Sergeant Robert Keyhoe of FREDERICK and Captain Paul Cyr of GEORGE landed in Brittany on 9/10 June. At the beginning of July a total of thirteen JEDBURGHS had been despatched, of which seven had originated from Algiers. Altogether ninety-three JEDBURGHS were deployed, with losses amounting to twenty-one, the equivalent of seven full teams.

The JEDBURGH concept was a very considerable shift in tactics for SOE and meant the adoption of a much more overt, paramilitary role than it had previously been accustomed to in France. An observer of these events is bound to ask whether this change represented an admission that the *réseaux* had failed in their purpose and had therefore been supplanted. Such a proposition can only be justified by a review of SOE's circuits still at liberty in the months leading up to D-Day and their performance thereafter. The results are quite surprising, for, according to a secret SFHQ map of 5 July 1944, there were only four areas considered to be under total control of the resistance and cleared of enemy troops on that date. They were in the *départements* of the Ardèche, Drôme, Savoie and Jura in the mountainous south-east of the country. That might be as expected, but the 'areas in which resistance has crystallised and intense activity is taking place' were limited to just five others, in the Morbihan, Indre, Vienne, Haute Loire, Hautes Pyrenées and Vosges.[8]

The circuits that SFHQ was in touch with at D-Day were too varied to fall into one single category. Some were huge, with more than a thousand *maquisards* under their command; others were tiny, consisting of just one individual operating alone. Some had no radio sets or method of communicating with SFHQ, although all could receive the BBC's prearranged coded messages. One, DIRECTOR, contained no one trained in England. Whether SFHQ was wise even to contemplate infiltrating more covert circuits into France is open to serious question, especially considering the parlous state of both F and RF Sections in January 1944, immediately prior to amalgamation. OSS had achieved little to speak of, and F Section was in dire trouble: its only successful networks were in entirely the wrong places. The PROSPER and SCIENTIST disasters had left very few arms caches available in the north and north-western parts of the country, where they were needed most. Elsewhere, only a fraction of the supplies delivered to Yugoslavia had gone to France. Even worse, the two key circuits in the area of most strategic importance, ARCHDEACON and MUSICIAN, had come under enemy control. That, of course, was not immediately realised and led to further losses, including no less than seventeen SOE agents arriving by air, and Alphonse Defendini, who landed by boat.[9]

F Section's difficulties were not immediately obvious, and the full impact of ARCHDEACON's penetration was not felt for some weeks. Indeed, the degree of skill exercised by the *Sicherheitsdienst* is demonstrated by the fact that the *funkspiel*'s first victim, François Michel (*Dispenser*), had disappeared the previous September. Thus, five months after the first sign that something was wrong with ARCHDEACON, F Section was still sending agents to it, oblivious to the danger. Nor was this the only manifestation of inadequate planning or bad organisation. There were cases of agents being despatched from England and Algiers with the same cryptonym, such as *Casimir* and *Justin*. There were also more fundamental issues, like the use of agents who spoke the language poorly, and the employment of members of the same family, an obvious security risk. George Millar was hindered by the strength of his Scots accent and John Young (*Gabriel*) was unmistakably a Geordie. A significant number of agents were Jewish and looked it. Pierre de Vomecourt recalls the case of André Bloch, who

happened to be Jewish and this was all too obvious in his appearance. To send us Bloch was yet another example of London's incredible ignorance of the realities of life in occupied France. Less than a month after he arrived he was denounced as a Jew by one of his neighbours. When the Germans came to his house to arrest him they howled with delight to find his transmitter. Expecting merely to arrest a Jew, they had found themselves a radio operator![10]

There have been dozens of other criticisms, too numerous to list here, from individual agents who have complained about sloppy briefings, inappropriate documentation and other hazards. Jacqueline Nearne actually knitted socks for her organiser, Maurice Southgate (as well as her brother and sister, who were also in SOE), because she suspected that the Germans could distinguish between French and English weaves. Nor were these more basic handicaps limited to F Section. RF was in an equally bad way, not least because of the political infighting between the Gaullists and the Giraudists, and the arrest in Lyons in July 1943 of the charismatic Jean Moulin and what was virtually the whole of the Gaullist underground leadership.

RF's relations with SOE were to turn particularly sour at this critical moment. A new political structure to co-ordinate the resistance had to be established quickly so as to avoid a power vacuum and a joint BCRA–RF mission, MARIE-CLAIRE, was prepared for the task. It was to consist of the two deputy heads of the Free French RF Section, Yeo-Thomas, and the BCRA, Pierre Brossolette. However, before they could be despatched, a bitter dispute arose. As Controller of Western Europe Robin Brook had insisted that any replacement for the CNR be less centralised and, for greatest security, managed externally, perhaps from London.

This proposal found no favour with the BCRA, which had devised an alternative strategy carving France into two zones, each to be run by its nominee. SOE only learned of this arrangement, which perpetuated the centralisation that had been the CNR's downfall, through its routine scrutiny of the BCRA's signals traffic. An objection was registered, and the BCRA undertook to delete the offending reference to the new *chefs de zones* from the encrypted message which had been submitted to SOE. However, when the new signal was produced for transmission, it was noted to contain an identical number of cipher groups, which strongly suggested that the BCRA had not in fact altered the content at all. SOE's resident crypto-grapher, the redoubtable Leo Marks, was called in, and he succeeded in breaking the French code in a single afternoon. Confronted with the evi-dence of its own duplicity, the BCRA responded with an accusation of bad faith and alleged that Brook had only managed to read the message by resorting to the cipher key kept in his safe, which had been lodged there, under very strict conditions, for emergency use only. Brook was able to refute the claim by demonstrating Marks's skill on another BCRA text, which proved the point but also served to exacerbate the situation further. Thus, when MARIE-CLAIRE did eventually get under way in September, the BCRA had virtually broken off official contact with RF Section in London.

Conditions were no better in the field. The first attempt to replace the CNR failed when a senior Gaullist, Claude-Bernard Serreules (*Scapin*), was arrested in Paris in September soon after having conferred with Brosso-lette and Yeo-Thomas. Worse, he was caught in possession of four months' worth of compromising radio signals, which identified most of the person-alities he had intended to reconstitute the CNR with. Most were promptly rounded up, putting RF Section at a further disadvantage when it came to prepare for D-Day.

RF Section was undaunted by these losses and, early in January, com-bined with SIS to send a high-powered team, UNION, to the south-east of France. Commanded by Pierre Fourcaud (*Sphère*) of SIS, it included Hutchison's deputy in RF, Thackthwaite, Peter Ortiz from OSS and a French wireless operator, C. Monnier. UNION made contact with the *maquis* of the Vercors plateau, in the mountains above Grenoble, and began to organise them. Two more RF advance parties followed to other guerrilla groups. A team of a dozen strong, CITRONELLE, went to the Ardennes under P. Bolladière (*Prisme*) in April and, in the middle of the following month, BENJOIN, three men led by B. Cardozo, dropped into the Massif Central. However, to ensure the integrity of the operation, neither RF Section nor the BCRA was ever fully indoctrinated into the secret of D-Day. Indeed, de Gaulle himself and all his staff were deliberately excluded from OVERLORD's planning and were only informed that it was imminent on the very eve of the attack. The fact that de Gaulle had only been told *after* some of his own troops, in the 3rd SAS regiment, had received their orders, was to be the cause of lasting bitterness.

Despite RF's problems, it was able to have nearly a hundred units equipped with wireless immediately after the invasion. Indeed, there were no less than nine other quite different clandestine organisations operating in France immediately after D-Day: SOE's regular F Section *réseaux*, of which there were twenty-five active on D-Day itself, all of varying sizes; the escape lines run separately by DF Section and MI9; the JEDBURGH parties reporting to SFHQ; SIS's own networks of agents, supplemented by the SUSSEX teams; squadrons deployed from the four SAS regiments, amounting in all to some two thousand troops; and the OSS Operational Groups (OGs). Surprisingly, SOE's EU/P Section played no part, although 100 Poles had been trained as part of BARDSEA with the intention of being dropped around Lille. The Polish expatriate community in the area had been active in the resistance and had developed MONICA, its own self-contained network. Although SOE had high hopes of mobilising MONICA, events and Polish politics conspired to keep the BARDSEA parties in England.

By D-Day the SAS had formed a brigade in Ayrshire, with three regiments ready for deployment in France, including the 1st and 2nd SAS, at Darvel and Prestwick respectively, having returned from the Mediterranean theatre. The 3rd and 4th SAS were French parachute battalions, and the 5th was a Belgian parachute company. All were to operate to great effect behind enemy lines with the JEDBURGHS and the local resistance, but they suffered considerable losses. The 4th SAS, which was dropped into Brittany during June, was reduced to half strength, and squadrons of the 1st SAS experienced an equally high casualty rate. Twenty-two men of A Squadron were killed in one incident alone, on 17 June, when their aircraft crashed while en route to HOUNDSWORTH south-west of Dijon. Very few SAS personnel survived the war as prisoners because German policy was to murder them.[11]

The SAS troops differed from the OSS OGs only in that the American units had a greater proportion of French-speakers; apart from that their weapons, training and tactics were broadly similar, although the OGs were controlled by SFHQ while the SAS had their own staff attached to 21st Army Group. A typical OG was composed of four officers, commanded by a captain, and thirty NCOs divided into two sections, with a wireless operator assigned to each. The OGs were originally designed to operate in Norway, which accounted for the high proportion of Norwegian Americans among their ranks, and the appointment of Harold P. Larsen as their commanding officer. After their arrival in December 1943, they were billeted at Forest Lodge, Aviemore, before being found a permanent home in January 1944 at Stronelairig near Inverness.

Although the OGs were intended to be deployed in Norway, the first project, a raid on Stord Lilleho Partes mine, codenamed BARTER, had to be abandoned for lack of transport across the North Sea. This setback did little to enhance OSS–SOE relations, since the Americans had donated several sub-chasers to SOE's base at Lerwick, ships that would have been ideal for mounting BARTER.

Not all the OGs were American. Two were entirely French, although under the overall command of OSS's Serge Obolensky, and were brought to Brock Hall, Weedon, from North Africa in April 1944. A Polish OG was also formed and trained alongside the BARDSEA parties at STS 63, but plans for a Danish OG, drawn up by the head of SOE's Scandinavian Section, Commander Hollingsworth, were eventually abandoned because of a shortage of suitable Danish Americans. A second plan for a raid to Norway, codenamed RANKIN B, was also dropped because of transport problems, so it was not until the end of July that the first OG, PERCY RED, was despatched, not to Norway, but to the Haute Vienne in central France.

PERCY RED, led by William F. Larson (*Leander*), did not get off to a very good start, which came as no surprise to the more superstitious members of the team who had already completed twelve jumps. Only one of the four aircraft found the drop zone, so most had to follow on the next night, with the last aircraft eventually getting to the target, south of Limoges, on 5 August. Once in contact with the local *maquis*, led by SALESMAN's organiser Philippe Liewer (*Hamlet*), who had been dropped with Violette Szabo for a second time on 6/7 June, PERCY RED linked up with JEDBURGH LEE and a thirteen-strong French SAS party, which dropped together from a Sterling bomber on 9/10 August. Together they armed and organised an estimated five thousand *maquisards* and negotiated the surrender of Limoges with the commander of the German garrison, General Gleiniger. Having taken prisoner several hundred (Russian) troops, PERCY RED was joined by another OG, ANTAGONIST, which, unusually, consisted of a single surgeon, Dr Fred Agee, who had flown in to treat the wounded *maquisards*. The OG continued to mop up isolated enemy units, before returning to London on 10 September via the roundabout route of Toulouse, Casablanca and Naples.

PERCY RED's experience was fairly typical of the six big OGs that followed it into the field, and even though they were composed chiefly of Scandinavian Americans who had intended to fight in Norway, their deployment in

France (listed in Appendix 3) was considered a great success for minimal loss of life. Only three OG members were killed, one of whom was the victim of a parachute accident. By the time PERCY RED had returned to England, ANTAGONIST and DONALD had already been withdrawn from the field. The last back was to be PERCY PINK on 10 October.

When attempting to assess the contribution made by SOE to the success of D-Day and, indeed, the Liberation itself, it should be noted that not even SFHQ fully understood at the time one aspect of its strategic role. As well as the general run of items singled out for sabotage, such as power cables, pylons and bridges, great emphasis had been placed on telephone lines as targets, and although SOE must have considered such operations useful, in that any interference with the enemy's communications grid is invariably helpful, it certainly never realised the vital nature of these particular targets. In fact, the Chiefs of Staff were especially anxious to destroy all the German landlines so as to force the enemy to rely more on their enciphered radio transmissions, which, as we now know, were the subject of an intensive and highly profitable programme of interception and decryption by GCHQ. The *Wehrmacht* had deployed five signals regiments in France, and all experienced unprecedented attention from the resistance during, and immediately after, D-Day. This was especially true of the unit stationed at Orléans, which suffered unrelenting disruption from HERMIT, SHIPWRIGHT and WRESTLER, so much so that by the time it was evacuated to Germany it had failed to restore any of its major telephone circuits.

Perhaps of equal long-term strategic significance was the disruption inflicted on the French railways. The intention was to isolate the northern part of the country and prevent enemy reinforcements from reaching the beachhead during the first critical hours of the invasion. No less than 950 incidents of sabotage were undertaken during the night of 5/6 June, and confirmation was received that night of 486 specific cuts. The lines continued to be blown, trains derailed and locomotives immobilised throughout the campaign and, in consequence, the crack 2nd SS *Das Reich* Panzer Division took seventeen days to reach Normandy from Toulouse, a journey which ought not to have taken longer than seventy-two hours. Combined with the comprehensive deception campaign known as FORTITUDE, which helped convince the German High Command that the landings were actually nothing more than a feint for a major Allied assault in the Pas-de-Calais, SOE's bridge-blowing and rail-cutting operations played a major part in ensuring D-Day's success.

Immediately after the landings SFHQ resumed normal service and sent more missions into the field: Pierre Liewer and Violette Szabo established

SALESMAN for the second time on 6/7 June, together with Robert Mortier and an American wireless operator, Jean-Claude Guiet. Three days after their arrival near Sussac *Louise* encountered an advance party of the SS *Das Reich* Panzer Division while in the car of a local *maquisard*. She took to the fields, armed with her sten gun, and held 400 Germans at bay while her ammunition lasted, but eventually she was wounded and arrested. Her companion escaped, only to be killed in Indo-China the following year.

Henri Borosch, formerly a DF wireless operator who had worked on the VIC escape line, was sent to start SILVERSMITH near Reims at the end of the month. Later PERMIT, HILLBILLY, WOODCUTTER, AUDITOR, LICENSEE and PEDAGOGUE were all established, but they were to be of short duration, most being overrun by Allied forces after they had linked up with JEDBURGHS and other irregulars.

By the Liberation F Section had lost more than forty circuits in France, thirty-one of which had been eliminated by the *Abwehr* and the *Sicherheitsdienst*. The total number of individuals to have been arrested is unknown, although the list on pages 126–30 is probably the most comprehensive yet published, but it is not necessarily complete.

●　　●　　●　　●　　●　　●

The liberation of Paris or, for that matter, France was not to be the end of the story for SOE. A tripartite body, the *Etat Major des Forces Françaises de l'Intérieur* (EMFFI), was created on 22 August 1944 under General Koenig to supervise the work of much of the clandestine units, but SFHQ continued in existence elsewhere to co-ordinate operations in Belgium and Holland. A separate EMFFI headquarters was established in Bryanston Square, where Colonels Carleton-Smith and Henry Coxe continued to run JEDBURGH teams into France. The last mission was despatched on 23 September, whereupon the OSS and SOE elements returned to their respective homes at 24 Grosvenor Street and Baker Street. The EMFFI was subsequently disbanded on 1 December.

Apart from the continuing administrative burden of winding down the organisation, there was a necessity to discover the fate of the many F Section agents who had disappeared. Much of this task fell to Buckmaster's Intelligence Officer, Vera Atkins, who travelled across Europe during late 1944 and 1945 trying to learn of their whereabouts. It was only through her research that SOE realised the full horror of what had befallen so many of its agents. Of the fifty women agents sent to France by F Section (three of them went twice), seventeen were caught. Of them, only three survived German captivity. Of the three women arrested by the French, two escaped and Elizabeth Reynolds was released by Allied forces in 1944. These grim statistics contrast with RF's total of eleven women agents sent into the field, all of whom survived.

While F Section was picking up the pieces, other important missions were being sent elsewhere in Europe in anticipation of a German collapse. On 12 September 1944 the first JEDBURGHS were despatched to Holland, but by the middle of the following month all had been overrun and withdrawn to England.

Elsewhere in Europe covert activity sponsored by SOE had reached a peak. The first mission to Poland had been dropped in February 1941 and since then there had been a trickle of men and supplies flown to General Rowecki's *Armia Krajowa*, the underground 'Home Army' based in Warsaw. Once Henry Threlfall had established a Polish Section office at Monopoli, under Force 139 cover, the number of flights flown to Poland escalated dramatically, but the distance involved was still daunting and close to the limit for the few Halifax bombers available.

The Polish government-in-exile largely managed its own resistance in Poland, using SOE's Polish Section for liaison and training. Alas, these lines of communication were to be muddled by the political complexities of inter-Allied relations and the difficulty of maintaining contact with the AK in German-occupied Warsaw. Nor was it immune to penetration. One of its networks, codenamed FAN, was found to contain a Gestapo agent, who compromised many of its operations before he was identified and executed. The Government itself was to be handicapped by the loss of its local commander, General Rowecki, who was arrested in June 1943, and the death of General Sikorksi a few days later.

When, on 1 August 1944, the AK called for a general uprising in the expectation of imminent liberation by the Red Army, it was to be cruelly disappointed. SOE's attempts to keep the street fighters supplied foundered after forty-one aircraft had been shot down, including fifteen of SOE's sixteen Halifax bombers with 1386 Flight based at Bari. Then Stalin ordered his men to stay on the Vistula's eastern bank, just a mile or so from Warsaw's suburbs, while the Poles fought on for a heroic sixty-three days. Altogether 193 missions were flown during the uprising, and some 400 tons of supplies were delivered, although a proportion of them fell into enemy hands.

Thereafter, SOE sent its first military mission to Poland, Operation FRESTON, to assess what resistance was left elsewhere on the ground. Led by Bill Hudson, of the BULLSEYE mission into Yugoslavia, it consisted of a Pole, Anton Popieszalski (who called himself Tony Currie), Peter Kemp (from Albania), Peter Solly-Flood (from Yugoslavia) and Sergeant-Major Galbraith. They landed near Cracow on 26/27 December, at the fourth attempt, and were eventually overrun by the Red Army in the middle of the following month. That, however, was only to be the beginning of their troubles, for they spent the following four weeks in Soviet custody and were not released for repatriation to George Hill in Moscow until mid-February.

Altogether 485 drops were made to Poland by SOE, and 318 (chiefly Polish) agents were dropped home. Very few were to survive the German occupation, the Warsaw uprising and then the NKVD's murder squads. The Polish Section was also to take a heavy toll of aircraft: no less than seventy-three were to be lost on Polish sorties.

The head of the Polish Section in London, Harold Perkins, himself went not to Poland but to Czechoslovakia, which, at this late stage of the war, also came under his aegis. His mission, with Major Pickles and Captain Auster, took him to Prague, where he declared himself the Chargé d'Affaires at the British Legation as soon as the Germans had withdrawn. SOE's other mission into Czechoslovakia, headed by John Sehmer (from ROUGHSHOD in Yugoslavia), disappeared after being discovered by an enemy patrol in the Hron valley on 26 December 1944. Sehmer had joined up with an OSS group, DAWES, led by Lieutenant Holt Green, and had celebrated Christmas with them at a hotel near Velny Bok, when a force of 250 German and Hinka guards surrounded them. Most of the OSS members of DAWES, including Green, are known to have been executed at Mauthausen on 24 January 1945, together with another OSS team, HOUSEBOAT, but Sehmer's fate is still unrecorded. The only other OSS mission to attempt the Yugoslav route into Austria, a three-man team dropped in August codenamed ORCHID, simply disappeared without trace, together with a band of partisans. They had crossed into the Eisenkappel region on 25 October and one member had been evacuated because of illness in December. Wireless contact had been maintained into January, and then there had been silence.

SOE's German Section, designated X, is still shrouded in mystery and very little has been written about it. Created late in 1940 under Major Thornley, it was to send representatives to Switzerland (Jock McCafferty), Sweden (Henry Threlfall) and Turkey (Eric Gedye). It would seem to have undertaken very little active work during much of its existence, under the leadership of Thornley, Field-Robinson or Gerald Templer, but when Dick Barry took over a renewed effort was made to recruit agent candidates. The country section was reorganised as a directorate with Miss Graham-Stamper in charge of an Austrian sub-section, designated X/AUS.

The first attempted drop was that of a Soviet, which ended in disaster (see page 71). The remainder were mainly Leftists from the Pioneer Corps recommended to OSS by SOE, and between September 1944 and the end of hostilities nineteen agents had completed successful missions. The attrition rate, however, was appallingly high. Of the twelve teams sent into Austria, seven were captured, one was killed and two were forced to flee into Yugoslavia. And of the seven radios sent into Austria, two were used in a Gestapo *funkspiel*. According to OSS's declassified history, 'Out of 34 teams safely infiltrated (into the Greater Reich) only seven came on the air.'[12]

The first joint SOE/OSS mission was DOWNEND on 2/3 September 1944. Jupp Kappius was a left-wing German political activist, who had fled to Austria in 1937 and thence to England, where he had eventually been recruited by the Labor Section of OSS's Secret Intelligence Division. Kappius's task was to re-establish himself in Bochum, where he had lived previously, and organise an intelligence network in the Ruhr. Having landed safely by parachute, he signalled that all was well by sending a coded message in a letter to an OSS postal address in Sweden. He was followed three weeks later by his wife Anne, who was infiltrated into Germany across the frontier from Switzerland at the end of September with Hilde Meisel (*Crocus*), who also shared the same political commitment as Jupp Kappius. Nothing more was heard of DOWNEND until mid-January 1945, when Anne Kappius returned to Switzerland disguised as a Red Cross nurse, carrying a thirteen-page report from her husband. She made one further sortie in mid-February and survived the experience. *Crocus* was not so lucky. She attempted to start a branch in Vienna and committed suicide when challenged by a border patrol while crossing back into Switzerland. Another agent, Willi Drucker (*Ragweed*), who crossed into Germany on New Year's Eve, was arrested soon after he had slipped into Germany overland, heading for Dortmund, having been betrayed by the local Gestapo chief whom OSS believed susceptible to bribery.

SOE's only official mission into the Greater Reich was CLOWDER, Alfgar Hesketh-Pritchard's trek through Yugoslavia to the Austrian border in 1944. He was accompanied part of the way by Peter Wilkinson, but the latter was recalled before they reached the frontier. Hesketh-Pritchard went on alone, but was never seen again, presumed killed by an enemy patrol or, more likely, murdered by local partisans.

SOE had no inclination to send agents into Germany because there was so little they could do. An initial attempt, about which little is known, ended in November 1944. The native population was so hostile, the police controls so tight, and the intelligence taken from the interception of enemy wireless signals so huge, that it was considered unlikely that JEDBURGHS or OGs could fulfil even a tactical role. Certainly SIS had abandoned the idea of running agents in Austria and Germany, and had none in place. Accordingly, X Section limited its activities to offering support to the OSS operation, centred on 70 Grosvenor Street in Mayfair, where a series of further operations was planned to exploit DOWNEND's success. In practical terms SOE's assistance was translated into the provision of sixteen recruits, most being members of the Pioneer Corps, with Leftist political leanings, and all of Austro-German origin. These were the initial candidates for OSS's ambitious plan to infiltrate agents either by air from Italy, or overland through Switzerland and Yugoslavia. However, the first mission, code-named DUPONT, consisted of three former Austrian prisoners of war captured in Italy and was led by Jack Taylor, a dentist by profession and an experienced OSS officer who had been a veteran of missions to Crete, Albania and Yugoslavia. DUPONT was dropped into Austria on 13/14 October, but had the misfortune to be arrested soon afterwards by the same well-informed Gestapo unit that had interrogated the survivors of DAWES and HOUSEBOAT.

None of OSS's other missions into Austria and Germany accomplished anything of significance. DILLON, a five-man team flown into Austria by Halifax from Brindisi on 28 December 1944, was betrayed by one of its own members. Surrounded by Gestapo agents on 17 February, only the traitor, Viktor Ruthi, and one other, Julio Prester, survived the shoot-out. The latter's radio was to be used for a *funkspiel*, which, due to an administrative oversight, was not detected. Prester sent his warning security check on thirteen separate occasions over three weeks, but its significance was not realised. Thus, a further team was despatched on 16 April near Klagenfurt and this pair was also arrested, but survived their short term of imprisonment before the Nazi collapse.

Also sent in during the early April period was DEADWOOD, a single agent who was caught on a train near Innsbruck by the Gestapo almost as soon as he arrived, and was the subject of a *funkspiel* which was detected instantly. A complex double-cross game developed, which resulted in the advancing Allied forces scooping up a complete Gestapo network masquerading as DEADWOOD, who, incidentally, survived the experience.

Next to go was GREENUP, with two OG-trained Americans, Frederick Mayer and Hans Wynberg, as wireless operator, and an Austrian deserter, Franz Weber. They dropped on 25 February near Innsbruck, but were arrested on 20 April after betrayal by a black-market contact. The GREENUP team subsequently played a key role in the surrender of the local German administration, but only after DEADWOOD had obligingly identified Mayer as a senior OSS officer empowered to negotiate terms on behalf of the Allies.

Two Berlin Communists, both of Czech origin, Toni Ruh and Paul Land, were dropped safely into Germany as HAMMER on 1/2 March and continued to maintain contact with OSS, communicating to aircraft at predetermined times at special rendezvous.[13] HAMMER was overrun by Soviet troops in Berlin on 24 April, but nearly two months of uncomfortable detention followed before the men were finally returned to American lines on 16 June. HAMMER was followed on 19 March by Karl Macht of CHISEL, who took off from RAF Harrington in bad weather, but neither he nor his A-26 bomber was ever seen again.

An alternative source of recruits for OSS was SOE's Belgian Section, which, working closely with the Belgian *Sûreté*, recommended candidates to a special OSS mission codenamed ESPINETTE. This collaboration resulted, on 20 March, in two Belgians, Emil Van Dyck and François Flour, being dropped near Munich on Operation PAINTER. Van Dyck had operated for OSS as a line-crosser during the Battle of the Bulge, and his companion was an SOE agent who had been imprisoned for his resistance work. They were to find jobs locally in an SS-run garage and, through their contacts in the Gestapo, were able to provide a useful enemy order-of-battle for the advancing Allied troops, which eventually overran them.

A second Belgian mission was CHAUFFEUR, which consisted of two SOE agents, Michel Delhandtshutter and André Renaix as wireless operator. Both had previously worked for an SOE circuit in Belgium, and Delhandts- hutter had been liberated from prison, where he had been serving a sentence for an unrelated matter, when Brussels was overrun. Renaix and Delhandtshutter were dropped near Regensburg on 31 March and they were to prove the most successful of all the teams sent into X Section's territory. CHAUFFEUR was also the first clandestine wireless link with the German interior. The team was to find shelter with some Allied prisoners of war, who gave them a measure of protection, as well as collected tactical intelligence, before being overrun.

One of the last OSS missions into what was left of the Greater Reich was DOCTOR, a two-man Belgian team consisting of Jean Smets, an SOE- trained agent, and Lucien Blonttrock, the wireless operator. They were dropped into the Austrian Tyrol, near Kufstein, on the sixth attempt on 23 March 1945 and quickly established themselves in the mountains, where they later received two pairs of Dutch agents, VIRGINIA and GEORGIA. All three were still at large when Allied troops entered Kitzbühl, and were to be the only OSS agents despatched from London who made successful radio contact.

When the war ended there were just three other teams operating in Germany. The LUXE I team had two unlikely characters: Ferdinand Appenzell, a German who had escaped from prison in France and had joined the underground while on the run, and Leon Lindau, also German, who had fought with the resistance in Lyons after having served in the French Foreign Legion. This improbable duo parachuted 'blind' on 4 April to Raisting in southern Bavaria, and were followed by a second pair of Germans, LUXE II, on 26 April. PICKAXE was the last to go in and was located in Landshut, near Munich, when the final surrender was announced. All performed minor, tactical roles, but accomplished very little of any lasting significance beyond disproving SOE's insistent claim that the infiltration of agents into Germany itself was a practical impossibility.

Conclusion

As the war in Europe came to a close Baker Street chose to wind up its affairs with inordinate haste, destroying documents wholesale and returning key personnel to civilian life with stern warnings about disclosing any information about what had become known as 'the racket'. Within Whitehall's intelligence bureaucracy a decision had been taken to make SOE disappear, retaining a small operations branch within a peacetime SIS, chiefly to prepare stay-behind networks in Scandinavia, Austria and Italy. The process by which this conclusion was reached is still shrouded in mystery. Certainly Anthony Eden was convinced, as late as November 1944, that there would be a peacetime need for a clandestine operations capability. He minuted to Churchill that although he would 'be sorry to see the abandonment of all machinery for "special operations" when the war is over', it would be essential to run SIS and SOE's successor together: 'Nothing but chaos can ensue if we try to have two secret organisations not under the same control working in foreign countries in peacetime.'[1]

Eden's professed enthusiasm for an SIS absorption of SOE was greeted with dismay by Sir Alexander Cadogan, who made this entry in his diary on 24 November 1944: 'I am concerned at the general drift that the F.O. should take over all these fantastic things. We aren't a Department Store . . . We are taking over remnants of M. of I., M.E.W., S.O.E. Are we competent to do so?'[2]

A small committee on the future of SOE was formed under the chairmanship of Victor Cavendish-Bentinck, then serving as the Chairman of the Joint Intelligence Committee, to determine Britain's post-war strategy, but the separation between SIS and SOE ceased on 15 August 1945, the day the war in the Far East effectively ended. The Chiefs of Staff took the opportunity of one of their regular meetings to authorise the amalgamation,[3] leaving the more difficult questions of how SIS should be structured, and whether it should come under the departmental control of the Ministry of Defence, until the conclusion of Sir Findlater Stewart's broader review of MI5 and SIS. The Cabinet's Defence Committee accepted the Chiefs of Staff's recommendations on 31 August 1945,[4] and Stewart Menzies promptly began the process of integration.

While these weighty deliberations were undertaken in Whitehall what remained of SOE's headquarters staff started the process of winding up the field organisation. A small office was opened in Paris in the Boulevard des Capucines to recommend the award of decorations and settle outstanding accounts submitted by what remained of the *réseaux*, and Vera Atkins made a painful journey to Germany to determine the fate of F Section's many women agents who had not returned from their missions. SOE's Special Training Schools were dismantled and returned to their owners, but Peter Follis was selected to provide SIS with a similar facility at a new site outside Gosport in Hampshire. Some other headquarters personnel, such as Terence O'Bryan Tear, Dayrell Oakley-Hill and Harold Perkins, also switched to SIS, as did some of the more accomplished field agents, among them Tony Brooks, Xan Fielding and Peter Kemp. By 30 June 1946 SOE's last operations in the Far East had been concluded and the organisation ceased to exist, the remaining files, which had survived a fire five months earlier, placed in SIS's custody, with only Professor Mackenzie authorised to examine them.

Determining the overall impact of SOE on the prosecution of the war, or the effect of the extraordinary hostility between SOE and SIS, is no easy task. Thousands of tons of *matériel* were successfully conveyed to resistance groups throughout the world, thereby fulfilling SOE's principal objective of supporting and sustaining home-grown guerrilla movements. But this was achieved at a considerable cost, both in terms of hardware lost to the enemy and a hitherto concealed rate of attrition for the personnel involved. On a strategic level it must be open to considerable doubt whether unconventional warfare, of the type practised by SOE, played any part in shortening the war. Certainly this is an assertion that has often been made, and Maurice Buckmaster for one is fond of quoting General Eisenhower on this subject, citing a period of nine months.[5] But is the claim really justified? It must be recognised that SOE's involvement in France during the critical days after the Normandy invasion was a significant contributory factor in the operation's success. The appalling obstacles placed in the path of the German counter-attack, with an entire armoured division being obliged to fight its way from village to village across France, in supposedly occupied territory, just to reach the newly opened front, are testimony enough to efficacy of Allied tactics of harrying the enemy before he had even reached the field of battle. But this, as we have seen, was predominantly the work of irregular formations composed of SAS troops, and whilst they were under the control of SFHQ, they played a paramilitary role quite unlike that adopted in earlier years by SOE.

Elsewhere it is more difficult to discern a pivotal function for SOE in regard to defeating the Axis. Indeed, in Yugoslavia, the scene of most of SOE's Southern European activities, the organisation had a very dubious part in confronting the enemy, but is directly implicated in the establishment of a totalitarian regime which used SOE-supplied weapons to impose a dictatorship and ruthlessly eliminate dissenters. The full details of the scale of the bloodletting have yet to emerge, and it was not until July 1990 that a few former Communists felt sufficiently safe to reveal the locations of some of the mass graves where initial estimates suggest that up to thirty thousand of Tito's opponents were butchered and buried. Michael Lees, of the FUGUE mission, believes that about 250,000, mainly Serbs, were slaughtered by the Communists, 'and while it was going on, Tito's Western Allied sponsors, who had enormously facilitated his grab for power but were now impotent to restrain him, either were hoodwinked some more or closed their eyes to the horrors'.[6] Whatever the exact statistics, far more Yugoslavs were killed with SOE weaponry than German or Italian troops, and in part this must be due to SOE Cairo. As Xan Fielding has commented, 'our Greek and Yugoslav sections suffered from muddled policy and lack of direction'.[7]

Whilst it is harder to demonstrate similar atrocities in Greece, there can be no doubt that SOE unconsciously fuelled a civil war and very nearly enabled a Communist take-over. Whether this was a manifestation of political naïveté, assisting in the creation of a power vacuum, the ideal conditions for a Communist coup, or something more sinister will probably never be known. That SOE meddled in Greek politics, and was manipulated by those seeking to include the country in a post-war Soviet Bloc, cannot be doubted. The question remaining is whether British military liaison personnel like Brigadier Myers were duped into allowing ELAS to get so close to gaining the upper hand, or whether Leftist elements in SOE Cairo deliberately conspired to outmanoeuvre those in the field, such as Hammond and Woodhouse, who expressed reservations as events unfolded. SOE certainly participated in Greek intrigue, isolated the monarchists and contributed to the creation of circumstances which were to be exploited by ELAS and nearly led to a pro-Soviet putsch. Instead, a bloody civil war was sustained by SOE weaponry and money. Once the Germans had withdrawn from Greece, Stanley Moss was amazed at the wealth of gold which the Communists found at their disposal. None of that money came from Russia; it was presented to the Communists by the Allies. For years the money had been poured into the country for the maintenance of guerrilla forces and the general pursuance of the war; but the Communists had used only a small proportion of it to fight the Germans.[8]

But was this political naïveté or a deliberate attempt to nudge Greece into the Soviet Bloc?

Elsewhere in Southern Europe, where SOE had been rather less active, the outcome was markedly different. In Romania, Bulgaria, Czechoslovakia and Hungary, SOE had played only a marginal role in the prosecution of the war and had exercised only minimal influence, if any at all, on the outcome. Certainly the liberating Red Army had little regard for SOE's efforts, for it arranged for the repatriation of the surviving SOE missions promptly and unceremoniously, with the single exception of Ivor Porter in Bucharest, whose continued presence in the capital was tolerated, no doubt because he was not perceived as a threat by the Russians.

Enthusiasm for SOE varied from country to country. The governments-in-exile of Norway, Denmark and Belgium expressed grave doubts about the wisdom of mounting what they regarded as highly provocative operations, which inevitably were followed by appalling reprisals exacted upon the civilian populations. Some politicians were also sceptical about the wisdom of sanctioning risky undertakings which exposed people who were already subjected to terrifying repression to further danger, and questioned whether it was appropriate to endorse the sabotage of what amounted to national industrial assets which would be pivotal to post-war reconstruction and economic recovery. The Foreign Office was also conscious of SOE's talent for indulging in counter-productive activity, which certainly never frightened the Axis, but did threaten to alienate non-combatant powers. The tendency had been demonstrated by the Rickman episode in Sweden and the Iron Gates fiasco in Romania, where Section D had mounted amateurish, ill-conceived operations, and the accident on the Gibraltar ferry showed that SOE had lost none of its ability to embarrass the Foreign Office. Not surprisingly, there was continued opposition to SOE's activities in neutral countries, and the fact that SOE even possessed a Swedish or Spanish country section was a closely guarded secret, particularly from the Ambassador in Madrid, Sir Samuel Hoare, who, like his counterpart in Lisbon, Sir Ronald Campbell, was constantly placing obstacles in the way of clandestine operations. Campbell's own record of intransigence, of course, dated back to his lack of co-operation in Belgrade.

As well as official hostility from the Foreign Office, SOE was constantly locked in unproductive conflict with SIS. The standard explanation for the strife, that the functions of intelligence-gathering and sabotage are incompatible, is too superficial, especially when the Americans, relative neophytes in the field, scarcely experienced the same kind of difficulties and accommodated secret intelligence and special operations within OSS. Indeed, BSC did the same in North and South America without friction. This implies that the motivation for the state of undeclared war that existed between SIS and SOE was historical in nature: that had the British been starting with a clean slate, they too might have adopted an American-style solution to the twin challenges of gathering information and fomenting resistance. So was this really a case of nothing more complicated than old-fashioned jealousy and rivalry? This seems unlikely, given that so many SIS officers took a leading role in SOE. After all, the first CD, Sir Frank Nelson, was himself an SIS officer, a fact frequently overlooked by historians who have accepted too readily his diplomatic cover in pre-war Basle at face value. Major Field-Robinson, George Hill, Lionel Loewe, Philip Johns and Eddie Boxshall, all SOE staffers, also had SIS backgrounds and were on close terms with their former colleagues. Moreover, the overwhelming majority of SIS's wartime personnel were wartime intakes, amateurs drafted in from the universities and others who had no earlier experience from which to have developed a prejudice. So why did so many become predisposed to a confrontational relationship with SOE?

One possible explanation was the quite widespread indoctrination within SIS of what has been termed the ULTRA secret. This description is always misleading because few people, anywhere, had a grasp of the full nature of GCHQ's cryptographic operation, or the extraordinary success it achieved. However, a very large proportion of SIS itself, including the whole of its largest branch, Section V, was dedicated to exploitation of material from this highly sensitive source. Some four hundred Section V officers handled GCHQ's counter-intelligence product, and the distribution mechanism for circulating all the other categories of decrypts was all firmly in SIS's control. In contrast, virtually nobody in SOE had even the slightest inkling of ULTRA's existence. Only CD, his deputy and, by accident rather than design, Brigadier Keble ever enjoyed access as a right, although in some limited theatres, such as the Balkans, a few selected staff officers like Hugh Seton-Watson were granted restricted access for a specific purpose, but never allowed to guess the extent of the entire programme. This inevitably put the SIS officers on to a different, exclusive plane in the intelligence environment, and burdened them with a responsibility to protect the 'family jewels' as well as the enhanced status which accompanied the access. This accounts for the superior air, interpreted as arrogance, which was detected by so many SOE officers in their dealings with their SIS counterparts. The latter tended to behave as if they knew something so secret it could not be imparted to the former. This, of course, was exactly the situation, yet the explanation must be more complex than simply that. After all, some senior SIS officers, such as Colonel A. G. Trevor-Wilson, established an entirely satisfactory rapport with their opposite numbers, apparently untainted by the mischief further up in Broadway's hierarchy. Unfortunately, it is now almost impossible to determine whether Trevor-Wilson himself enjoyed access to ULTRA, but in all likelihood he did, which rules out an explanation of the sour SOE/SIS relationship as somehow linked to knowledge of signals intelligence, or the lack of it.

The fact is that the uneasiness which characterised their relations dated back to Section D and there is no single rule that holds good throughout the world. In some territories, such as Algiers, there was co-operation. In Denmark SOE actually fulfilled SIS's functions, with the latter's (reluctant) acceptance. There were varying degrees of collaboration elsewhere in Western Europe and something approaching open warfare in London, Cairo and the Far East.

There has been a tendency for observers to blame Claude Dansey, SIS's manipulative Deputy Chief with overall responsibility for French liaison, for many of the ills that befell SOE. The most popular claim is to suggest that he deliberately exploited SOE for his own purposes, which, though poorly defined, usually imply a ruthless and calculating determination to use the organisation as an expendable instrument of strategic deception. Such a proposition does not stand up to detailed examination in the two related cases cited most often: the attempts in 1943 to persuade the enemy that a second front was imminent, and the duplicity of Henri Dericourt, SOE's air operations controller, and maybe a double agent run by SIS against the SD. Analysis of the deception campaign for 1943 shows that deliberate sacrifice was not on the agenda as a means of duping the German High Command, and the evidence of *Gilbert*'s connections with SIS is both modest and entirely circumstantial. More likely is Professor Foot's rationale that Dericourt had a highly developed sense of self-preservation and did whatever he felt necessary to accomplish his mission and survive. Whatever Dericourt's faults, the fact remains that he supervised over fifty flights in and out of enemy-occupied territory and never lost an aircraft. Whilst one might speculate about the human cost of this success, and wonder about his involvement in the collapse of PROSPER or the exact nature of his relationship with the SD, nothing of subtance has ever emerged to tie him in with Dansey or SIS's French sections. Nor is there any evidence that the two men ever met, or even knew of each other. The controversy, such as it is, centres on a single disputed night in London when Dericourt's movements cannot be accounted for, and some ambiguous remarks made by him concerning his contacts with what he termed 'British Intelligence'. However, as many of the uninitiated fail to discriminate between the separate branches of what is often (but erroneously) perceived as a single body, Dericourt can be forgiven for his inexactitude, an understandable slip which may owe as much to language differences as anything else.

Dericourt's inability to distinguish between SIS and SOE was a handicap shared by the Germans, but not, significantly, by the Italians, who succeeded in exploiting SOE's weaknesses to a much greater degree than their Axis partners. The dreaded OVRA, the Italian security service, ran numerous double agents in the Italian campaign and was generally well-informed about SOE in particular. In contrast, the Germans' piecemeal approach meant a fragmented effort with little or no attempt to collate information obtained from interrogations conducted in different theatres. Whereas the Italians centralised their efforts, the *Abwehr* ran quite separate operations from several different centres. This is illustrated by the *Abwehr*'s attack on Britain, which was run from *Abstelles* in Hamburg, Brussels, Paris, Lisbon and Madrid, with minimal overall control from Berlin.

The unpalatable truth is that even with their unco-ordinated efforts the Germans achieved very considerable success against SOE. In France, Belgium and Holland in particular, where the *Sicherheitsdienst* and the *Abwehr* were competing against each other, they brought large parts of the total resistance network under their control. Views differ about how they accomplished this, but Baker Street's apparent inability to distinguish between messages from agents operating under enemy control and those still at liberty was to have tragic consequences. The head of SOE's coderoom, Leo Marks, is one of those who believes he knows how the failures occurred.[9]

Marks's entry in SOE had been entirely accidental. The son of Ben Marks, the Charing Cross Road bookdealer, he had been transferred to Ozanne's Signal Section in June 1942 having completed a cipher course run by GCHQ at Bedford. He suggests that SOE mistakenly believed he was actually the son of Sir Simon Marks, then Chairman of Marks and Spencer, and had agreed to employ him so as to gain access to the Marks and Spencer staff canteen. More likely, Marks had been recognised as a gifted, if eccentric, cryptographer. Marks quickly learned the ropes and spotted two intrinsic flaws in SOE's wireless procedures. The first was the security check, which he regarded as a worthless guide to whether an agent was operating under duress. The enemy had grasped the principle very quickly and had been known to have simply forced agents into revealing their particular check. Conversely, many agents transmitting under stress in the field either accidentally omitted their check or placed it in the wrong part of the message. Either way, the check did not constitute, as previously claimed, a reliable method of discriminating between agents. Indeed, as has been seen, N Section took a conscious decision in the case of Hubertus Lauwers to continue the contact even though his signal had been logged as missing his security check.

Marks's second damning criticism concerned SOE's reliance on poem codes. Working on advice proffered by SIS when the Signal Section had been created, Ozanne had supplied each agent with a short poem which was to be the basis of their individual code. However, once the enemy became aware of the system, it was all too easy for them to extract the full text from an agent and construct their own texts. Thus, on Marks's advice, SOE abandoned the poem codes in February 1943 and adopted a new system based on random numbers generated by a team of 400 women code clerks and printed on silk handkerchiefs. For many agents this improvement had come too late.

SOE's reliance on a defective communications system was not the only breach of security to have handicapped the organisation. A continuing theme throughout SOE's wartime operations was the apparent willingness of senior officers to place themselves at risk by operating in the field. The examples are legion: Nicholas Bodington in France, Brigadier Barker-Benfield in Greece, Mostyn Davies in Bulgaria, Jack Hughes-Smith in Crete and Peter Boughey in Hungary. All of these missions were, of course, sanctioned from Baker Street, which raises doubts about how the organisation's hierarchy viewed its staff and the expendability of its agents. Certainly SFHQ's determination to build circuits in France prior to D-Day came close to recklessness with agent after agent being despatched to a thoroughly compromised ARCHDEACON. It is only when the contribution of the para-militaries, the SAS, the JEDBURGHS and the OGs are taken into account that the often tragic heroism of individual *résistants* can be put into a strategic perspective. Dozens of SOE organisers displayed extraordinary personal gallantry on many occasions throughout the Nazi occupation of Europe. But whether they ever received the logistical support or political backing from SOE itself that they so handsomely merited is an issue which can only be resolved by the wholesale declassification and release of all the still-secret wartime archives. Based on the evidence available at present, both SIS and

SOE stand indicted of prosecuting an undeclared war against each other with the same, if not more, venomous enthusiasm as the official conflict waged against the common enemy. Nor was this some minor, bureaucratic sideshow. It was to help ensure that much of Eastern Europe remained under totalitarian domination for a further forty-five years after the Nazi defeat.

APPENDIX I
SOE's Organisation, Structure and Personnel

SOE's complex structure, a pyramid headed by the Council and based on the country sections and directorates, evolved throughout its short existence. These structure plans illustrate SOE's internal organisation at two stages in its development, in July 1943 and October 1944, and represent a 'snapshot' of the principal staff in London. It identifies, for the first time, each of SOE's component parts, together with the names of those serving in each Section on the two dates selected.

SOE reflected the business background of its senior management, with the Council operating as a board of nine directors with a further five ex-officio members. Each presided over his own line of command, down through three broad branches: the country sections, the support directorates and the overseas missions.

In order to preserve secrecy and continuity, each SOE post was represented by an individual symbol, starting with CD. Taking the Polish Section as an example, the overall head of the regional branch for Poland, Czechoslovakia and Hungary was Harold Perkins, known as MP, who was assisted by two senior staff officers, MPJ and MPF. The Polish country section itself, designated MPP, was commanded by Major Pickles with various subordinates taking responsibility for particular functions, such as Operations (MPC), Training (MPG), Movements and Supplies (MPN) and Intelligence (MPX.1). In each sub-section FANY personnel fulfilled specialist duties, with an ensign handling Intelligence (MPL) and Couriers (MPK). Thus, throughout an SOE staff officer's career, he was likely to have used more than one symbol. As a security precaution communications and internal memoranda referred to a person's acronym in preference to a surname.

July 1943

Members of the Council

CD	Chief of SOE and Chairman of the Council	Charles Hambro
V/CD	Vice-Chief of SOE	Major-General C. Gubbins DSO, MC
A/CD	Assistant Chief of SOE, President of the Personnel Board, Director of Personnel Services, Intelligence, Security and Liaison	Air-Commodore A. R. Boyle CMG, OBE, MC

D/FIN	Director of Finance and Administration	Group Captain J. F. Venner
AD	Director of HQ Staff of Overseas Groups and Missions	Colonel G. F. Taylor CBE
AD/Z	Director of Research, Development and Supply	Colonel F. T. Davies
AD/E	Director of London Group	Brigadier E. E. Mockler-Ferryman CBE, MC
D/PLANS	Liaison with Planning Staffs of other government departments and head of Council Secretariat	Colonel R. H. Barry
MS	Director of Signals	Colonel F. W. Nicholls OBE

Ex Officio Members

AD/3	Director of Cairo Group	Lord Glenconner
BB/100	Director of Delhi Group	Colin H. Mackenzie
AD/N	Naval Director	Rear-Admiral A. H. Taylor CB, OBE
K/AIR/P	Liaison Officer (Policy) between SOE and Air Ministry, and Air Adviser	Air-Commodore H. N. Thornton MBE
K/POL	Political Adviser	W. E. Houstoun-Boswall CMG, MC

PPS to SO

| A/DS | Lieutenant-Colonel H. N. Sporborg |
| AD/S1 | V. M. Cannon-Brookes |

London Group

| AD/E | Brigadier E. E. Mockler-Ferryman CBE, MC |

Air Operations

| AL | Wing-Commander J. C. Corby |

Training

| MT | Lieutenant-Colonel J. T. Young MC, DCM, TD |

Scandinavia and Baltic States

Sweden, Denmark, Finland and Baltic States

S	G. O. Wiskeman
S1	Major H. McL. Threlfall
SG	Sir George Binney
S2	D. P. Coleridge

Denmark

SD	Pay Lieutenant-Commander R. C. Hollingworth RNVR
SD/1	R. Spink
SD/T	Captain R. L. Taylor
SD/D	Miss M. de Fries
SD/R	Lieutenant J. A. Ray

Norway

SN	Lieutenant-Colonel J. S. Wilson OBE
SN/A	Captain P. F. S. Douglas DSO
SN/A1	Lieutenant Keith H. Cochrane
SN/A2	Major R. C. Holme (Retd) DSO
SN/P	Lieutenant J. Chaworth-Musters RNVR
SN/S	Major W. F. Ram
SN/S1	Captain F. K. M. Carver
SN/S2	Lieutenant F. R. B. Hoskier

SN/T	Captain P. W. Boughton-Leigh	FB	Major N. R. Bodington MBE
SN/T1	Flight Lieutenant Lord Ventry	FP	Captain R. A. Bourne-Paterson
SN/1	Captain H. A. Nyberg	FG	Captain S. Jepson
SN/O	Major J. C. Adamson	FH	Captain J. P. C. Le Harival
SN/O1	Lieutenant Sir G. S. M. Pollock, Bart RN	FM	Captain G. H. Morel
SN/US	Lieutenant F. Cromwell	FQ	Captain J. D. Coleman
		FQ1	Captain H. C. Peace
		FV	Miss V. Atkins
		FN	Captain G. R. Noble

Switzerland, Italy, Sicily, Corsica and Sardinia

	FL	Flight Lieutenant A. Simon
	FL5	Lieutenant R. L. Searle
J	Major C. L. Roseberry
JA	Squadron Leader H. G. Crawshaw
JD	F. H. Norrish
JH	Miss Lane

J	Major C. L. Roseberry	FL7	Miss P. McFie
JA	Squadron Leader H. G. Crawshaw	FL8	Ensign B. Myer
JD	F. H. Norrish	F/RECS	Miss H. Hudson
JH	Miss Lane		Miss P. Torr

Low Countries, France, Fighting France

Fighting France

		RF	Lieutenant-Colonel J. R. H. Hutchison
D/R	R. E. Brook		
D/RA	Major J. H. F. Collingwood MBE	RF(P)	Flight Lieutenant F. F. E. Yeo-Thomas
D/RO	Flight Officer J. McA. Wollaston	RF(O)	Captain R. A. Johnson MC
D/RV	G. N. Vansittart	RF(I)	Lieutenant A. R. H. Kellas
D/RX	Miss M. A. K. Wilson	RF(AQ)	Flying Officer H. M. G. Clark
DR/US	Captain P. van der Stricht	RF(Q)	Captain T. L. O'Bryan Tear
GM	Lieutenant-Colonel L. Franck	RF(A)	Lieutenant P. J. F. Storrs
		RF(T)	Lieutenant H. E. Bramwell
		RF(T1)	Flying Officer G. Whitehead
		RF(W/T)	Ensign K. Moore

Clandestine Communications

D/F	Major L. A. L. Humphreys	RF(L)	Captain H. H. A. Thackthwaite
D/FB	Flight Lieutenant R. M. Archibald		
D/FP	Lieutenant F. R. Pickering		
D/FS	Captain U. B. Walmsley	**Holland**	
D/FO	Captain P. J. Harratt	N	Major S. Bingham
D/FM	E. Croft-Murray	NO	Captain R. A. Wells
D/FJ	Captain G. T. Lynch	NC1	Lieutenant A. Shewing
D/FE	E. V. H. Rizzo	NC2	A. C. Parr
		NT	Captain J. D. Killick
		NS	Captain A. G. Knight
		NL	Junior Commander S. I. Bond

France

F	Lieutenant-Colonel M. Buckmaster	NA	Captain W. E. Mills
		NP	B. H. Oliver

Belgium

T	Major C. T. Knight
TG	Captain G. T. R. Thompson
TH	Major E. H. Amies
TD	Captain R. I. Dobson
TL	Lieutenant J. G. Kidd
TX	Captain R. L. Raemaekers
TF	Lieutenant P. J. Ferry
TM	Flight Officer Cameron
TR	Lieutenant A. M. F. J. Robinson
TB	Lieutenant H. P. Verhaegen
TK	Lieutenant Edward Brooks
TC	Lieutenant L. G. Boudin
TQ	ASO E. M. Morrison

Poland, Czechoslovakia and Hungary

MP	Lieutenant Colonel H. P. Perkins
MP1	Major E. P. F. Boughey
MP/US	

Poland

MP	Lieutenant-Colonel H. P. Perkins
MPX	Major R. Truszkowski (Pol. Int.)
MPX1	Captain L. H. Massey
MPT	Captain G. I. Klauber (Ops)
MPM	Captain A. Morgan
MPG	Captain C. T. Gregor (Training)
MPJ	Ensign J. R. Aldis
MPK	ASO North (Courier)
MPS	J. A. D. Timms ⎫ Wireless
MPR	Captain H. R. Adams ⎭ Section

Poles, Minorities

EU/P	Major R. Hazell
EU/P1	Major C. B. Ince
EU/P2	Captain H. H. Cochran
EU/P3	Captain R. R. Sadler

EU/P4	
EU/P5	Major R. H. Egdell
EU/P6	Captain C. H. Edwards

Czechoslovakia

MY	F. E. Keary
MYA	Captain P. R. Auster (Ops)
MYD	Miss E. O'Donnell (Int.)

Hungary

MPH	Captain O. L. Uren

Germany and Austria

X	Major R. H. Thornley
X/A	Miss E. B. Graham-Stamper
X/A1	Mrs M. Holmes
X/G	Major W. Field-Robinson
X/1	Lieutenant F. Boothroyd
X/S	Lieutenant C. Brown

Iberia and Spanish Morocco

H	Major L. J. W. Richardson
HH	Major J. A. S. Hamilton
HL	Captain K. M. D. Mills
HS	H. E. Steiner

Cairo Group

Yugoslavia and Bulgaria

D/H.170	Major E. C. Last

Romania, Greece, Crete and Albania

D/H.109	Major E. G. Boxshall

Communications

M	Colonel F. W. Nicholls OBE
D/HV	Lieutenant-Colonel J. S. A. Pearson

Middle East, Turkey and Persia

Personnel and Supplies

D/HX	F. H. B. Nixon

Delhi Group

AD/O   John Keswick

India, Burma, China and Australia
B/B   Major C. A. L. Guise MBE

Directorate of Finance and Administration

D/FIN	Director	Group Captain J. F. Venner
AQ	Assistant Director of Administration	Major A. G. Howe

Directorates of Intelligence, Security and Personnel Services and Liaison Officers

A/CD	Air-Commodore A. R. Boyle CMG, OBE, MC	
AD/P	Deputy to A/CD and Director of Security	Commander John Senter RNVR

Directorate of Services

AD/Z   Colonel F. T. Davies

London HQ

Scientific Research
DSR   Professor D. M. Newitt FRS

Supplies
E   Lieutenant-Commander E. A. Milne RNVR

Country Stations

Devices (Station XII)
E/D   Lieutenant-Colonel L. J. C. Wood

Arms (Station VI)
E/CA   Captain E. I. Rowat

Camouflage
D/CAM   Major J. E. Wills

Director of Missions

AD/O   John Keswick

Africa – East and West, and Madagascar
W   Major J. E. Benham

Americas
U   Major W. E. Hedley-Dent

Russia
D/P   Major A. D. Seddon

Summer 1943

SOE Headquarters Staff

CD   Sir Charles Hambro

D/CD   J. Hanbury-Williams

    COS Colonel G. Taylor
    Asst Lieutenant-Colonel Guinness
            Major Sweet-Escott
            Major Sheridan

    Director of Intelligence ——————— Security Section
    Air-Commodore A. R. Boyle   Liaison, Service Depts
                               Intelligence Division
                               Liaison with PWE, MO1

    Director of Operations, ——————— Scandinavia, Holland, Belgium,
    Western and Central Europe   France, Switzerland, Italy, Germany,
    Brigadier C. Gubbins   Poland, Czechoslovakia

                               Operations
                               Training
                               Signals
                               Special Raiding Force

    Director of Missions ——————— Iberia, North Africa, West and
    Area A   East Africa
    Lieutenant-Colonel Brian Clarke

    Director of Missions ——————— Balkans and Middle East,
    Area B   Russia
    Lord Glenconner

    Director of Missions ——————— India, Far East,
    Area C   North and South America
    W. J. Keswick

    Director of Services ——————— Arms and RE Supplies
    Lieutenant-Colonel Davies   Research
                                   Distribution
                                   Production

                               W/T Supplies
                                 Station Equipment
                                   Research/Production

    Director of Finance ——————— Finance
    and Administration   Administration
    W/C Venner

19 October 1944

Members of the Council

CD	Chief of SOE and Chairman of the Council	Major-General C. Gubbins DSO, MC
V/CD	Vice-Chief of SOE	H. N. Sporborg
D/CD	Deputy Chief of SOE	M. P. Murray
A/CD	Assistant Chief of SOE, President of the Personnel Board, Director of Personnel Services, Intelligence, Security and Liaison	Air-Commodore A. R. Boyle CMG, OBE, MC
D/FIN	Director of Finance and Administration	Group Captain J. F. Venner
AD/E	Director of London Group	Brigadier E. E. Mockler-Ferryman CBE, MC
AD	Director of Far East Group	Colonel G. F. Taylor CBE
A/DH	Director of Mediterranean Group	Colonel D. J. Keswick
AD/Z	Director of Research, Development and Supply	Colonel F. T. Davies
CD/S	Chief Staff Officer to CD and V/CD, liaison with Chiefs of Staff Organisation	Colonel R. H. Barry OBE
D/SIGS	Director of Signals	Brigadier F. W. Nicholls OBE

Ex Officio Members

D/H	Director of Cairo Group	Major-General A. W. M. Stawell CBE, MC
BB/100	Director of Delhi Group	Colin H. Mackenzie
AD/N	Naval Director	Rear-Admiral A. H. Taylor CB, OBE
AD/A	Air Adviser	Air Vice-Marshal A. P. Ritchie CBE, AFC

PPS to SO

AD/S1	V. M. Cannon-Brookes
AD/SW	Lieutenant-Commander C. E. H. Smith

German Directorate

AD/X	Colonel R. H. Barry
ADX/PA	Miss L. Wauchope
AD/X1	Lieutenant-Colonel R. H. Thornley

GS and Liaison

X/S	Major G. Prentice
X/S1	S/O P. Haines WAAF

Intelligence

X/INT	Major J. Hayward
X/DOC	Captain F. Boothroyd
X/DOC.1	Lieutenant D. Davenport FANY
X/INT.1	Captain F. W. Hornsby
X/INT.2	Lieutenant H. K. Annett

Plans

X/PLANS	
X/TGT	Captain J. D. Helps
X/TGT.1	Junior Commander H. M. Lishman ATS

Air Liaison

K/AIR	Squadron Leader H. M. Potter

A and Q

X/AQ	Major L. M. Smith
X/ADM	Captain L. Eardley
X/ADM.1	
X/Q	Captain C. V. Russell
X/Q.1	Sub des Salles d/Epinoix
X/REG	Miss M. Morse

Germany

X/GER	Major W. Field-Robinson
X/GER.1	Captain A. Kier
X/GER.2	Captain A. H. Campbell
X/GER.3	
XGER.C.	Mrs P. Graham

Austria

X/AUS	Miss E. B. Graham-Stamper
X/AUS.1	Mrs M. Holmes
X/AUS.4	Captain D. M. Dobell

Poles

EU/P	Major C. B. Ince
EU/P1	Captain J. D. Cole
EU/P2	Junior Commander E. Johnstone ATS
EU/PA	Junior Commander J. March ATS

Iberia and Spanish Morocco

H	R. G. Head
H2	Captain W. J. C. Berington
HR	Lieutenant J. A. Robertson

Directorate of Organisation and Staff Duties

D/CD	Director	M. P. Murray

Directorate of Staff Duties and Administration

General Administration and 'Q' Matters

D/AQ	Major J. S. Dodd

Provision and Administration of Personnel

D/AG	Major P. H. T. Kenyon

Directorates of Intelligence, Security and Personnel Services and Liaison Officers

A/CD	Director	Air-Commodore A. R. Boyle CMG, OBE, MC
AD/P	Deputy to A/CD and Director of Security	Commander J. Senter RNVR

Directorate of Finance and Administration

D/FIN	Director	Group Captain J. F. Venner
AG	Assistant Director of Administration	Lieutenant-Colonel A. G. Howe

Overseas Groups and Missions

AD	Director	Colonel G. F. Taylor CBE
AD/4	Deputy Director	Lieutenant-Colonel L. F. Sheridan

Far East Region

B/B	Lieutenant-Colonel G. Egerton Mott

Americas

U	Major W. E. Hedley-Dent

Russia and Africa Sections

D/P	Major J. E. Benham

Mediterranean Group

A/DH	Director	Colonel David Keswick
A/DH.1	Deputy Director	Lieutenant-Colonel L. J. W. Richardson

Balkans and Middle East

D/HT	Lieutenant-Colonel D. Talbot Rice MBE

Yugoslavia and Bulgaria

D/H170	Major E. C. Last
D/H930	Mrs R. G. Seawright

Romania, Greece, Crete and Albania

D/H109	Major E. G. Boxshall
D/HA	Major E. B. M. Pirie
D/H61	Major D. Oakley Hill

Middle East, Turkey and Persia

D/HX	Major F. H. B. Nixon

Massingham

AMX	Major E. H. Sherren

Poland, Czechoslovakia and Hungary

MP	Lieutenant-Colonel H. B. Perkins
MPJ	Captain J. R. Aldis, FANY (Regional Admin.)

MPF	Lieutenant N. H. Empson-Ridler, FANY (Regional Admin.)

Wireless Section

MPR	Major H. R. Adams
MPR.1	R. P. Heatley
MPS	J. A. D. Timms

Poland

MPP	Major M. J. T. Pickles
MPC	Captain R. G. Colt-Williams MC (Ops)
MPG	Captain C. T. Gregor (Training)
MPN	Lieutenant J. C. D. Pickford RNVR (Movements and Supplies)
MPX.1	Captain L. M. Massey (Intelligence)
MPL	Ensign P. Harrison, FANY (Intelligence)
MPK	Sergeant S. Kay, FANY (Couriers)

Czechoslovakia

MY	F. E. Kerry
MYA	Captain P. R. Auster (Ops)
MYT	Lieutenant D. Ff Thomas

Hungary

MPH	
MPH/POL	H. J. Bruce
MPH.1	
MPH.2	F. G. Redward
MPH.3	Major J. Faure-Field
MPH.4	Miss V. Fone
MPH.5	Flight Lieutenant R. Railton

Switzerland and Italy

J	Lieutenant-Colonel C. L. Roseberry
JD	F. H. Norrish
JK	Sub M. Judge ATS
JH	Mrs J. Paget
JL	Captain M. E. V. Blake

Directorate of Research, Development and Supplies

AD/Z	Director	Colonel F. T. Davies

London Headquarters

Scientific Research

DSR	Professor D. M. Newitt FRS

Supplies

E	Commander E. Milne RMVR

Directorate of Signals

D/SIGS	Brigadier F. W. Nicholls OBE

Low Countries, France and Allied French

France

F/ADM	Major I. K. Mackenzie
F/OPS.1	Captain N. Fraser-Campbell, FANY
F/FIN	I. D. Lloyd (Finance)
F/REC	Lieutenant A. Willis (Records)
F/REC.1	Miss P. Cole
F/REG	Miss E. Alexander

Allied French

RF	Lieutenant-Colonel L. H. Dismore
RF/P	Major C. S. Rogerson
RF/P1	Captain R. S. Walker
RF/AQ	Flight Lieutenant H. M. G. Clark
RF/A	Junior Commander M. M. Fox
RF/D	Junior Commander M. E. Gurney
RF/C	Captain J. H. Childs
RF/C1	Flight Officer A. Barrie

Belgium and Holland

LC	Pay Commander P. L. Johns RN
LC/INT	Mrs Domville

Holland

N	Major R. I. Dobson
N/1	Captain C. F. Dadley
N/OPS	Captain A. G. Knight
N/OPS.1	Lieutenant D. G. Mortlock (US)
N/DOC	Captain A. C. Parr
N/A	Captain W. E. Mills
N/WT	Captain B. H. Oliver
N/WT.1	Ensign W. A. Thomas, FANY
N/T	Junior Commander S. I. Bond
N/T.1	Captain A. Shewing
N/CON	Lieutenant H. Hooper
N/FLAT	Vol A. Palmer, FANY

Belgium

T	Lieutenant-Colonel E. H. Amies
T/PLANS	Major W. A. Murphy
T/OPS	Lieutenant C. P. Tivey
T/WT	Captain A. M. F. Robinson
T/WT.1	Captain J. Doneux
T/WT.2	S/O E. M. Morrison
T/CON	Lieutenant A. B. K. O'Connor
T/RECS	Miss D. Jackson

Clandestine Communications

D/F	Lieutenant-Colonel L. A. L. Humphreys
DF/OPS	Squadron Leader R. M. Archibald
DF/PLANS	Major G. T. Lynch
DF/AQ	Captain S. Dolton
DF/REC	Captain J. C. Whitaker
DF/WT	Captain the Hon. A. G. Samuel

DF/DOC   Captain A. Hall
DF/SEA.1 Lieutenant P. J. Ellam
DF/Y   Miss D. O. Butterfield

Jedburgh Section
DR/JED   Lieutenant-Colonel
          D. L. G. Carleton-Smith
DR/   Captain H. E. P. Buck,
JED.AQ   FANY

Poles (Minorities)

EU/P   Major C. B. Ince
EU/P1   Captain J. D. Cole
EU/P.Q   Junior Commander E.
          Johnstone
EU/P.A   Sub. S. Key
EU/P.A.1 Junior Commander J.
          March
EU/P.DOC Major C. H. Edwards
          (Stn XIV)
EU/   Miss N. Brock
P.DOC.1
EU/   Miss J. Ridland
P.DOC.2
EU/   Captain C. F. Roberts
P.DOC.3   (Stn XIV)

Scandinavian Region

DS   Lieutenant-Colonel J. S.
          Wilson OBE
DS/US   Lieutenant-Commander
          G. U. Vetlesen USNR
DS/US.A   Mr Morrison
DS/G   Major J. Mann
DS/G.1.
DS/INT   Captain T. Jonsson
DS/   Captain P. Brightman
INT.US
DS/INT.1 Lieutenant B. Burrus,
          FANY
DS/RAF   Squadron Leader
          D. K. de G. Faulks
DS/RG   Miss J. Armstrong

Sweden
SS   Major P. H. Thompson

SGB   Lieutenant-Commander
          B. Bingham MBE, DSC,
          RNR
SG1   P. Coleridge

Denmark
SD   Pay Lieutenant-
          Commander R. C.
          Hollingworth RNVR
SD/PA   Miss M. de Fries
SD/1   Major H. L. Lasson
SD/US   Major K. Winkelhorn, US
SD/G   Major A. R. T. Garrett
SD/AIR   Flight Officer F. Townson,
          WAAF
SD/OPS   Captain Verschoor, US
SD/OPS.1 Lieutenant G. F. Juncker
SD/INT   Lieutenant S. A. P.
          Truelsen
SD/DT.1
SD/WT   Ensign D. M. Schieldrop,
          FANY
SD/AQ   Captain R. L. Taylor
SD/A   Lieutenant G. C. Bowden
SD/Q   Lieutenant A. Blanner
          RMVR
SD/Q1   J. Cross, US

Norway
SN.1   Lieutenant-Commander
          Sir George M. Pollock,
          Bart, RN
SN/US   Captain A. Brogger
SN/INT   Captain J. M. D. Carr
SN/DT.1
SN/   Mrs A. N. Walker
INT.RECS
SN/   Major R. C. Holme DSO
TRANS
SN/OPS   Captain Keith Cochrane
SN/AIR   Captain E. J. Fraser-
          Campbell
SN/AIR.1 Lieutenant B. Myer,
          FANY
SN/AIR.2 Sergeant Major M.
          Barnett
SN/WT   Lieutenant K. R. Turner

SN/SQ	Major F. K. M. Carver
SN/Q	Captain F. R. B. Hoskier
SN/S	Sergeant T. J. Hudson
SN/T	Major P. W. T. Boughton-Leigh
SN/T.1	Flight Lieutenant Lord Ventry

SOE Overseas

Algiers	John Munn
	John Anstey
	Douglas Dodds-Parker
Athens	Nicholas Hammond
	David Pawson
Belgrade	Tom Masterson
Berne	Jock McCaffery
Cape Town	Richard Broad
Chunking	John Keswick
	Peter Petro
Darwin	John Chapman-Walker
	Thomas Cook
Freetown	Philip Leake
Gibraltar	Hugh Quennell
	Harry Morris
Istanbul	Norman Davies
	Frank Stirling
	Gardyne de Chastelain
	William Harris-Burland
Lagos	Francis Glyn
Lisbon	Jack Beevor
	Alexander Glen
	L. H. Motimore
Luanda	Leopold Manderstam
	Hedley Vincent
Madrid	David Muirhead
	Eric Piquet-Wicks
	David Babington Smith
Moscow	Robert Guinness
	George Hill
New York	Richard Coit
	Ivar Bryce
	H. A. Benson
	David Keswick
	Mostyn Davies
Singapore	Valentine Killery
Stockholm	Peter Tennant
	Ronald Turnbull
	George Larden
	William Montagu-Pollock
	Thomas O'Reilly
Tangier	Edward Wharton-Tigar
Tunis	Alexander Anstruther
	Francis Brooks Richards
Vancouver	Hamish Pelham-Burn
Washington	Bartholomew Pleydell-Bouverie

APPENDIX 2
SOE's Special Training Schools

SOE developed a sophisticated network of special training schools to provide paramilitary, wireless, tradecraft and parachute courses for prospective agents. Before going into the field, each underwent a three-part programme, starting with a physically demanding series of exercises in Scotland and progressing through the various specialist centres to the 'finishing schools' and holding camps located in requisitioned country mansions.

Training Section

Paramilitary Schools (Group 'A')

STS 21	Arisaig House, Arisaig, Inverness-shire	Lieutenant-Colonel A. D. Balden
STS 22	Rhubana Lodge, Morar, Inverness-shire	Major G. Maxwell
STS 23	Meoble Lodge, Morar, Inverness-shire	Major N. M. Maclean
STS 23b	Swordland, Tarb Bay, Morar, Inverness-shire	Major N. M. Maclean
STS 24a	Inverie House, Knoydart, Mallaig, Inverness-shire	Major I. D. Parsons
STS 24b	Glaschoille, Knoydart, Mallaig, Inverness-shire	Major I. D. Parsons
STS 25a	Garramor House, Morar, Inverness-shire	Major R. S. Millar
STS 25b	Cammusdarrach, Morar, Inverness-shire	Major R. S. Millar
STS 25c	Traigh House, Morar, Inverness-shire	Major R. S. Millar

Finishing Schools (Group 'B')

STS 31	The Rings, Beaulieu, Brockenhurst, Hants.	Lieutenant-Colonel S. H. C. Woolrych OBE
	The House in the Wood, Beaulieu, Brockenhurst, Hants.	Lieutenant-Colonel S. H. C. Woolrych OBE
STS 32a	Harford House, Beaulieu, Brockenhurst, Hants.	Captain A. R. Hinde
STS 32b	Saltmarsh, Beaulieu, Brockenhurst, Hants.	Captain A. R. Hinde

STS 32c	Blackbridge, Beaulieu, Brockenhurst, Hants.	Captain A. R. Hinde
STS 33	The House on the Shore, Beaulieu, Brockenhurst, Hants.	Captain W. J. Corrie
STS 34	The Drokes, Beaulieu, Brockenhurst, Hants.	Captain R. Carr
STS 35	The Vineyards, Beaulieu, Brockenhurst, Hants.	Captain W. Clark
STS 36	Boarmans, Beaulieu, Brockenhurst, Hants.	Captain F. W. Rhodes DSO
STS 37a	Warren House, Beaulieu, Brockenhurst, Hants.	Captain R. H. Harris MC
STS 37b	Clobb Gorse, Beaulieu, Brockenhurst, Hants.	Captain R. H. Harris MC

Operational Schools (Group 'C')

STS 2	Bellasis, Box Hill Road, Dorking, Surrey	Major A. M. Boal
STS 3	Stodham Park, Liss, Hants.	Major J. W. Richardson
STS 5	Wanborough Manor, Puttenham, Guildford, Surrey	Major E. J. Castello
STS 6	West Court, Finchampstead, Wokingham, Berks.	
STS 40	Howbury Hall, Nr Waterend, Beds.	Major P. J. Tidmarsh
STS 41	Gumley Hall, Market Harborough, Leics.	Major J. H. Dumbrell
STS 42	Roughwood Park, Chalfont St Giles, Bucks.	Major V. E. Blomfield
STS 44	Gorse Hill, Witley, Godalming, Surrey	Major P. S. Smith
STS 45	Hatherop Castle, Fairford, Glos.	Major D. Hart
STS 47	Anderson Manor, Blandford, Dorset	Major R. J. Metherell
STS 50	Water Eaton Manor, Oxford	

Signals Section

STS 52	Thame Park, Thame, Oxon.	Major H. J. Byrne
ST 53a	Grendon Hall, Grendon-Underwood, Aylesbury, Bucks.	Major D. Phillips
ST 53b	Poundon House, Poundon, Bicester, Oxon.	Major J. Adams
STS 54a	Fawley Court, Henley-on-Thames, Oxon.	Major F. G. Homan
STS 54b	Belhaven School, Dunbar.	Major F. G. Homan

Polish Section

STA 18	Frogmore Farm, Watton-at-Stone, Herts.	Lieutenant-Colonel A. M. Kennedy MC

STA 19	Gardner's End, Ardeley, Stevenage, Herts.	Lieutenant-Colonel A. M. Kennedy MC
STS 20a	Pollard's Park, Nightingale Lane, Chalfont St Giles, Bucks.	Lieutenant-Colonel A. M. Kennedy MC
STA 20b	Pollard's Wood Grange, Nightingale Lane, Chalfont St Giles, Bucks.	Lieutenant-Colonel A. M. Kennedy MC
STS 43	Audley End House, Audley End, Saffron Walden, Essex	Lieutenant-Colonel A. M. Kennedy MC
STS 46	Chicheley Hall, Newport Pagnell, Bletchley, Bucks.	Major J. W. Harper
STA 14	Briggens, Roydon, Essex	Major C. H. Edwards
STS 63	Warnham Court, near Horsham, Sussex	Major R. H. Egdell MC

Norwegian Section

STS 26a	Drumintoul Lodge, Aviemore, Inverness-shire	Major D. P. Hilton
STS 26b	Glenmore Lodge, Aviemore, Inverness-shire	Major D. P. Hilton
STS 61	Gaynes Hall, St Neots, Hunts.	Major C. S. Hampton

Parachute Schools

STS 51a	Dunham House, Charcoal Lane, Dunham Massey, Altrincham, Cheshire	Major C. J. Edwards MBE
STS 51b	Fulshaw Hall, Alderley Road, Wilmslow, Manchester	Major C. J. Edwards MBE
STS 7	Winterfold, Cranleigh, Surrey	Major G. A. Brown
STS 17	Brickendonbury, Hertford, Herts.	Lieutenant-Colonel G. T. T. Rheam
STS 39	Wall Hall, Aldenham, Herts.	Major W. B. Gallie
ME 65	Milton Hall, Milton, Peterborough, Northants.	Lieutenant-Colonel F. V. Spooner

APPENDIX 3
JEDBURGHS

JEDBURGH	Date of Despatch	Personnel/Codename	Area of Operations
ALAN	12 August	Captain S. N. Cannicott/*Pembroke* Lieutenant A. Gairaud/*Ariage* Corporal F. de Heysen/*Kroner*	Saône et Loire
ALASTAIR	September	Major O. H. Brown/*Kent* Lieutenant R. Maitre/*Donegall* Sergeant G. N. Smith/*Lincoln*	Epinal
ALEC	9/10 August	Lieutenant G. G. Thomson/*Cromarty* Lieutenant B. Allet/*Oxford* Sergeant John A. White/*Colorado*	Loire et Cher
ALEXANDER	12 August	Lieutenant Stewart J. Alsop/*Rona* Lieutenant R. Thouville/*Leix* Sergeant Norman R. Franklin/*Cork*	Creuse
ALFRED	September	Captain L. D. MacDougall/*Argyll* Lieutenant G. de Wavrant/*Aude* Sergeant A. W. Key/*Wampaum*	Besançon
AMMONIA		Captain Benton Austin/*Gaspard* Captain R. Coute/*Ludovic* Sergeant J. Berlin/*Martial*	
ANDY	11/12 July	Major R. A. Parkinson/*Fife* Commandant J. Vermeulen/*Carlow* Sergeant R. Loosmore/*Lundy*	Haute Vienne
ANTHONY	14 August	Lieutenant Mason B. Starring/*Nebraska* Captain C. Deprez/*Perth* Sergeant John L. Bradner/*Pfennig*	Saône et Loire
ARCHIBALD			
AUBREY	11 August	Captain G. Marchant/*Rutland* Lieutenant J. Telmon/*Kildare* Sergeant I. Hooker/*Thaler*	Seine et Marne
BASIL	September	Major T. A. Carew/*Sutherland* Captain Raincourt/*Ambreve* Sergeant J. L. Stoyka/*Ore*	Jura/Doubs
BENJAMIN	September	Major A. J. Forrest/*Stirling* Lieutenant P. Marchand/*Ulster* Lieutenant J. Camouin/*Serre*	Autun
BERNARD	September	Captain Waller	Autun

JEDBURGH	Date of Despatch	Personnel/Codename	Area of Operations
BRIAN	August	Major F. Johnston/*Illinois* Captain R. Francompte/*Orkney* Sergeant N. A. Smith/*Ura*	Nancy
BRUCE	14 August	Major William E. Colby Lieutenant J. Favel Lieutenant L. Giry	Yonne
CECIL	September	Major D. J. Neilson/*Delaware* Captain A. Frayan/*Lys* Sergeant R. Wilde/*Centavo*	Jura/Doubs
DANIEL	5/6 August	Captain K. G. Bennett/*Aportre* Lieutenant P. de Schonen/*Argentier* Sergeant R. Brierley/*Florin*	Côtes du Nord
DESMOND		Captain William Pietsch/*Sherry* Captain Bourriot/*Shetland* Sergeant W. Baird/*Hampshire*	Poitiers
DIAMOND			Haute Vienne
DOUGLAS	5/6 August	Captain R. A. Rubinstein/*Augure* Lieutenant J. Ronglou/*Anachore* Sergeant J. D. Raven/*Half Crown*	Morbihan, Brittany
DOUGLAS II	15/16 September	Captain R. A. Rubinstein/*Augure* Captain J. Ronglou/*Anachore* Sergeant John van Hart/*Half Crown*	Aisne/Doubs Jura
FELIX	8/9 July	Captain J. J. Marchant/*Somerset* Captain J. Kerneval/*Carnarvon* Sergeant P. M. Calvin/*Middlesex*	Côtes du Nord
FRANCIS	9/10 July	Major C. Ogden-Smith/*Dorset* Captain G. le Zachmeur/*Durance* Sergeant A. J. Dallow/*Groat*	Finistère
FRANK	September	Captain A. Massoni/*Dumbarton* Captain I. Isaac/*Westmorland* Sergeant T. Henney/*Cheshire*	Finistère
FREDERICK	9/10 June	Major A. W. Wise/*Kinross* Captain P. Aguirac/*Vire* Sergeant Robert R. Kehoe/*Peseta*	Guincamp, Brittany
GAVIN	11/12 July	Major D. Jeanclaude/*Shilling* Captain William B. Droux/*Sixpence* Lieutenant G. Masson/*Halfpenny*	Northern part of Ille et Vilaine
GEORGE	9/10 June	Captain P. Erard/*Save* Captain Paul Cyr/*Wigton* Lieutenant C. Lejeune/*Rupee*	Redan, Brittany
GEORGE II	7 September	(same as GEORGE)	Bordeaux
GERALD	18/19 July	Captain S. J. Knerly/*Suffolk* Captain J. L. Beaumont/*Norfolk* Sergeant B. E. Friele/*Selkirk*	Morbihan, Brittany
GILBERT	9/10 July	Captain C. G. Blathwayt/*Surrey* Lieutenant P. Charron/*Ardèche* Sergeant N. Wood/*Doubloon*	Finistère

JEDBURGH	Date of Despatch	Personnel/Codename	Area of Operations
GILES	8/9 July	Captain B. M. Knox/*Kentucky* Captain P. Lebel/*Loire* Sergeant G. H. Tack/*Tickie*	Finistère
GODFREY	September	Lieutenant J. Forbes/*Rhode Island* Lieutenant J. Morhange/*Roscommon* Sergeant F. Hanson/*Roxburgh*	Saône et Loire
GREGORY	4 September	(same as DANIEL)	Jura/Doubs
GUY	11/12 July	Captain A. Dhomas/*Dronne* Captain A. A. Trofimov/*Gironde* Lieutenant J. Deschamps/*Dordogne*	Southern part of Ille et Vilaine
HAMISH	12/13 June	Lieutenant R. M. Anstett/*Alabama* Lieutenant L. Blanchere/*Louisiana* Sergeant L. J. Watters/*Kansas*	Châtellerault, Indre
HAROLD	15/16 July	Major V. E. Whitty/*Ross* Lieutenant R. Rimbaut/*Tyrone* Sergeant H. Verlander/*Sligo*	Vendée
HARRY	6/7 June	Captain D. D. Guthrie/*Denby* Lieutenant P. E. Dupont/*Gapeau* R. Legrand/*Centime*	Mountains north of Autun
HENRY	September	Lieutenant R. E. Moore/*New Mexico* Lieutenant S. Montcler/*Anglesey* Sergeant V. M. Rocca/*West Virginia*	Jura/Doubs
HILARY	17/18 July	Lieutenant E. Marchant/*Charente* Lieutenant Philip E. Chadbourne/*Nevada* Lieutenant R. Pariselle/*Kupek*	Finistère
HORACE	17/18 July	Major J. Summers/*Wyoming* Lieutenant G. Levalois/*Somme* W. Zielake/*Dime*	Finistère
HUGH	5/6 June	Captain L. Legrand/*Franc* Captain W. R. Crawshay/*Crown* C. C. R. Mersiol/*Yonne*	Châteauroux, Indre
IAN	20/21 June	Major John Gildee/*Oklahoma* Lieutenant Y. Deslorme/*Maine* Sergeant Lucien Bourgoin/*Mayo*	Poitiers, Vienne
IVOR	6/7 August	Captain J. H. Cox/*Monmouth* Lieutenant Y. M. Dantes/*Selune* Sergeant Lewis F. Goddard/*Lundy*	St Amand, Cher
JACOB	12 August	Captain V. A. Gough/*Arran* Lieutenant G. Baraud/*Connaught* Sergeant K. Seymour/*Skye*	Vosges
JAMES	10/11 August	Lieutenant John K. Singlaub/*Mississippi* Lieutenant D. Leb/*Michigan* Sergeant Anthony J. Denneau/*Massachusetts*	Corrèze

JEDBURGH	Date of Despatch	Personnel/Codename	Area of Operations
JULIAN	10/11 August	Major R. H. Clutton/*Stafford* Lieutenant M. Brouillard/*Vermont* Sergeant T. S. Menzies/*Essex*	Indre et Loire
LEE	9/10 August	Captain Charles E. Brown/*Rice* Captain N. Viguier/*Sous* Lieutenant A. Chevalier/*Reis*	Haute Vienne
MAURICE	September	Captain C. M. Carman/*Utah* Lieutenant H. Dumesnil/*Virginia* Sergeant F. J. Cole/*Georgia*	Autun
MONTY			Haute Vienne
NICHOLAS	August	Captain J. C. Maude/*Leicester* Lieutenant H. Puget/*Brecknock* Sergeant M. A. Whittle/*Northumberland*	Besançon
PAUL	August	Major E. Hood/*Shropshire* Lieutenant F. Cormier/*Durthe* Sergeant K. J. W. Brown/*Limerick*	Jura
PHILIP	August	Captain J. Derouen/*Kintyre* Lieutenant R. A. Lucas/*Caithness* Sergeant G. Grgat/*Leinster*	Cher
QUENTIN		Captain W. S. Fenton/*Cornwall* Lieutenant J. Lassere/*Wicklow* Sergeant R. Dawson/*Merioneth*	Finistère
QUININE	August	Major R. McPherson/*Anselme* Lieutenant M. Bourdon/*Aristide* Sergeant O. Brown/*Félicien*	Allier
RONALD	5/6 August	Lieutenant Shirley R. Trumps/*Boursier* Lieutenant J. Dartigues/*Bouton* Sergeant Elmer B. Esch/*Pound*	Finistère
RUPERT	September	(same as PHILIP)	Besançon
STANLEY	September	Captain O. Craster/*Yorkshire* Lieutenant R. Carliere/*Meath* Sergeant E. J. Grinham/*Worcestershire*	Cher
TIMOTHY	September	Captain L. Ambel/*Nesque* Lieutenant R. D. Mundinger/*Marcelin* Sergeant D. A. Spears/*Escaut*	Aisne/Jura
TONY	September	Major R. Montgomery/*Dollar* Lieutenant M. Devailly/*Ecu* Sergeant J. E. McGowan/*Quarter*	Finistère
VEGANIN		D. Gardner	

Source Notes

Introduction

1 Information from Sir Charles's daughter, Pammie. He died at his home in St John's Wood, London, on 28 August 1963 having destroyed all his secret papers.

2 'Resistance Movements in the War', RUSI Lecture, 28 January 1948, published in the *RUSI Journal*, vol. 93, pp. 210–23.

3 The Gubbins biography, written by Joan Bright Astley and Peter Wilkinson, is scheduled for publication in 1992 by Leo Cooper.

4 *Now It Can Be Told*, made by the RAF Film Unit for the Central Office of Information, was subsequently released under the title *School for Danger*.

5 'I do not claim that the incidents described in these pages are completely factually accurate,' *Specially Employed* (Batchworth, 1952), p. 7.

6 Jean Overton Fuller, *Double Webs* (Putnam, 1958). Following publication Dame Irene Ward tabled the following motion in the House of Commons on 12 November 1958:

> Special Operations Executive and Official Secrets Act Enquiry: That this House is of the opinion that the present publication of *Double Webs*, by Jean Overton Fuller, Putnams, and *Death Be Not Proud*, by Elizabeth Nicholas, Cresset Press, demands an investigation into the effectiveness of the Special Operations Executive and the operation of the Official Secrets Act; that the success stories of Special Operations Executive written by Colonel Buckmaster, head of the French Section, and others, have led the public to believe that an amateur wartime organisation, bravely manned and devotedly served both by British and French agents, was a match for the German Intelligence Service; that had the Official Secrets Act been adequately enforced by authority and proper care exercised to protect in Great Britain and France the reputation of those who became the unwilling victims of Nazi German success, much painful recrimination would have been avoided, but that under the circumstances the question of whether the Air Movements Officer of the Special Operations Executive, the central figure in the book *Double Webs*, was a German agent working in a British organisation, must be cleared up; that although the disclosure of German penetration of the Dutch Section of Special Operations Executive was the subject of an international inquiry, the fact that this penetration extended from Holland to a vitally important area in France, causing the arrest of many men and women, has been deliberately concealed, has led to disclosures damaging to our security and to our relationships with those friends in France in the years of danger going unchallenged and without official factual comment; this House, therefore, urges Her Majesty's Government to publish a book giving an authoritative account of the successes and failures of the Special Operations Executive.

7 Jean Overton Fuller, *Madeleine* (Gollancz, 1952).

8 Elizabeth Nicholas, *Death Be Not Proud* (White Lion, 1958). 'Compelled by anger, by deep emotion, by compassion,' Miss

Nicholas catalogued the loss of seven F
Section women agents and asked 'how it
was possible that so many groups, involving
so many people, that should have been
entirely watertight were in fact integrated
to a degree where penetration of one meant
penetration of all' (p. 19). She concurred
with the opinion of an unnamed
intelligence officer who asserted that 'SOE
agents were frequently called upon to
undertake missions which involved a risk
far beyond the potential value of the work
they might perform or the information they
might obtain' (p. 23).

Despite the co-operation offered to an
earlier author, Jerrard Tickell, by Major
Norman Mott of the War Office when he
had written *Odette* (Chapman & Hall,
1949), Miss Nicholas was refused access to
what remained of SOE's files and 'any
information, even on the most
straightforward matters' (p. 285).

9 House of Commons, 15 December
1958, Hansard 757–8. Cordeaux was not
the only Member of Parliament with
experience of SOE. Christopher Mayhew
(see his autobiography, *Time To Explain*;
Hutchinson, 1987) was on the Opposition
benches and Dame Patricia Hornsby-
Smith, then a minister in the Home Office,
had been Lord Selborne's assistant when
he was Minister of Economic Warfare with
responsibility for SOE.

10 Professor M. R. D. Foot, *SOE in
France* (HMSO, 1966). References in the
first edition to Odette Sansom GC (pp. 209,
251, 337, 430–1) were replaced in
subsequent editions. The most extensive
deletions concern Foot's controversial
conclusion that 'the number [of women
SOE agents] who were ever seriously
tortured is small'. He insisted that the
'stories of torture come from the prurient
imaginations of authors anxious to make
their books sell' and singled out *Carve Her
Name with Pride* by R. J. Minney (George
Newnes, 1956) as being 'completely
fictitious' in describing Violette Szabo as
having undergone 'atrocious torture' (p.
156). This entire passage was removed.

Although Szabo did exist and was
captured by the enemy, there have been
several cases of bogus spies. *The Man Who
Wouldn't Talk*, the story of George Dupré
by Quentin Reynolds (Random House,
1953), is a classic of the genre. After
publication Dupré was exposed as a
fantasist. Similarly, Greville Wynne
invented a girlfriend based on Miss Szabo
in *The Man from Odessa* (Robert Hale,
1981), pp. 78–80.

Peter Churchill was particularly sensitive
to the accusation in Foot's first edition (pp.
208, 209, 252) that he had acted
negligently in the field and had been
caught with 'over thirty' (or 'over forty',
depending upon the edition) wireless
messages and thereby had caused the
arrest of the Baron de Malval, who,
understandably, was highly indignant at
Churchill's behaviour. The relevant
passage was amended following Churchill's
legal action.

11 Interview with Brian Stonehouse, 3 July
1990.

12 Boxshall was succeeded as the Foreign
Office's SOE Adviser by Christopher M.
Woods MC and the present incumbent,
Gervase Cowell, to whom I am grateful for
his generous help.

13 At the time of *SOE in France*'s
publication Brooks had been seconded to
Lord Mountbatten's enquiry into prison
security following the escape from
Wormwood Scrubs of George Blake. His
name, however, was omitted from the
published version of the report (Cmmd
3175).

14 Perhaps aware of Foot's suspicions,
Cookridge claimed in the preface to *Inside
SOE* (Arthur Barker, 1966) that when *SOE
in France* was released by HMSO in May
1966, his own book had already been
printed, thus failing to address the
suspicion that he had obtained a copy of
Foot's proofs from Colonel L. G. (Sammy)
Lohan, the then Secretary of the 'D'
Notice Committee, who had himself served
in SOE.

Cookridge, who was a *Daily Telegraph*
parliamentary lobby correspondent,
experienced a 'protracted tussle with the
security authorities' (p. xiii) while
researching his book, but it is widely

believed that he had benefited from his friendship with Lohan, who was later to be dismissed in 1967 for his indiscretion with another Fleet Street journalist, Chapman Pincher.

Cookridge was the name adopted by Edward Spiro, a Viennese Jew and left-wing activist, who was extracted from Dachau in 1938 after representations were made by the British newspaper for which Spiro had worked. When he first arrived in England Spiro was billeted in Cookham, Berkshire, whence he chose his new name before joining the Ministry of Economic Warfare.

15 E. H. Cookridge, *They Came from the Sky* (Heinemann, 1965), with a foreword contributed by Maurice Buckmaster. The following year Buckmaster contributed an appendix (p. 602) to *Inside SOE*, in which he launched a fierce counter-attack on Elizabeth Nicholas and Jean Overton Fuller and their 'monstrous and intolerable accusations' that SOE had 'deliberately sent our agents into the hands of the Germans' (p. 603).

16 R. A. Bourne-Paterson, *The 'British' Circuits in France*. Unpublished, but a complete copy has been acquired by the author.

17 Correspondence with Professor William Mackenzie, 7 July 1990.

18 Correspondence with Sir Robin Butler, 18 July 1990.

19 Charles Cruickshank, *SOE in Scandinavia* (OUP, 1986) and *SOE in the Far East* (OUP, 1983).

1 The First Two Years

1 Jack Beevor, *SOE: Recollections and Reflections* (Bodley Head, 1981), p. 15.

2 For Best's version of this episode see *The Venlo Incident* (Hutchinson, 1950).

3 For an account of Beatty's interests in the Trepca Mine see Edward Wharton-Tigar, *Burning Bright* (Metal Bulletin Books, 1987).

4 See Merlin Minshall's *Guilt Edged* (Bachman & Turner, 1975), p. 152. Another account of the same episode can be found in Geoffrey Household's

autobiography *Against the Wind* (Michael Joseph, 1958), p. 107, and David E. Walker, *Lunch with a Stranger* (W. W. Norton, 1957), p. 85.

5 Cruickshank, *SOE in Scandinavia*, p. 56.

6 Biggs was released in October 1941 and flown to Scotland. He later worked for his pre-war friend Jacques de Guélis in SOE's F Section.

7 See John Codrington's obituary, *Sunday Telegraph*, 30 April 1991.

8 Chidson's mission was the basis of *Adventure in Diamonds* (Evans Bros, 1955) written by his Section D colleague, David E. Walker.

9 For an account of the Auxiliary Units see David Lampe's *The Last Ditch* (Putnam, 1968) and Andrew Craft's *A Talent for Adventure* (SPA, 1991).

10 For Stuart Macrae's own account see *Winston Churchill's Toyshop* (Walker & Co., 1971).

11 For Clayton Hutton's own account see *Official Secret* (Max Parrish, 1960).

12 Churchill refers disparagingly to 'the kind of silly fiascos which were perpetrated at Boulogne and Guernsey' in a memorandum to the Secretary of State for War on 23 July 1940 in *The Second World War* (Cassell, 1950), vol. II, p. 572. However, on 6 July he had demanded from General Ismay 'a proper system of espionage and intelligence along the whole coast', *ibid.*, p. 218.

13 For Alan Warren's account see Richard Gough's *SOE Singapore 1941–2* (William Kimber, 1985), pp. 14–17.

14 Bickham Sweet-Escott, *Baker Street Irregular* (Methuen, 1965), p. 123.

15 Gubbins, RUSI lecture, p. 221.

16 Dalton to Halifax in Dalton's autobiography, *The Fateful Years* (Frederick Muller, 1957), p. 368.

17 David Dilks (ed.), *The Diaries of Sir Alexander Cadogan* (Cassell, 1971), p. 312.

18 The SOE Charter was based on Chamberlain's paper, circulated as WP (40)271 and approved by the War Cabinet on 23 July. It thereupon became War Cabinet Paper COS (40) 27(0). Although Foot observed that SOE's founding charter had been 'treasured by SOE' (p. 8), it was

in fact mislaid and no copy exists in SOE's archive.

19 The Prime Minister's letter to Dr Dalton survives in SOE archive as File No: 2/340/3.0.

20 Professor Harry Hinsley, *British Intelligence in the Second World War* (HMSO, 1979) vol. I, p. 278. Although the five-volume official history series deals extensively with SIS, MI5 and GCHQ, there are only a few passing references to SOE.

21 Sweet-Escott, *op. cit.*, p. 24.

22 For details of Dunderdale's career, see his obituary, *The Times*, 27 April 1991.

23 Foot, *SOE in Scandinavia*, p. 56.

24 M. R. D. Foot refers briefly to Inverlair in *SOE in France*, and the subject of SOE's secret prison was pursued in fictional terms by George Markstein in *The Cooler* and this author in *The Blue List*. Located just south of the A86 between Spean Bridge and Tulloch station, it is now in private hands.

25 Foot, *SOE in France*, p. 65.

26 *Ibid.*

27 Eric Piquet-Wicks, *Four in the Shadows* (Jarrolds, 1957), p. 19.

28 *Ibid.*, p. 20.

29 Colonel Passy (Dewavrin's nom de guerre), *Deuxième Bureau Londres* (Editions Solar, 1954), p. 146.

30 See Philippe de Vomécourt's *Army of Amateurs* (Doubleday, 1959) and *Who Lived To See the Day* (Hutchinson, 1960).

31 Beevor, *op. cit.*, p. 152.

32 See Marcel Jullian, *HMS Fidelity* (W. W. Norton, 1957).

33 For an account of Albert-Marie Guerisse, better known by his nom de guerre of Pat O'Leary, see M. R. D. Foot's *MI9* (Bodley Head, 1979).

34 Roman Garby-Czerniawski's version of INTERALLIÉ is *The Big Network* (George Ronald, 1961). See also Hugo Bleicher's memoirs, *Colonel Henri's Story*, edited by Ian Colvin (William Kimber, 1954); Michael Soltikow, *The Cat* (MacGibbon & Kee, 1957); Gordon Young, *The Cat with Two Faces* (Putnam, 1957); Mathilde-Lily Carré, *I Was the Cat* (Souvenir Press, 1959); Lauran Paine, *Mathilde Carré, Double Agent* (Robert Hale, 1976).

35 Hinsley, *op. cit.*, p. 278.

36 Maurice Buckmaster, *They Fought Alone* (W. W. Norton, 1958), p. 20.

37 de Vomécourt, *Army of Amateurs*, p. 91.

38 For Ben Cowburn's account, see *No Cloak No Dagger* (Jarrolds, 1960).

39 For Christopher Burney's memoirs see *Solitary Confinement* (Clerke & Cockeran, 1952).

40 J. C. Masterman describes the *Brutus* case in *The Double Cross System of the War of 1939–45* (Yale University Press, 1972) without identifying Garby-Czerniawski as *Brutus*, who was then Minister of Information in the Polish government-in-exile.

41 For a first-hand account of ALLIANCE see Marie-Madeleine Fourcade's *Noah's Ark* (E. P. Dutton, 1974).

42 Buckmaster's tale of Nigel Low is not corroborated from any other accounts of SOE's operations in France; see *They Fought Alone*, pp. 46–9.

43 Portal quoted in Foot, *SOE in France*, p. 13.

44 SOE War Diary, p. 204, quoted in *ibid.*, p. 153.

45 Reginald Fletcher, *The Air Defences of Britain* (Harmondsworth, 1938).

46 Warington-Smyth quoted by Foot, *SOE in France*, p. 66.

47 Adrian Gallegos, *From Capri to Oblivion* (Hodder & Stoughton, 1959).

48 Peter Kemp, *No Colours or Crest* (Cassell, 1958); *The Thorns of Memory* (Sinclair-Stevenson, 1990).

49 Kemp, *The Thorns of Memory*, p. 150.

50 Kemp, *No Colours or Crest*, p. 29.

---

2 A Branch of the Secret Service?
SOE in the Middle East

1 Gubbins's introduction in *SOE in the Balkans*, in Phyllis Auty and Richard Clogg (eds), *British Policy Towards Wartime Resistance in Yugoslavia & Greece* (Macmillan, 1975), p. 3.

2 For an account of the Middle East Intelligence Centre see John Connell's *The House at Herod's Gate*, (Sampson Low, 1946).

3 Nigel Clive, *A Greek Experience 1943–48* (Michael Russell, 1985), p. 21.

4 *Ibid.*
5 Sweet-Escott, *op. cit.*, p. 73.
6 Christopher Sykes, *High-Minded Murder* (Home & Van Thal, 1944). The principal villain in this tale of incompetence and infighting in Cairo's secret departments is a certain Captain Walter Anstey, who is revealed as an enemy agent.
7 General Wavell cited in Sweet-Escott, *op. cit.*, p. 95.
8 Christopher Sykes, *A Song of a Shirt* (Derek Verschoyle, 1953). Published by a recently retired SIS officer, who included Patrick Leigh Fermor, Donald Downes and Randolph Churchill on his list, Sykes's story is set in wartime Cairo and describes the prevalent intrigues at GHQ (ME).
9 See Julian Amery's *Sons of the Eagle* (Macmillan, 1948) and *Approach March* (Hutchinson, 1973). For a detailed analysis of BULLSEYE see Milan Deroc's *British Special Operations Explored* (Columbia University Press, 1988) and Mark Wheeler's *Britain and the War for Yugoslavia, 1940–1943* (Columbia University Press, 1980).
10 F. W. D. Deakin, *The Embattled Mountain* (OUP, 1971), p. 129.
11 General Simovic quoted by Deakin, *ibid.*, p. 129.
12 W. S. Churchill, *Marlborough* (Harrap, 1937).
13 For details of the Vickers espionage case, see Allan Monkhouse's own account, *Moscow 1911–33* (Gollancz, 1933), p. 281.
14 Ennals's role in Section D in Belgrade is referred to by his undercover colleague David E. Walker in *Lunch with a Stranger*, p. 137.
15 For Stuart's background see Roy Maclaren's *Canadians behind Enemy Lines* (University of British Columbia, 1982), p.134.
16 James Klugmann, *History of the Communist Party of Great Britain* (Lawrence & Wishart, 1968). His *Times* obituary (26 September 1977) makes no mention of his post-war membership of the CPGB's executive committee or his wartime service in SOE's Yugoslav Section.
17 M. R. D. Foot, *SOE 1940–46* (BBC Publications 1984), p. 146.
18 See *The Rape of Serbia* (Harcourt Brace, 1990), p. 154.

19 Signal from Colonel Bill Cope (of the NERONIAN mission): PRO File WO 202/143.
20 PRO File WO 202/131.
21 PRO File WO 202/140.
22 *Ibid.*
23 *Ibid.*
24 George Taylor in Auty and Clogg, *op. cit.*, p. 214.
25 *Ibid.*, p. 210.
26 *Ibid.*, p. 211.
27 *Ibid.*
28 *Ibid*, p. 226.
29 Fitzroy Maclean, *Eastern Approaches* (Cape, 1949), p. 281.
30 *Ibid.*, p. 279.
31 *Ibid.*, p. 280.
32 Deakin, *op. cit.*, p. 203.
33 FO memorandum dated 19 November 1943, PRO File WO 201/1561.
34 George Hill, *Go Spy the Land* (Cassell, 1932) and *Dreaded Hour* (Cassell, 1936).
35 'Socially dangerous elements' in Russian is *sotsial 'no-opasnye elementy.*
36 Major Field-Robinson was the former SIS Head of Station in Paris who had maintained contact with the legendary anti-Bolshevik Sydney Reilly and was, therefore, himself probably well known to the NKVD; see Robin Bruce Lockhart, *Ace of Spies* (Stein & Day, 1967), p. 88.

3 Suspicion and Misgiving: Scandinavian Operations

1 Sir Alexander Cadogan quoted by Cruickshank, *SOE in Scandinavia*, p. 63.
2 *Ibid.*, p. 56.
3 For the best account of the capture of the *Krebs* see David Kahn's *Seizing the Enigma* (Houghton Mifflin, 1991).
4 For David Howarth's account see his book *The Shetland Bus* (Thomas Nelson, 1951).
5 For details of Flemington see Ron Hogg, 'The Shetland Isles', *After the Battle*, no. 67, pp. 18–20.
6 Hinsley, *op. cit.*, vol. IV, p. 95.
7 For Marshall-Cornwall's account see *War and Rumours of War* (Leo Cooper, 1984), p. 204.
8 See Gubbins's 'SOE and Regular and Irregular Warfare' in Michael Elliott-

Bateman (ed.), *The Fourth Dimension of Warfare* (Manchester University Press, 1970), p. 89. For accounts of FRESHMAN see John D. Drummond, *But For These Men* (Elmfield Press, 1962); Dorothy Baden-Powell, *Operation Jupiter* (Robert Hale, 1982); Richard Wiggan, *Operation Freshman* (William Kimber, 1986); Thomas Gallagher *Assault in Norway* (Harcourt Brace, 1975).
9 Gubbins, *ibid.*, p. 90.
10 *Ibid.*
11 Chiefs of Staff, 20 March 1943, COS (43) 142 (0), in CAB 80/68, quoted by David Stafford in *Britain and European Resistance 1940–45* (Macmillan, 1980), p. 248.
12 *Ibid.*
13 Stewart Menzies quoted by Cruickshank, *SOE in Scandinavia*, p. 68.
14 Gubbins quoted by Cruickshank, *ibid.*, p. 134.
15 *Ibid.* p. 100.
16 Hinsley, *op. cit.*, vol. II, p. 278.
17 See H. Montgomery Hyde's *The Quiet Canadian* (Hamish Hamilton, 1962) and the wholly inaccurate *A Man Called Intrepid* by William Stevenson (Harcourt Brace, 1976). David Stafford's *Camp X* (Lester & Orpen Dennys, 1986) gives a more balanced account of BSC's activities.
18 Ivar Bryce, *You Only Live Once* (Weidenfeld & Nicolson, 1975).
19 See Leopold Manderstam's *From the Red Army to SOE* (William Kimber, 1985).

4 'Der Englandspiel': SOE in Holland, Belgium and Czechoslovakia

1 Erik Hazelhoff, *Soldier of Orange* (Holland Heritage Society, NY, 1980), p. 146.
2 For accounts of ANTHROPOID see Alan Burgess, *Seven Days at Daybreak* (Companion Book Club, 1960); Callum Macdonald, *The Killing of Reinhard Heydrich* (Macmillan, 1989); Edouard Calic, *Reinhard Heydrich* (Morrow, 1982); Miroslav Ivanov, *The Assassination of Heydrich* (Hart-Davis, MacGibbon, 1973);

G. S. Graber, *The Life and Times of Reinhard Heydrich* (Robert Hale, 1989); Jan Wiener, *The Assassination of Heydrich* (Grossman, 1969); Gunther Deschner, *Heydrich: The Pursuit of Total Power* (Orbis, 1981).
3 Frantisek Moravec, *Master of Spies* (Bodley Head, 1975), p. 211.
4 Ab Homburg was later killed when his fighter was shot down in April 1945.
5 Parliamentary Commission of Enquiry, vol. 4a, p. 852.
6 Private correspondence. A slightly inaccurate version is given by Cecil Hampshire in *The Secret Navies* (William Kimber, 1978), p. 33.
7 Quoted by Nicholas Kelso in *Errors of Judgement* (Robert Hale, 1988), p. 151.
8 *Ibid.*, p. 152.
9 Van Bilsen was incorrectly identified as a collaborator and assassinated.
10 Pieter Dourlein, *Inside North Pole* (William Kimber, 1953), p. 190.
11 Philip Johns, *Within Two Cloaks* (William Kimber, 1979), p. 142.
12 *Ibid.*, p. 143.
13 *Ibid.*
14 Parliamentary Commission of Enquiry, vol. 4a, p. 878.

5 A Deep and Abiding Jealousy: French Operations

1 Foot, *SOE in France*, p. 79. A total of 1,350 SOE agents (excluding members of the Operational Groups) were dropped into France by parachute.
2 Cookridge, *Inside SOE*, p. 604, mentions F Section sending 480 agents to France, of whom 130 were caught.
3 Henri Michel, *The Shadow War* (Deutsch, 1972), p. 123.
4 Buckmaster, *op. cit.*, p. 21.
5 *Ibid.*, p. 52.
6 The Comte de Marenches and Ockrent, *The Evil Empire* (Sidgwick & Jackson, 1978), p. 15.
7 R. A. Bourne-Paterson, p. iv para. 22.
8 Peter Churchill described his experiences in *Of Their Own Choice* (Hodder & Stoughton, 1952), *Duel of Wits* (Elmfield Press, 1953) and *Spirit in the Cage* (Hodder & Stoughton, 1954).

9 See Bleicher, *op. cit.*

10 Harold Cole's case is best described in Brendan M. Murphy's *Turncoat* (Harcourt Brace, 1987).

11 Robert Marshall, *All the King's Men* (Collins, 1988).

12 Jean Overton Fuller has written about Dericourt extensively, including: *The German Penetration of SOE* (William Kimber, 1975) and *Dericourt: The Chequered Spy* (Michael Russell, 1989).

13 Frank Pickersgill's case is studied in Maclaren, *op. cit.*

14 Foot, *SOE in France*, p. 321.

15 For Yeo-Thomas's account see Bruce Marshall's *The White Rabbit* (Houghton Mifflin, 1952).

16 The counter-intelligence handbook has recently been released by Cloak & Dagger Publications under the title *A History of the German Secret Services and British Counter-Measures* (Utah, 1986).

17 Eddie Chapman's remarkable career is described in Frank Owen, *The Eddie Chapman Story* (Messner, 1954) and Eddie Chapman, *The Real Eddie Chapman Story* (Library 33, 1956).

18 Lily Sergueiev's version is in *Secret Service Rendered* (William Kimber, 1968). It may not be entirely accurate as there is now reason to believe that she may have been operating for the NKVD as well as the *Abwehr*. Her uncles were the White Russian General Evgenni Miller, who was kidnapped and assassinated in September 1937, and Nikolai V. Skoblin, a senior NKVD agent in Paris. Despite the evidence of the NKVD's complicity in Miller's murder, Lily Sergueiev insisted the Nazis had been responsible for it (p. 13).

19 Foot, *SOE in France*, p. 308.

6 A Hot Humid Summer: SOE in North Africa and the Balkans

1 Ivor Porter, *Operation Autonomous* (Chatto & Windus, 1989), p. 72.

2 For a detailed appreciation of *Bodden* see Denis Smyth's 'Screening Torch: Allied Counter-Intelligence and the Spanish Threat to the Secrecy of the Allied Invasion of French North Africa in November 1942', in *Intelligence and National Security*, vol. 4, no. 2, April 1989, p. 335. Smyth's contention that Operation FALAISE never took place is contradicted by Wharton-Tigar and Beevor *op. cit.*, p. 131. In 'The Bodden Line: A Case-study of Wartime Technology', Thomas T. Smith (Intelligence and National Security, vol. 6, no. 2, April 1991, p. 447) argues that infra-red technology was probably not involved in Operation FALAISE.

3 See Wharton-Tigar, *op. cit.*

4 For Charles MacIntosh's recollections see *From Cloak to Dagger: An SOE Agent in Italy 1943–45* (William Kimber, 1982).

5 Carleton S. Coon, *A North Africa Story* (Gambit, 1980), p. 131.

6 Kermit Roosevelt, *The War Report of the OSS*, vol. 1, declassified 1976, p. 94.

7 See Sir Douglas Dodds-Parker's *Setting Europe Ablaze* (Springwood, 1983).

8 Admiral Darlan's assassination is still a matter of controversy; see Peter Tomkins's *The Murder of Admiral Darlan* (Weidenfeld & Nicolson, 1965).

9 *The Diaries of Sir Alexander Cadogan*, p. 493.

10 Frederick Winterbotham, *The Ultra Secret* (Weidenfeld & Nicolson, 1974), p. 99. Curiously Winterbotham had omitted any reference to his presence in Algiers at the time of Darlan's murder in his previously published memoirs *Secret and Personal* (William Kimber, 1969), which makes only passing mention of the incident (p. 165).

11 Dodds-Parker, *op. cit.*, p. 123.

12 *Ibid*, p. 24.

13 See Donald Hamilton-Hill's *SOE Assignment* (William Kimber, 1973).

14 Gerald Holdsworth's activities are described by Patrick Howarth in *Undercover* (Routledge & Kegan Paul, 1980).

15 Sir Anthony Quayle, *A Time to Speak* (Barrie & Jenkins, 1990), p. 260.

16 Amery, *Sons of the Eagle*, p. 49.

17 David Smiley, *Albanian Assignment* (Chatto & Windus, 1984), p. 56.

18 Kemp, *No Colours or Crest* and *The Thorns of Memory*.

19 Brigadier 'Trotsky' Davies, *Illyrian Adventure* (Bodley Head, 1952), p. 137.
20 Correspondence with David Smiley 1990.
21 Roosevelt, *op. cit.*, vol. 2, p. 125.
22 *Ibid.*
23 *Ibid.*, p. 127.
24 *Ibid.*
25 *Ibid.*
26 Jasper Rootham, *Miss Fire* (Chatto & Windus, 1946), p. 144.
27 A War Cabinet memorandum dated 14 October 1943 (PRO File CAB/122/762) suggests twenty-eight other ranks from Canada and the United States were currently serving with eight British Military Liaison Missions in Yugoslavia.
28 Lindsay Rogers, *Guerilla Surgeon* (Collins, 1957), p. 153.
29 William M. Jones, *Twelve Months with Tito's Partisans* (Bedford Books, 1946).
30 Deakin, *op. cit.*, p. 218.
31 Michael Lees, *Special Operations Executed* (William Kimber, 1986) and *The Rape of Serbia* (Harcourt Brace, 1990).
32 Basil Davidson, *Partisan Picture* (Bedford Books, 1946) and *Special Operations Europe* (Gollancz, 1980).
33 Maclean, *op. cit.*
34 Michael Davie (ed.), *The Diaries of Evelyn Waugh* (Weidenfeld & Nicolson, 1976), p. 575.
35 Sweet-Escott, *op. cit*, p. 212.
36 See Porter, *op. cit.*, p. 99.
37 PRO File FO 371/44000 R7756.
38 PRO File FO 371/44000 R8070.

7 Pass Down the Blame: SOE in Greece

1 See Nicholas Hammond's *Venture into Greece: With the Guerrillas 1943–44* (William Kimber, 1983).
2 C. J. Hamson, later Professor of Comparative Law at Trinity College, Cambridge.
3 See C. M. Woodhouse's *Apple of Discord* (W. B. O'Neill, 1985).
4 Xan Fielding, *Hide and Seek* (Secker & Warburg, 1954), p. 179. Fielding had previously written *The Stronghold* (Secker & Warburg, 1953), in which he also described his experiences in Crete.
5 *Ibid.*, p. 61.
6 *Ibid.*, p. 109.
7 *Ibid.*, p. 106.
8 Kreipe was not 'the German general in command on the island' (Foot, *SOE 1940–46*, p. 234). In fact the commander of the Fortress of Crete was General Bruno Brauer. Both Brauer and Müller were sentenced to death for war crimes in Athens in December 1945. Kreipe was merely the local divisional commander.
9 W. Stanley Moss, *Ill Met by Moonlight* (Harrap, 1950), p. 86.
10 Sir Ian Moncreiffe in the prologue to *ibid.*, p. 15.
11 General Kreipe was quartered in the Villa Ariadne, which, by coincidence, had been John Pendlebury's pre-war home, see Dilys Powell's *The Villa Ariadne* (Hodder & Stoughton, 1974).
12 E. C. W. Myers, *Greek Entanglement* (Hart-Davis, 1955), p. 14.
13 Hammond, *op. cit.*, p. 76.
14 C. M. Woodhouse, *The Struggle for Greece 1941–9* (Hart-Davis, 1976), p. 26.
15 Myers, *op. cit.*, p. 100.
16 *Ibid.*
17 Denys Hamson, *We Fell among Greeks* (Cape, 1946), p. 149.
18 Hammond, *op. cit.*, p. 174.
19 *Ibid.*
20 *Ibid.*, p. 59.
21 Myers, *op. cit.*, p. 216.
22 *Ibid.*
23 Woodhouse, *Apple of Discord*, p. 157.
24 For details of David Balfour's extraordinary career see Peter Blyth's *The Man Who Was Uncle* (Arthur Barker, 1975).
25 Pan Kanellopoulos cited by Woodhouse, *The Struggle for Greece*, p. 28.
26 Myers, *op. cit.*, p. 262.
27 Fielding, *Hide and Seek*, p. 98.
28 Woodhouse, *Apple of Discord*, p. 38.
29 Lieutenant-Commander Cumberlege DSO was murdered at Flossenbürg just two days before the German surrender.
30 Hubbard's death on 14 October 1944 is described in Stefano's Sarafis's *ELAS: Greek Resistance Army* (Merlin Press, 1980), p. 202; see also Hammond, *op. cit.*, p. 142.
31 Myers signal, 24 February 1943.

32 Sheppard signal, quoted by Myers, *op. cit.*, p. 127.
33 Woodhouse, *The Struggle for Greece*, p. 36.

8 Exorbitant Cost: The Oriental Mission

1 Sir George Moss quoted by Cruickshank, *SOE in the Far East*, p. 81.
2 F. Spencer Chapman, *The Jungle Is Neutral* (Chatto & Windus, 1949), p. 14.
3 Sir Josiah Crosby, quoted by Cruickshank, *SOE in the Far East*, p. 71.
4 The other six were headed by Pat Garden, a tin miner. His mission included Frank Quayle, Clarke Haywood, Robert Chrystal and William Robinson, the last of whom died. The other teams were led by A. J. Wynne, an irrigation engineer; T. M. Smyllie, a police officer who was to be killed; John Reid, a timber engineer who died in Changi in May 1944 and who had been accompanied by Harte Barry; and two planters, T. D. Mackay and D. D. Matthews, who retreated to Sumatra where he was captured. The fate of Pat Noone remains a mystery (see *Rape of the Dream People* [Hutchinson, 1972] by his brother Richard). His last reported sighting was by a former British district officer, John Creer, late in 1943.
5 See Boris Hembry's obituary, *Daily Telegraph*, 28 September 1990.
6 Chapman, *op. cit.*, p. 41.
7 John Cross, *Red Jungle* (Robert Hale, 1957), p. 17.
8 *Ibid.*, p. 97.
9 *Ibid.*, p. 216.
10 Clark-Kerr in PRO File WO 208 129 HN 00745.
11 Cruickshank, *SOE in the Far East*, p. 79.
12 *Ibid.*, p. 81.
13 *Ibid.*

9 Too Many Plans: The India Mission

1 Marquess of Linlithgow quoted in Cruickshank, *SOE in the Far East*, p. 87.
2 *Ibid.*
3 *Ibid.*

4 *Ibid.*, p. 94.
5 Andrew Gilchrist, *Bangkok Top Secret* (Hutchinson, 1970, p. 144.
6 For a detailed account of RIMAU see Ronald McKie's *The Heroes* (Harcourt Brace, 1950).
7 Cruickshank, *SOE in the Far East*, p. 252.
8 Ian Trenowden, *Operations Most Secret* (William Kimber, 1978), p. 124.
9 Cruickshank, *SOE in the Far East*, p. 202n.
10 Terence O'Brien, *The Moonlight War* (Collins, 1987), p. 264.
11 Loi Teck's role as a double agent lasted for some years, but eventually he was evacuated by the Special Branch in March 1947 and resettled with a new identity in Hong Kong.
12 For further details of OATMEAL see General Ibrahim bin Ismail's *Have You Met Mariam Yet?* (Westlight, 1984), p. 33.
13 Correspondence from Squadron Leader Brookes, 4 February 1980.
14 Hinsley, *op. cit.*, vol. v, p. 208.
15 Cruickshank, *SOE in the Far East*, p. 206.
16 Squadron Leader Brookes has disputed previous accounts of this air operation, including Trenowden's in *Operations Most Secret*, p. 159.
17 For an account of the mutual hostility of the British residents during the Malayan Emergency, see Noel Barber's *The War of the Running Dogs* (Weybright & Talley, 1971), p. 39.

10 Bitter and Unfruitful Argument: SOE in South-East Asia

1 Gilchrist, *op. cit.*, p. 87.
2 Cruickshank, *SOE in the Far East*, p. 89.
3 For Ritchie Gardiner's obituary see *The Times*, 29 September 1990.
4 O'Brien, *op. cit.*, p. 114.
5 Cruickshank, *SOE in the Far East*, p. 165.
6 O'Brien, *op. cit.*, p. 187.
7 Eden cited by Cruickshank, *SOE in the Far East*, p. 179.
8 Gilchrist, *op. cit.*, p. 71.

9 The operational codename for the invasion of Phuket, selected by a member of Mountbatten's planning staff with a highly developed sense of humour, was ROGER, but an objection was raised on the ground that no codename should contain a clue to the location of the target. When the issue went to the War Cabinet, Churchill listed several other equally entertaining alternatives, but restored ROGER.

10 Boulle, author of *Bridge on the River Kwai*, attempted to infiltrate Hanoi from Kunming, but was arrested by the Vichy French authorities in October 1942 and sentenced to life imprisonment for treason. He subsequently wrote an account of his experiences, *The Source of the River Kwai* (Vanguard Press, 1967), which was translated by Xan Fielding.

11 Cruickshank, *SOE in the Far East*, p. 150.

12 Peter Murphy's controversial relationship with Mountbatten is described by Richard Deacon in *The Greatest Treason* (Century, 1989). Murphy had been up at Cambridge with Mackenzie and this connection may have assisted Murphy's transfer to India.

13 O'Brien, *op. cit.*, p. 125.

14 Cruickshank, *SOE in the Far East*, p. 162.

15 *Ibid.*, p. 150.

16 *Ibid.*, p. 162.

17 *Ibid.*, p. 217.

18 Roosevelt, *op. cit.*, vol. 2, p. 375.

19 *Ibid.*

20 *Ibid.*, p. 378.

21 *Ibid.*, p. 393.

22 *Ibid.*, p. 394.

23 *Ibid.*, p. 410.

24 *Ibid.*, p. 444.

25 *Ibid.*

11 Clandestine Bodies: SOE in 1944

1 Foot, *SOE in France*, p. 34.

2 Hinsley, *op. cit.*, vol. v, p. 287.

3 Churchill, *The Second World War*, vol. v, p. 620.

4 As a consequence of MI5's advice de Gaulle was always very circumspect in his dealings with Soustelle. See Soustelle's *Times* obituary (8 August 1990), which refers to the 'mystery about his personal relations with de Gaulle who seemed always to have reservations about his one-time principal lieutenant'. For further details of the compromising GRU material, see the CIA's declassified account of *The Rote Kapelle*.

5 Unbeknownst to SOE, Virginia Hall's true name, together with details of her first mission, had been supplied to the Germans by SIS over a *funkspiel* radio link late in 1943, just weeks before she was scheduled to go back into the field. Fortunately, on this occasion, no harm was done and Miss Hall completed her mission without undue incident.

6 There is some doubt about the composition of LIONTAMER. M. R. D. Foot identifies an E. Lesout and an M. Lepage as ARCHDEACON's victims, but makes no mention of *Guillaume*. However, OSS records list Maurice Lanis, E. Lesout and *Guillaume*.

7 Preamble to *OSS War Diary* (Garland Publishing, 1989).

8 SFHQ map, *ibid*.

9 Alphonse Defendini arrived by the VAR sea line, but was captured in Paris and was sent to Buchenwald.

10 de Vomécourt, *An Army of Amateurs*, p. 100.

11 Prisoners taken from Operation LOYTON at Moussey were all shot, and over two hundred villagers were arrested in reprisals. Only seventy villagers survived the concentration camps. Also, D Squadron 1st SAS suffered heavy casualties in the Forêt de Fontainebleau south of Paris during Operation GAIN after the betrayal of its base by a double agent.

12 Roosevelt, *op. cit.*, vol. 2, p. 285.

13 Communications depended upon the JOAN–ELEANOR transceiver, which linked agents on the ground via a voice channel to aircraft circling directly overhead.

Conclusion

1 Eden's memorandum, 23 November 1944, in COS (44) 381 1st(0), in PRO File CAB 79/89.

2 *The Diaries of Sir Alexander Cadogan*, p. 683.

3 COS (45) 198th, in PRO File CAB 79/37.

4 COS (46) 58th, in PRO File CAB 79/47.

5 Maurice Buckmaster's introduction to Cookridge's *They Came from the Sky*, p. 2.

6 Lees, *The Rape of Serbia*, p. 329.

7 Fielding, *Hide and Seek*, p. 99.

8 Stanley Moss, *A War of Shadows*, p. 75.

9 Leo Marks, 5 March 1991.

Index

Abbott, G. W., 39, 40, 126
Abel, 229
Abélard, 227
Abrahams, Sir Arthur, 16
Abwehr, 36, 42, 76, 94–104,
    108–11, 122, 123, 131,
    153, 239
ACOLYTE, 227
ACROBAT, 109, 129, 130
ACTOR, 122, 225, 228
Adam, 225
Adams, H. R., 258, 263
Adams, J., 268
Adamson, J. C., 257
Adèle, 128
ADRIAN, 225
Agazarian, Francine
    (*Marguerite*), 112
Agazarian, Jack (*Marcel*),
    122, 126
Agee, Dr Fred (*Antagonist*),
    225, 237
Aguirac, P. (*Vire*), 271
Ah Lam, 177
Aimé, 128
Air Liaison Section (AL),
    23, 46, 135
  Head of, *see* Allerton
Airey, (Sir) Terence, 15, 54,
    55
Aksel, 77
Alabama, 272
Alain, 127
ALAN, 270
ALASTAIR, 270
Albanian Section, 70, 147
  Head of, *see* Cripps, Leake
Albert, 126, 224
Alblas, Aart, 97
Alceste, 130
Aldis, J. R., 258, 263
ALEC, 270
ALEXANDER, 270

Alexander, E., 264
Alexander, Gen., 164
Alexandre, 130, 155
Alexandre, Raoul, 119, 126
Alfred, 127, 218
ALFRED, 270
Alice, 128
Allard, E. A. L., 126
Allerton, Lord, 46
Allet, B. (*Oxford*), 270
ALLIANCE, 41, 42, 278
Almond, Sgt, 77
ALMONER, 66
Alphonse, 223
Alsop, Stewart J. (*Rona*), 270
Alston, Gordon, 67
ALUM, 145
AMAZON, 145
Ambel, L. (*Nesque*), 273
Ambreve, 270
Ambroise, 126
Amery, Julian, 10, 56, 57,
    61, 140, 141, 143, 278,
    281
Amery, Leo, 184
AMF Section, 135
Amies, E. Hardy, 101, 258,
    264
AMMONIA, 270
Amps, Jean (*Tomas*), 126
Anachore, 271
Anderson, Sir John, 8
Anderson, Pat, 85
Andorsen, 77
André, 127
Andrew, Finlay, 212
Andringa, Leonard, 94, 95
ANDY, 270
Anfora, 186
Angier, Norman, 15
Anglesey, 272
Anglo-Dutch Section, 185,
    211, 212

Head of, *see* Mollinger
Annan, W. R., 192, 211
Annett, H. K., 261
Annette, 110, 224
Anselme, 273
Anstett, R. M. (*Alabama*),
    272
Anstey, John, 137, 210, 266
Anstey, Walter, 55, 278
Anstruther, Alexander, 134,
    266
ANTAGONIST, 89, 225, 237,
    238
Antagonist, 225
Antelme, France (*Antoine*),
    119, 126
ANTHONY, 270
ANTHROPOID, 89–91, 280
Anti-Fascist Organisation
    (AFO), 201ff.
ANTIMONY, 91
Antoine, 126, 224
Anton, 112
Antonescu, Ion, 152, 154
Aphlett, P. J., 126
Aportre, 271
Appenzell, Ferdinand, 245
Appleyard, Geoffrey, 86
APPRECIATION, 193, 204,
    205
Aptaker, Bernard, 228
AQUATINT, 130
Aramis, 228
Archambaud, 112, 115, 129
ARCHDEACON, 120, 127,
    228, 233, 253, 284
ARCHERY, 76
ARCHIBALD, 270
Archibald, A., 26
Archibald, R. M., 257, 264
Ardèche, 271
Ardinian, 11
Argentier, 271

Argyll, 270
Argyropoulos, Col, 169
Ariage, 270
Aristide, 225
Armand, 227
Armia Krajowa (AK), 28, 240
Armstrong, Charles, 66, 68, 69, 142, 144, 148
Armstrong, J., 265
Armstrong, Lord, 5
Arnaud, 129
Arnault, Claude (*Neron*), 219
Aron, J. M., 126
Arun, 207
Arran, 272
Aristide, 224, 273
Astley, Joan Bright, 275
Atherton, Terence, 58, 59, 70
Arthur, 128
Ashwell, Paul, 208
ASYMPTOTE, 130
Atherton, Terence, 144
Atkins, Vera, 123, 239, 247, 257
Attlee, Clement, 19
Aude, 270
AUDITOR, 239
Augure, 271
Auster, P. R., 241, 258, 263
Austin, Benton (*Gaspard*), 270
Austin, P/O, 58
AUTHOR, 129, 227
AUTOGIRO, 33, 38, 43, 126, 127
AUTONOMOUS, 70, 153–5
Auxiliary Units, 13, 17, 173, 277

Baatsen, Arnold, 93, 94
Babington-Smith, David, 226
Bablik, Josef, 91
Badoglio, Pietro, 138
Badois, 130
Bailey, S. William (Bill), 10, 11, 56, 66, 69, 84, 155
Baird, W. (*Hampshire*), 271
Baissac, Claude de (*David*), 224, 225
Bakirdzis, Euripedes, 52, 70
BALACLAVA, 137

Balden, A. D., 267
BALDHEAD II, 188
BALDHEAD III, 188
Baldwin, Oliver, 15
Baldwin, Stanley, 7
Balfour, David, 169, 281
Balharry, Jack, 206
Bally, G., 230
Balmaceda, Giliana, 112
Baraud, G. (*Connaught*), 272
Bardet, Roger (*Chaillan*), 110, 114, 121, 124
BARDSEA, 236
BARGEE, 129
Barjot, Pierre, 42
Barker-Benfield, Karl, 54, 168, 170, 253
Barkham, Geoffrey, 164
Barnes, Dick, 164
Barnes, Sir Edward, 187
Barnes, Tom, 165–7
Barnett, M., 225, 265
Barrett, Denis (*Honoré*), 126
Barrie, A., 264
Barry, James, 179
Barry, Richard H., 24, 31, 241, 256, 261, 282
BARTER, 237
Bartos, Alfred, 91
Baseden, Yvonne (*Odette*), 126, 225
BASIL, 270
Basin, Francis (*Laurent*), 126
BASS, 127
Bassett, M. (*Ludovic*), 225
Bastien, 111, 126
Bathurst, Ben, 206
BCRA, *see Bureau Central de Renseignements et d'Action*
Bearsted, Lord, 10
Beatty, Sir Chester, 9, 56, 132
Beaumont, J. L. (*Norfolk*), 271
Beaumont-Nesbitt, Paddy, 17
Beauregard, Alcide, 126, 229
Bec, P. E., 126
Bedell Smith, Walter, 138
Beekman, Yolande (*Mariette*), 126, 227
Beevor, Jack, 34, 266, 277, 280
BEGGAR, 225, 228

Begué, Georges (*George One*), 33–5, 37, 120, 126
Behrisch, Arno, 13
Belgian Section (T), 23, 24, 88, 101–3
  Head of, *see* Amies, Knight
BELIEF, 210
Benham, J. E., 259, 263
BENJAMIN (Czechoslovakia), 88, 91
BENJAMIN (JEDBURGH), 270
BENJOIN, 127, 225, 235
Bennett, John, 10, 54, 57, 60, 61
Bennett, K. G. (*Aportre*), 271
Bennington, Cmmdr, 191
Benoist, Robert (*Lionel*), 126, 225, 227
Benoit, 107, 128
Benson, Henry A., 65, 266
Berge, G., 32
Berington, W. J. C., 266
Berlin, J. (*Martial*), 270
BERNARD, 270
Bernard, 33
Bernard, Maj., 102
Bertholet, René, 35
Bertrand, 115, 129
Best, Sigismund P., 8, 277
BETTY, 176
Beukema, Karel, 96
Beyts, Bill, 188
Bieler, Gustave (*Guy*), 126, 227
Biggs, Ernest, 12, 277
BILLOW, 204
bin Ismail, Tan Sri Ibrahim, 282
Bingham, B., 265
Bingham, Seymour, 26, 98–100, 103, 104, 257
Binney, Sir George, 256
BIOSCOPE, 91
BIRD, 143
Bishop, 126
Bishop, Adrian, 51, 55
Bitner, 34
BIVOUAC, 91
Black, Ivan, 39, 40
Blacker, Stewart, 15, 16
Blackmore, Sgt, 145
Blaise, 227
Blaizot, Gen., 208, 209

Blake, M. E. V., 263
Blanchere, L. (*Louisiana*), 272
Blanner, A., 265
Blathwayt, C. G. (*Surrey*), 271
Bleicher, Hugo, 36, 40, 110, 113, 121, 277, 280
Blizard, Charles, 94, 98, 100, 104
Bloch, André, 234
Bloch, Denise (*Ambroise*), 126, 225
Bloch, Pierre (*Draftsman*), 126
Blomfield, V. E., 268
Blonttrock, Lucien, 244
Bloom, Marcus (*Bishop*), 126
Blunt, Anthony, 62, 221
Boal, A. M., 268
Bob, 130, 229
Bodden, 132
Bodington, Nicholas R., 3, 26, 39, 113, 114, 118, 121
Boemelberg, Karl, 113
Boemermann, Wilbur, 225
Boiteux, Robert (*Nicholas*), 224, 228
Bolladière, P. C. (*Prisme*), 235
Bond, S. I., 257, 264
Bonnier de la Chapelle, Fernand, 135
Bony, Pierre, 108
Boothroyd, F., 258, 261
Boris III, King, 151
Borosch, Henri, 239
Borrel, Andrée (*Denise*), 111, 116, 119, 125, 126
Bouchard, Henri (*Noel*), 224
Bouchardon, André (*Narcisse*), 126, 219
Boudin, L. G., 258
Boughey, E. Peter F., 10, 62, 71, 155, 156, 243, 258
Boughton-Leigh, P. W. T., 257, 265
Boulle, Pierre, 208, 283
Bourdon, M. (*Aristide*), 273
Bourgoin, Lucien (*Mayo*), 272
Bourriot, Capt. (*Shetland*), 271
Bourne, (Sir) Alan, 17, 29

Bourne-Paterson, R. A., 5, 105, 106, 108, 230, 257, 277, 280
Boursier, 273
Bouton, 273
Boutron, Jean, 42
Bowden, G. C., 265
Bowlby, Cuthbert, 55
Boxshall, Edward G., 4, 61, 250, 258, 263
Boyle, Archie R., 259–62
Bracken, Brendan, 19
Bradley, Joe, 161
Bradner, John L. (*Pfennig*), 270
Bramwell, H. E., 257
BRANDON, 134
Brauer, Gen., 281
Braunfels, 186
Brecknock, 273
Bremner, Col, 187
Brey, Oscar de, 98, 104
BRIAN, 271
BRICKLAYER, 126
Brierley, R. (*Florin*), 271
Brightman, P., 265
BRILLIG, 206
Briscoe, Henry, 26
BRISSEX, 230
British Security Co-ordination (BSC), 83, 84, 133, 151,
Chief of, *see* Stephenson
Broad, Richard, 266
Brock, N., 265
Brogger, A., 26, 265
BRONX, 112
Brook, (Sir) Robin E., 31, 39, 234, 235, 237
Brooke, Sir Alan, 39
Brooker, Bill, 84
Brookes, Sqdn Ldr, 194
Brooks, Edward, 258
Brooks, Tony (*Alphonse*), 223, 224, 247, 282
Broome, Richard, 178, 186, 189
Brossolette, Pierre, 234
Brouillard, M. (*Vermont*), 273
Brouville, Comte de (*Théodule*), 225
Brown, C., 258
Brown, Charles E. (*Rice*), 273
Brown, G. A., 269

Brown, John, 73
Brown, K. J. W. (*Limerick*), 273
Brown, O. (*Félicien*), 273
Brown, O. H. (*Kent*), 232, 270
Browne, Gordon, 133
Browne-Bartolli, Albert (*Tiburce*), 225, 227
Broz, Josip (Tito), 56, 144–6, 148, 248
BRUCE, 271
Bruce, H. J., 263
Bruce Lockhart, Robin, 278
Bruce-Mitford, Terence, 158
Brucker, Herbert (*Sacha*), 225
BRUTUS, 278
Bryce, Ivar, 83, 84, 266, 280
Buchenwald, 126–8
Buchowski, Jan, 47
Buck, H. E. P., 265
Buckmaster, Maurice, 2, 5, 26, 31, 38, 43, 93, 106–8, 124, 137, 229, 230, 247, 257, 275, 277, 278, 280, 284
Budge, Vincent, 54, 70
Buhn, Carl, 81
Buizer, Johannes, 95
Bukkens, Sjef, 96
Bulgarian Section, 71, 151
Head of, *see* Davies
BULBASKET, 232
BULLSEYE, 57, 63, 66, 240, 278
BUNKUM, 188
Burdeyron, Noel (*Gaston*), 40, 126
Bureau Centrale de Renseignements et d'Action (BCRA), 222, 230, 234
Burgess, Guy, 62
Burma Section, 181, 185, 191, 195–203
Head of, *see* Forrester, Gardiner
Burney, Christopher, 40, 126, 278
Burrus, B., 265
Burton, John, 47
Butch, 225
BUTLER, 120, 127, 129
Butler, Ewan, 54

Butler, Sir Robin, 5, 277
Butterfield, D. O., 265
BUZZARD, 64
Byck, Muriel (*Violette*), 126
Byerly, Robert, 119, 126
Byrne, H. J., 268

Cabard, R., 33
Cabral, Jose, 186
Cadett, Thomas, 30, 31, 33, 38, 107
Cadogan, Sir Alexander, 18, 19, 47, 73, 136, 245, 277, 278, 281, 284
Cadogan, Bruce, 126
Cairncross, John, 62
Caithness, 273
Calosso, Umberto, 52
Calthrop, Edward, 101
Calvin, P. M. (*Middlesex*), 271
CAMEL, 200, 201
Cameron, F/O, 258
Campbell, A. H., 262
Campbell, John, 159
Campbell, Sir Roland, 155, 248
Camouin, J. (*Serre*), 270
Cammaerts, Francis (*Roger*), 224, 227
CANDLE, 208
Cannicott, S. N. (*Pembroke*), 270
Cannon-Brookes, V. M., 256, 261
Capel-Dunn, Denis, 280
Cardozo, B., 235
Carew, T. A. (*Sutherland*), 200, 270
Carleton-Smith D. L. G., 239, 265
Carliere, R. (*Meath*), 273
Carlow, 270
Carman, C. M. (*Utah*), 273
Carnarvon, 271
CARP, 109
CARPENTER, 189, 193
CARPENTER II, 190
Carr, Frank, 28
Carr, J. M. D., 26, 265
Carr, R., 268
Carré, Mathilde, 36–40, 110, 277
CARTE, 109, 110, 114, 121, 124, 126

Cartigny, J., 35
CARVER, 225, 228
Carver, F. K. M., 256, 265
Casabianca, 137
Casimir, 234
Castellano, Guiseppe, 138
Castello, E. J., 268
Caton, 224
Cauchi, Eric (*Pedro*), 126
Cauvin, Maj., 179
Cavell, Edith, 111
Cavendish-Bentinck, Victor, 209, 246, 280
Caza, Roger (*Emanuel*), 224
CECIL, 271
Célestin, 130, 224
Centaur, 146
Centavo, 271
Centime, 272
Central Intelligence Agency (CIA), 283
César, 227
Cesari, 137
Chadbourne, Philip E. (*Nevada*), 272
Chaillan, 110, 114, 121, 124
Chamberlain, Neville, 19, 60, 277
CHANCELLOR, 225, 229
Chapman, Eddie, 123, 281
Chapman, Robert, 58
Chapman-Walker, John, 189, 197, 266
CHARACTER, 202
Charente, 272
Charlet, Blanche (*Christiane*), 126
Charron, P. (*Ardèche*), 271
Chastelain, Gardyne de, 10, 12, 56, 153, 266
CHAUFFEUR, 244
Chaworth-Musters, James, 24, 74, 75, 256
Cheshire, 271
Chesshire, Jim, 141
CHESTNUT, 127
Chiang Kai-shek, 212
Chichaev, Ivan, 71
Chidson, Monty, 9, 10, 277
Child, Douglas, 26
Childs, J. H., 264
China Section, 181, 185, 195, 212–13
CHISEL, 244
Christiane, 126

Christoffersen, 82
Christophe, 130
CHRISTOPHER, 225
Chrystal, Robert, 282
Churchill, Odette, *see* Sansom
Churchill, Peter (*Michel*), 3, 109, 121, 126
Churchill, Randolph, 148, 278
Churchill, Winston S., 1, 16, 17, 60, 67, 68, 75, 148, 154, 221
CIA, *see* Central Intelligence Agency
Cicero, 128
CINEMA, 127
Circlitira, Dennis, 160, 164
CITRONELLE, 235
CLARENCE, 101
CLARIBEL, 74, 79
CLARIDGES, 151, 152
Clark, H. M. G., 257
Clark, W., 268
Clarke, Brian M., 173, 187, 260
Clark-Kerr, Sir Alexander, 181
Claudine, 127
CLAYMORE, 74, 75, 80
Clayton, Iltyd, 50
Clech, Marcel (*Bastien*), 111, 126
Clement, 229
Clement, Georges (*Edouard*), 126
CLERGYMAN, 126, 225, 227
CLEVELAND, 101
Clive, Nigel, 51, 278
CLOWDER, 242
Clutton, R. H. (*Stafford*), 273
Cnoops, A. J., 103
Cochet, Gen., 109
Cochran, H. H., 258, 265
Cochrane, Keith H., 256
Codrington, John, 13, 277
Cohen, Gaston (*Justin*), 224, 228
Cohen, Kenneth, 22–4, 30, 41, 43, 230
Coit, Richard, 83, 266
Colby, William E., 271
Colditz, 126–8, 141, 156
Cole, F. J. (*Georgia*), 273

Cole, Harold, 110, 281
Cole, J. D., 262, 265
Cole, P., 264
Coleman, J. D., 224, 257
Coleridge, D. P., 256
Coleridge, P., 265
Colin, 128, 228
Collingwood, J. F. H., 257
Colorado, 270
Colt-Williams, R. G., 263
COMBAT, 129
Combe-Tennant, Maj., 231
Combined Operations,
  Chief of, 17
Communist Party of Great
  Britain (CPGB), 64, 209,
  221
CONJURER, 128
CONSENSUS, 70, 71, 140,
  171
CONSENSUS II, 141
Conway, Capt., 26
Cook, John, 140, 165, 171
Cook, Thomas, 266
Cookridge, E. H., 5, 105,
  106, 276, 277
Coon, Carleton, 133
Cooper, Lt, 183
Cope, Capt., 26, 278
Coppin, Edward (*Oliver*),
  126
Corbett, Bill, 137
Corbin, Charles, 225
Corby, J. C., 256
Cordeaux, John, 34, 94, 276,
  280
Cork, 270
Cormeau, Yvonne (*Annette*),
  224
Cormier, F. (*Durthe*), 273
Cornwall, 273
Cornwall, Sgt, 145
Corrie, W. J., 268
Corsair, Tony, 143
CORSICAN, 126–8, 130
Cosmo, 229
Cottani-Chalbur, Vera de,
  111
Cotterill, Maurice, 177
Cottin, Roger (*Albert,
  Bernard*), 33, 40, 127
Counasse, Emile (*Caton*), 224
Coupek, Jindrich, 91
COUPLING, 206, 207
Courtauld, George, 10, 24

Coustenoble, Maurice, 42
Coute, R. (*Ludovic*), 270
Cowburn, Ben (*Benoit*), 40,
  107, 112, 276
Cowell, Gervase, 276
Cox, J. H. (*Monmouth*), 272
Coxe, Henry B., 231, 232,
  239
CPGB, *see* Communist Party
  of Great Britain
Craster, O. (*Yorkshire*), 273
Crawford, Albert, 158
Crawley, 42
Crawshaw, H. G., 257
Crawshay, William W.
  (*Crown*), 54, 61, 272
Cretan sub-section, 159–64
  Head of, *see* Simmonds,
  Stevens
Cripps, Maj., 10, 54
Crnjanski, Pavle, 58
Crockatt, Norman, 16
Crocus, 242
Croft, Andrew, 15, 25, 75,
  79, 137
Croft-Murray, E., 257
Cromarty, 270
Cromwell, F., 257
Crosby, Sir Josiah, 174, 176,
  283
Crosby, M. C. M., 232
Cross, J., 265
Cross, John, 179, 282
Crown, 272
Cruickshank, Charles, 5,
  194, 277, 278, 280, 283,
  284
Culioli, Pierre, 111, 116
Cumberledge, Michael, 159,
  171, 282
Cummins, Steven, 174
Cupal, Ludvik, 91
Curda, Karel, 89, 91
Currie, Tony, 240
Cutting, Robert F., 230
Cyr, Paul (*Wigton*), 232,
  271
Czech *Deuxième Bureau*, 90
  Head of, *see* Moravec
Czech Section (MY), 88–90
  Head of, *see* Wilkinson

Dachau, 125–8, 276
Dadley, C. F., 264
Dafoe, Colin, 150

Dakic, Spasoje, 59
Dalley, John, 175
Dallow, A. J. (*Groat*), 271
Dalton, Hugh, 18, 19, 39,
  48, 53, 59, 183, 277
Damerment, Madeleine
  (*Solange*), 119, 127
Dandicolle, Jean, 127
Daniel, 130
DANIEL, 271
Danish Section (SD), 80–82
  Head of, *see* Hollingworth
Dansey, (Sir), Claude, 22,
  23, 30, 124, 222, 251
Dantes, Y. M. (*Selune*), 272
Darby, O., 177
D'Arcangues, Jacques, 122
Darlan, Emile, 135, 136,
  281
Darling, Georges, 116, 127
Dartigues, J. (*Bouton*), 273
Davenport, D., 261
David, 226
Davidson, Basil, 10, 54, 60,
  67, 147, 155, 156, 282
Davidson, Douglas, 61
Davies, F. Tommy, 15, 24,
  56, 84, 256, 259, 260,
  264
Davies, Mostyn, 71, 83, 150,
  253, 266
Davies, Norman, 10, 54, 266
Davies, 'Trotsky', 140, 142,
  143, 281
Davis, Bradley, 42
DAWES, 241, 242
Dawson, R. (*Merioneth*), 273
Day, Maj., 26
Dayan, Moshe, 50
DEADWOOD, 243
Deakin, Sir F. William, 54,
  56, 60, 67–9, 145, 147,
  150, 278, 282
Death Be Not Proud, 2
D-Day, 220, 222–7, 233,
  235, 236, 253
Dédé (Défence), 127
Dédé (Maingard), 225
Défence, Marcel (*Dédé*), 127
Defendini, Alphonse, 127,
  283
de Fries, M., 265
Delaney, Guy, 160
Delaware, 271
DELEGATE, 127

Delhandtshutter, Michel, 244
Delignant, Daniel, 35
Demand, G., 219
Denby, 272
Dening, Esler, 209
Denise, 111, 126
Denneau, Anthony J. (*Massachusetts*), 272
Deniset, François, 119, 127
Deprez, C. (*Perth*), 270
Dericourt, Henri (*Gilbert*), 2, 112–15, 121–5
Derouen, J. (*Kintyre*), 273
Deschamps, J. (*Dordogne*), 272
Deslorme, Y. (*Maine*), 272
DESMOND, 225, 271
Dessing, George, 94, 99
Detal, J. T. J., 127
DETECTIVE, 129, 130, 227
Deuxième Bureau, 45, 114, 136
Deuxième Direction, 102
Devailly, M. (*Ecu*), 273
de Vomécourt, *see* Vomécourt
Devonshire, G. E., 175
De Vries, M., 256, 265
Dewavrin, André, 29–32, 277
Dewe, Walther, 101
DF Section, 23, 24, 31, 34, 35, 38, 112
  Head of, *see* Humphreys
Dhomas, A. (*Dronne*), 272
DIAMOND, 271
Diancono, H. L. A. (*Blaise*), 227
Diane, 224, 228
Dickens, Sgt, 188
DIETICIAN, 225
DIGGER, 225
DILLON, 243
Dillon, Edward, 159
Dime, 272
Dimu, 128
DIPLOMAT, 225, 227
DIRECTOR, 227, 233
Director of Military Intelligence (DMI), 17
DISCLAIM, 58, 144
Dismore, L. H., 26, 264
Dispenser, 116, 128

DITCHER, 227
Dixon, Lt, 26
DMI, *see* Director of Military Intelligence
Dobell, D. M., 262
Dobrski, Julian, 54
Dobson, R. Ivor, 101, 103, 264
Dodd, J. S., 262
Dodds-Parker, (Sir) Douglas, 15, 135–7, 266, 281
Dollar, 273
Dolton, S., 264
Dominique, 129
Domvile, Patrick, 10, 54, 55
Domville, Mrs, 264
DONALD, 225, 238
Donegall, 270
Doneux, J., 264
DONKEY, 199
DONKEYMAN, 114, 126–8, 223
Donovan, William, 134, 214, 218
Dordogne, 272
Dorset, 271
Dorsey, H. A., 232
Doubloon, 271
DOUGLAS, 271
DOUGLAS II, 271
Douglas, P. F. S., 256
Dourlein, Pieter, 98–100, 103
Dowlen, Robert (*Richard*), 127
DOWNEND, 242, 243
Downes, Donald, 278
Draftsman, 126
Dragivec, Veljko, 56
DRAGONFLY, 123
Drew-Brook, Tommy, 84
Driberg, Tom, 221
Dronne, 272
Drooglever, Knees, 96
Droux, William B. (*Sixpence*), 271
Druce, G. A. J., 26
Druchenfels, 186
Drucker, Willi (*Ragweed*), 242
Dubois, Albert (*Hercule*), 127
Dubourdin, Georges (*Alain*), 127
Duchessa D'Aosta, 86

Duclos, P. F., 127
Duffy, Garry, 70, 140
Dugmore, Maj., 150, 151
Duke, Florimond, 156
Dulling, Kenneth, 26
Duluguet, Marc, 122
Dumbarton, 271
Dumbrell, J. H., 268
Dumont-Guillemet, René (*Armande*), 225, 227
Dunbabin, Thomas, 53, 54, 160, 164
Dunderdale, Wilfred, 23, 26, 277
Dupond, Yvan (*Abélard*), 225, 227
DUPONT, 242
Dupont, P. E. (*Gapeau*), 272
Dupré, George, 275
Dupré, Roger, 122
du Puy, Comte, 127
Durance, 271
Durthe, 273
Dumesnil, H. (*Virginia*), 273
Dutch Section, *see* Netherlands Section
Dvorak, Oldrich, 91

EAM, 160–72
Eardley, L., 262
Earle, Pierce (*Locker*), 225
Ecu, 273
Eddy, William, 134
Eden, Anthony, 17, 39, 61, 154, 201, 205, 245, 284
Eden, R. J. R., 54
EDES, 164, 166, 172
Edmonds, Arthur, 166, 167
Edwards, C. H., 258, 265, 269
Egdell, R. H., 258, 269
Egerton Mott, G., 186, 197, 262
Ehrenfels, 186, 187
Eifler, Carl, 200, 215
Eisenhower, Dwight D., 247
ELAS, 160, 248
Elie, 127
Elizabeth, 129
ELK, 202
Elkin, E. F., 177
Ellam, P. J., 265
Elliott, Kavan, 58, 144
Ellis, Toby, 132
El-Masri, Aziz, 52

Elwell, Charles, 97
Emanuel, 224
Emile, 229
Emmanuel, King Victor, 138
Emmer, Jan, 97
Empson-Ridler, N. H., 263
ENAMEL, 66
End, 108
Englandspiel, 99, 100, 103,
    104
Ennals, David, 62
Ennals, John, 26, 62, 151,
    278
Ennals, Martin, 62
Epinois, 262
Erard, P. (*Save*), 271
Eritrea, 182
Ernest, 128
Erskine, David, 54, 61
Escampador, 159
Escape and Evasion Service
    (MI9), 110, 111, 161,
    239
Escaut, 273
Esch, Elmer B. (*Pound*), 273
Escoute, M., 127
ESPINETTE, 244
Essex, 273
Estèphe, 225
Etienne, 130
Eugène, 129
EU/P Section, 23, 36, 47,
    236
    Head of, *see* Hazell
Eustache, 227
Everson, Reg, 160
EVIDENCE, 191
EXCERPT, 146
Experimental Station Z, 190
Eyre, John, 65, 139

FABULOUS, 35
Fairbairn, Dan, 84
Faithfull, Sgt, 150
FALAISE, 132
FAN, 240
FANY, *see* First Aid Nursing
    Yeomanry
Farley, Wally, 72
FARMER, 129, 130, 224, 226
Farmer, John (*Hubert*), 225
Farrant, Ralph, 16
Farrish, Slim, 146
Faulks, D. K. de G., 265
Faure-Field, J., 263

Favel, J., 271
Fearfield, Tony, 204
Félix, 127
FELIX, 271
Fenner, Claude, 149
Fenton, W. S. (*Cornwall*),
    273
Fenwick, Basil, 26
Ferry, P. J., 258
Field, Gerry, 141
Field, Simon, 12
Field-Robinson, W., 72,
    241, 250, 258, 262, 278
Fielding, Xan, 143, 160–2,
    172, 247, 248, 281, 284
Fife, 270
Filou, Prof., 151
Fincken, Jack, 38, 40, 127
Finlay, Jack, 189, 197
Finlayson, D. (*Guillaume*),
    127
FIREMAN, 225, 228
First Aid Nursing Yeomanry
    (FANY), 93, 261, 263,
    264
Fleming, Ian, 51
Fleming, Peter, 15, 51, 137,
    158
Fletcher, Reginald, 31, 46,
    278
Fletcher, Walter, 213
FLIMWELL, 198
Floege, Ernest (*Alfred*), 127
Floiras, August (*Albert*), 224
Flour, François, 244
Flossenbürg, 129
Flower, Raymond (*Gaspard*),
    111
Foley, Frank, 74
Follis, Peter, 247
Fone, V., 263
Foot, M. R. D., 4, 29, 65,
    105, 106, 119, 124,
    276–82, 284
FOOTMAN, 225, 227
Forbes, J. (*Rhode Island*),
    272
Force *133*, 139, 152
    136, 180, 195, 199–202,
    210–13
    137, 189, 197
    139, 139, 147
    266, 139, 147
    333, 139
    399, 148

Forman, A., 33
Forrest, A. J. (*Stirling*), 270
Forrester, R. E., 185, 197,
    198
FORTITUDE, 238
FORWARD, 214
Fourcade, Marie-
    Madeleine, 42, 278
Fourcaud, Pierre (*Sphère*),
    235
Fox, Marcel (*Ernest*), 127
Fox, M. M., 264
Frager, Henri (*Louba*), 114,
    127, 223, 224
Franc, 272
FRANCIS, 271
Franck, Louis, 10, 83, 86,
    151, 152, 257
Franco, Francisco, 47
Francompte, R. (*Orkney*),
    271
FRANK, 271
Frank, Karl Hermann, 89
FRANKLIN, 133
Franklin, Norman R. (*Cork*),
    270
Fraser, Gordon, 54, 61
Fraser, Hon. Hugh, 164
Fraser, Ingram, 82, 83
Fraser-Campbell, N., 264,
    265
Frayan, A. (*Lys*), 271
Fréderic, 225
FREDERICK, 232, 271
Free French Section (RF),
    *see République Français
    Section*
FREELANCE, 225, 228
French Indo-China Section,
    182, 183, 185, 195, 197,
    208–10
    Head of, *see* Langlade
French Section (F), 23, 24,
    29, 31, 33–43, 45, 59,
    93, 96, 105–30, 137, 220
    Head of, *see* Humphreys,
    Marriott, Buckmaster
FRESHMAN, 77, 78
Friele, B. E. (*Selkirk*), 271
FUGUE, 145, 150, 248
Fuller, Horace, 232
Fuller, Jean Overton, 2, 113,
    275, 277, 281
FUNGUS, 146, 149
FUNNEL, 191

Gabcik, Josef, 89, 91
Gabriel, 130, 234
Gaby, 129
Gael, 219, 224
Gaertner, Friedle, 112
Gaetan, 128
Gaillot, H. H. (*Ignace*), 127
GAIN, 283
Gairaud, A. (*Ariage*), 270
Galbraith, Sgt-Maj., 241
Gale, Roland, 158
Gallegos, Adrian, 47
Gallie, W. B., 269
Gallienne, Simon, 26
Galvin, Jim, 212
Gambier, R. M., 191
Ganay, J. L. de, 225
Gande, W. J., 182
Gane, 36
Gano, Stanislaw, 31
Garby-Czerniawski, Roman, 36, 41, 277
GARDENER, 228
Gardiner, Ritchie, 196, 197, 282
Gardner, D., 273
Garel, François, 127
Garnons-Williams, Capt., 209
Garrett, A. R. T., 265
Garrow, Ian, 26
Gaspard, 111
Gaston, 126
Gaulle, Charles de, 16, 35, 59, 131, 135, 208, 210, 221, 222, 234, 235, 283
Gaulle, Madame de, 13
GAVIN, 271
Gavin, Jim, 174, 182, 186
GCHQ, *see* Government Communications Headquarters
Gedye, Eric, 241
Geelen, P. A. H., 127
GEORGE, 232, 271
GEORGE II, 271
George, Hans, 123
George, King of the Hellenes, 158, 169
George One, 126
Georges 53, 130
GEORGIA, 244
Georgia, 273
Georgescu, Rica 153, 154
GERALD, 271

Gerbrands, Peter, 103
Gerik, Vilem, 91
German Section (X), 72, 241-5
Head of, *see* Templer
Gestapo, 63, 108, 118, 119, 122, 151, 156, 226, 228, 229, 240, 243
Gibson, Archie, 152, 154
Gibson, Harold, 155
Gielgud, Lewis, 32
Giffey, Frank, 51
Gilbert, 2, 251
GILBERT, 271
Gilchrist, (Sir) Andrew, 195, 205, 282
Gildee, John (*Oklahoma*), 272
GILES, 272
Gill, Harry, 12
Gill-Davies, Col, 212
Gilmour, B. W., 232
Ginzburger, Pierre, 222
Giraud, André, 109
Gironde, 272
Giry, L., 271
Gizycki, Christine, 10
Glading, Percy, 7
Gleiniger, Gen., 237
Glen, (Sir) Alexander, 10, 266
Glenconner, Lord, 54, 60, 170, 256, 260
GLOVER, 127, 219, 225
Glyn, Francis, 135, 266
Gneisenau, 38
Godber, Frank, 207
Goddard, Lewis F. (*Lundy*), 272
GODFREY, 272
Goeland Shipping Company, 11, 153
Goetz, Josef, 114
GOLF, 102
GONDOLIER, 225, 227
Goodfellow, Basil, 173, 185
Goodfellow, Patrick, 197
Goodfellow, Preston, 134
Goodwill, Arthur, 10, 49, 54
Gordon-Creed, Geoffrey, 166, 167
Gough, V. A. (*Arran*), 272

Government Communications Headquarters, 62-4, 69, 74-5, 122, 123, 131, 132, 250, 252
Grabovsky, Bohuslav, 91
Graham, L. Lee, 128
Graham, P., 262
Graham, Richard, 177
Graham-Stamper, E. B., 139, 241, 258, 262
Grand, Laurence, 9, 17, 49
Grandclément, André, 122
Greek Section, 70, 140, 159-72
Head of, *see* Stevens, Budge
Green, Holt, 241
GREENHEART, 129
Greenlees, Kenneth, 61
Greensleeves, P. J., 132
GREENUP, 243
Greig, Maj., 188
Gregg, Ralph, 15
Grégoire, 128
Gregor, C. T., 258, 263
Grell, William G., 230
Grgat, G. (*Leinster*), 273
Grierson, G., 46
Grinham, E. J. (*Worcestershire*), 273
Groat, 271
Gross Rosen, 126-9
Grover-Williams, C. (*Sébastien*), 127
Gruen, Hans, 103
Gubbins (Sir) Colin McV., 1, 14, 31, 49, 60, 78, 81, 187, 208, 209, 223, 231, 260, 261, 275, 277-80
Guélis, Jacques de, 45, 137, 276
Guerisse, Albert-Marie, 34, 277
Guiet, Jean-Claude, 239
Guillaume, 127, 228, 284
Guinness, Robert, 71, 196, 210, 266
Guiraud, R. J. (*André*), 127, 225
Guise, C. A. Leonard, 86, 187, 259
GUNNERSIDE, 78
Gunther, John, 134
Gurney, M. E., 264

Gustave, 225
GUSTAVUS, 189, 192
GUSTAVUS EMERGENCY, 190
Guthrie, D. D. (*Denby*), 272
Guy, 126, 227
GUY, 272

Haakon, King, 16
Haas, Jan de, 95
Habib Singh, Jemadar, 188
Haines, W., 261
Half Crown, 271
Halfpenny, 271
Halifax, Lord, 8, 18, 19, 277
Hall, A., 265
Hall, C. E., 150
Hall, Virginia (*Diane*), 40, 112, 224, 228, 284
Hambro, Sir Charles, 1, 7, 24, 25, 59, 60, 67, 73–5, 107, 134, 260
Hamilton, J. A. S., 47, 258
Hamilton J. T., 127
Hamilton, William, 164, 167
Hamilton-Hill, Donald, 137, 147, 281
HAMISH, 272
Hamlet, 237
HAMMER, 244
Hammer, Mogens, 81
Hammond, Nicholas, 52, 70, 158, 166, 168, 281
Hampton, C. S., 269
Hamson, C. J. (Jack), 53, 158
Hamson, Denys, 167, 281
Hanau, Julius, 9, 10, 49, 86
Hanbury-Williams, J., 260
Hands, Andy, 140
Hankey, Lord, 17, 18
Hannah, J. P., 191
Hansen, Hans, 81
Hanson, F. (*Roxburgh*), 272
Harcourt, Lord, 54, 137
Hare, Hon. Alan, 143
Hargreaves, Micky, 144, 150
HARLING, 164, 165, 171, 172
HARLINGTON, 198, 199
HAROLD, 272
Harper, J. W., 269
Harratt, P. J., 257
Harratt, R. H., 268
Harris-Burland, William, 11, 12, 153, 266

Harrison, P., 263
HARRY, 272
Hart, D., 268
Hart, Maj., 190
Harvey, Bill, 177
Hasluck, Margaret ('Fanny'), 54, 70
Hawksworth, Capt., 144, 150
Hayes, Charles (*Yves*), 127
Hayes, Graham, 86
Hayes, Jack B. (*Victor*), 127
Hayward, J., 261
Haywood, Clarke, 282
Hazelhoff, Erik, 280
Hazell, Ronald, 23, 31, 258
Head, R. G., 26, 262
HEADMASTER, 126, 127, 129, 224, 226
Heath Lt, 181
Heatley, R. P., 263
HECKLER, 130
Hector, 130
HECTOR, 130
Hedgehog, 159
Hedley-Dent, W. E., 259, 263
Helps, J. D., 262
Hembry, Boris, 177, 186, 283
HENNA, 58
Henney, T. (*Cheshire*), 271
Henquet, Roger (*Robert*), 225
HENRY, 272
Herbert, Mary (*Claudine*), 127
Hercule, 127
Héritier, Richard, 127
HERMIT, 225, 229, 238
Herriot, Edouard, 124
Hesketh-Pritchard, Alfgar, 242
Heslop, Richard (*Xavier*), 224, 227
Heydrich, Reinhard, 89, 280
Heysen, F. de (*Kroner*), 270
Hibberdine, John, 141, 143, 208
Hibbert, Lt, 141
HILARY, 225, 272
Hill, Bbr, 141
Hill, George, 71, 242, 250, 266, 278
HILLBILLY, 239

Hiller, George (*Maxime*), 225, 227
Hilton, D. P., 269
Hinde, A. R., 267, 268
Hinsley, Sir Harry, 22
Hirtz, R. D., 225
HISTORIAN, 129, 130, 225, 228
Hitchen, J. W., 54, 61
Hitler, Adolf, 51
Hjeltness, Melvin, 225
Hoare, Sir Sam, 47, 86, 132, 248
HOATHLEY I, 146, 149
Hobbs, Tom, 207, 208
Hodgart, Matthew, 85
Hogg, Quintin, 14
Holdsworth, Gerald, 13, 28, 29, 137, 139
Holland, John, 14, 17
Hollingworth, Ralph C., 80, 237, 256, 265, 281
Holme, R. C., 256, 265
Holmes, Mrs M., 258, 262
Holmes, Sir Ronald, 182
Holst, Madge, 35
Homan, F. G., 268
Homburg, Ab, 92, 280
Home Defence (Security) Executive, 8, 19–21
Chairman of, *see* Swinton
Honoré, 126
Hood, E. (*Shropshire*), 273
Hooper, Harry, 264
Hope, Norman, 13
HORACE, 272
Hornsby, F. W., 261
Hornsby-Smith, Dame Patricia, 276
Horthy, Miklós, 155
Hoskier, F. R. B., 256, 265
HOUND, 200
HOUNDSWORTH, 236
HOUSEBOAT, 241, 243
Household, Geoffrey, 15, 277
HOUSEKEEPER, 219
Houseman, John, 164
Houstoun-Boswall, W. E., 256
Howard, Col, 150
Howard, Sir Michael, 194
Howarth, David, 25, 76, 280, 281
Howarth, Patrick, 278

Howe, A. G., 259, 262
Hoxha, Enver, 140, 143, 144
Hruby, Jan, 91
Hubbard, Lt, 171, 282
Hubble, Desmond, 127
Hubert, 128, 225
Hudson, Charles (*Simon*),
    127, 256
Hudson, Christopher, 183,
    187
Hudson, Duane T. (Bill),
    10, 11, 56–9, 65, 66, 69,
    148
Hudson, H., 257
Hudson, T. J., 266
HUGH, 225, 232
Hughes-Smith, Jack, 253
Hugon, Antoine, 42
Humphreys, Leslie, 10, 22,
    26, 31, 33, 35, 38, 257,
    264
Hungarian Section (MPH),
    71, 155, 156, 221
    Head of, *see* Boughey
Hunter, Anthony, 146
Hutchison, (Sir) James
    R. H., 26, 120, 257
Hutton, Clayton, 16, 277
Hyde, Harford M., 10, 280
Hyde, Louis (*Fréderic*), 225
HYDRA, 58, 144

IAN, 272
Iberia and Spanish Morocco
    Section (H), 47, 48, 132,
    133
    Head of, *see* Richardson
Igland, 77
Ignace, 128
Illinois, 271
Ince, C. B., 26, 258, 262,
    265
India Mission, 184–217
    Head of, *see* Mackenzie
Indian Communist Party,
    185
Indo-China Section, 208–10
Industrial Intelligence
    Centre (IIC), 18
INFLUX, 207
Inman, Roger, 54, 61
INTERALLIÉ, 35–41, 43,
    110, 121, 125, 277
Inter-Services Liaison
    Department (ISLD)

Middle East, 55, 169
    Head of, *see* Bowlby
Far East, 173, 177, 179,
    180, 190–4, 198, 204,
    205, 216
    Head of, *see* Pile
Inter-Services
    Reconnaissnce
    Department (ISRD), 189
Inter-Services Research
    Bureau, 24
'Inter-Service Signal Unit
    6', 135
INTRANSITIVE, 91
INVENTOR, 126, 128
Ionides, David, 61
Ionides, Michael, 54
Isaac, I. (*Westmorland*), 271
Isadore, 127
ISLD, *see* Inter-Services
    Liaison Department
Italian Military Intelligence
    Service (SIM), 138
Italian Secret Police
    (OVRA), 252
Italian Section (J), 23, 100,
    138
    Head of, *see* Roseberry
IVOR, 272

Jack, Archie, 150
Jackson, E., 264
JACOB, 272
Jacobi, Gerard, 123
Jacqueline, 112, 129
Jacquot, 224
Jambroes, George, 96
JAMES, 272
James, Helen, 110–12
Janyk, C., 127
Jaques, Victor, 207
Jasinek, Lubomir, 91
JAYWICK, 283
Jazwinski, Jan, 27
Jeanclaude, D. (*Shilling*),
    271
Jebb, Gladwyn, 18, 59
JEDBURGH, 200, 202, 223,
    230–2, 236–9, 253
Jefferis, (Sir) Millis, 16
Jempson, F. J., 101
Jepson, Selwyn, 110, 257
Jewish Agency, 13, 50
JOAN-ELEANOR, 284
JOCKEY, 127, 128, 224, 228

Joe, 128
Joew, 120, 128
Johannessen, Poul, 81
Johansson, Elsa, 13
Johns, Philip L., 101–3,
    250, 264, 280
Johnson, Owen (*Gael*), 219,
    224
Johnson, R. A., 257
Johnston, F. (*Illinois*), 271
Johnstone, E., 262, 265
Joint Intelligence Committee
    (JIC), 79, 246
    Chairman of, *see*,
    Cavendish-Bentinck
Jones, George (*Isadore*), 127,
    226
Jones, G. D., 224
Jones, Sydney (*Félix/Elie*),
    127
Jones, William, 146, 147,
    282
Jonge, Ernst de, 97
Jongelie, Cmmdr, 96
Jonovic, Yovan, 56
Jonsson, T., 265
Jordaan, Han, 94, 95
JOSEPHINE, 32, 33, 44
JOSEPHINE B, 33
Judge, M., 263
JUGGLER, 130, 228
JULIAN, 273
Jumeau, Claude, 127
Juncker, G. F., 265
Justin (Cohen), 224, 228
Justin (Rake), 225

Kadulski, Marian, 47
Kane, Claude Jumeau, 128
Kanellopoulos, Pan, 170,
    277
Kansas, 272
Kappius, Anne, 241
Kappius, Jupp, 241
Kay, S., 263
Kayser, Robert, 110
Keary, F. E., 26, 258
Keat, 192
Keble, C. M., 54, 60, 63,
    67, 141, 156, 166, 170,
    250
Kell, Sir Vernon, 7
Kellas, A. R. H., 257
Kemp, Peter, 15, 47, 141–3,
    207, 240, 247, 281

Kempei'tai, 176, 191–3
Kendall, F. W., 182
Kennedy, A. M., 268, 269
Kennedy, John, 15
Kent, 270
Kentucky, 272
Kenyon, P. H. T., 262
Kergolay, Comte A. de
   (*Joew*), 120, 128
Kerneval, J. (*Carnarvon*),
   271
Kerry, F. E., 263
Keswick, David J., 107, 135,
   261, 263, 266
Keswick, W. John, 212, 259,
   260, 266
Key, A. W. (*Wampaum*), 270
Key, S., 265
Keyhoe, Robert R. (*Peseta*),
   232, 271
Keyser, Maj., 26
Khan, Noor Inayat
   (*Madeleine*), 2, 118, 119,
   125, 127, 275
Kidd, J. G., 258
Kier, A., 262
Kiffer, Raoul, 36, 110, 125
Kildare, 270
Killery, Valentine, 173, 186,
   266
Killick, J. D., 257
Kindl, Vaclav, 91
King's Flight, 44
Kinross, 271
Kintyre, 273
Klauber, G. I., 258
Kliemann, Maj., 123
Klooss, Barend, 94
Klop, Dirk, 90
Klugmann, James, 54, 61,
   64, 65, 151, 278
Knierly (*Suffolk*), 271
KNIFE, 16
Knight, A. G., 257, 264
Knight, Claude T., 26, 88,
   258
Knight, Donald, 148
Knight, Maxwell, 221
Knight, Peggy (*Nicole*), 128
KNOTHEAD, 214
Knott, Jack, 178, 182
Knox, B. M. (*Kentucky*), 272
Kolarik, Ivan, 91
Kombol, Nikola, 150
Kong, 206

Kooker, I. (*Thaler*), 270
Kopkow, Horst, 123
Kouba, Bohuslav, 91
Koutsoyiannopoulos, Capt.,
   70, 165
Krafft, Mathilde, 111
Krain, 186
Krebs, 75
Kreipe, Gen., 163
Kroner, 270
Krutki, Bernard, 36
Krzymowski, Stanislaw, 28
Kubis, Jan, 89, 91
Kupek, 272

Labit, Henri (*Leroy*), 35, 127
LABOURER, 126–8, 229
LACKEY, 126
Lady, 12
Lafont, Henri, 109
Lagier, Raymond, 30
Lalatovic, Mirko, 56, 57
Laming, Richard V., 90, 94,
   100
Lancastria, 228
Lancelot, 199
Land, Paul, 244
Landes, Roger (*Aristide*),
   224, 225
Lane, Miss, 257
Lang, Derek, 167
Langard, E. (*Dimu*), 128
Langdon, 128
Langelaan, George
   (*Langdon*), 124, 128
Langlade, François de, 174,
   185, 197, 208, 210
Langley, Arthur, 14
Langley, James, 26
Lanis, Maurice (*Colin*), 128,
   228, 284
Larcher, M. L., 128
Larden, George, 79
LaRosée, James (*Estèphe*),
   225
Larsen, Harold P., 236
Larson, William F.
   (*Leander*), 225, 237
Lassen, Anders, 86
Lassere, J. (*Wicklow*), 273
Lasson, H. L., 265
Last, E. C., 26, 258, 263
Latour, Jacques, 128
Laurent (Basin), 126
Laurent (Steele), 130

Lausucq, Henri (*Aramis*),
   224, 228
Lauwers, Huub, 92–4, 99,
   253
Laval, Pierre, 135
Lawrence, Arthur, 15, 50
Lawrence, T. E., 14
Layton, Sir Geoffrey, 174,
   188
Leake, Philip, 70, 86, 141,
   266
Leander, 237
Leb, D. (*Michigan*), 272
Lebel, F. (*Loire*), 272
Le Chene, Marie (*Adèle*),
   128
Le Chene, P. L. (*Grégoire*),
   128
Leccia, M., 128
Ledoux, Georges (*Tir*), 128
Ledoux, Jacques, 119, 128
LEE, 237, 273
Lee, Lionel (*Mechanic*), 119,
   128
Lees, Michael, 147, 248,
   282, 285
Lefebvre, René, 110, 122
Lefort, Cicely (*Alice*), 128
Lefrandt, Cmmdr, 212
Legare, Thomas (*Sack*), 225
Légion Belge, 101
Legrand, L. (*Franc*), 272
Legrand, R. (*Centime*), 272
Le Harival, Jean C., 128,
   257
Leicester, 273
Leigh, Vera (*Simone*), 128
Leigh Fermor, Patrick, 158,
   278
Leinster, 273
Leix, 270
Lejeune, C. (*Rupee*), 271
Lencement, R., 44, 128
Leopold, 129
Lepage, Fernand, 101
Lepage, M., 128
Leroy, 127
Lesage, J. E. (*Cosmo*), 229
Lesar, Sgt, 150
Lesout, E. (*Tristan*), 128,
   228
Letac, Joel (*Joe*), 32, 128
Letac, Yves, 128
Letty, Angus, 97
Levalois, G. (*Summer*), 272

Levant Fishing Patrol, 139
LEVEE, 45
Levine, Edward, 128
L'Herminier, Capt., 137
Liba, Shika Bin, 177
LICENSEE, 239
Liewer, Philippe (*Clement*), 229, 237, 238
LIKEWISE, 193
Likomba, 86
Litalien, Joseph (*Jacquot*), 225
Limerick, 273
Lincoln, 270
LINCOLN, 133
Lindau, Leon, 245
Lindberg, Konrad, 12, 74
LINDSEY, 225
Lindsey, Peter, 181
Lindstrom, Sgt, 150
Linge, Martin, 75
Linlithgow, Lord, 184, 283
Lionel, 126
LIONTAMER, 127, 128, 228, 284
Lise, 110, 129
Lishman, H. M., 262
LLAMA, 64
Llewellyn, Lord, 151
Lloyd, I. D., 264
Lloyd, Lord, 18
Lockwood, Chester, 167
Lodge, Maj., 212
Loewe, Lionel, 90, 250
Lohan, L. G. Sammy, 276, 277
Loire, 272
Loi Teck, 175, 282
Lomenech, Daniel, 29
LONGSHANKS, 186, 187
Loosmore, R. (*Lundy*), 270
Louba, 223
Louise, 130, 229, 239
Louisiana, 272
Loustaunau-Lacau, Georges, 41
Lovett-Campbell, L. V., 199
Low Countries Section (LC), 103
    Head of, *see* Johns
Low, Nigel, 43, 278
Lowe, J. G. D., 192, 211
LOYTON, 284
Lucas, 127
Lucas, R. A. (*Caithness*), 273

Lucien, 225
Ludovic, 225
Lukastik, Vojtech, 91
Lundy, 270, 272
LUXE, 245
Lyall, Archie, 10
Lynch, G. T., 257, 264
Lyon, Robert, 128, 224, 227
Lys, 271
Lyttelton, Oliver, 131

Macalister, John (*Valentin*), 115, 116, 128
MacArthur, Douglas, 189
Macartney, Wilfred, 7
McBain, G., 128
McCaffery, Jock, 138, 241, 265
McCarthy, Denis, 188
McCrindle, Eric, 198
MacDougall, L. D. (*Argyll*), 270
McFie, P., 257
McGowan, J. E. (*Quarter*), 273
MacIntosh, Charles, 133, 281
McIntyre, Capt., 166
Mackay, T. D., 282
Mackenzie, Colin H., 184–6, 196, 197, 206, 210, 256
Mackenzie, Ian, 58, 150
Mackenzie, I. K., 225, 264
McKenzie, John, 128
Mackenzie, Steven, 29
Mackenzie, Prof. William, 5, 247, 276, 284
McLallen, Maj., 232
Maclean, Sir Fitzroy, 63, 67–9, 142, 148, 149, 278, 282
Maclean, N. M., 267
McLean, Billy, 70, 141, 143, 171
McMillan, Capt., 179, 180
Macmillan, Harold, 3
McMullen, J., 203
McPherson, R. (*Anselme*), 273
Macrae, Stuart, 14, 277
MAD DOG, 47, 48
Madeleine, 127
Maessen, 97
MAHOUT, 200

Maid Honor, 86
Maine, 272
Maingard, René (*Dédé*), 225
Maingot, Graham, 13
Maisky, Ivan, 63
Maitre, R. (*Donegall*), 270
Malaya Section, 185
    Head of, *see* Goodfellow
Malayan Communist Party, (MCP), 175, 176
Mallaby, Richard, 138
Mallet, Sir Victor, 79
Malraux, Claude (*Cicero*), 128
Malval, Baron de, 276
Manderstam, Leopold, 86, 266, 280
Manesson, Jean, 128
Maniu, Juliu, 70, 153
Mann, J., 265
Manning, Capt., 26
Manuel, André, 30
Marcel, 112
Marcelin, 273
March, J., 262, 265
Marchand, Joseph, 225, 227
Marchand, P. (*Ulster*), 270
Marchant, E. (*Charente*), 272
Marchant, G. (*Rutland*), 270
Marchant, J. J. (*Somerset*), 271
March-Phillips, Gus, 86
Marenches, Comte de, 108
Marguerite, 112
Marie, 225, 229
MARIE-CLAIRE, 234, 235
Mariette, 126, 227
Marissal, Jean, 102
Marks, Hugh, 80
Marks, Leo, 235, 252, 253, 285
MARKSMAN, 219, 227
Markstein, George, 277
Marquet, Adrien, 101
Marriott, Henry, 24, 38, 106
Marsac, André (*End*), 108, 110
Marshall, Robert, 113, 125
Marshall-Cornwall, (Sir) James, 77, 279
Masson, G. (*Halfpenny*), 271
Martial, 270
Martin, John, 13, 25
Martin, Maurice (*Adam*), 225
Martin, W. B., 190

Martinot, P. M., 128, 228
MARYLAND, 139
MASON, 225, 228
Mason, Michael, 10, 137
Massachusetts, 272
Massey, L. H., 258, 263
MASSINGHAM, 135, 137–9
Massoni, A. (*Dumbarton*), 271
Masterman, J. C., 278
Masterson, Tom, 10, 54, 154, 266
Mata Hari, 176
Matthews, D. D., 283
Mathieu, René (*Aimé*), 128
MATRIARCH, 211
Mattei, Pierre (*Gaétan*), 128
Maude, J. C. (*Leicester*), 273
Maugenet, Albert (*Benoit*), 128
Maunsell, Raymund, 55
MAURICE, 273
Mauthausen, 42, 141, 241
Maxime, 227
Maxwell, Gavin, 85, 267, 280
Maxwell, Terence, 53–6, 60, 176
MAY, 190
Maydwell, Charles, 54, 70, 153
Mayer, Frederick, 243
Mayer, John A., 128, 229
Mayfield, Brian, 16
Mayhew, Christopher, 276
Mayo, 272
MCP, *see* Malayan Communist Party
Meath, 273
Mechanic, 128
Meisel, Hilde, 242
Meldrum, Sgt, 179
Menzies, Sir Stewart, 22, 80, 136, 247, 280
Menzies, T. S. (*Essex*), 273
Merioneth, 273
MERLIN, 64
Merlin, 199
Merritt, Lt, 141
Merritt, Sgt, 179
Mersiol, C. C. R. (*Yonne*), 272
Mesnard, 227
Metaxas, Ioannis, 157
Metherell, R. John, 54, 55, 268

Metianu, Silviu, 70, 153
Meyer, P. E., 225
Michel, 109, 126
Michel, François, (*Dispenser*), 116, 128, 233
Michel, Henri, 105
Michigan, 272
MICKLEHAM, 213
Micklethwaite, Guy, 140
Middlesex, 271
MIDWAY, 133
MI5, *see* Security Service
MI6, *see* Secret Intelligence Service
MI9, *see* Escape and Evasion Service
Mihailovic, Draza, 56, 60, 62–6, 68, 69, 144–8
Mikkelsen, Max, 81
Miks, Arnost, 91
Miles, Brig., 139
Milhaud, Roger (*Aimé*), 129
Miljkovic, Sgt, 58
MILL, 101
Millar, George (*Emile*), 225, 229, 234
Millar, R. S., 267
Miller, Francis P., 230
Miller, James, 62
Millett, Stephen, 230
Mills, Cyril, 30
Mills, K. M. D., 47, 258
Mills, W. E., 257, 264
Milne, E. A., 259, 264
Milner, Fred, 84
Milorg, 76
MINISTER, 126, 128, 225, 228
Ministry of Economic Warfare, 59, 209, 246
Minister of, *see* Dalton
Mink, Anton, 98, 104
Minney, R. J., 276
Minshall, Merlin, 11, 277
MI(R), 14–18, 48–51, 55, 56, 75, 173
Misselbrook, Sgt, 176
Mississippi, 272
MISSIVE, 204
Mitchell, Leslie, 25, 26, 74
Mockler-Ferryman, E. E., 256, 261
Molenaar, Jan, 94, 96
Mollinger, Frits, 185, 197, 211

Moncreiffe, Ian, 163, 282
MONICA, 236
MONK, 129, 130
MONKEY, 138
MONKEYPUZZLE, 111, 112
Monkhouse, Allan, 62, 278
Monmouth, 272
Monnier, C., 235
Monroe, Sgt, 151
Montagu-Pollock, William, 79
Montcler, S. (*Anglesey*), 272
Montgomery, R. (*Dollar*), 273
MONTY, 273
Moore, K., 257
Moore, R. E. (*New Mexico*), 272
Mooy, Arie, 96
Moravec, Frantisek, 90, 280
Morel, Gerard H., 120, 129
Morgan, A., 144, 258
Morgan-Giles, Morgan, 139
Morhange, J. (*Roscommon*), 272
Morris, Harry, 47, 266
Morrison, E. M., 258, 264, 265
Morse, M., 262
Mortier, Robert, 239
Mortimore, L. H., 266
Mortlock, D. G., 264
Morton, (Sir) Desmond, 18, 19, 62, 83
MO Section, 24, 46
Head of, *see* Dodds-Parker
Moss, Sir George, 173
Moss, W. Stanley, 162, 163, 208, 248, 282, 283, 285
Mott, Norman, 275
Moulin, Jean, 234
Mountbatten, Lord Louis, 201, 208–10, 276, 284
MUD, 190, 191
Muirhead, David, 47, 266
Müller, Gen., 277, 282
MULLET, 192
MULLIGATAWNY, 151
Mulsant, Pierre, 129, 225
Munck, Ebbe, 80, 81
Mundinger, R. D. (*Marcelin*), 273
Munn, John, 135, 266
Munro, P. H., 212
Munthe, Malcolm, 15, 25, 79

Murphy, J. J. V. F. Peter, 209, 283
Murphy, W. A., 264
Murray, M. P., 261, 262
Musgrove, Col, 232
MUSICIAN, 126, 130, 228, 233
Mutin, 29
Myer, B., 257, 265
Myers, Edmund, 71, 142, 164, 166, 168–70, 172, 248, 281

Nadine, 129
Narcisse, 126, 219
NATION, 202
Natzweiler, 125
Nearne, Eileen (*Rose*), 129, 225
Nearne, Jacqueline, 234
Neave, Airey, 26
Nebraska, 270
Nedeljkovic, Radoje, 58
Neel, Tony, 140, 143
Neilson, D. J. (*Delaware*), 271
Nelson, Sir Frank, 1, 12, 22, 24, 38, 50, 53, 71, 74, 80, 183, 250
NEPTUNE, 220
Neron, 219
NERONIAN, 65, 278
Nesque, 273
Netherlands Section (N), 23, 24, 90–101, 103, 104, 120, 229, 253, 275
Head of, *see* Bingham, Blizard, Laming
Neunier, Jean (*Mesnard*), 227
Nevada, 272
New Mexico, 272
Newitt, Prof. D. M., 26, 269, 264
Newman, Isadore (*Pépé*), 129
Newnham, Maurice, 85
NEWSAGENT, 225, 227
Newton, Alfred (*Arthur*), 129
Newton, Harry (*Hubert*), 129
NICHOLAS, 273
Nicholas, 228
Nicholas, Elizabeth, 2, 274–7, 280, 282
Nicholls, Arthur, 141

Nicholls, F. W., 256, 258, 261, 264
Nicholson, N. F., 213
Nicole, 127
Nielson, Peter, 81
Niermayer, Willem, 97
Nimmo, Jimmy, 198
Nixon, F. Hilton B., 10, 13, 258, 263
NKVD, 65, 71
Noble, G. R., 257
Noel, 224
Noone, Patrick, 282
Norfolk, 271
Norman, Gilbert (*Archambaud*), 112, 129
Norrish, F. H., 257, 263, 265
North, ASO, 258
Northrop, Anthony, 143
Northumberland, 273
Novikov, Kirill, 154
Now It Can Be Told, 2, 274
Norwegian Section (N), 74–80
Head of, *see* Hambro, Wilson
NUTHATCH, 64
Nyberg, H. A., 257

O 24, 188, 211
Oades, R. C. E., 54, 61
Oakley-Hill, Dayrell, 143, 247, 263
OATMEAL, 193, 194, 283
O'Brien, Terence, 192
O'Bryan Tear, Terence L., 247, 257
Obolensky, Serge (*Butch*), 225, 237
O'Connor, A. B. K., 264
Odette, 126
O'Donnell, E., 258
O'Donovan, Patrick, 58, 59
O'Dwyer, A. B., 183
Office of Co-ordination of Information (OCI), 133
Office of Strategic Services (OSS), 84, 133–6, 145, 146, 149, 206, 213–16, 218, 219, 228–30, 232, 241–5
Chief of, *see* Donovan
OSS *101*, 200, 214, 215

OSS *303*, 215
OSS *404*, 215
OSS *505*, 215
Ogden-Smith, C. (*Dorset*), 271
Ogilvie-Grant, Mark, 171
Olav, 77
OLDELL, 74
Olive, 130
Oliver, 126
Oliver, B. H., 257, 264
Oliver, Philip, 208
Olivier, 129
Olsen, H. W., 77
Olsen, Roland, 82
Opalka, Adolf, 89, 91
Operational Groups (OG), 223, 225, 236–8
Orabona, 129
Oranowski, Zygmunt, 27
ORATOR, 128
Orde Dienst, 96, 99, 100
Ore, 270
O'Reilly, Thomas, 79, 266
Oriental Mission, 173–83
Head of, *see* Killery
Orkney, 271
Ortiz, Peter J., 218
Ortt, Felix, 97
OSS, *see* Office of Strategic Services
OSSEX, 230
Ostojic, Zaharije, 56, 57
O'Sullivan, Paddy (*Stocking*), 225
OUT DISTANCE, 89, 91
OVERCLOUD, 120, 127, 128
OVERLORD, 228, 229, 235
OVRA, *see* Italian Secret Police
Oxford, 12
Oxford (Allet), 270
OYSTER, 63
Ozanne, Maj., 252

Padumananda, Prasert, 206
Paget, Mrs J., 263
Paget, Sir James, 83
PAINTER, 244
Palmer, A., 264
Palmer, Anthony, 15, 25
PANICLE, 207
Papaderos, Stelio, 160
Papanicholis, 162
Paquebot, 129

Pardi, Paul, 129
Pariselle, R. (*Kupek*), 272
Parker, Ralph, 10
Parkinson, R. A. (*Fife*), 270
Parlevliet, Herman, 95
Parr, A. C., 257, 264
PARSON, 119, 126, 127, 130
Parsons, I. D., 267
Passmore, Brian, 177
Passport Control Office (PCO), 8
Passy, *see* Dewavrin
PAT, 111, 119
Patrice, 129
PATRICK, 225
Patterson, Capt, 150
Pau, 206
PAUL, 273
Paul (Peulevé), 129
Paul (Poitras), 225
Paul, King of Yugoslavia, 142
Paulette, 129
Pavelka, Frantisek, 88, 91
Pavlic, Paul, 145
Pawson, David, 52, 54, 56, 70, 266
PCO, *see* Passport Control Office
Pe, Thein (*Merlin*), 199
Peace, H. C., 257
Pearson, C. W., 177
Pearson, D. M., 129
Pearson, James, 61
Pearson, S. A., 258
Pechal, Oldrich, 91
PEDAGOGUE, 129, 239
Pedersen, Frithof, 12, 74
PEDLAR, 121
Pedro (Cauchi), 126
Pedro (Simon), 130
Pel, H. G., 188, 197
Pelham-Burn, Hamish, 85, 266
Pellay, Marcel (*Paquebot*), 129
Pembroke, 270
Pendlebury, John, 158, 282
Pépé, 129
PERCENTAGE, 88
Percival, A. E., 175, 194
PERCY PINK, 225, 238
PERCY RED, 237, 238

PEREGRINE, 64
Perkins, Donald, 10, 52
Perkins, Dudley, 160
Perkins, Harold P., 26, 88, 241, 247, 258, 263
Perkins, John, 46
PERMIT, 239
Perth, 270
Pertschuk, Maurice (*Eugène*), 129
Peseta, 271
Peters, Frederic, 85
Petersen, Knud, 81
Peterson, Sir Maurice, 19
Petro, Peter, 266
Petropavlovsky, Vladimir, 181
Peulevé, Harry (*Paul*), 121, 129, 224, 227
Pfennig, 270
Philby, H. A. R., 143
PHILIP, 273
Philip, Aidan, 51
Philippe, 232
Philipson, Ft Lt, 26
Phillips, Doug, 165
Phillips, D., 268
PHONO, 120
PHUKEO, 208
PHYSICIAN, 112
PICKAXE, 245
Pickering, F. R., 26, 257
Pickersgill, Frank (*Bertrand*), 115–17, 120, 129, 281
Pickford, J. C. D., 263
Pickles, M. J. T., 241, 263
Pierlot, H., 59, 101, 102
Pierre, 103
PIERRE-JACQUES, 130
Pilditch, Sir Denys, 186
Pile, Wg Cmmdr, 173
PILGRIM, 133
PIMENTO, 126, 223, 224
Piquet-Wicks, Eric, 30, 266, 277
Pirie, E. B. M., 263
Pirie, Ian, 158
PLANE, 109
Planning Section, 231
Head of, *see* Rowlandson
Plewman, Elaine (*Gaby*), 129, 227
Pleydell-Bouverie, Bartholomew, 84, 137, 266

Plowden, Humphrey, 13
Pointon, A. C. Peter, 185, 197, 203
Poitras, Edwin (*Paul*), 225
Polish Section (MP), 88
Head of, *see* Perkins
Political Warfare Executive (PWE), 59, 125
Pollard, Hugh, 10
Pollitt, Harry, 221
Pollock, Sir George, 26, 50, 53, 54, 257, 265
POLLUX, 74
Ponsonby, James, 132
Pool, Francis, 159
Popieszalski, Anton, 240
Portal, Sir Charles, 43, 44, 278
Porter, Ivor, 70, 131, 153, 154, 281
Pospisil, Frantisek, 91
Posse, Countess Emelie, 79
POSTMASTER, 86, 87
Potter, H. M., 262
Potucek, Jiri, 91
Poulain, Edmond, 42
Pound, 273
Prentice, G., 261
Prester, Julio, 243
PRESTON, 240
Prévost, Lucien, 122
PRICHARD, 203
Pridi, Luang, 203–5
PRIEST, 129
Prinz Eugen, 38
PRIVET, 115
Profumo, John, 3
Prometheus, *see* Bakirdzis
Prometheus II, *see* Koutsoyiannopoulos
PROSPER, 106, 110–12, 115, 126, 128–30, 226, 233, 251
PRUNUS, 129
Puget, H. (*Brecknock*), 273
Pugh, Lewis, 186, 187
Punt, Laurens, 98, 104
PWE, *see* Political Warfare Executive

Quarter, 272
Quayle, (Sir) Anthony, 139, 143, 281, 283
Quennell, Hugh, 47, 132, 266

QUENTIN, 273
QUININE, 273

Rabagliati, Euan, 26, 92, 96, 97, 100
Rabinovitch, Alec (*Arnaud*), 129
RACKETEER, 225, 228
Raczkowski, Czeslaw, 28
Radema, Evert, 97
Radio Security Service (RSS), 76, 123
Raemaekers, R. L., 258
Rafferty, Brian (*Dominique*), 129, 224, 226
Ragweed, 242
Railton, R., 263
Raincourt, Capt. (*Ambreve*), 270
Rake, Denis (*Justin*), 225
Ram, W. F., 256
Rand, G. W., 177
RANJI, 150, 153
RANKIN B, 237
Rapotec, Lt, 58
Ras, Gosse, 94
Rashid Ali, 51
RAVEN, 64
Raven, J. D. (*Half Crown*), 271
Ray, J. A., 256
Reade, Arthur, 157, 162
Rechermann, Charles, 129
Redding, Claude, 39, 40, 129
Redward, F. G., 263
Ree, Harry (*César*), 224, 227
Reeves, Lt (*Olivier*), 129
Regan, Sgt, 179
Regnier, Jean, 225
Reid, John, 282
Reile, Oscar, 123
REINDEER, 202
Reis, 273
RELATOR, 47, 48, 86
REMARKABLE, 190, 191
REMORSE, 213
Renaix, André, 244
Renault-Roulier, Gilbert, 29, 230
Rendell, Sandy, 164
REPARTEE, 150
République Français Section (RF), 31, 33, 43, 59, 105, 107, 114, 120

Head of, *see* Hutchison, Piquet-Wicks
RESIDENCY, 192, 211
RETALIATE, 211
Reynolds, Elizabeth (*Elizabeth*), 129, 240, 276
Rheam, George T. T., 85, 269
Rhode Island, 272
Rhodes, F. W., 268
Rice, 273
Richard, 127
Richards, F. Brooks, 135, 137, 266
Richardson, Charles, 15
Richardson, L. J. W., 47, 132, 258, 262, 268
Rickman, Alexander, 10, 12, 25, 28, 83, 277
Riddell, Richard, 141
Ridland, J., 265
Riedl, Otmar, 88, 91
Rietschoten, Jan van, 95, 103
RIMAU, 282
Rimbaut, R. (*Tyrone*), 272
RINGLET, 137
RINUS, 102, 103
Ritchie, A. P., 261
Rivet, Louis, 23, 136
Riviere, Gabriel, 42
Rizzo, E. V. H., 34, 257
ROACH, 109
Robert, 225
Roberts, C. F., 265
Roberts, Douglas, 15
Roberts, Trooper, 141
Robertson, E. J., 26
Robertson, J. A., 262
Robin, 115
Robinson, A. M. F. J., 258, 264
Robinson, Sgt, 145
Robinson, William, 282
Rocca, V. M. (*West Virginia*), 272
Roche, Raymond, 129
Rodney, Frederick, 42
Rodolphe, 227
Roger, 227
ROGER, 284
Rogers, Lindsay, 147, 282
Rogers, Sgt, 150
Rogerson, C. S., 264

Rolfe, Lilian (*Nadine*), 129, 225
Rommel, Erwin, 65, 164
Rona, 270
RONALD, 273
Ronglou, J. (*Anachore*), 271
Roosevelt, Franklin D., 133, 208, 214
Roosevelt, Kermit, 143, 281, 282, 283
Rootham, Jasper, 146, 147, 150, 282
Roper-Caldbeck, Terence, 84
Rose, 128, 225
Roscommon, 272
Roseberry, C. L., 26, 138, 257, 263
Rosher, Maj., 176
Ross, 272
Rottball, Christain, 81
ROUGHSHOD, 241
Rouneau, M., 225
Rousset, Marcel (*Léopold*), 129
ROVER, 229
Rowat, E. I., 259
Rowden, Diana (*Paulette*), 129
Rowecki, Gen., 240
Rowlandson, N. W., 231
Roxburgh, 272
Royal Air Force, 139, 206, 207, 222
Special Duties Squadrons, 44, 45, 48, 58, 137, 202
Royal Navy,
HMS *Clyde*, 137
HMS *Fidelity*, 34, 43, 46, 47, 277
HMS *Maidstone*, 137
HMS *Severn*, 193
HMS *Tactician*, 192, 204
HMS *Tally Ho*, 190
HMS *Taurus*, 188
HMS *Templar*, 192, 211
HMS *Thorn*, 58
HMS *Thule*, 180
HMS *Thunderbolt*, 159
HMS *Tigris*, 32
HMS *Torbay*, 160, 212
HMS *Triumph*, 56
HMS *Truculent*, 192
HMS *York*, 162

Royal Victoria Patriotic
  School (RVPS), 101
Rubinstein, R. A. (*Augure*),
  271
Rucker, Maj., 135
RUDDER, 139
Rudelatt, Yvonne
  (*Jacqueline*), 112, 129
Ruh, Toni, 244
Rupee, 271
RUPERT, 273
Rusbridger, James, 125
Russell, C. V., 262
Russell, David, 70, 146, 153
Russian Section, 71
  Head of, *see* Seddon
Ruthi, Viktor, 243
Rutland, 270

Sabatier, Gilbert, 135
Sabotage Service, *see* Section
  D
Sabourin, Roger, 130
Sacha, 225
SACRISTAN, 126, 127
Sadler, R. R., 258
SAINT, 224, 228
St Genies, Baron de
  (*Lucien*), 127, 225
SALESMAN, 109, 225, 229,
  237
Salis, John de, 54
Salt, (Dame) Barbara, 132
Samuel, Hon. A. G., 264
Sandford, Dan, 54
Sansom, Odette (*Lise*), 3,
  110, 121, 130
SAPLING, 141
Sarrette, Paul, 130, 225, 227
Sartin, John, 177
SAS, *see* Special Air Service
SATIRIST, 130
SAVANNA (France), 32, 35,
  44
SAVANNA (Yugoslavia), 150
Save, 271
Savy, W. J., 225
Sawyer, Corp., 181
Scandinavian Section (S),
  23, 24, 25, 80, 82, 137
  Head of, *see* Hambro,
  Hollingworth, Stagg
Scapin, 235
Scappe, Hidde, 91
Schaerrer, Henri, 42

Scharnhorst, 38
Scheepens, Jan, 211
Schieldrop, D. M., 265
Schneidau, Philip, 36, 43,
  44
Schock, A. L., 130
SCHOLAR, 126, 225, 228
Schonen, P. de (*Argentier*),
  271
Schrage, Wiek, 92
Schwatschko, A., 130
SCIENTIST, 122, 127, 224,
  226, 233
Sclater, Arthur, 77
SCONCE, 141
Scorgie, Capt., 150
Scott, Capt., 166
Scott, Kenneth, 150, 151,
  208
Scott-Harston, J. C., 15
SCULLION II, 127, 129, 219
SCULPTOR, 141
Seagrim, Hugh, 181, 196
Seahorse, 130
Seailles, Pierre, 224
SEALING WAX, 120
Sealog, 47
Searle, R. A., 257
Seawolf, 47
Seawright, R. G., 262
Sébastien, 127
Sebes, Hendrik, 94
Secret Intelligence Service
  (SIS), 1, 3–10, 18–31,
  35, 37, 40–3, 46–8, 52,
  55–8, 61–3, 67, 72,
  74–9, 82, 90, 97–101,
  103, 104, 124, 131–8,
  144–6, 150–2, 157–61,
  169–73, 176, 179,
  190–4, 196–200, 209,
  216, 222, 235, 243,
  246–53
  Chief of, *see* Menzies,
  Sinclair
Section D, 9–14, 17–19,
  22, 28, 48–51, 53, 55,
  56, 60, 61, 70, 71, 82,
  84, 101, 140, 155, 159,
  167, 249, 251
Security Intelligence Middle
  East (SIME), 125
  Head of, *see* Maunsell
Security Section, 231
  Head of, *see* Senter

Security Service (MI5), 122,
  221
  Director-General of, *see*
  Kell
Seddon, A. D., 71, 259
Sehmer, John, 146, 241
Selborne, Lord, 39, 59, 68,
  155, 187, 223, 276
Selby, Neil, 145, 150
Selection Trust, 9
Selkirk, 271
Selune, 272
Senter, John, 77, 259, 262
SEQUENCE, 206
SERBONIAN, 150
Sereni, Enzo, 52
Sergueiev, Lily, 123, 181
Serre, 270
Serreules, Claude-Bernard
  (*Scapin*), 235
Service Action (SA), 30
Service de Renseignements, 23,
  30, 136
Seth, Ronald,
Seton-Watson, Hugh, 10,
  61, 250
Sevenet, Henri (*Rodolphe*),
  130, 224, 227
Seymour, Charles, 26
Seymour, George, 141
Seymour, K. (*Skye*), 272
SFHQ, *see* Special Forces
  Headquarters
Sharrett, Moshe, 13, 50
Shaw, A. P. (*Olive*), 130
SHELBURNE, 29
Sheppard, Robert (*Patrice*),
  130
Sheppard, Rufus, 70, 166,
  172
Sheridan, Leslie F., 260,
  262
Sherren, E. H., 26, 135,
  263
Sherwood, Sgt, 77
Shewing, A., 257, 264
Shilling, 271
Shiloah, Reuven, 50
Shinko, Stevan, 58
SHIPWRIGHT, 225, 232, 238
Shropshire, 273
Shufflebotham, Sgt, 182
Shwei, Tin (*Lancelot*), 199
Siam Section, 203–8
  Head of, *see* Pointon

Sicherheitsdienst, 8, 63, 108, 113, 118, 121, 122, 125, 233, 239, 252
Signal Section, 73, 179
Head of, *see* Nicholls, Ozanne
Sikorski, Gen., 240
SILVER A, 89, 91
SILVER B, 89, 91
SILVERSMITH, 239
SIM, *see* Italian Military Intelligence Service
Simcox, Anthony, 141
SIME, *see* Security Intelligence Middle East
Simmonds, Tony, 159
Simon, 127
Simon, A., 257
Simon, Jean (*Pedro*), 130
Simon, Octave (*Badois*), 130
Simone, 128
Simovic, Gen., 57
Sinclair, Sir Hugh, 7
Sinclair, Jack, 130
Sinclair, John, 134
Sinclair, Ronald, 153
Singh, Habib, 188
Singlaub, John K. (*Mississippi*), 272
Singlet, 229
Sirois, A. (*Gustave*), 225
SIS, *see* Secret Intelligence Service
Sisselaar, Lt, 211
Sixpence, 271
Skacha, Vladimir, 91
Skepper, Charles (*Bernard*), 130
SKIDDAW, 86
Skilbeck, Cuthbert, 84
Skye, 272
SKYLARK, 74
Sligo, 272
Slim, Gen. Bill, 200, 201
Slocum, Frank, 28, 29
Small, Harry, 208
Smets, Jean, 244
Smiley, David, 70, 140, 141, 143, 171, 281, 282
Smith, Brian O., 179
Smith, Bryce, 208
Smith, C. E. H., 261
Smith, Col, 232
Smith, G. N. (*Lincoln*), 270
Smith, L/A, 145

Smith, L. M., 262
Smith, N. A. (*Ura*), 271
Smith, P. S., 268
Smith-Hughes, Jack, 54, 159
Smolenski, Jozef, 27
Smuts, Gen., 16
Snark, The, 112
Sneum, Thomas, 82
SOE, *see* Special Operations Executive
Solange, 119
Solly-Flood, Peter, 150, 241
Somerset, 271
Somme, 272
Solway, 219
SONGKLA, 208
Soskice, Victor (*Solway*), 219
Soustelle, Jacques, 222, 283
Southgate, Maurice (*Hector*), 130, 228, 234
SPARTAN, 231
Spears, D. A. (*Escaut*), 273
Special Air Service (SAS), 232, 236, 247, 248, 253
Special Forces Headquarters (SFHQ), 218, 219, 248
Special Operations Executive (SOE),
Director of, *see* Gubbins, Hambro, Nelson
Special Training Schools (STS), 17, 85, 247
STS 2 Bellasis, 86, 89, 268
3 Stodham Park, 85, 268
5 Wanborough Manor, 31, 86, 268
6 West Court, 231, 268
7 Winterfold, 269
14 Briggens, 269
17 Brickendonbury, 85, 269
18 Frogmore Farm, 268
19 Gardner's End, 269
20a Pollard's Park, 269
20b Pollard's Wood Grange, 269
21 Arisaig House, 267
22 Rhubana Lodge, 267
23 Meoble Lodge, 267
23b Swordland, 267
24a Inverie House, 267

24b Glaschoille, 267
25a Garramor House, 267
25b Cammusdarrach, 267
25c Traigh House, 267
26a Drumintoul Lodge, 76, 279
26b Glenmore Lodge, 76, 26
31 The Rings, 267
32a Harford House, 267
32b Saltmarsh, 267
32c Blackbridge, 268
33 The House on the Shore, 268
34 The Drokes, 268
35 The Vineyards, 268
36 Boarmans, 268
37a Warren House, 268
37b Clobb Gorse, 268
39 Wall Hall, 269
40 Howbury Hall, 268
41 Gumley Hall, 86, 231, 268
42 Roughwood Park, 268
43 Audley End House, 86, 269
44 Gorse Hill, 268
45 Hatherop Castle, 86, 231, 268
46 Chicheley Hall, 86, 269
47 Anderson Manor, 268
50 Water Eaton Manor, 268
51a Dunham House, 85, 135, 231, 269
51b Fulshaw Hall, 269
52 Thame Park, 85, 268
53a Grendon Hall, 268
53b Poundon House, 268
54a Fawley Court, 76, 84, 231, 268
54b Belhaven School, 268
61 Gaynes Hall, 86, 269
63 Warnham Court, 269
65 Milton Hall, 231, 232, 269
101 Singapore, 173, 174
102 Ranath David, 146, 151, 158
103 Oshawa, 84, 133
Spencer Chapman, Freddie, 175, 189, 276, 277, 283
Spiliotopoulos, Col, 169
SPINDLE, 110, 126, 129

Spink, R., 256
SPIRITUALIST, 228
Spiro, Edward, *see*
  Cookridge
Spooner, Frank V., 232, 269
Sporborg, Harry N., 25, 30,
  31, 38, 43, 45, 73–5,
  113, 119, 256, 261
Sporre, Corre, 92
Springhall, Douglas, 65
SPRUCE, 127, 226
Srazil, Stanislav, 91
Stafford, 273
Stagg, Frank, 25, 82
Staggs, Albert, 130, 226
Stalin, Josef, 157
STANLEY, 273
Starring, Mason B.
  (*Nebraska*), 270
Starceviv, Ivan, 150
Starheim, Odd, 74
Stark, Freya, 51
Starr, George (*Hilaire*), 224,
  226
Starr, John (*Bob*), 2, 121,
  130, 229
Starves, Alec, 160
STATIONER, 129, 229
Stawell, W. A. M., 54, 139,
  147, 152, 168, 170, 171
STEEL, 212
STEEL A, 91
Steele, Arthur (*Laurent*), 130
Steiner, H. E., 258
Stephenson, H. N. C., 180
Stephenson, Sir William, 83
STEPMOTHER, 141
Stevens, John, 54, 70, 158,
  159, 168
Stevens, Richard, 8, 9, 90
Stewart, Sir Findlater, 246
Stewart, Gavin, 185, 186,
  196, 197
Stilwell, Joseph, 200, 215
Stirbey, Prince Barbu, 62,
  154
Stirling, 270
Stirling, Bill, 16
Stirling, Frank, 10, 56, 266
Stockbridge, Ralph, 159
STOCKBROKER, 126, 130,
  227
Stocking, 225
Stonehouse, Brian (*Célestin*),
  4, 130, 224, 276

Storrs, P. J. F., 257
Stott, Donald, 166, 167
Stoyka, J. L. (*Ore*), 270
STRIKE OX, 83
Strong, Kenneth, 138
STS, *see* Special Training
  Schools
Stuart, Bill, 62, 145, 150,
  278
Stuart, Sir Campbell, 1, 20
Stubbington, W. H., 177
Student, Karl, 159
Studler, André, 130
Subha, Prince, 207
Suffolk, 271
SUGARLOAF, 211
Summers, J. (*Wyoming*),
  272
Sûreté de l'Etat, 101
  Head of, *see* Lepage
Surrey, 271
SURVEYOR, 119, 126, 130
SUSSEX, 230, 236
Suttill, Francis (*Prosper*),
  111, 112, 130
Svarc, Jaroslav, 91
Svasti, Prince Subha (*Arun*),
  207
SWALLOW, 78
SWEEP, 212
Sweet-Escott, Bickham, 10,
  13, 17, 22, 62, 67, 152,
  164, 260, 277, 278, 282
Sweet-Escott, Louisa, 164
Swinton, Lord, 9
Syers, Kenneth, 150
Sykes, Bill, 84, 232
Sykes, Christopher, 55, 56,
  278
Sylvestre, 130, 226
Szabo, Violette (*Louise*), 130,
  229, 237–9, 276

Tabet, Henri, 36
Tack, G. H. (*Tickie*), 272
Taconis, Thys, 92, 94
Tagore, Rabindranath, 196
Tai Lai, 181, 213
Tailcoat, 225
Talbot, Sir Gerald, 10, 52
Talbot Rice, David, 263
Tambour, Germaine
  (*Annette*), 110 115
Tamplin, Guy, 54, 170
TANK, 143

Taylor, A. H., 256, 261, 262
Taylor, Capt., 209
Taylor, George F., 9, 10, 50,
  60, 67, 134, 187, 196,
  256, 260, 261
Taylor, Jack, 243
Taylor, R. L., 256, 265
Teague-Jones, Reginald,
  133
Teesdale, E. B., 182
Tell, 228
Templer, (Sir) Gerald, 241
Tempo, 150
Tennant, (Sir) Peter, 25, 266
Ter Laak, Johannes, 97
TERRIER, 202
Terwindt, Beatrix, 98
Tessier, P. R., 130
TETHER, 212
Thackthwaite, H. H. A., 257
Thaler, 270
Théodore, 228
Théodule, 225
Thomas, D. F., 263, 264
Thomas, Sir Shenton, 175
Thompson, Frank, 71, 150,
  151
Thompson, G. T. R., 258
Thompson, L/A, 145, 150
Thompson, P. H., 265
Thompson, Robert, 182
Thomson, G. G. (*Cromarty*),
  270
Thornhill, Cudbert, 51, 52,
  55
Thornley, R. H., 26
Thornton, H. N., 256
Thouville, R. (*Leix*), 270
Threlfall, Henry McL., 80,
  139, 152, 241, 256
Tiburce, 227
Tickell, Gerard, 276
Tidmarsh, P. J., 268
Tilman, Bill, 141
Timms, J. A. D., 258, 263
TIMOTHY, 273
TIN, 91
Tissier, P. R., 130
Tito, *see* Broz
Tivey, C. P., 264
Tomlinson, Tommy, 150
Tonkin, J. E., 232
Tonnet, Capt., 103
TONY, 273
Tooke, Colin, 185

Tormonde, 12
Torr, P., 257
Torrance, J. Watt, 15, 25
TORCH, 48, 131, 134, 220
TORTURE, 35
Tosayanonda, Kris, 206
Tovey, Jack, 193
Townson, F., 265
Training Section, 77, 231
  Head of, *see* Wilson, Young
Trappes-Lomax, Capt.,
  177
Trayhorn, F., 141
TREASURER, 129, 225, 228
Trebilcock, H. L., 232
Tremlett, Innes, 175, 187,
  197
Trevor-Wilson, A. G., 136,
  251
Tristan, 128, 228
Trofimov, A. A. (*Gironde*),
  272
TROMBONE, 44
Trotobas, Michael
  (*Sylvestre*), 130, 226
TROY, 34, 35
Truelsen, S. A. P., 265
Truszkowski, R., 258
Turberville, Denis (*Daniel*),
  130
Turcanu, Nikolai, 70, 150,
  153, 154
Turck, Georges (*Christophe*),
  45, 130
Turnbull, Ronald, 79, 266
Turner, Capt., 26
Turner, K. R., 265
Turrell, Guy, 160
Tweeds, 225
TYPICAL, 63, 145, 147, 150
Tyrone, 272
Tyson, John, 231

Ubbink, Johan, 98, 99, 103
Ullmann, P. S. (*Alceste*), 130
Ulster, 270
ULTRA, 63, 64, 67, 122, 250,
  251
Ulysses, 228
UNION, 129
Ura, 271
URCHIN, 126
Uren, Ormond L., 65, 71,
  221, 258
Utah, 273

Vaclik, Josef, 89, 91
Valentin, 115, 128
Vallee, François, 130
Vallet, Lucien, 42
Valrimont, M., 222
van Bilsen, Frans, 99, 280
Vanden Heuvel, Frederick,
  98
van der Giessen, Aat, 97, 98
van der Meerssche, Gaston,
  102
van der Post, Laurens, 183
van der Reyden, Wim, 97,
  104
van der Streicht, P., 257
van Driel, 92
van Dyke, Emil, 244
van Hamel, Lodo, 90, 91
van Hamert, Gerard, 95
van Hart, John (*Half Crown*),
  271
van Hattem, Johan, 91
van Os, Gerard, 102
van Schelle, Jan D., 84, 103
van Serveyt, Maj., 102
Vansittart, G. N., 257
Vansittart, Sir Robert, 220
van Steen, Antonius, 95
van t'Sant, François, 88
VAR, 128
Varnier, Lt, 33
Vautrin, Col, 103
Venner, John F., 256,
  259–62
VEGANIN, 225, 273
VENTRILOQUIST, 126, 224
Ventry, Lord, 257, 265
Vercoe, Capt, 145, 150
Veress, Lazlo, 155
VERGER, 126, 128
Verhaegen, H. P., 258
Verlander, H. (*Sligo*), 272
Vermeulen, J. (*Carlow*), 270
Vermont, 273
Verschoor, Capt., 265
Vetlesen, G. V., 265
Vickers Company, 62
Victor, 127
Viguier, N. (*Sous*), 273
VILLA RESTA, 58
Villeneuve, Col de, 23
Vincent, Hedley, 86, 265
Vining, Charles, 84
Violette, 128
Vire, 271

VIRGINIA, 244
Virginia, 273
Vogt, Ernst, 121
Vomécourt, Jean de, 33, 34,
  40
Vomécourt, Philippe de, 33,
  34, 39–41, 277, 283
Vomécourt, Pierre de (*Lucas;
  Antoine*), 33, 34, 37, 38,
  127, 224
Vukmanovic, Vetozar, 150

Wagstaff, Fred, 179
Walker, A. N., 265
Walker, David, 12, 152
Walker, R. S., 264
Walker, Sgt, 150, 151
Wallace, David, E., 168,
  168, 277, 278
Wallace, D. T., 32
Waller, Capt., 270
Walmsley, U. B., 26, 257
Walters, Leon, 40
Wampaum, 270
Ward, Dame Irene, 3
Warinton-Smyth, Nigel, 46,
  278
Warrell, John, 208
Warren, Alan, 17, 173, 277
Watney, Cyril, 225, 227
Watrous, Capt., 139
Watters, L. J. (*Kansas*), 272
Watts, Capt., 145
Wauchope, L., 261
Waugh, Evelyn, 148
Wavell, Gen. Archie, 51, 55,
  278
Wavrant, G. de (*Aude*), 270
WEASEL, 202
Weber, Hans, 243
Weatherly, Robin, 148
Wedemeyer, Gen., 212
Wegner, Anton, 103
Wells, R. A., 257
Welsh, Eric, 26, 78
Wemyss, Vic, 176, 206
Wesselow, Roger de, 32
Westmorland, 271
West Virginia, 272
Wharton-Tigar, Edward,
  132–4, 213, 266, 277, 281
WHEELWRIGHT, 219, 224,
  226
WHISKY, 71
Whitaker, J. C., 264

White, John A. (*Colorado*), 270
White, Matthew, 164
Whitehead, G., 257
WHITE LADY, 101
Whittington-Moe, E. R. W., 15
Whitty, V. E. (*Ross*), 272
Wicklow, 273
Wiggington, Cmmdr, 54
Wigston, 271
Wilde, R. (*Centavo*), 271
Wilkinson, Ernest (*Alexandre*), 15, 130
Wilkinson, George (*Etienne*), 130, 225
Wilkinson, Peter, 13, 23, 88, 242
Williams, Peter, 96
Williamson, Cpl, 70, 140
Willis, A., 264
Wills, J. E., 259
Wilmott, Len, 65
Wilson, John S., 32, 77, 256, 265
Wilson, M. A. K., 257
Wilson, William D., 54, 61
Windham-Wright, Capt., 26
Wingate, Orde, 199, 214
Wingate, P., 166
Wingender, C. J., 197
Winkelhorn, K., 265
Winn, Roland, 206
Winter, T., 130
Winterbotham, Frederick W., 281
Wise, A. W. (*Kinross*), 271

Wiskeman, George O., 26, 79, 256
Witherington, Pearl (*Marie*), 225, 229
WIZARD, 225, 228
Woerther, A. V., 130
Wollaston, J. McA., 257
Wood, (Sir) Ernest, 14
Wood, L. J. C., 259
Wood, N. (*Doubloon*), 271
WOODCUTTER, 130, 239
Woodhouse, Hon. C. Monty, 54, 158, 165, 166, 169, 171, 172, 282
WOODPECKER, 64
Woods, Christopher M., 276
Wooler, Ray, 135
Woolrych, S. H. C., 267
Worcestershire, 273
Worms, Jean (*Robin*), 115, 130
WRESTLER, 225, 229, 238
Wrestler, 225
Wright, A. F., 211
Wright, Capt., 192
Wright, Jim, 179
Wright, Peter K., 61
Wright, Sgt, 176
Wroughton, W., 150
WRYNECK 1, 64
Wuchan, 182
Wyberg, Hans, 243
Wynne, Greville, 276
Wyoming, 272

Xavier, 219, 227
Xenos, Demetrius, 158

YAK (Operation), 64
YAK (ULTRA key), 51
YANKEE, 133
Yeo-Thomas, Forest F. E. (*Seahorse*), 26, 114, 121, 130, 234, 257, 281
Yin Kok, Ngit, 204
Yonne, 272
Yorkshire, 273
Young, James, 231
Young, John (*Gabriel*), 130, 234
Young, J. T., 256
Young, P. E., 190
Yugoslav Section, 61, 62, 147–51
  Head of, *see* Bennett
Yves, 127

Zabielski, Jozef, 28
Zachmeur, G. le (*Durance*), 271
Zaharoff, Sir Basil, 62
Zapletal, Libor, 91
Zavorka, Frantisek, 91
Zeff, Edward (*Georges 53*), 130
Zembsch-Schreve Capt. (*Pierre*), 103, 130
Zemek, Jan, 91
Zielake, W. (*Dime*), 272
ZINC, 91
Zinoviev Letter, 7
Z Organisation, 7, 8
Zog, King, 140, 142
Zomer, Hans, 92, 97